TRAINING MANUAL FOR REAL ESTATE SALESMEN

TRAINING MANUAL FOR REAL ESTATE SALESMEN

DAVID STONE

PRENTICE-HALL, INC.
Englewood Cliffs, N.J.

© 1965 by
DAVID STONE

ALL RIGHTS RESERVED. NO PART OF THIS BOOK MAY BE REPRODUCED IN ANY FORM, BY MIMEOGRAPH OR ANY OTHER MEANS, WITHOUT PERMISSION IN WRITING FROM THE PUBLISHER.

Library of Congress
Catalog Card Number: 64-22806

Seventh Printing . . . April, 1985

PRINTED IN THE UNITED STATES OF AMERICA

THE AUTHOR

David Stone is one of the earliest trail-blazers in the Trade-In field. Since 1954 he has devoted most of his efforts to developing the mechanics of selling and trading real estate, and the program he put into action has been highly successful in expanding his business. Yearly gross sales are consistently over thirty million dollars.

The details of his own 30 million dollar program and many other programs mapped out in this unique new book are the result of his own experience and the experience of many other brokers and salesmen who cooperated with him in the research and preparation that went into writing this definitive work.

Dedication

To my mother and father whose interest has been a source of great inspiration to me in all my endeavors, and to my family who shared my hours of labor in preparing this book.

Acknowledgments

The many ideas contained in this book represent the accumulated thoughts of fellow Realtors and associates to whom I am extremely grateful for their unselfish sharing of experiences, observations, and conclusions. It is characteristic of this profession for its practitioners to give freely of their knowledge in order that others might benefit. I am especially indebted to the California Real Estate Association and its progressive leaders who have generously permitted me to work with them on educational conferences, seminars, and research projects for which the Association has gained national recognition. The list of people to whom I am indebted for the material in this manual would be of such length that I am forced to omit it completely. To all my friends in the real estate, homebuilding, and mortgage industries who have aided me in compiling this training manual, I offer my sincere and lasting thanks.

The Author

HOW THIS BOOK WILL LEAD YOU TO GREATER REWARDS IN REAL ESTATE

This <u>Training Manual for Real Estate Salesmen</u> represents nearly seven years of organizing a sales training program for the real estate company I currently manage: Stone & Schutte, Inc. of San Jose, California. It contains hundreds of proven ideas for selling real estate which were gathered from my own experiences and those of leading brokers and salesmen around the nation. While burning midnight oil with fellow Realtors, I have exchanged and shared most of the techniques contained in this book, which I have written as a practical guide to the real estate business for both new and seasoned salesmen.

The reader will learn where to look for saleable listings and how to obtain them at prices and terms which assure their ultimate sale. He will absorb ideas about prospecting for buyers and sellers through advertising, telephone, contact and personal canvassing. The topic of telephone answering is given special consideration since it is generally neglected in most real estate training material. Our student will learn how a successful salesman selects and shows real estate to a qualified customer, controlling the sequence of events leading to the sale. Closing the sale, both with the buyer and the seller, is the very heart of our training program and gives the reader numerous proven ideas, examples, and techniques to help him master this all important phase of real estate selling. The subject of building a referral business has been left untouched in most real estate publications, but because it is vital to a salesman's ultimate success, I have devoted an entire chapter to the topic.

The financing of real property is a technical, but extremely important, subject which is reviewed for the reader interested in the fundamentals of creating sales by using borrowed capital. In the concluding sections of this book, we offer the reader a glimpse at the many specialized phases of our business which await him when he matures in his career of real estate selling. The complete Bibliography at the end of the book provides a ready reference to the outstanding publications available to aid the salesman in his research necessary to perfect his knowledge of the more technical fields available. The glossary of real estate terms and phrases should also prove helpful to both beginner and expert when confronted with unfamiliar real estate expressions.

The author believes that the opportunities and the competition of the real estate business are greater today than they have ever been in previous periods. As a consequence, real estate selling demands more knowledge, skill, and dedication from those who would rise above the masses of unsuccessful people attracted to this expanding enterprise. As an avid student of real estate, I sincerely hope this training manual provides you with enough stimulating ideas to lead you to the rewards you envision!

The author,

Dave Stone

CONTENTS

1 Welcome to the Real Estate Profession . 1

   Think, Eat, and Sleep Real Estate . Start with your attitude . Other Reasons for Real Estate Transfer

2 Get on Your Mark, Get Set 7

   How to Manage Your Time . How to Manage Yourself . Carry a Notebook Think Success . Prepare Your Tools . Your Wardrobe and Appearance . Other Tools You Will Need . Become Dedicated to Your Goals . Open the Floodgates of Enthusiasm

3 Meet Your Employees: The Sellers of Real Estate! . 20

   First: The Seller Has the Greater Need and Pays the Commission . Second: The Property Is a Magnet to Attract Buyers and Sellers . Third: The Seller Becomes a Vital Center of Influence . Prospecting for Listings . Selecting an Area to Canvass . Developing Your Ten Acres of Diamond . Phone Solicitation to Obtain Listings. "For Sale by Owner" Ads . Extend Yourself . Always Use Names . Sources of Listings . Develop a Nose for News . Ask the Right Questions Every Day . Selling Owners on Your Services . Conclusion

4 How to Obtain and Service Saleable Listings . 49

   Your Listing Appointment . Preparation Before You Leave the Office . Appraisal Knowledge Important . Inspecting the Neighborhood Around the Property . Learning to Appraise Depreciation Factors . Inspecting the Property . Categories and Sample Questions . Keep Your Objectives in Mind . A Word of Caution About Price . Reviewing the Facts You Have Gathered . Appraising and Pricing the Property . Cost Replacement Appraising . Determining the Net Equity . There Is No Magic in Pricing Real Estate . How to Evaluate the Marketability of Your Listing . The Listing Presentation . Your Review Will Never End . Use the Price Range Approach . How to Talk Terms . Prepare the Sellers for the Selling Process . Post Servicing of the Listing . Types of Listing Contracts . Summary

5 How to Obtain Prospects from Advertising . 85

   How to Handle Floor Time Responsibilities . Learn to Be Independent . Preparing Good Advertising Copy for Classified Ads . How Prospects

5 How to Obtain Prospects from Advertising (Cont'd)

Select Ads . The Importance of Headers and Lead Lines . Use a Theme in Your Copy . Tell Them Enough, But Not Too Much. Do Not Use Abbreviations . Use Effective Layout . Repetition Has Value Also . Honesty and Truthfullness in Advertising . How to Plan Your Daily Advertising . Writing an Ad for 3562 Rosedale . How to Handle Telephone Inquiries . List Comparables for Every Ad . Use a Prospect Card to Record the Facts . Obtain and Use the Caller's Name . Develop an Effective Series of Probing Questions . How to Use These Questions in an Actual Interview . It's a Smile-a-Phone!

6 Know Your Prospects and Your Properties . 115

Your Counselling Session with the Carters . A Word About the Art of Communication . You Are Ready to Discuss the Showing of Property . Other Points to Remember About Qualifying Interviews . How to Select the Right Properties for Showings . The Romance of Selecting a Home . Do Not Give the Prospect Too Many Choices . Keep the Emotional Needs of the Buyer in Mind . Most Customers Want More Comfort and Convenience . Do Not Be Influenced by Your Own Preferences . There Are No Perfect Homes! . Pre-Inspect the Homes You Plan to Show . Don't Miss Out on the Why . Plan the Showing Sequence for Maximum Effect . While Inspecting Property Always Look for New Business . Prepare for Your Appointment with the Carters

7 Showing Properties to Buyers . 133

Drive Courteously . What to Talk About . Be Sure It Is the Right Home Before Beginning the Close . You Arrive at 461 Harrison . Do Not Rush Through a Showing . Never Defend the Property . Listen . Demonstrate Benefits . Ten Good Rules to Remember . The Value of Showmanship . Develop Empathy . The Difference Between New and Used Homes . Plan Your Tour Through Home to Accent Hotspots

8 Obtaining the Offer . 145

Building the Buying Temperature . Master Your Fears First . Assume the Sale . Make It Painless for Your Customer . Obtain "Yes" Responses . Closing by Defensive Persuasion . Overcoming Closing Objections . The Fallacy of the Magic Moment . Where to Close the Sale . Moments When Silence Is Golden . Back to the Carters . Now Begin Writing Portions of Your Purchase Agreement . Always Put It in Writing . Use Closing Questions . What Do They Want to Think Over? . Feed Back the Positive Comments . Let Them Tour the Home Alone . Take the Cushion Away from the Buyer's Offer . Ask for and Obtain Large Deposits . The Nature of the Earnest Money . Buyers Must Justify Their Action or Inaction . Handling and Processing Deposits . Writing Valid Contracts . Summary . A Few Special Notes on Closing Sales . The Psychology of the Closing Session . The Courage to Make or Break the Sale . With Offer in Hand

Contents

9 Closing the Seller . 174

How to Phone the Seller . Think It Through First . Cooperating with Listing Salesmen . Educating the Seller . Who Carries the Ball? . Cover Contingencies First . Always Stay Calm and Confident . Review What You Have Done . Cover All the Details . Reduce to Simplest Terms . The Seller is Now a Buyer . How to Command the "Think It Over" Rebuttal . Your Contract Is Confirmed . Other Closing Techniques to Remember . Conveying Acceptance to the Buyer . Handling Counter-Offers . All Changes Must Be Initialed . Your Night's Work Is Done

10 How to Build a Personal Referral Business . 195

Servicing After Your Sale . Check List of Escrow Details . Closing the Escrow or Completing the Transfer . Building a Referral Business . Where Are You Going? . What Are Your Motives? . A Matter of Mathematics . The Center of Influence Theory . Working Your Gold Mine . Never Forget Their Name . Lost Sales But Not Lost Clients . Gifts and Remembrances . Don't Neglect Problems . Always Keep Everyone Informed . Stay on Target

11 Financing Your Real Estate Sales . 212

Basic Types of Residential Financing . Regulations and Policies Governing FHA Insured Loans . VA Loans and Eligibility . Creative Use of Financing Instruments . Instruments Used in Mortgage Financing . Qualifying the Buyer for Financing . Summary.

12 Expanding Your Real Estate Opportunities . 240

Selling Investment Properties . The Importance of Property Information Forms . The Four Tests of an Investment: Liquidity, Stability, Appreciation, Yield . Leverage . Analyzing Equity Yields . Tax Advantages in Real Estate Ownership . Depreciation--The Investor's Benefactor . Accelerated Depreciation Provisions . Tax-Free Exchanges . Listing and Selling Apartment Units . Why Do People Buy Apartments? . Determining the Price . Motels, Hotels, Trailer Parks . Commercial - Industrial Buildings and Leases . Selling Business Opportunities . Selling Land, Farms, and Ranches . Exchanging--The Creative Transfer of Property . Property Management . Appraising . Approaches to Value in Appraising . Factors of Depreciation Considered in Appraising . The Appraiser's Role . Mortgage Specialities Available . Other Specializations in Real Estate . Chart Your Future with Care . Be Active in Your Real Estate Association . Developing Your Sales Personality . Use Your Knowledge Wisely . Sincerity: A Priceless Quality . How Is Your Personality? Smile More Often . Look and Act Successful . Approach and Be Approachable . You and Your Voice . Energy and Health . Learn to Know Yourself . Aim for the Stars

Glossary . 281

Bibliography . 316

Index . 328

TRAINING MANUAL FOR REAL ESTATE SALESMEN

WELCOME TO THE REAL ESTATE PROFESSION

As a real estate salesman you will be representing a product in which all of us believe. Salesmen in other fields are not as fortunate. Frequently they must educate their prospects to the advantages of investing in their basic commodity before they can establish common ground on which to continue a sales presentation. Most of your clients will accept real estate ownership as worthwhile and desirable. As the legend of Simon Legree suggests, the landlord in American folklore has never been a very popular person. You will soon learn that when you talk to people about owning their own homes you are unleashing a basic motivation to be free of landlords and free of the controls others can exert over their lives. Since the time of our Pilgrim forefathers, Americans have been taught to value the right to own and improve the "free land," and thus to be free themselves.

Will Rogers is credited with the sage observation: "All one has to do to become rich in this country is to find out where the people are going, get there first, and buy land."

The great American humorist was expressing a simple truth about the real estate business. When God made the world, He created every bit of land that will ever exist on this earth, and this automatically means an increasing demand for a fixed commodity. As real estate salesmen, we need only to know where that demand will be directly felt to realize a substantial return for our clients and ourselves. Use of this principle has built many of the great fortunes of this nation.

So you want to sell real estate? Well, you have selected an occupation which has much to offer you and the people you will serve. However, I would offer you a word of caution before you begin. If you are to be among those who survive the rigors of the first few months in this business and go on to attain the pinnacles of personal success awaiting the mature professional, you must prepare yourself for hard work. Selling real estate, despite what you may have heard, is not a gravy train! Whether or not you achieve the satisfying results you expect will depend entirely upon your personal ability and your willingness to implement natural talents with determined dedication to your chosen career. It is true that nothing worthwhile is ever accomplished without real effort.

WELCOME TO THE REAL ESTATE PROFESSION

The real estate business is certainly no exception to this proven rule. The potential listings and sales which lie on the horizon of your real estate future will not be yours without daily, personal application of the proven principles of real estate selling. We know this to be a truth, and thus this training manual has been developed. It has been written to help you become an effective and successful real estate salesman by giving you the advice and experience of many successful realtors.

By now we assume you have carefully weighed your decision to enter the real estate field and are determined to make a success of it. If, by chance, you have not, now is the time to do so! Achievement in this occupation is a direct result of using creative salesmanship with daily, consistent effort. In real estate selling you write your own pay check. Unfortunately, many thousands have entered and left the business without ever knowing financial success. The majority of these failed because they were unable or unwilling to expend the energy and thought necessary to attain the accomplishments they envisioned. Most real estate transactions are not the result of coincidence and luck. They are the result of persistent efforts by competent real estate salesmen dedicated to solving the problems of buyers and sellers who want and need professional assistance in the acquisition and disposal of real property.

THINK, EAT, AND SLEEP REAL ESTATE

Genuine interest in your business and in the people whose needs it serves will be the key to your success. When you look at a piece of real property you should be able to use your creative talent to envision the possibilities for its highest and best use. By training yourself to see the potential business around you and using your ingenuity to develop that business, you will produce sales which others have left unnoticed. Such effort will be well rewarded. There are few enterprises into which inexperienced salesmen can enter and in a few months attain the high financial levels to which some real estate men rise. Why is this so? Because there is no limit to one's success other than his own personal effort. Unlike other professions, there is no rigid, prescribed course of apprenticeship which must be served before substantial earnings are realized, although there is a period of learning and experience which varies from individual to individual.

You will find that as a real estate salesman you will be drawn into the inner circle of the family consultants who provide services to their clients during periods of change and personal stress. The family doctor, lawyer, and insurance representative are among the leading members of this fraternity. You will derive great satisfaction from your work if you understand and appreciate your role as a real estate counselor. Professional real estate salesmen should be genuinely interested in the needs of their customers and clients and win their confidence as friendly advisors where real estate transfers are concerned. It is only on this basis that you can build a solid, continuing referral business with which to sustain and improve your real estate career.

WELCOME TO THE REAL ESTATE PROFESSION

START WITH YOUR ATTITUDE

Now is the time to begin developing the right mental attitude about your business and about the people with whom you will be working. Do not think of your career as one of selling property. In reality it is a business of <u>selling people.</u> If you learn to understand the motivations and needs of the people who come to you for service, and if you are sincerely able to help these people, the results will be almost automatic. <u>You will sell real estate to people!</u> At times you will be confronted with seemingly irrational clients whose emotional reactions to a real estate transaction tend to confuse the issues and make your task even more difficult and complex than it should be. You must learn to accept this as natural and be the master of the situation by being patient and understanding. It is a known fact that most residential real estate transfers come at times when family life is strained by outside influences in one way or another. The normal emotional balance maintained by a family is generally upset by the very need to transfer to a new location. People resist change. They do not like to be uprooted or transplanted. Their reactions will often reveal the insecurity which such changes have precipitated. You must learn to understand that this is a natural reaction which results when anyone is forced to go through a major change in the accustomed pattern of his life for which he is unprepared. Your attitude and confidence will pull both you and the client through the ordeal. I certainly do not want to infer that all real estate transactions are unhappy ones or the result of disturbing influences, but you should appreciate fully the strains which real estate transactions often produce.

Why do people buy or sell? Often it is because some external cause has forced a change in personal and family life. For example, people sometimes sell because of:

1. DEATH—When death occurs there are usually requirements to settle the estate, pay inheritance taxes, and there is a reduction of family space requirements.
2. DIVORCE—Separation of mates in a marriage nearly always produces the need to dispose of the community property or at least provide for the liquidation of the interests of one of the parties.
3. ILLNESS—Frequently chronic illnesses, such as heart conditions, or allergies, will cause people to sell their homes to accomodate these circumstances.
4. FINANCIAL PRESSURES—This is one of the more important reasons why people sell. It is especially true in younger families which have over-extended their credit to purchase a home and have found themselves in a tight financial situation where the equity of their home is their only recourse to meet their obligations.

WELCOME TO THE REAL ESTATE PROFESSION

5. LOSS OF EMPLOYMENT — Selling a home again is often necessary for those out of work who need their equities to continue meeting their living expenses or change of location for new employment areas.
6. EMPLOYMENT TRANSFER — This is certainly one of the predominant reasons for selling in America today. Large corporations frequently transfer their personnel, and employees often accept positions with other companies which offer the opportunity to improve their position.

These are some of the reasons why property must be transferred. Obviously, the real estate salesman who is asked to assist in solving these relocation problems must be able to understand the feelings of his clients. Indeed, he should consider it a privilege to help them during these periods of adjustment.

OTHER REASONS FOR REAL ESTATE TRANSFER

Of course, not all real estate transfers result from unhappy circumstances. Many do spring from events which are wonderful experiences for those involved. For example, consider these causes:

1. MARRIAGE — The young couple launching the marital ship needs shelter and frequently must find either an apartment or a small home.
2. BIRTH — Every addition to a family certainly increases the need for family living space.
3. PROMOTION — As homeowners can afford more living comfort as a result of business success, they will normally seek it.
4. EXPRESSION — Creative individuals often are looking for greater individuality to be expressed in the home they purchase and around which they mold their family life.
5. UNEXPECTED WEALTH — Any windfall producing financial surplus will create a desire to change status, which such new wealth justifies.
6. PRESTIGE — The "snob appeal" of living in just the "right" neighborhoods and with the "right" neighbors will frequently, with certain groups, provide a major incentive to move up in class status. Also, with important positions often there is the necessity of presenting living facilities that are compatible with their business requirements.

Whatever the underlying motivation, the real estate counselor who understands the significance of his role will demonstrate a genuine and sympathetic interest in the needs and desires of his clients. He will find ways to utilize his knowledge and talents to serve the many and varied people who call upon him for professional advice. Such a salesman welcomes the responsibilities of this public demand for his knowledge and talents. He also learns to cultivate the mental attitude which characterizes the true professional, <u>that of putting customer interests ahead of personal interests.</u>

WELCOME TO THE REAL ESTATE PROFESSION

You will learn, in the months and years ahead, that the challenges and opportunities in this business of selling real estate are boundless; but you will also learn that they must be earned. You can be proud to be a part of America's number one industry. Your counterparts in every city of our land have contributed to the great creative real estate developments by influencing capital, investors, builders, and others to buy and develop the land. A piece of land is just a piece of land until someone sees its potential and utilizes it for a magnificent hotel, business building, service station, farm, or home. Value is created and enhanced—it does not just happen! Next time you view a tall building in a metropolitan city, remember that it was just an idea in someone's mind before it became a reality. Realize also that the idea had to be <u>sold</u> to bankers, investors, owners, developers, and the public before it could finally rise into existence. From such creative contributions have come most of the wonderful things we enjoy today, and you are part of the industry which does more to improve and develop a man's environment than any other: <u>the real estate industry.</u>

It has been rightly said that the real estate profession is one of the last great frontiers of our free enterprise system. Today's real estate opportunities are greater than ever before in history. You have chosen an exciting business in one of its most exciting periods. I sincerely hope you will remain among those who carve successful careers from the fertile field of real estate selling and share in the sense of personal achievement they have gained. It will be worth it!

STUDY QUESTIONS FOR CHAPTER ONE

<u>Questions:</u>

1. What aspects of the real estate business interest you? Why might you want to sell real estate as a career?
2. What advantages do you have over other commodities when you represent real estate for sale?
3. How is real estate ownership related to the history of governments and man's struggle for independence?
4. Why is your mental attitude important to your success in this business?
5. What are the basic motivations of those who buy and sell real estate?
6. Where would you like to be five years from now in terms of your personal goals and how will real estate selling help you attain these objectives?

<u>Projects:</u>

1. On a sheet of paper list the advantages of real estate ownership and then think of all the disadvantages you can find. Compare and analyze them.

WELCOME TO THE REAL ESTATE PROFESSION

2. If you are now associated with a real estate company, ask your broker or supervisor to cover the following topics with you:
   a. The history of your company, its objectives, and future plans.
   b. What are the policies of your office? If the office has a policy book, read it and discuss any policies that are not clear to you.
   c. What services does your company offer its customers and clients? What departments exist within the company which will help you achieve your goals and improve the quality of service you render your clients?
   d. If your firm has a contract with its salesmen, review its terms and ascertain the obligations and responsibilities of both broker and salesman.
   e. Learn the location and use of all files, supplies, research materials, forms and other things offered by your broker to assist you in selling real estate.
   f. List the advantages you and your broker can offer those who seek or need your help.
3. Ask your broker for permission to read any of the books he may have available to provide you with a better understanding of the real estate business. If he should have a copy of Hobart Brady's <u>Real Estate, It's Wonderful</u> (published by the Institute of Real Estate Brokers of the National Association of Real Estate Boards), ask permission to read this choice description of the real estate profession. For other recommended books, see the Bibliography for this training manual.

2

GET ON YOUR MARK, GET SET . . .

A real estate salesman without definite plans and objectives is like a rudderless ship which can be easily tossed about by stormy seas and broken upon rocky shoals. Just as the rudder is the guiding force by which ships, large or small, are directed to predetermined destinations, well defined goals and daily plans are the stabilizing power which help us steer our course to a specific achievement plateau. The time to establish your goals is now, at the beginning of your career. By doing so you will automatically find your daily efforts directing you toward your envisioned rewards.

Today's real estate market is a highly competitive one, demanding the very best from salesmen who hope to achieve economic success. Let no one mislead you! Most real estate salesmen do not earn as much money as they should, and many do not even make a good living for themselves. Why? Because they are often unprepared to make the investment in time and energy that is necessary to become successful. It has been said that a good real estate office cannot afford a salesman who is just "average," because "average" in this business is actually "very poor." For every real estate salesman who genuinely works at his business, there are ten "desk-warmers" waiting for success to drop into their laps. This is true simply because it is so easy to enter the real estate field after abandoning or retiring from some other occupation. "Desk-warmers" abound in this business, but they do not earn a reasonable living and they are very costly for any broker to maintain. There is a Chinese proverb which expresses this point very well:

Confucius say: "Man will go hungry who waits all day for roast duck to fly in mouth."

Contrary to popular opinion, the sales leaders in the real estate business must practice sound business management principles and devote considerable thought and effort to their activity in order to stay out in front. Their work must be planned! Their goals well defined! How about your goals? Do you know why you want to sell real estate? Ask yourself what you hope to gain from your efforts in this profession, then determine when and how you expect to reach these objectives. Don't be afraid to commit yourself to a specific level of achievement - that's the only way to rise above the "average." Write your goals down on paper and place them where you can, from time to time, review them. Set time limits on each of them and measure your progress daily. If you do this, your mind will begin directing its powerful energies toward these accomplishments and it will help you stay on course in the attainment of your goals. If you will firmly ingrain your desired objectives in your conscious mind, your subconscious processes will assist you in finding ways to reach them!

HOW TO MANAGE YOUR TIME

Of all the factors which can influence the degree of business success you can enjoy, none is more important than the management of your time. Time is the one thing you have in common with all real estate salesmen, but how you use that time is yours to decide. You can fill the hours set aside for business with creative productivity, or waste them in useless and profitless motions. In either case, the results will be readily evident in your commission checks and bank balance.

When I was a youngster in grade school, one of my teachers had me memorize a little saying which adequately emphasizes the value of time:

LOST

Somewhere between sunrise and sunset, yesterday,
One golden hour!
It was set with sixty ruby minutes,
And each in turn studded with sixty diamond seconds.
No reward is offered,
For this golden hour is lost forever!

Time is a fleeting phantom which, when we chase it, fades before us and disappears into the past. The only way time becomes real is when we fill it to the brim with activity and life! Then it takes on dimension and purpose, giving shape to our lives and definition to our existence. There are certainly plenty of ways to waste time just as there are hundreds of ways to fill it with pleasurable and creative tasks. Step into any real estate office and I will show you examples of both.

Some salesmen come to the office and spend valuable hours reading newspapers, chatting with fellow salesmen about sales "almost" made, and drinking extra cups of coffee on extended "coffee breaks"; others devote these same hours to calling clients, inspecting listings, and creating new business. Some of these men will conclude the day with a sense of achievement and well-being; the others with a feeling of frustration and discouragement.

HOW TO MANAGE YOURSELF

No real estate salesman should ever be without hundreds of things to do each day to build his business. There is the matter of prospecting for new business and caring for old business, of reviewing client files, and inspecting properties. There are customers to call, sales to close, real estate to show and people to see; but none of these things will ever get done unless we form the right habit patterns in the use of our time. You have heard of people who are "in a rut." These are individuals whose habit patterns have helped them dig "an open-ended grave"! Their objectives are no longer in sight and they find it difficult to see over the sides of the meaningless groove they have cut for themselves. Once, when traveling a small country road in Kansas, I happened upon a sign which read:

CAUTION: BEFORE PROCEEDING, PICK YOUR RUT.....
YOU WILL BE IN IT FOR THE NEXT TEN MILES!

To our reader we might apply a parody of this admonition:

CAUTION: BEFORE PROCEEDING, CHOOSE YOUR COURSE....
YOU WILL BE TRAVELING IT FOR MANY YEARS TO COME!

Now is the time to begin forming the right habit patterns and the right mental attitudes which will help pave your road to success. Cultivate the sound habit of planning your daily activities and learn to guard your time as you would your money and your reputation. Do not permit others to encroach on your time with idle gossip and useless horseplay when you are in your place of business. When you walk through the front doors of your office, be prepared to conduct yourself as a professional who knows his value and purpose. Take time to organize your desk, your work, and your schedule of activities for the day. Remember that "time is money" and wasting it is just as senseless as wasting money. Every hour of your working day should be directed toward efforts which will produce a reasonable return for the time invested. If you want to be more than just an "average" salesman, practice outlining each day in advance, <u>protecting your time from those things or persons who would misdirect your efforts.</u>

One of the ways you can assure yourself of better time scheduling is simply to list the tasks and goals each morning while your mind is alert and your day ahead of you. (See the DAILY WORK PLAN form.) In the very process of listing the many things you want to do, you will develop a sense of urgency about the important tasks which will help you take direct action in attaining them. In addition, there is a side benefit in this systematic scheduling of daily activities. It frees your mind from the responsibility of trying to remember routine details and gives you freedom to achieve your creative goals without burdensome worries.

GET ON YOUR MARK, GET SET...

DAILY WORK PLAN

Day _____
Date: _____
Floor _____ A. M. ____ P. M. ____

1. Appointments:

8:00 _____	2:30 _____
8:30 _____	3:00 _____
9:00 _____	3:30 _____
9:30 _____	4:00 _____
10:00 _____	4:30 _____
10:30 _____	5:00 _____
11:00 _____	5:30 _____
11:30 _____	6:00 _____
12:00 _____	6:30 _____
12:30 _____	7:00 _____
1:00 _____	7:30 _____
1:30 _____	8:00 _____
2:00 _____	8:30 _____

2. Buyers to call: _____
   _____
   _____

3. Sellers to call: _____
   _____
   _____

4. Listings to   A. _____
   Inspect   B. _____
                 C. _____

5. Ads to write: _____

6. Letters to write: _____

7. Listing Service   A. Signs _____
                     B. Keys _____
                     C. Lock-Box _____
                     D. Other _____

8. Daily Progress   A. Sales _____
                     B. Listings _____
                     C. New contacts _____

9. REMARKS: _____
   _____
   _____
   _____
   _____
   _____

My father once impressed upon me the value of doing things that needed to be done at the scheduled time. It was my task to water the cows each day before I left for school, and on one occasion, I neglected to perform this chore. Unconsciously it worried me while in school all day, and when I returned home I knew the task would still be waiting for me. Mentally I was expecting the worst, and when my father confronted me I was sure my procrastination would be punished. When he saw how conscience stricken I was, he said:

"Son, you have punished yourself today by carrying those buckets of water all day long!"

How many of us "carry buckets of water all day" when we could relieve our minds from the tiresome worries of such nagging tasks by simply taking direct action or putting it on paper where we could refer to it at the proper time. Mental energy can literally be drained by needless procrastination and useless worry when we do not organize our time and take direct action at the opportune moments. If you postpone the trivial tasks that should be done immediately, you sap the creative power which should be dedicated to more profitable and enjoyable assignments. <u>Direct action</u> is frequently the best cure for a clogged mind and a lethargic attitude. When responsibilities cannot be performed immediately, it is certainly better to reduce them to written memoranda than to clutter the mind with them.

CARRY A NOTEBOOK

I recommend to you the consistent use of a daily notebook which is always in your possession. A notebook of pocket size is a substitute memory. It can be used to jot down all the little things you want to remember as they occur to you throughout the day. It will help to free your mind so you can concentrate on more important objectives until the appropriate time to review your notes. Regular and systematic use of the pocket notebook will help you to avoid embarrassment and unhappy episodes which stem from carelessness or neglect. It will also become, as we shall discuss later, an important tool in the building of a solid referral business.

Whatever system you select, keep it simple. No system is of value if it consumes so much time or is so complicated it discourages you from adhering to it. Set a regular time to review your notes and to outline your program. I have always preferred the early morning hours for the purpose of organizing daily activities. Even before leaving home I list my work objectives and goals so that, when I arrive at the office, my plan of action is well-defined and ready for initiation. This procedure takes only thirty minutes or so, but it is one of the most productive portions of the day. It gives me an opportunity to review quietly and objectively the unfinished business from yesterday, the new business for today, and the personal goals which I want to review.

I have heard men complain because there are only twenty-four hours in the day. This is a fallacy! I know individuals who pack 30, 40, or more hours into the day by learning to use every moment to advantage.

You have heard the saying:

"If you want a task done always give it to the busiest man!"

Why? Because busy, successful people have learned how to manage their time and can always find ways to include new tasks by conserving energy and time through use of efficient methods. Most of these people have learned to organize their work and they frequently "empty their brains on paper" so as to reschedule and review daily plans. Just seeing the things that are to be done in a black and white form helps them to re-evaluate their plans and eliminate unnecessary details.

Another secret in learning to use time wisely is to budget it among all the various types of activities which must be performed in order to stay on course. For a real estate salesman this includes time to inspect listings, obtain new ones, review prospect lists, cultivate new ones, show properties, and follow up sales. If time is consumed on only one phase of the business to the exclusion of the others, invariably one's progress is impeded until the other activities are renewed. Learn to keep a good balanced relationship between each of the necessary tasks involved in your real estate career and you will find there will be fewer peaks and valleys to your personal income. These suggestions should help you "plan your work and work your plan" so as to pack more profitable hours into your working day.

THINK SUCCESS

Psychologists and educators have clearly established that nothing will influence the success or failure of an individual more readily than his own mental attitude. William James, recognized by many as the father of American psychology, made this profound observation nearly 70 years ago:

> The greatest discovery of our generation is that a man can alter his life by altering his attitude of mind!

In reality, however, this is not a new discovery. The Bible centuries ago recorded that "as a man thinketh in his heart, so is he" and Marcus Aurelius, Roman emperor, wrote in his <u>Meditations</u>: "The World in which a man lives is determined by how he thinks." Your thoughts, attitudes, and dreams tend to influence and project what you are and what you will become.

To be a successful salesman you need energy and enthusiasm. Both of these attributes are directly affected by one's mental attitude. In fact, <u>without the right mental stimuli a person cannot be enthusiastic nor energetic.</u> Your attitude affects the way you feel and the way you react to others. What you think about is evident in your actions, your speech, and your appearance. Since selling is primarily the art of communication at its very best and depends upon the matching of minds to influence decisions, one must be mentally alert and emotionally prepared to engage in such mental exchanges. Unless you can project positive results by thinking positive thoughts with optimistic attitudes, you will find the majority of your clients cold and unresponsive. Your actions will be mirrored in their reactions. Nothing is more vital to your career than the development of positive, optimistic thoughts about your business, your clients, your properties, and your whole life. You are in a business which is primarily concerned with people and their problems. This means you will at times be exposed to disagreeable situations. Unless you have the right mental approach toward these people, you will be tempted to do or say things which can adversely affect your business. Understanding the motivations of others and having the patience to work with them is essential to the realization of your objectives. You cannot influence and motivate others if your own attitudes and emotions are not in balance and under control.

There are many excellent books on this subject and since space does not permit us to discuss this topic thoroughly, I recommend to you the reading of any or all of the following, as well as similar books. (See Bibliography.)

The Power of Positive Thinking	Norman Vincent Peale
Think and Grow Rich	Napoleon Hill
How to Win Friends and Influence People	Dale Carnegie
How to Live 365 Days a Year	Dr. John A. Schindler
Your Subconscious Power	Charles Simmons

In addition, buy a copy of the recording: The Strangest Secret Ever Told, by Earle Nightengale. It will give you new inspiration and insight into your hidden powers which are controlled by your thoughts and attitudes.

PREPARE YOUR TOOLS

Now that your workday and your mental equipment are ready for business, how about your other tools? What tools, you ask? Well, let's begin with your traveling office: your car. Is it ready to receive your first customer? Is it clean? Neat? Ready for use? Reasonably new? I have known salesmen whose cars always looked like they were just on the way to the dump yards or just returning. Front and back seats would contain an assorted collection of listing books, newspapers, maps, and miscellaneous bits of paper and trash. Customers who have to push such things aside to find a place to sit cannot be impressed favorably with the salesman who owns such a collection. The automobile is a vital tool in your selling profession and it should be ready at all times to serve its purpose. You never know when your next customer will appear on the scene and want to see your listings. The car should be ready to receive him.

While we are discussing cars, let's talk about the kind of car you should drive. There is no reason why a real estate salesman should drive an old jalopy or an antique model. First of all, if he has confidence in his selling ability and in himself he will want to own and drive a neat, modern, and efficient automobile which will make a favorable impression on his clients. Remember, nobody wants to deal with an unsuccessful man! To a real estate salesman, his automobile is like his office and should reflect the image of success and stability which is necessary to attract business. When you first enter this business, consider the type of image your car projects and if it does not do the job, plan to change it soon.

Next comes your desk at the office. Does it look like the desk of a professional salesman? Or does it look like that of a local pack-rat who has accumulated a little bit of everything for the past year? A cluttered desk reflects a cluttered mind and is a deterrent to efficient activity. Customers who enter your office will receive an impression of you and your company by the facilities and the desks they see. What will be their impression of you and your business? When you leave the office at the conclusion of the day, learn to clean off the top of your desk and to arrange your papers neatly in the desk drawers or brief case so that you are ready for tomorrow's business. This will have a stimulating effect on your attitudes toward your occupation. Leaving your desk cluttered has the same effect on you that leaving dirty dishes in the sink has on the housewife who must face them early the next morning.

YOUR WARDROBE AND APPEARANCE

You have undoubtedly heard the saying: "First impressions are often lasting impressions!" This is certainly true. Your clients will immediately form an impression of you by inspecting your appearance and bearing. What kind of impression will it be? Do you look the part of a successful, professional business person? Do your clothes and personal appearance reflect the "image" you want them to see? Would your banker, lawyer, or insurance adviser dress as you do? If not, the chances are you are not projecting the best possible "image" to inspire confidence.

Your personal wardrobe is a major part of your sales personality and for that very reason it should be selected with great care. If your present one is inadequate, I highly recommend that you add the right suits and accessories to bring it up to professional standards. You cannot afford not to look your best at all times. If you look successful and act successful, the chances are you will be successful. Others will have only as much respect for you as you have for yourself. If you want people to listen to you and place confidence in you, dress and carry yourself in the manner which gives you the right to speak with authority.

This principle also applies to the matter of personal cleanliness and good grooming. Regular haircuts, shoe shines, manicures, and other habits of personal care should be followed religiously. Dress and act like a professional businessman worthy of customer respect and confidence. In my offices I insist that the salesmen wear business suits of a conservative style and color with white shirts and ties. The women, although allowed more freedom by custom, are asked to wear business suits or other combinations which are appropriate for business. Except for certain resort communities where the living modes are designed to reflect the environment, salesmen should not wear sport shirts, slacks, string ties, or casual clothes. A good rule to follow is to ask yourself:

Would my banker wear similar clothes in his place of employment?

OTHER TOOLS YOU WILL NEED

Now let's review the other working tools you may need in order to conduct your real estate business properly. Here are some of the more important ones; you should acquire these at the outset of your employment.

1. Listing Binder or Book. You will need a binder or book in which to insert all listings, properly catalogued, for easy reference when needed. Check with your broker regarding size and type used in your office.
2. Brief Case. Since you must carry with you various brochures, listings, contracts, maps, and other materials, you should have a neat brief case organized to accommodate these tools.
3. Tape Measure. You will be inspecting and measuring properties to determine room measurements and footage. A 50 to 100 foot tape is about the right size.
4. Screwdriver, Pliers. Part of your task will include putting up and taking down "For Sale" and "Sold" signs. Screwdrivers, pliers, nuts, and bolts should be kept in the trunk of your car for this purpose.
5. Appointment Book. Since your real estate life is centered around daily appointments, you will need a book or desk calendar in which to record them.
6. Map or Map Book. Most metropolitan areas have real estate districts established by local board or custom. Maps or map books are normally available identifying these districts and streets.
7. Filing Box. You will want to set up a follow-up system to build a referral business and maintain contact with clients. A 3 x 5 filing box with index cards is an easy method of doing so.

GET ON YOUR MARK, GET SET...

8. Listing Forms. You should maintain a good supply of all forms and contracts used in listing property, ready for use when required.
9. Selling Forms. Gather a supply of deposit receipts, blank checks, assignment forms, straight notes and all other documents authorized by your broker for use in selling property.
10. Mortgage Amortization Tables. You will need to compute monthly payments and interest rates for a variety of loans and a pocket amortization schedule is necessary for this purpose.
11. Mortgage Yield Guide. To compute the pay-off amounts on mortgages and deeds of trust and yields based on discounts, you can use a mortgage yield guide book.
12. Title Policy Schedule of Fees. Your title company can give you a schedule of fees, including revenue stamp information and other closing costs.
13. List of Mortgage Companies. Ask your broker to furnish you with a list of the various mortgage companies in your area and the people to contact for loan commitments.
14. Residential Cost Handbook. Various companies publish cost handbooks which provide data for computing square foot costs of construction on different types of properties. They are helpful in appraising by cost-reproduction methods.
15. Listing Kit. Some real estate firms have developed listing kits which contain visual aids, pictures, ads, and other material to help convince sellers to list property with a particular company. You can easily assemble one yourself if your broker does not already have one for you.
16. Company Policy Manual. If your broker has a policy manual, you should read it carefully and know what it says. Larger firms today are convinced such written guides are necessary to eliminate misunderstandings.
17. Keys, Lock-Boxes, Signs, etc. There are many other items you will need and you should go over the list with your broker or sales manager to be sure you have everything necessary to do a professional job.

All of these tools are important parts of your equipment which should be organized and ready for use each day. Together with your desk, telephone, and other facilities, these implements add to your effectiveness as a real estate salesman.

BECOME DEDICATED TO YOUR GOALS

You can make plans, have the right attitude and know all there is to know about real estate selling, but you must have one more ingredient

GET ON YOUR MARK, GET SET... 17

to assure success. That little ingredient is <u>persistent dedication to your goals and objectives</u>. It takes daily determination and a willingness to work diligently in order to be consistently successful. It is the constant plugging away, day in and day out, that keeps you on the path toward your envisioned achievements. No farmer worth his salt would think of sowing a field of seed and leaving it to take care of itself without watering, cultivating, or harvesting. Likewise, no real estate salesman worth his salt would do a lot of prospecting and then take a mental vacation from the responsibility of servicing and cultivating these prospects. Thomas Edison said: "Success is 99% perspiration and 1% inspiration." I cannot vouch for those percentages, but I can vouch for the fact that it takes consistent effort to achieve any worthwhile goal.

    Determination to be a professional real estate salesman should be a primary objective that is with you each day of your career. If you picture yourself as already being successful, you will probably become successful. Mr. Patterson of the National Cash Register Company is credited with having developed the first canned sales talk and he proved any salesman using it enough times each day would sell more cash registers than those who did not. Why? Because the law of averages goes to work for men who say and do the right things often enough with the right people. If you will be persistent you will obtain listings and make sales. Insurance salesmen know about the law of averages as well as the law of numbers. They are taught to make a prescribed number of "cold turkey" calls each day in order to use the laws to find enough qualified insurance prospects from which they can make at least one appointment. The same rule will apply to the real estate business. Until you have developed a substantial referral business in the early stages of your career, you must rely on the "cold turkey" prospects which your efforts uncover. If you see and show enough property you will generally sell enough property.

    The great real estate salesmen and brokers whom I personally know are all men who love their businesses. They talk it, live it, and dream about it. They are dedicated to their goals and they accept every opportunity to use their talents and knowledge in their business. They do the things that come naturally to them, and these little things combine to make big business. Early in your career, take a tip from these successful men and start talking about your business to the people you meet every day: the service station attendant, the grocer, druggist, insurance man, and neighbors. Do not be afraid to talk about your profession. You will learn that the majority of people are interested in real estate and many of them are planning to do something about it <u>today</u>. Business is all around you, just waiting to be developed!

OPEN THE FLOODGATES OF ENTHUSIASM

    By becoming genuinely interested in real estate you will increase your personal enthusiasm. Enthusiasm springs from great personal interest in a subject. If you want to become more enthusiastic just act enthusiastic about your job, your properties, and your clients. If you do, you will become an enthusiastic professional.

The two greatest obstacles to selling are:

FEAR and INDECISION - both your fear and indecision and that of your clients. You cannot overcome a customer's doubts until you have first conquered your own. If you do not believe in the product, the value, the need, or the prospect, the buyer is certainly not going to believe in you or the merits of your proposition. If you would instill confidence in your buyer's hesitant actions, act confident and enthusiastic. Demonstrate your own convictions by radiating optimism and enthusiasm.

You have heard the story about the person who was afraid until he began to whistle, and soon the act of whistling drove away his fear. So it is with all fear; positive actions and positive thoughts drown out the doubts and indecisive attitudes. Act as though you were never more confident in your life and those around you will begin to feel better too. Such emotions are contagious.

Now that you have your tools and your mental attitudes primed for business, let's:

> GET SET....
> GET ON YOUR MARK....
> AND GO!

QUESTIONS AND PROJECTS FOR CHAPTER TWO

Questions:

1. Why are personal goals important to individual success?
2. What things can you do to assure the best use of your time?
3. Why does listing your daily activities at the beginning of the day help you in executing them and conserving your time?
4. How can a pocket notebook assist you in performing your various tasks?
5. Do you believe in the "power of positive thinking"? How can you cultivate your mental attitudes in order to become more successful?

Projects:

1. Review the various tools of the trade listed on pages 15-16 and check them against your own equipment. Obtain the others needed to complete your personal working materials.
2. On a sheet of paper, list your various goals and relate them to the daily objectives you must fulfill in order to realize their achievement.
3. During the coming week, list on paper at the end of each day how you spent every hour of that day. Then ask yourself these questions:
   a. Did I use my time wisely today?
   b. Could I have accomplished more with better organization?

GET ON YOUR MARK, GET SET...

    c. How many hours did I waste?
    d. Were my actions today decisive and direct or indecisive and ineffective?
    e. How can I accomplish more tomorrow through better planning?
4. Begin inspecting property, gathering market data, and reviewing current listings as directed by your broker.
5. Read at least one inspirational book that will help you raise your sights and reach your goals.

3

MEET YOUR EMPLOYERS:
THE SELLERS OF REAL ESTATE!

Can you imagine a supermarket without groceries, a service station without gas, or a bank without money? It is just as difficult to picture a successful real estate office without listings! Saleable listings are the basic trading stock, the bread and butter, and the profit, of any real estate office. There is no substitute for good listings. There is no magic formula for securing them. Good listings are obtained through hard work, creative effort, and constant attention to the problems of sellers, but there is no activity more vital to a real estate salesman's career than procuring and servicing listings.

Unfortunately, most salesmen fail to fully appreciate the importance of cultivating real estate sellers. Instead, they have a strong tendency to spend the majority of their time with prospective buyers and only a small amount of it with sellers. In my opinion, this is a serious mistake. I believe sellers are the key to our business and therefore deserve primary consideration and attention. To begin with, what other businesses secure their merchandise with as little capital outlay as this one? Most retailers must invest substantial sums of money in the stock which they must have to stay in business, but real estate salesmen (to achieve the same results) need only obtain saleable, exclusive listings. In essence we use our clients' capital to maintain an inventory for us! This is certainly a prime advantage enjoyed by real estate salesmen, and we should not only recognize this fact but, equally important, we should realize the responsibilities we assume in representing these properties. Sellers trust us with their most valuable possessions and we, in turn, owe them our best professional service. This means conscientious application of our knowledge and talents, together with a fair amount of our time being devoted to solving the seller's real estate problems. When we fail to obtain results, everyone loses. When we make a sale, everybody wins.

There are three major reasons why sellers are important to your career. Let's analyze each of them:

FIRST: THE SELLER HAS THE GREATER NEED AND PAYS THE COMMISSION

The fact that sellers do pay most commissions deserves consideration. Although there is nothing to prevent the buyer from paying a commission, the seller normally assumes this responsibility because he does have the greater need. A buyer usually has many properties from which to choose, whereas the seller has only one to sell. Under an exclusive listing program, the seller is tied to you, while the buyer is free to work with anyone he chooses. The prospect can shop the market with many real estate salesmen (and often does) while the seller is entirely dependent upon your professional attention to his needs.

SECOND: THE PROPERTY IS A MAGNET TO ATTRACT BUYERS AND SELLERS

Just as buyers are drawn to the retail shops displaying the best merchandise, homebuyers learn to seek real estate firms handling the types of property in which they are interested. Prospective purchasers often scout neighborhoods which appeal to them, calling the real estate offices whose signs are evident in the district. The more "For Sale" signs your office displays on property, the more calls it will receive from such customers. My experience has proven to me that calls resulting from these signs are generally from prospects who are already partially sold on the neighborhoods and exteriors they have seen and this makes it easier to qualify and sell them. This factor is more important in real estate selling than in other businesses because no two pieces of real property are exactly alike. There is only one of a kind for any real estate offering, and location is an intrinsic part of the value which is created by the building and its surrounding amenities.

Alert real estate salesmen and brokers, who know the value of having exposure in the market place, will do everything possible to attract the best listings in the most saleable real estate districts. The more listings you have in a given neighborhood, the more you will probably obtain. Sellers of other homes will be watching the activity in their area and will select the office which appears to be doing the best job of listing and selling real estate in their neighborhood. This is true regardless of the size of the real estate firms operating in the total area or whether or not they have friends in the real estate business. Sellers are interested in the activity around their home, not on the other side of town. Once you obtain a good listing, it immediately becomes a magnet which can pull other sellers and buyers to you and to your office. Remember this point when you list property and learn to take advantage of this natural exposure by every means available. Let the world know you have a new listing!

THIRD: THE SELLER BECOMES A VITAL CENTER OF INFLUENCE

Have you ever cast a small pebble into a lake and watched the resulting ripples develop into increasingly larger circles until they became small waves which washed the shoreline? A real estate salesman who becomes a seller's representative can easily create a similar effect. Just as the property is a magnet to draw the interest of buyers, so the seller becomes a center of influence among his neighbors, friends, and associates. This can be a center of influence for either good or bad, depending entirely on the quality of service rendered by the salesman and his alertness in cultivating the owner's goodwill. As will be emphasized in Chapter Ten, building a solid referral business should be a prime objective of any real estate salesman who expects to make a career of this business. You will often find it easier to build a lasting relationship with sellers than with buyers because you have more time to do so. Sellers are with you for several weeks or months prior to consummation of a transaction, whereas the buyers are usually sold and closed within a few days. If you fully appreciate the importance of the seller's support and confidence you will expend the extra effort necessary to win his approval. The seller has friends, relatives, neighbors, and business associates who may be interested in the property. Whether they are or not, they are certainly potential future clients and worth knowing on a referral basis. If you are always alert to the opportunities of a listing salesman, you will harvest other real estate transactions from each new listing. When you <u>list</u> a property, learn to <u>enlist</u> the seller as a member of your referral team. Doing this requires special interest on your part in the seller and his problems, but it will pay big dividends over the years to come and all of your sellers will become a constant source of new business. The ripples of action which you started with the listing will spread into larger and larger centers of influence like that small pebble cast into a pond.

These, then, are the three prime reasons why listing property is the most important activity in which a real estate salesman can engage. The real estate salesman or office which controls the largest number of saleable listings will do the largest volume of business. In any brokerage office it is the duty of every man on the selling team to contribute his share of listings each month. I believe every salesman should have a minimum goal of three new listings a month and should devote enough time to this phase of his business to achieve this goal. It is not difficult to obtain new listings if you know where to look and are willing to invest the time needed to do a competent job of prospecting for them.

PROSPECTING FOR LISTINGS

Paraphrasing the late General MacArthur's famous quotation, someone once said: "Old real estate salesmen never die; they just grow listless!"

MEET YOUR EMPLOYERS

This is true because a real estate salesman without listings is like a car without wheels - he can't move! In the very beginning of his career, a neophyte salesman should concentrate his efforts on the art of prospecting for, and obtaining well-priced listings. It is also the easiest way to learn the business. Just meeting people at their homes and learning to evaluate property will shorten the time required to attain maturity as a real estate professional. "Where do I begin?" you ask. The simple, obvious answer is, "Begin in the neighborhoods and communities where your potential sellers live!" There is still no method of prospecting more direct and effective than meeting the owners in their homes. Canvassing for listings in selected districts quickly exposes you to people and properties, and without these two ingredients you will never succeed. Since everyone who owns a home is a prospective seller at one time or another, you need only contact enough property owners in order to uncover some of those who are currently thinking of selling. It is the most direct and effective method to build a listing inventory when you are just beginning a real estate career.

SELECTING AN AREA TO CANVASS

If your broker allows you a choice of real estate districts for your personal canvassing efforts, try to pick one which evidences substantial activity. Review the office records or the sales reports published by multiple listing services to determine which areas are the "high turnover" sections of your city. After all, if you are going to expend considerable time to build a listing portfolio you might as well spend it where the return will be the highest. Some sections just do not sell as rapidly as others. Generally, you will want to concentrate in the neighborhoods which are in high demand and in the price range most buyers can afford. Those areas which are higher priced are often more limited in sales activity due to the economics involved. The low priced districts, on the other hand, may not be very desirable for the average buyer due to environmental disadvantages. The medium price range for your market area will usually have the highest consistent turnover.

Once you have selected a section to canvas, preferably a minimum of 8 to 10 blocks, you should gather as many facts as possible about property values and activity in that area. This information is obtained from office files or real estate board publications. List each known sale, expiration, current listing, and past appraisal for the homes within your proposed canvassing territory. Using a reverse telephone directory [1], copy the names and addresses of all residents in the same order you intend to work the area. With this information you are now ready to call the owners

---

[1] In metropolitan areas a subsidiary of the telephone company normally furnishes such directories at a nominal cost. Inquire at your telephone company business office.

by name and are prepared to discuss with them actual property sales and listings in the neighborhood. With a little research, you have become an "expert" on the property values and sales conditions in your "ten acres." The next step is direct exposure in the market place.

"What should I say when I go to the door?" Well, there are many approaches, but whatever you decide to say should be briefly rehearsed in advance to give you self-confidence when actually meeting a homeowner for the first time. You do not need to be afraid of doing or saying the wrong thing. As in swimming, just jump in and you will find it is not nearly as "cold" as you had imagined. After all, people are basically friendly and when you demonstrate sincere interest in them they will generally reciprocate. After a few doors, you will begin to relax and enjoy this direct exposure to potential sellers.

DOOR OPENERS THAT WORK

Example 1

"Good morning, Mrs. Greene. I'm Bill Brice of Stone & Schulte, Realtors. Our firm is making a survey to determine which homes may be coming up for sale soon in this neighborhood. Do you know of anyone who is thinking of selling?"

Example 2

"Hello, I'm Jerry Jones of A.B.C. Realty. Recently, our real estate office sold the Brown's residence at 1189 Highland Drive and while advertising for customers we had so many prospective inquiries from buyers who desire to live in this neighborhood that we decided to make a special effort to locate additional homes to show them. Do you know of anyone in this area who might be thinking of selling?"

Example 3

"Good afternoon! Are you the owner of this lovely home? (pause) Well, I'm Joe Barber of Thompson and Thompson, Realtors. My firm has just appointed me the office representative for this real estate district and my first task is to get acquainted with the owners. Have you lived here long?"

Example 4

"Good morning! Are you Mrs. Olsen? (pause) I'm John Dobbs of the real estate firm of Thomas E. Jones and Company. I just wanted to stop by this morning, Mrs. Olson, and acquaint you with your new neighbors. You see, we just sold the home formerly owned by Mr. and Mrs. Gratton to Mr. and Mrs. Johnson. We wanted to be sure they are properly welcomed into the neighborhood. They have two lovely teenage children, Jill and Kathy, who will be attending the Willow Glen High School. Do you have children their age?"

In every case, always try to ascertain the resident's name before calling and use it frequently in your conversation. This helps to break down any barriers which might otherwise exist. Also, remember to talk in terms of the homeowner's interests, not your own. With a little experience you can make door to door canvassing an interesting and profitable method of obtaining listings. Some realtors prefer "spot canvassing" to the systematic coverage of an area. Under this method, you cruise a neighborhood looking for people working in their yards or relaxing where they can be seen. When you spot someone, you park in front, get out and approach the owner with a comment like this:

Example 5

"Good morning! I wonder if you could help me? I'm Bob Mason of Hanson & Company, local realtors. Recently, I was told there was a party on this street who was planning to sell his home soon. Do you know of someone who is thinking of selling?"

The advantage to this type of canvassing is simply that it is informal and it is often easier to strike up a conversation with an owner who has been working in his yard because he appreciates the opportunity to rest and he is usually in a relaxed frame of mind. The salesman who uses this method often finds he can extract much more information from these owners than from those situations where he is standing on the outside looking in.

Example 6

When you locate a property that has recently sold or is still for sale, you will find the following approach very helpful:

"Good morning, Mrs. Smith. I'm John Jones of Colonial Realty. I understand you recently purchased this home. I am gathering facts about the neighborhood property values as our company is appraising several properties in this area. Would you mind answering a few questions for me? How much did you pay for this home? Did you buy it under FHA terms?"

This approach is extremely successful in obtaining information about property, particularly when you are appraising for new listings in the area. We have successfully used this method in our company when extracting information for our Trade-In Housing Program. If you have a Trade-In Program to offer, consider using the following modification.

Example 7

"Good morning, I'm Ronald Rhoades of Rhoades Realty Company, I wonder if you would mind answering a few questions for me? Our company is making a Guaranteed Trade for Mr. and Mrs. Finch up the street and we need a few facts about the neighborhood. I see you have your home for sale. Would you mind telling me if you have had a great deal of activity? How much are you asking for your home?"

Obviously, while gathering this information <u>you are selling yourself, your firm, and your services</u>. Furthermore, <u>you have mentioned that you have a Trade-In Program</u> which may be of interest to this particular party. Before using this particular approach, however, please consult with your broker as to the rules and regulations with your Real Estate Board in reference to discussing property values with owners whose homes are listed with other brokers.

With a little practice you can develop your own presentation which will be most natural and effective for you. The main thing to remember is to be sincere, polite, and pleasant. You are trying to build relationships with the owners in your area so that future business will flow to you rather than to someone else. Like a farmer, you must plant the seeds, cultivate and water them so that eventually you can harvest the crop.

DEVELOPING YOUR TEN ACRES OF DIAMONDS

The chances are you will find yourself going in nine directions at the same time when you first enter the real estate business. This is typical of new salesmen! They tend to see too much property, in too short a time, and in too many areas. As a result they become confused and often very frustrated. You cannot learn <u>all</u> there is to know about the properties for sale in your city when you first go to work. Don't try! It is much wiser to limit your exploration to a small segment of the market and concentrate on knowing that portion so well you will extract immediate returns for your effort. New salesmen would do well to put blinders on themselves and aim their course in one specific direction at a time. When you first begin to inspect the listing inventory in your office and on the multiple listing service, eliminate all but that group of properties which is in the section where you expect to start your activity. <u>Begin by learning to do a thorough job on a small section of the market rather than trying to spread yourself so thin you can do only a poor job on all of it.</u> To be successful today you must be a <u>professional</u> and a <u>specialist</u>. It is no longer sufficient to merely have a glib tongue and a fast hand. You must know properties well enough that when you show them to prospective buyers you will close the sales with confidence. Therefore, it is far better to know a great deal about ten individual listings than a little about 100. It is wiser to select an area in which you like to work and to become a specialist within that district than to try to cover the whole county with a meager knowledge of properties and values.

As you launch your business career, remember this advice and do not try to accomplish and learn everything about all properties in the first few months of your new occupation. Take one step of the ladder at a time and concentrate your activity in those areas and with those properties where your return will be the greatest! This specialized approach will pay handsome dividends if it is consistently followed. Ask your broker or sales manager to assign you a small district and then begin immediately to perform the following assignments on a weekly, programmed schedule:

1. Personally canvass at least one full block each week, talking to the owners of real estate and building a file of follow-up information.

2. Check weekly for any new listings for sale which have appeared in your district and catalogue this information for special attention.

3. Inspect all new multiple listings which have come on the market in your area. Separate these into a special section of your own listing book so they will receive immediate action.

4. Check the area for any new exclusives of other real estate firms and request permission to inspect and work on these properties.

5. Look for new "For Sale By Owner" signs which may appear in your area and make prompt contact to begin building relations.

6. Report to the rest of the sales staff any information about your area and its listings which will help your office to sell the properties involved.

7. Watch for any changes in the status of property which would indicate intent or need to sell. Vacant homes, neglected properties, moving vans in the area, are signs of change which you should explore.

8. Keep a permanent record of all the listings which sell, expire, or change hands in your area so that you have your own comparable file for this section of the city.

9. When any property is sold by your office in your area, immediately contact the homeowners on each side of the property and advise them of the change. This gives you another opportunity to plant your seeds for future business. "Choose Your Neighbor" cards can be mailed when a new listing is obtained and "Know Your Neighbor" cards when it is sold.

10. Obtain from county recorder, tax assessor, or title company a plot map of this district, together with the recorded names of all current owners. Systematically contact them by direct mail, telephone, and personal canvassing. Especially note any absentee owners (as shown on tax assessor records) and contact them by mail or phone. These out-of-town owners frequently need real estate help.

All of the above activities, if performed regularly, will contribute to your rapid development as a specialist in this real estate district. As a direct result you will begin selling homes in the area, listing new ones for sale, and increasing your sphere of influence within that market perimeter. I can personally guarantee your success in listing property if you follow this program faithfully. Your listings will increase in your "ten acres of diamonds" and so will your income!

PHONE SOLICITATION TO OBTAIN LISTINGS

Although it is not as effective or as personal as direct contact with the homeowners, many salesmen are able to use the telephone to screen potential leads for listing appointments. In terms of conserving time, you can cover more homeowners in the same period than by door-to-door canvassing. A telephone campaign, to be effective, must be directed to specific prospects and be well-rehearsed. Here is a list of some of the common sources one might select in making telephone calls.

1. For Sale By Owner ads
2. Expired listings
3. Foreclosure notices
4. Divorce notices
5. Regular coverage of a given district
6. Spot coverage of a given district

Sources of the necessary information to cover these categories would include the following:

1. Newspapers and legal publication columns
2. Regular telephone directory
3. Reverse telephone directory (lists by street address rather than names)
4. City directories
5. Expired listing files
6. Office comparable files
7. County records or tax assessor files of ownership

Telephone solicitation is an art in itself. One salesman whom I hired several years ago took my advice to make 10 telephone solicitation calls each day. As a result, during his first month in the business he came up with four new listings and two sales. He later figured each call he had made was worth $11.46 to him. He made all of his calls to the neighbors surrounding the homes our office had recently sold. Working from the reverse telephone directory to obtain the right addresses and names, his conversation over the phone went something like this:

Example 8

"Hello! Is this Mrs. Jones? (Pause) This is Ray Baxton of Stone & Schulte, Inc., Realtors. Possibly you noticed our "Sold" sign on the property near you at 1521 Western Boulevard? We wanted you to know that we have sold the home and your new neighbors will be Mr. and Mrs. Parton from Cleveland, Ohio. They plan to move in about the fifteenth of this month. While we were advertising this property for sale, Mrs. Jones, we attracted several prospective buyers who wanted to live in that area. I wonder if you might know of anyone else who is planning to sell?"

Again, remember that it is better to always use personal names in calling people because there is no faster way to establish a friendly relationship.

Another telephone campaign which we successfully conducted involved the use of the reverse telephone directory and a city directory. By comparing a city directory of four years ago with a current reverse directory, our salesman would note those names which still appeared in the area. Working on the assumption that the average person lives in one place about four years, we [2] limited our calls to those who had been in one location at least that long. We were able to determine those who qualified by making a simple comparison between the two directories.

A quick review of the names of the occupants which appeared in both directories at the same address would give our salesman the ones he wanted to call. His conversation would then go like this:

Example 9

"Hello! Is this Mrs. Carter? (pause) This is Tom Starr of Stone & Schulte, Realtors. I was just going through my records and noticed how many of your neighbors have moved away since you originally purchased your home on Ventura Drive. Do you realize that over half of those who were there when you moved in have now bought elsewhere? Let's see now ... you've been there four, or is it five years?" At this point the owner will always interrupt to furnish the correct number of years involved and frequently will volunteer other information about the changes in the neighborhood. Our salesman would play it by ear and try to ascertain whether or not the Carters had thought of joining the exodus to other neighborhoods and better properties. If properly handled, the owner would often believe he knew our salesman and that in some manner he must have been connected with the original purchase. For

---

[2] This is the California average. Some areas are substantially longer.

every ten or twelve calls made, at least one potential listing appointment would be made.

This is creative and effective use of the telephone to obtain prospective listings. A prepared "sales pitch" is preferable when you are trying to control a brief telephone conversation. If you try one yourself, write it down on paper and rehearse it until you feel it is reasonably natural and smooth. Then pick up the phone and try your luck. Remember that in telephone solicitation the results from any single call are of no consequence. It is only in making a substantial number of calls that real results can be obtained. The law of averages will work for you providing you make enough calls each day so the total is sufficient to provide an average. If you talk to enough homeowners about their real estate problems and needs, you will find many who can use your services.

"FOR SALE BY OWNER" ADS

"For Sale By Owner" ads are still among the very best sources of listings. After all, these people have already decided to sell, and it is now only a question of when and how. However, since every real estate salesman will also have the same idea, you will be challenged to find an effective means of contacting these owners. Put yourself in the owner's shoes for a moment and try to think of his problems from his viewpoint. If you would take yourself out of the category of just another salesman looking for a commission, you must be able to communicate to the seller your interest in solving his problems. Your objective in calling owner ads should be to put yourself and your company in a special classification with this owner, one which the owner will remember when it comes time to turn to professional help. It is useless to just ask the seller for his business, unless you first impress him with the reasons why he should give you his listing. What can you do for him? Why does he need you? What can you do that your competitors can not?

One of the best ways to impress the owner is to be the <u>first one that calls</u>. To do this, you should get the first edition of your newspaper every day and promptly search out new owner ads, placing your calls immediately. Another approach which we have found effective is to use our trade-in program as an "opener."

<u>Example 10</u>

"Hello! Am I speaking to the owner of the property advertised in today's newspaper? (pause) This is Tom Starr of the Guarantee Department of Stone & Schulte, Realtors. Mr. Stone asked me to call you and explain our guaranteed trade-in plan because he felt you might need our services in the event you found a buyer for your home. You know, most buyers today must first sell one home before they can buy another one. This is where our guaranteed equity plan comes into the picture. If this prospective buyer needs to trade or sell his home before he can buy yours, we have the knowledge and services to make that possible."

The reason this approach is so successful is that it puts our salesmen and the firm in a "special" category with "special" services which helps the seller remember us. Also, I do not believe in trying to list the property over the phone nor discourage the seller from selling it himself. After all, he has made up his mind to try, and I do not want to insult his intelligence by telling him this is impossible. You and I know that some sellers are able to move their own properties while others are not. We always wish the seller luck and try to obtain an appointment to see his home in the event he should later need our help. Most do-it-yourself fans must first try it alone before they list with a realtor, and you will only damage your own image if you degrade their chances of succeeding. The key to this business is simply to stay in touch, and then strike when the iron is hot! You should continue to call these owners until their homes are sold, listed with you or with some other office.

EXTEND YOURSELF

Another effective approach with owner ads is to volunteer advice and service in the event the owner obtains his own buyer. It has always been my conviction that when you courteously advise the "do-it-yourself seller" that you wish him success and firmly plant the idea that you will help him if help is needed, you will be remembered when he finally gives up and seeks professional help. If he should be fortunate enough to succeed in selling his own home, your free advice is not lost because you will win a friend and another center of influence working for you. Here is how you might handle that call:

Example 11

"Hello! Is this the owner of the property advertised in today's Journal News? (pause) This is Dick Bryant of Stone & Schulte, Realtors. I'm sure, by now, you have probably had several real estate salesmen call to list your property. Well, although I would also like that privilege, that is not the primary purpose of this call. Since you just put your home on the market, I know you will want to try your luck at selling your home yourself for a few days. I hope you succeed. If you should be fortunate enough to find a prospective buyer in the next few days, I would be very happy to give you any advice I can offer about arranging financing and closing procedures. When you do decide to call a realtor, I would appreciate the opportunity of explaining the many services our firm of Stone & Schulte can offer."

If the seller does take up the offer to give free advice and help in a sale, we extend it willingly, as it gives us another opportunity to build relations with potential buyers and sellers of the future.

In any telephone solicitation campaign, I recommend use of a daily follow-up system to assure best results. Also, after a call has been placed, a hand-written card or note should be mailed to the owner. This can be a simple one like these:

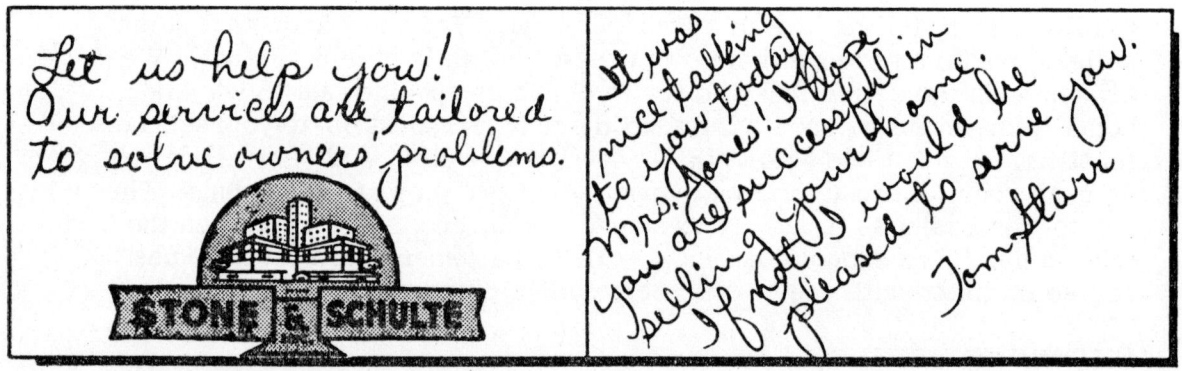

Or a business card clipped to a company brochure with a note on the back of the business card:

The secret in handling for sale by owner phone solicitation is to always express genuine interest in the problems of the owners involved and then follow-up any contacts made until results are realized.

ALWAYS USE NAMES

If you would be remembered and respected, use the name of your client and your own frequently in the conversation. If you want to retain the interest of the person on the other end of the line, use his name several times during the call. If you want him to remember you, then im-

MEET YOUR EMPLOYERS 33

press upon him your name and the name of your firm. Keep both of these objectives in mind and never close the conversation without repeating both names. It is sometimes helpful to associate your name with some common object and use it in an illustrated context to further indelibly impress it on the seller. For example, Tom Starr would say:

"Remember, Mrs. Green, to ask for Tom Starr! That's Starr as in sky!"

Corny? Yes, but effective! One of our salesmen was named John Bahl and he would say:

"That's Bahl - like baseball, basketball, and football."

We will have more to say on the subject of telephone technique in Chapter Five, but now is the time to begin practicing the art of making people remember you whenever you talk with them - with or without a telephone.

SOURCES OF LISTINGS

On the next few pages I have catalogued for you the principal sources of new listing business. I know that you will not be able to use them all at any one time, but over a period of time you can gradually explore each of them to increase your effectiveness in prospecting for listings.

1. **For Sale by Owner Ads from Newspapers**
This has been extensively reviewed in this chapter. It is obviously a major source since the people involved have already decided to sell and it is only a matter of convincing them they need professional service. Phones, direct mail, and personal contact should all be used to follow these leads.

2. **Telephone Solicitation by Real Estate Districts**
As explained in this chapter, this is also among the better means of locating potential sellers. To be effective, however, the caller must have a plan and be consistent in his efforts to make enough calls each day to locate the prospective clients.

3. **Door-To-Door Solicitation in the Areas in Demand**
This is still one of the best methods for a new salesman to use in prospecting for listings. He learns properties, people, and marketing factors which will later help him in his career.

4. **Neighbors of Listings Taken**
Still a prime source. As we have emphasized, you should always take advantage of the exposure to new business which surrounds the properties you list and sell. Both phone and personal contact should be considered, plus the mailing of "Choose Your Neighbor" cards.

5. "For Sale By Owner" Signs

These are always a challenge to any "red blooded" real estate salesman and should be handled by personal contact to stress the advantages of professional service.

6. Expired Listings

In any market area there are always a number of listings which expire unsold, although the owners wanted to sell. Any salesman who knows how to explain the "facts of life" to sellers and present his services in the best manner can usually obtain relistings of these properties. However, care should be exercised to reintroduce them with the right price and terms.

7. Out-of-Town Owners

Owners who live some distance from their properties are often at a disadvantage in the matter of management and protection of their interests. When you learn of an out-of-town owner, call or write to him and suggest the use of your services in selling the property and reinvesting in real estate closer to his present home. You can determine out-of-town ownership from the tax rolls, title records, or neighborhood information.

8. Direct Mail to Prime Real Estate Areas

When you systematically promote your services to the public, you invariably produce results. Direct mail may not be as effective as phone solicitation or direct canvassing, but it provides the groundwork for such campaigns. The most effective mail programs have a news value, such as announcing new neighbors or special services.

9. Advertising for Specific Properties to List

Well-worded ads placed in the classified columns of your local newspaper under "Listings Wanted" will sometimes produce results. It is best to be specific when using this type of advertising. For example:

> Wanted, a 3 bedroom, 2 bath split level in the
> Willow Glen area priced below $30,000. Call
> CYpress 7-3757 - S&S Realtors.

10. Moving Companies Can Provide Leads

You can often arrange to share information about properties for sale and potential transfers with key men of various van and storage companies. These two businesses enjoy a common interest in real estate moves, and can profit from a reciprocal exchange of names and addresses. Also, remember that people who store furniture are sometimes prospects for new properties.

MEET YOUR EMPLOYERS

11. "Furniture For Sale" Ads

People who sell furniture, frequently do so before they market their homes. They may plan to move out of town, and this step is one they take to facilitate that move.

12. Business Transfer Notices

Relocation of industry or promotion of key personnel to other offices can provide ready made clients if you are alert to these changes and make prompt contact with the parties involved. Watch the newspapers for such notices or cultivate "pipelines" within the major companies operating in your market area to stay abreast of these employment changes.

13. Contractors of Custom Homes

Homebuilders can use competent real estate sales representation. This is particularly true of the builder who specializes in custom or expensive homes, since the market for these is limited to a smaller segment of the total housing field and greater exposure to reach the select clientele is required to obtain results. Realtors with trade-in plans for the resale properties involved will have even more to offer such contractors.

14. Advertising and Promoting a Trade-In Plan[3]

I have proven that many sellers who plan to relocate will first inquire about our advertised "Exchange-A-Plan" trade-in service before exploring the potential move. Through the use of newspaper ads, brochures, direct mail, radio, and billboards we have created a recognized service which attracts public response from potential sellers. A salesman can use this tool with all types of prospective sellers.

15. Acquaintances and Contacts at Business and Social Clubs

Wherever you meet people you have opportunities to cultivate potential clients. If you belong to clubs, churches, civic or social groups, be sure those in these associations know you are in the real estate business. Remember that most people would rather entrust their properties to those they know and trust than to strangers.

16. News Items Regarding Marriages and Divorces

By reviewing the newspapers for daily items of interest concerning people and their lives, you can uncover opportunities to help those involved solve their real estate problems related to these events. News items about marriages, divorces, estate settlements, business changes, and so forth, are always valuable leads for the ambitious real estate salesman.

---

[3] See HOW TO OPERATE A REAL ESTATE TRADE-IN PROGRAM by David Stone (Englewood Cliffs, N.J.: Prentice-Hall, 1962).

MEET YOUR EMPLOYERS

17. <u>Bank and Trust Department Contacts</u>

   Most banks handle estate-properties for clients and also advise owners about their real estate holdings. If you have a banker friend or another primary contact within a bank, cultivate him for the referral leads these institutions can provide.

18. <u>Attorneys - Estates and Foreclosures</u>

   Nearly all attorneys handle some real estate transactions in their professional relationship with clients. This is especially true when death or divorce is involved. The disposition of estates becomes the attorney's business when his clients request help. If you have demonstrated your professional interest and ability to such attorneys, you can in turn, benefit from the referrals they can give you.

19. <u>Mortgage Companies - All Types</u>

   Mortgage companies derive their existence from the placing and servicing of real estate loans. Thus, there is nothing more natural than the development of a working relationship between realtor and mortgage solicitors. Whenever notices of default must be filed or delinquencies published, the need of a real estate counselor's services is indicated. By contacting those involved you can often arrange to sell the properties and save the credit of the mortgagors.

20. <u>Legal Notices in Newspapers</u>

   The legal columns of court recorder type newspapers provide many leads for real estate salesmen. Notices of pending foreclosures, estate sales, record of liens, and similar items can lead to potential listings. However, this type of business is often very entangled and the novice will usually find the problems involved greater than the time and attention warrants.

21. <u>Building and Loan Associations</u>

   Savings and loan companies enjoy a major position in the real estate market and are thus an influential source of business. The firms with whom you are conducting business can reciprocate by providing you with recommendations and referral leads to those clients who need real estate service. New builders often need real estate representation and they may consult their local savings and loan officer regarding these problems while arranging the necessary construction capital.

22. <u>Doctors, Dentists, and Other Professional Men</u>

   Doctors, dentists, and similar professional men invest in real estate to offset their relatively high personal income and to build financially sound futures for themselves. Consult your own physician about his needs and then ask about his friends. Syndicates are often involved which buy and sell considerable real estate.

23. Barbers, Milkmen, Route Men, and Postmen

People who travel in various businesses around the best neighborhoods where listings are available can supply you with information about potential moves. Milkmen often know when one of their customers intends to move. Other route men, such as laundry solicitors and door-to-door salesmen, run across leads for property listings which can be turned over to you if you have cultivated their cooperation. Even your barber hears about potential moves, since he talks to people while they are in his barber chair. All you have to do is also talk to these same sources and show your interest in the cases they discuss. When you obtain a lead, never fail to thank the one giving it.

24. Past Business Acquaintances and Associates

When you first enter the real estate industry you should make a list of everyone you have ever known or been associated with in previous occupations. Send them announcement cards about your association with a real estate office. People like to help beginners. Do not be afraid to develop such sources; they can be very valuable.

25. Insurance Company Representatives

Today, life insurance companies counsel their clients on their entire investment portfolio, and real estate holdings are part of their program to build life insurance protection for the liabilities and assets involved. Thus, these salesmen know much about the plans of their clients and can recommend courses of action when asked. Your own insurance man may be in a position to furnish you important leads from his clientele.

26. Personnel Officers of Key Industries in Your Area

Here is a source that can pay real dividends. With industries moving their employees from one state to another and with more emphasis on recruiting specialized help, the number of transferees increases each year. Industrial counselors try to help their employees in the matter of real estate purchases and liquidation. They can and do recommend certain real estate firms or salesmen when they believe this is in the best interest of the employee. Trade-in programs are of value in creating interest with industrial accounts.

27. Neglected Properties Which Need Attention

When driving through neighborhoods, keep your eyes open for properties that appear in need of care. These are often the indication of rented or financially depressed properties whose owners might well consider selling to eliminate the problems.

28. Former Clients Who Purchased or Sold Property Through You

After you have been in business six months or longer, you should have some buyers and sellers on whom you can call for referral business.

When you have been in business for several years, these same people may plan to resell due to changing needs, and those leads should come to you - providing you have maintained regular contact with them. There is no substitute for contact when you are trying to build a referral business.

29. Talk to Merchants with Whom You Do Business

Your grocer, service station attendant, druggist, and the many other people you and your family use daily for other services and supplies are valuable centers of influence who can steer business to you if you let them know you are interested in receiving it. You must ask for it as they will seldom think to inform you if you do not.

30. Every Prospect Who Calls You Regarding Buying

Many of the people who contact you regarding property you have for sale are also potential sellers. Be sure to remember this fact when discussing their needs and ask them about their present residences as a simple matter of practice.

31. Vacant Properties

Whenever you see a vacant home that is not already listed for sale by some other broker, your curiosity should be aroused and your interest fanned sufficiently to cause you to investigate the situation. Many listings can result from such inquisitiveness.

32. Building Permits

Watching building permits and checking with the applicants can turn up need for professional help. This is especially true when the permit is for a single family residence and is filed by the applicant. It may be a private party arranging to build a new home before his present one is sold. A listing on the older property can be yours with a little investigative effort.

33. Armed Service Personnel Contacts

Service men are frequently transferred and some of them need real estate help. If you have centers of influence within such military bases that can keep you posted about proposed transfers, you may be in a position to take advantage of them. Even the telephone directory provides the names and ranks of many military residents.

34. Ministers and Parish Counselors

A minister or priest is frequently asked for advice when family or financial difficulties arise. We do not suggest you commercialize your religious affiliations, but we do recommend that your minister or priest know your occupation and your specialized services. They may prefer recommending the services of an honest believer than entrust to strangers the real estate matters with which their parishioners are concerned.

35. Accountants and Tax Consultants

Those who are directly concerned with the financial problems of real estate owners and who must advise their clients about selling, refinancing, or exchanging their holdings can be outstanding sources of business for real estate men. This is particularly true for investment and commercial properties where tax and depreciation factors affect the need to buy and sell property. Start with your own tax advisor and make sure you are receiving the benefit of his referrals for the clients he serves.

36. Architects, Interior Decorators, and Designers

Architects and decorators often receive advance notice of the intention to build, buy, or sell. They can refer business to favored real estate men, and you should be able to cultivate a few of them for your personal referral activity.

37. Institutional Advertising of All Types

The image of your firm and yourself can be more firmly implanted in the minds of the buying and selling public through various institutional advertising media. Before you invest in such promotional campaigns, ask yourself whether or not it will project the right image of your company, is effective, and in good taste.

38. Recommendations from Friends, Relatives, Customers

As your business career progresses, you should receive more and more referrals from those you have known and served. It will only happen, however, if you have earned it and taken care of the relationships involved. Remember the basic rule: "Never let your customers forget you, and don't ever forget your customers." (See Chapter Ten.)

This impressive compilation of potential listing sources is still only a partial one. It has been estimated that there are more than 100 ways to develop new listings. Whenever you exhaust your own ideas or need new inspiration about where to look for potential listings, turn to this section of our manual and review the ideas outlined here.

DEVELOP A NOSE FOR NEWS

Prospecting for listings is like being a good newspaper reporter. The real estate salesman needs to have a "nose for news." By keeping your ear to the ground for the first hint of a good listing, you can use your ingenuity and perseverance to obtain it before your competition does. This includes inspecting neighborhoods, reading newspapers, listening to the activity in your area, and just being on the alert for the changing conditions which precede the need to sell. Drive different routes to your office each day and watch for new "For Sale By Owner" signs or other prospecting signals. As a real estate salesman you are involved in the daily, changing drama of life in your city. Learn to think about this drama and the part you can play in it. Cultivate your listing sensitivity.

Why do people sell? Because change is a part of life. I awake this morning and have no plans to sell. At noon my employer calls me into his office and informs me I am being transferred to the new plant in Milwaukee. At 5:00 that day I am looking for a realtor to sell my home! Yes, changing events create changing real estate needs and your task is to find the people who are caught up in this moving current of life and offer your professional services for their benefit. People sell to settle estates, pay taxes, improve their way of life, or solve financial difficulties. They move to better themselves or to provide more suitable environments for their offspring. They transfer real estate as a means of increasing recognition or insuring security. Buying and selling real estate is an integral part of the moving story of life being enacted thousands of times each day in your city and mine. All you need to do in order to obtain more listings is to open your eyes and see the needs which motivate sellers to sell and buyers to buy.

ASK THE RIGHT QUESTIONS EVERY DAY

You will be amazed how easy it is to list property when you put forth a little extra effort to ask the right questions and meet the right people. It has been wisely said that there is more money to be made in asking the right questions than in knowing the right answers. When you talk to people, ask questions and you will be surprised how much information can be extracted about property and the people who own it. When you develop a lead, follow it up immediately before it grows cold or some other agent obtains the listing. When a customer tells you he is thinking of selling next spring instead of now, put the information into a follow-up file and contact the prospective seller at the proper time. Results come from doing many little things correctly every day!

When I started in the real estate business there were no training manuals and very few training programs of any kind. I had to learn the business by trial and error. My father simply said to me: "Go out and ring door bells, meet the people, and you will find the business." He was right. I did just that. I worked a section of the real estate market around our first small office known as the Burbank District. I talked to owners and tenants alike and learned much about the property and the people who lived there. Each thirty days or so, I would repeat my rounds and each time a few more listings came my way. Gradually I knew personally many of the people who lived in "my ten acres of diamonds." Relationships developed which produced many profitable real estate transactions and led to continued growth for both myself and my clients. There is no substitute for meeting people!

SELLING OWNERS ON YOUR SERVICES

Often, after obtaining a listing appointment, you will still be in competition with other realtors or brokers as well as with some "do-it-yourself fans." To overcome the obstacles such competition creates, I recommend investing some time in preparing for the listing interview and in the development of an outline presentation you can recall mentally when it is needed. Begin by asking yourself: "Why should the seller want to list with me? What can I do for him? If he is trying to sell his own home, what can I do for him that he cannot do for himself?" When you have the answers, memorize the key points to your arguments and outline them for future use. This provides you with a mental rack on which to hang each point and enables you to remove the prepared items when they are needed to convince potential sellers they should employ you.

Start your outline by remembering that <u>no seller is interested in your services if all you are going to do for him is what he can do for himself</u>! Any seller can advertise his own property, put up a for sale sign, or hold his home open for inspection. If this is all you promise to do, he doesn't really need you in order to sell his property.

Did you ever try to sell your own home? If so, you probably can recall some of the problems you encountered. Put yourself in the shoes of the typical seller for a moment and imagine the problems with which he is confronted. Here is a list of the major problems involved when sellers try to locate their own purchasers without the aid of professional real estate service.

1. <u>They price property at unrealistic prices.</u>

    Since they do not really understand how to arrive at market values, most sellers working on their own are tempted to over-price their properties in order to have a cushion in case they have to come down. This frequently discourages prospective buyers who go elsewhere because they do not know how to negotiate price and terms.

2. <u>Speculators can prey on untrained sellers.</u>

    When an owner is without professional counsel he may not be able to determine whether or not an offer to buy is legitimate or reasonable. Some investors make their living by buying directly from unsuspecting property owners.

3. <u>Legal entanglements can occur through careless actions.</u>

    Sellers who are without professional guidance can, and often do, find themselves tied with unexpected red tape which might have been avoided if they had consulted a knowledgeable real estate broker.

4. <u>He must attract many buyers to find one.</u>

    Eliminating the many unqualified property prospects and the shoppers is a task few sellers are really prepared to handle. After a few days of tramping people through their homes, sellers are often disgusted or impatient and tempted to sell to unqualified prospects at low prices.

5. Arranging financing for the buyer is a problem.

Sellers seldom understand the various types of financing tools available to the buyer to facilitate the sale. Thus, unless the buyer has all cash, the seller may turn away customers who want to use FHA, VA, or other financing. In fact, the prospects themselves often do not know how to arrange the best financing.

6. Prospects respond to advertising different from their needs.

When the seller advertises his home, he generally will attract people who are looking for something better than he has to offer. Prospects tend to call on ads for homes considerably less than they can afford, because they are looking for bargains. Thus, the buyer for a particular home is probably responding to an ad for another home, but there is no way for the prospect to be cross-fed to the owner-seller since he is not using the services of a qualified agent.

7. Prospects who call on owner ads always want to know both price and location.

Obviously, the seller must reveal both of these facts. This eliminates many potential prospects who might have been sold had they been qualified and shown by an experienced negotiator. Also, if the prospect drives to the property and decides not to come in because of exterior appearances, he may be lost because his impression is limited to the external exposure although the interior was what he wanted.

8. Sellers find it difficult to negotiate with buyers.

If a buyer says to the owner: "Will you take less?" how can he reply? If he says, "Yes," the next question is "How much less?" If he says "No," he may lose the buyer although an agent could have negotiated the sale. The problem is one of protecting his own interests while trying to help the buyer make a decision. This is one of the most important reasons for using experienced real estate negotiators.

9. Homes must be open to the public at all hours.

It can be a nerve-racking experience to an owner who cannot go anywhere in the evenings or on weekends because buyers want to look at his home. Trying to maintain some semblance of normal home life when you must be at the property constantly and answer phone calls continuously is an inconvenience many owners do not appreciate.

10. The wife and children encourage danger while alone.

Consider the fearful disadvantage of the housewife who must show her property to strange men whose motives she cannot question when they request permission to inspect her home while the husband is away!

If an agent were involved, he would be in attendance and could screen away the undesirables as well as protect the interests of the seller. This is reason enough for any husband to want to hire a reputable real estate salesman.

This list covers only a few of the obstacles any "do-it-yourself" property owner may encounter. Look them over again. Now prepare your own outline of arguments to use when calling on "for sale by owner" clients. Here is an example of how you might contact such an owner:

Example 12

"How do you do! Are you Mr. Jones?" (pause) "I'm Sam Brown with Perkins Realty. I talked to you yesterday about your home selling problems. Have your sold your home yet?" (pause)

"May I see your home? Possibly I can make some suggestions that will be of benefit to you."

After gaining access and making a brief inspection, you are seated in the livingroom discussing the situation with Mr. and Mrs. Jones.

"You do have a lovely home, Mr. and Mrs. Jones. I imagine you will regret leaving it, since it is obvious you have spent much time and money in maintaining it!" (Pause. Here you are trying to find the motive for selling.)

"I am certain you are well acquainted with Perkins Realty. We have effectively represented sellers like yourselves for many years and we appreciate the problems involved in attempting to sell your own home. You see, Mr. Jones, when a prospect replies to your ad or stops at your For Sale sign, you seldom have an opportunity to qualify him, know his financial means, or understand his motives. Also, because you are forced to reveal the address and price of your property over the phone, some of them will drive by and inspect the exterior of the home without ever coming inside. This is like judging a book by its cover, isn't it Mr. Jones?" (Pause)

"Our experience has proven to us that most prospects are not interested in the home about which they inquire. This may seem strange to you, but we believe it is because most prospects are looking for bargains and respond to ads that are less than what they can really afford. The chances are, the potential prospect for your home is replying to somebody else's advertisement, but there is no way that prospect can be directed to your home. Our firm advertises many properties daily, each of which is pre-selected to cover the broad range of property types available in our office. This way we attract a large number of new buyers and, after proper qualifying and counselling, we show them the best homes suited to their needs. In this manner we show and sell most of the homes listed with our company.

"If you place your residence in my hands, I will see that all qualified prospects are shown the property and no addresses will be given out for buyers who just want to drive by. We will get them inside so they can inspect all of its outstanding features. Further, we are able to arrange all kinds of financing for the buyer and show him how he can qualify for the terms. This is a very vital factor in any real estate sale today since few people have all cash for the purchase price.

"You know, Mr. Jones, there are some other very important considerations you should make. For example, have you thought about the dangers to which your wife and family might be subjected in your absence while showing the home to strangers? There have been some unhappy consequences for sellers in similar circumstances. Also, I know you must now keep your home open at all hours of the day or night and even stay home on weekends in order to show it. If we were your agents, you could forget about being home or having to answer phones. No buyers will go through the property without one of our bonded sales representatives in attendance." (Pause)

"Consider also, Mr. Jones, the importance of avoiding legal entanglements that can often result in loss of time and money. When we represent you, our staff of experts in escrow work, financing, and sales takes over to protect your interests. Many years of experience have built the reputation Perkins Realty enjoys as the real estate company that knows its business.

"Finally, I would like to point out the problems I know you are experiencing in trying to negotiate price and terms with prospects. They will seldom tell you what they really want, or why they object to something, because you are the owner. On the other hand, if they ask for a reduction, you do not know how far to go in commiting yourself. Our trained negotiators can fill that important function so as to close the sale at the best possible dollar to yourselves. If the client owns another property, we can even take this home in trade at no extra cost to you. These are just some of the services which we offer our real estate clients. If you employ me, I will represent your property to all the other agents in town and to the public through them, so we can sell your home for the right price and quickly."

This typical presentation is loaded with vital facts which should interest any seller. If not, it will certainly leave the door open for repeat calls until they either list or sell. The key to this presentation is in selling the benefits the owner will realize when he employs you. As in all selling, you must sell the benefits to the client, not to yourself.

CONCLUSION

In this chapter you have learned the importance of real estate sellers to your career. We have extensively explored ways to prospect for listings and given you a list of practical sources to be developed. Finally, we have shown you how to sell the individual owner on using your services by pointing out the benefits you can render, doing for him what he cannot do for himself. All of these factors are important, but they will only pay dividends if you know how to list the property at the right price and terms so it will sell. This is the subject we discuss in the next chapter.

MEET YOUR EMPLOYERS 47

QUESTIONS AND PROJECTS FOR CHAPTER THREE

Questions:

1. Give at least three reasons why sellers are vitally important to a real estate salesman's career.
2. What five questions can you ask every seller of property to help uncover additional business?
3. Of the 38 sources for obtaining listings given in this chapter on pages 33/40, which five do you believe will be the more important to you in your initial prospecting activity?
4. What are some of the advantages of working an assigned area for continuous prospecting for listings?
5. What research should you complete before beginning any canvassing campaign in a pre-selected area?
6. Name three good sources of leads for prospecting by telephone for new listings.
7. What services do you and your company offer sellers that make it advantageous for them to consider listing with you rather than a competitor?
8. How can you develop centers of influence to help you find new listings?
9. Why is the property a magnet to help you attract new business and how can you use this fact to advantage?
10. Give three good approaches you can use when canvassing for listings from door to door. Give three you can use when prospecting by telephone.

Projects:

1. Select your private listing area as assigned to you by your broker.
2. Research all the following facts about this area in prepartion for your canvassing activity:
    a. Obtain copies of the plot or tract maps of this area from County Recorder's office or a title company.
    b. On separate pages list or reproduce all known sales, listings, appraisals, and cancellations within this district for the past 12 months or longer.
    c. List all current properties for sale (whether they are listed by your office or other brokers) and record all known facts about the activity on these properties.
    d. Inspect all properties for sale in your area (if permissible with listing brokers) and introduce yourself to the owners as "The District Representative" from your office who has been assigned to this section as a specialist in its real estate activities.
    e. Using reverse telephone directories, city directories, or any other source available, canvass by telephone or personally contact the owners living in your section. Use some of the techniques for prospecting reviewed in this chapter.

  f. Cover your district with direct mail campaigns of various types as approved by your broker.
  g. Maintain a record of all your contacts and your research material, building a listing book for continuous reference and follow-up.
   This is your "ten acres of diamonds" for cultivation and harvesting in the months and years ahead.
3. Clip out all "For Sale By Owner" ads in your area and begin contacting them with daily follow up until sold or listed.
4. Drive your area daily and search for owner For Sale signs. Apply the techniques covered in this lesson to approach such owners.
5. Select your best centers of influence for personal development and begin planting the seeds necessary to obtain future listing business from these sources.
6. Make a complete list of the services you and your company are prepared to offer sellers and then analyze how you can capitalize on these professional advantages to convince sellers they should use your services.
7. Ask your broker or supervisor for an explanation of the various research files available for your listing activities and comparable records necessary to obtain market data. Also learn how to use city directories, reverse telephone directories, and other such sources of prospects.
8. Explain and define the following, and know your office policies on each:
 a. open listings
 b. exclusive agency listings
 c. net listings
 d. multiple listings
 e. exclusive right to sell listings
9. What are the office policies on listings concerning the following points:
 a. Minimum acceptable listing period?
 b. Maximum protection period after listing expires?
 c. Acceptable commission rate?
 d. Handling a cancellation, extension, or reduction?
 e. If MLS fees are involved, who pays them?
10. Visit the County Recorder's Office, Planning Commission, and Tax Assessor's office to learn how to use these sources of information for accurate research when listing property or gathering market data.

4

HOW TO OBTAIN AND SERVICE
SALEABLE LISTINGS

      Now that you have learned where to prospect for good listings and how to use proven sales techniques in securing the interest and attention of potential sellers of property, you are ready to venture forth into your real estate market and begin listing homes. In this chapter we will outline for you the steps to be taken in preparing for a professional listing presentation and emphasize the importance of conditioning owners to the facts of real estate selling in order to assure results. It is not enough to just list property. To be profitable for you and beneficial to sellers these listings must attract the interest of salesmen and buyers. Unless you can produce a sufficient number of realistic and marketable listings, you will be wasting your time in the real estate business, and your sellers will be unhappy with you and your broker. There are few things which are more detrimental to this business than the damage inflicted by careless, non-professional real estate sales people who will take any listing at any price hoping someone will wave a magic wand and sell the property for them. Many multiple listing services find their inventories constantly log-jammed with over-priced merchandise due to the lax listing policies of member brokers and salesmen. When more than 50% of the listings taken finally expire unsold, the public image of our profession and the thousands of lost hours wasted penalize the conscientious men and women who desire to become professional listers.
      The existence of real estate markets in which a high percentage of property owners attempt to solve their own real estate problems can be directly charged to those brokers and salesmen who violate the basic principles and professional knowledge needed in listing and selling real property. If we are faced with an increasing number of "For Sale By Owner" signs and ads in our market areas, we have only ourselves (the industry) to blame! If the seller believes he can do a better job than we can, it is because we have either failed him in the past or have not convinced him we are worth the price he pays for professional service. A recent survey among sellers of property in Los Angeles County who had attempted to sell their own homes revealed the fact that the majority had

previously used real estate brokers on other transactions and had been disappointed in the results and the treatment they received.[1] This startling fact should make all of us in the real estate business more conscious of the great need for professional attitudes and actions by ourselves and our associates.

YOUR LISTING APPOINTMENT

With this in mind, let us help you prepare for a listing appointment you have obtained through your prospecting efforts. Mr. and Mrs. Kenneth Ervin have been referred to you by a builder contact as the result of their purchase of a new home in the Blue Hills Estates subdivision, and you have made an appointment to visit them at their home this evening at 7:00. You made the appointment for this time in order to provide several hours for gathering facts and making a pre-inspection trip to the property. Also, you want to contact them when they are in a relaxed frame of mind, after their evening meal. You know it is important to have the sellers together when you make your sales presentation because you are going to have many things to say which should be heard by both of them. Selling real property generally requires the mutual consent of all parties involved, and you must know that husband and wife agree on price, terms, occupancy, and other vital matters affecting this proposed transfer.

You have set aside three hours this afternoon to make your first inspection and to gather the facts needed for your presentation this evening. There are two primary reasons why you should use the two-visit approach to the listing appointment. The first is simply to give yourself an opportunity to inspect the property in an unhurried fashion and to gather the facts about the parcel so you can return to the privacy of your office and digest what you have uncovered before reaching any conclusions. The second is related to the importance of showmanship in any selling situation. You will want the seller to realize you are a professional and that your decisions are based on sound facts, not snap judgments. I realize that it is entirely possible for you to know property values reasonably well after you have made even a few sales and taken some listings in a given neighborhood. You may be able to walk in the front door of a home and quickly decide the approximate price range. <u>However, the seller cannot appreciate such hasty reactions</u> and since your prime task is to win the confidence of the seller so he will accept your recommendations concerning price, terms, and the other important matters pertaining to your listing service, you need to establish a foundation of trust on which your relationship with the seller can be soundly constructed.

---

[1] See the research studies of Dr. William Case, University of California at Los Angeles, Real Estate Research Dept.

HOW TO OBTAIN AND SERVICE SALEABLE LISTINGS 51

There will be some situations when you must take the listing on a single call, and on these occasions you will have to consolidate the steps we set forth in this chapter so as to accomplish your objectives. This will generally require from two to three hours for a combined presentation and inspection call. Many salesmen make the mistake of attempting to take the listing too quickly and the result is often an over-priced listing. Even if it is correctly priced, the salesman will seldom have spent sufficient time to develop the good client relationships needed for later negotiation and follow-up contacts. Most important is the ultimate objective of every professional salesman to build a solid referral business for future success. This can only be done if proper time and attention is taken at the beginning of business relationships.

PREPARATION BEFORE YOU LEAVE THE OFFICE

If your office has been in business for a number of years, your broker has undoubtedly developed extensive property appraisal files from which to gather vital facts concerning real estate activity in your area. Every broker knows the value of maintaining such records as they are essential tools in listing property, as well as in handling repeat business. If your broker does not maintain such records, then you can probably compile your own from the following sources:

1. Multiple listing bulletins or records showing sales and listings sold through its service.
2. Summary books available from certain real estate publishing firms which identify real estate activity for major market areas.
3. Lending institutions whose files and records contain many FHA, VA, and conventional appraisals.
4. Title and escrow companies whose files and recorded documents reveal records of title transfer.
5. County Recorder's office or Tax Assessor's office where chain of title is maintained, and values established.
6. Your own inspection of current properties for sale, sold, and expired from listing records of your office and other brokers in the area.

From all or some of these sources you can compile a fairly accurate picture of the market situation in the neighborhood surrounding the residence which you are going to inspect. This information should be copied on a suitable form which you can use with the sellers. (See the "Competitive Property Report Form" on page 52.) The form used by our salesmen has proven to be a valuable tool in conditioning sellers to accept the truth about the real estate market. It provides space for 18 comparable or competitive properties: <u>6 sold</u>, <u>6 expired</u>, <u>6 currently for sale in the area.</u> Actual dates, prices, and names are inserted to authenticate the record and provide both seller and salesman with the necessary facts to make a decision about the listing price of the subject

STONE & SCHULTE, INC.
COMPETITIVE PROPERTIES REPORT FORM

Property: 3562 Rosedale Ave
Address:
City: Your Town, USA
Area Code: CBN Tract No. 1304
Subdivision Name: Rosedale Gardens Lot No. 114

Date: Jul 6, 19— Dept. Residential
Assigned to:
Suggested Price: $18,500
Property Code: 6-3-2-H-D-S

STREETS IN PROJECT
- Rosedale Bl
- Mardell Ln
- Gardenia Dr
- Blossom Dr
- Blossom Ave
- Cherry Ave

SOLD PROPERTIES

1. 3560 Rosedale — Brought: Jenkins / Sold: Frank Jewell
Listing Price: 19,450 Date: Jan 16, 19—
Selling Price: 18,250 firm Date: June 3, 19—
Code: 6-3-2-H-D-S

4. 3463 Mardell — Brought: Smith / Sold: Johnson
Listing: 17,950 Date: Apr 18, 19—
Selling: 17,400 Date: Jun 21, 19—
Code: 5-2-1½-H-D-S

7. 3420 Mardell — Brought: Owens / Sold: O'Malley
Listing: 18,750 Date: Mar 10, 19—
Selling: 18,450 Date: May 5, 19—
Code: 6-3-2-1½-H-D-S

10. 3216 Gardenia — Brought: Barker / Sold: Garcia
Listing: 18,250 Date: Feb 4, 19—
Selling: 19,150 Date: May 26, 19—
Code: 6-3-1-H-D-S

13. 2803 Blossom Ave — Brought: Madison / Sold: Hunter
Listing: 18,950 Date: Dec 11, 19—
Selling: 18,300 Date: Mar 22, 19—
Code: 6-4-2-H-D-S

16. 3517 Bascal — Brought: Hines / Sold: Sorsen
Listing: 17,950 Date: Jan 15, 19—
Selling: 17,750 Date: Apr 8, 19—
Code: 5-2-1½-H-D-S

EXPIRED LISTINGS

2. 2432 Rosedale — Browning
Listing: 19,500 Date: Jun 3, 19—
Code: 6-3-2-H-D-S

5. 3196 Gardenia — Pershing
Listing: 19,950 Date: Apr 18, 19—
Code: 6-3-2-H-D-S

8. 3450 Mardell — Henderson
Listing: 19,250 Date: Feb 16, 19—
Code: 6-3-2-H-D-S

11. 3176 Cherry — Johnsen
Listing: 18,400 Date: Mar 22, 19—
Code: 5-3-1-H-D-S

14. 3463 Bascal — Larkmann
Listing: 19,950 Date: Jan 4, 19—
Code: 5-2-1½-H-D-S

17. 2933 Blossom — Beckmann
Listing: 15,950 Date: Dec 6, 19—
Code: 6-3-2-H-D-S

CURRENT LISTINGS

3. 2375 Rosedale — Winklemann
Listing: 18,950 Date: Jun 25, 19—
Code: 6-3-2-H-D-S

6. 2859 Cherry — Becker
Listing: 18,500 Date: Jul 3, 19—
Code: 6-3-2-H-D-S

9. 3743 Blossom — Jacobs
Listing: 19,300 Date: May 13, 19—
Code: 6-4-2-H-D-S

12. 3563 Mardell — Edwards
Listing: 19,250 Date: Apr 6, 19—
Code: 5-3-1½-H-D-S

15. 3754 Blossom — Backster
Listing: 17,950 Date: Jun 22, 19—
Code: 5-2-1-H-D-S

18. 2156 Cherry — Summers
Listing: 18,800 Date: May 15, 19—
Code: 6-3-2-H-D-S

property. The size and type of home are coded for easy reference:

> Code: 6 - 3- 2 - H - D- S

This tells our salesman that the home in question has six rooms, 3 bedrooms 2 baths, hardwood floors, a double garage, and shake roof. Even with this limited description there is generally enough information to help evaluate the relative differences in property values for various floor plans in this community. Since most homes in the medium and modest price ranges are former subdivision homes built in the post-war years, a salesman can quickly compare similar models built by the same developer and determine approximate values involved. In many appraisal files, the real estate firm posts the original selling prices of each model in a tract and thereafter brings the information about resale and appraisal up to date as new transactions occur within the project. <u>There is no substitute for a complete and accurate appraisal record to assist new salesmen in learning property values.</u>

APPRAISAL KNOWLEDGE IMPORTANT

Listing property effectively is a matter of relating many aspects of the real estate market to the particular property under consideration. As a competent real estate salesman you should be as knowledgeable as possible about the real estate trends in the areas you serve. You should know population figures and the trends of increase or decrease. You should be familiar with industry, employment patterns, average income of your buyers, and the availability of employment for new residents. From your local Chamber of Commerce or other information centers you can obtain data about utilities, taxes, churches, banks, and building activity. The vacancy factor in various sections of your community and the availability or shortage of certain types of property should influence your reactions to any given piece of property. As you conduct your daily real estate business, gather and store these bits of information about your market area. It is never too early to begin gathering a fund of knowledge about property values. A new real estate salesman owes it to himself and his clients to know the major factors which will influence real estate values.[1]

I have developed an additional analysis form to assist salesmen in listing property correctly. It is known as "The Total Market Analysis Report." (See page 54.) Once each month we summarize the activity currently experienced in each of the various real estate districts surrounding our offices. We list in total units the number of homes for sale by area; the current turnover rate is shown in terms of 30- and 90-day periods. We also list the number of units which have expired unsold

---

[2] See "Appraising," Chapter 12, p. 240.

TOTAL MARKET ANALYSIS REPORT -- JULY 19-

AREA	OFFICE Listings	MLS Listings	SOLD 30 Days	EXPIRED 30 Days	AVERAGE PRICE	PERCENT Sold	MSL SUMMARY Preceding Calendar Year			
							Listed	Sold	Expired	Percent Sold
BUR	8	39	9	10	$18,233	23%	207	115	92	56%
CBN	18	127	39	37	18,847	31%	837	271	566	32%
CPL	28	105	33	23	20,536	31%	610	219	391	36%
CMV	20	148	38	39	20,478	26%	762	461	301	60%
EFH	21	104	24	28	15,664	23%	565	217	348	38%
LG-SAR	26	253	83	101	28,754	33%	465	161	304	34%
MFR	18	52	8	8	14,463	15%	258	88	170	34%
NSJ	13	21	2	7	17,975	10%	127	62	65	41%
WSJ	10	25	14	10	16,978	56%	185	109	76	60%
SCA	17	68	20	18	18,837	29%	585	274	311	47%
WGN	16	96	36	26	23,664	36%	668	282	386	42%
TOTALS	195	1038	306	307	$18,760	29%	5269	2259	3010	43%

Aug. 1, 19 -

HOW TO OBTAIN AND SERVICE SALEABLE LISTINGS

during this time. The results are often dramatic visual aids which help to convince sellers they have competition.

<u>Sellers can understand competition. They do not understand "comparables."</u> Nothing is really comparable to "my" property, because I have certain amenities my neighbors' homes do not possess. But I can easily realize there are only so many buyers for the total number of homes on the market in my neighborhood and that some of them will sell while others will not.

In areas where the ratio of listings taken to sales consummated is high, this tool can help you convince an owner to price his home at or below the market in order to avoid the competitive problem. Let me emphasize the value of such visual aids to a listing salesman. <u>Most sellers and buyers do not accept the real estate salesman as a professional and therefore they tend to distrust his verbal representations.</u> When you produce printed or written facts and present them in a confident and authoritative fashion, you remove these doubts and open paths to a successful understanding with the owners.

INSPECTING THE NEIGHBORHOOD AROUND THE PROPERTY

You are now ready to leave your office and inspect the neighborhood surrounding your proposed listing. At this point I would like to stress the importance of neighborhood influence on real estate values. The only thing permanent in real estate is change. Every piece of property is affected by the conditions in the area in which it is located, as well as by the immediate influence of adjacent parcels. When you sell a property you are not selling just a single piece of real estate, but rather a neighborhood, an environment, and a way of life. Prospective buyers will be observing the homes, lawns, yards, and people who live in the district where you propose to place them. You must also learn to study these same factors when you list property, and to evaluate in advance the probable effect upon your proposed listing. As you drive around the neighborhood close to the property you are concerned with, you will be interested in the status of the area as it is today, not what it was yesterday. Properties and property conditions change daily. Some are sold, old ones are removed, others deteriorate, and more come on the market for sale. Prior to inspecting the home, you thus decide to drive each of the blocks adjacent to the property and look for the following things:

1. New For Sale signs that have appeared since you were last there and which may not have been reported to your office. If other brokers have obtained new listings in the area, you will want addresses and phone numbers to call for further information when you are back at your office.

2. The exterior appearance and condition of the properties listed on your competitive property report form, noting observations about the relative differences involved. Those still on the market, competing for the same buyer your prospective seller may

require, should be inspected closely for comparative purposes. If the listing brokers cooperate in this matter, I even recommend actually going into the listings that are still for sale and gathering additional facts about the properties from their owners.

3. The condition of the neighborhood as to maintenance, pride of ownership, and general appearance. Also study the effect any adverse influence such as freeway construction, deteriorated properties, number of For Sale signs, vacancy factors, and misused parcels might have had on property values.

4. If new subdivisions are operating in the immediate vicinity, be certain to check these also and note price ranges, values, and terms as they will also affect the resale market in the area. New homes are competition for used homes and the sellers of property should be educated to this fact.

LEARNING TO APPRAISE DEPRECIATION FACTORS

One of the prime factors in determining the value of real estate is to correctly relate the forces which combine to cause loss in property values. These factors are frequently difficult to evaluate, but their importance cannot be underestimated. There are three principle sources of depreciation:

1. Physical Deterioration

    This covers those things which represent the lowered values resulting from wear and tear and normal usage. This includes termite damage, decay, paint erosion, and many similar items of physical change which occur as property grows old or is not well maintained.

2. Functional Obsolescence

    The intrinsic design and use of a property often limits its desirability as changing styles, conveniences, and needs are accented by newer, more modern structures. The inherent qualities built into the plan of a building become, in time, disadvantages to those desiring the latest features. The depreciation in value resulting from the nature of the building itself is said to be "functional obsolescence." This is nothing, more or less, than a reflection of the current tastes of the real estate buyer as shown in market trends.

3. Economic Obsolescence

    External factors affecting values adversely are said to result from depreciation by economic obsolescence. Adjacent properties, deteriorating neighborhoods, changes in zoning, traffic patterns, and other factors combine to produce adverse effects on certain properties. In learning to appraise and list

HOW TO OBTAIN AND SERVICE SALEABLE LISTINGS

property correctly, you should be alert to these influences and learn to weigh them carefully when pricing property.

INSPECTING THE PROPERTY

You are now ready to make your first inspection of the home of Mr. and Mrs. Ervin. Since you made an appointment with the sellers to be there between 2:30 and 3:00, you plan to arrive on time. Nothing is more aggravating to a seller than the frustration of waiting for a real estate salesman long after the appointment time has passed. The owner may have made other plans, and the relationships you want to create can go right out the window before you even arrive if you do not exercise common courtesy about keeping appointments. If you must be late for any reason, you are always as near as a telephone call, and you should place one promptly to advise the owner about the delay. Being punctual is part of being professional.

Now as you approach the front door of the Ervin's property, you notice that the lawns and shrubs are neatly edged and trimmed, that there are sprinklers in the front yard, and the gutters are painted and cleaned. As you prepare to ring the bell, your trained eye takes in the window sills, door trim, and the hardware on the front door. You are aware these are items which any prospective purchaser is likely to notice. In this case, you note the trim around the window sills has been recently painted but the front door hardware is worn from use. Unconsciously you have already formed an impression about the Ervins, even though you have not met them. Property is another extension of personality and the way it is maintained reveals much about the people who own it. You are reasonably certain they are clean, home-loving people who take basic pride in their possessions.

Mrs. Ervin answers the door and you introduce yourself, explaining as you do so that this first visit is to obtain the basic facts about the home so you can intelligently review the findings before you return this evening. You ask Mrs. Ervin if she would be kind enough to locate the various documents pertaining to the property. These include:

1. The deed, contract of sale, or other documents establishing ownership.
2. The payment books for any mortgages involved.
3. The policy of title insurance (if one was issued when they purchased).
4. Fire insurance policies.
5. Real estate tax statements.
6. Any other papers they may possess which affect the status of title.

While she is gathering these, you begin taping the exterior of the home to compute the square footage on your work sheet. You sketch the outline of the home as you make your computations. In case you have never taped a home before, let me briefly explain the steps. Starting at one corner of the home, going in one direction completely around the property, measure each side and place your figures on your graph paper. When you have measured the exterior and all the indentations, complete the total footage by squaring the various sections of the home and deducting the porch and other indentations.

The Ervin's home has 1356 square feet, plus a garage with 378 square feet. While making the trip around the exterior, you also kept your eyes open for any condition which might affect the value of the property. This includes watching for water rot, termite problems, damaged materials, and poor construction (physical deterioration). Homes not sufficiently elevated above the ground will often evidence water damage and termite infestation. When you come to the meter box, you open it and look for tags that indicate dates of construction, lot number, and completion dates. Often you can find these still hanging there or in a concealed spot in the garage. In older homes, the age of the property can be approximated from the date stamped on the underlid of the commode. All plumbing fixtures of this type have the date they were manufactured stamped somewhere on the rims of the toilet lids.

When you return to the living room, Mrs. Ervin has located the papers you requested. Before looking at them, you ask her if she would mind showing you through the home to permit you to gather the rest of your facts. This gives you an opportunity to ask questions while obtaining the information needed. As you tour the home, you will do the following things:

1. Measure all major rooms (bedrooms, livingroom, and family room).
2. Inspect closets, cabinets, heaters, and service areas.
3. Carefully check bathrooms, noting condition and quality of plumbing fixtures.
4. Observe the condition of paint, trim, color, and neatness of home as they might affect the average buyer.
5. Study the decor and furnishings of the home and their effect on marketability.
6. List the personal property items to be included by the owner in the price.
7. Study the floor plan and relate its acceptability to similar priced merchandise in the area.
8. In general, note all items which will detract from value as well as those which will add to value.

While making these observations and measuring the home, you can begin planting ideas to help condition the seller to the obsolescence factors you have detected in the home. Checking the information on the clipboard worksheet, you make semi-obvious comments:

HOW TO OBTAIN AND SERVICE SALEABLE LISTINGS 59

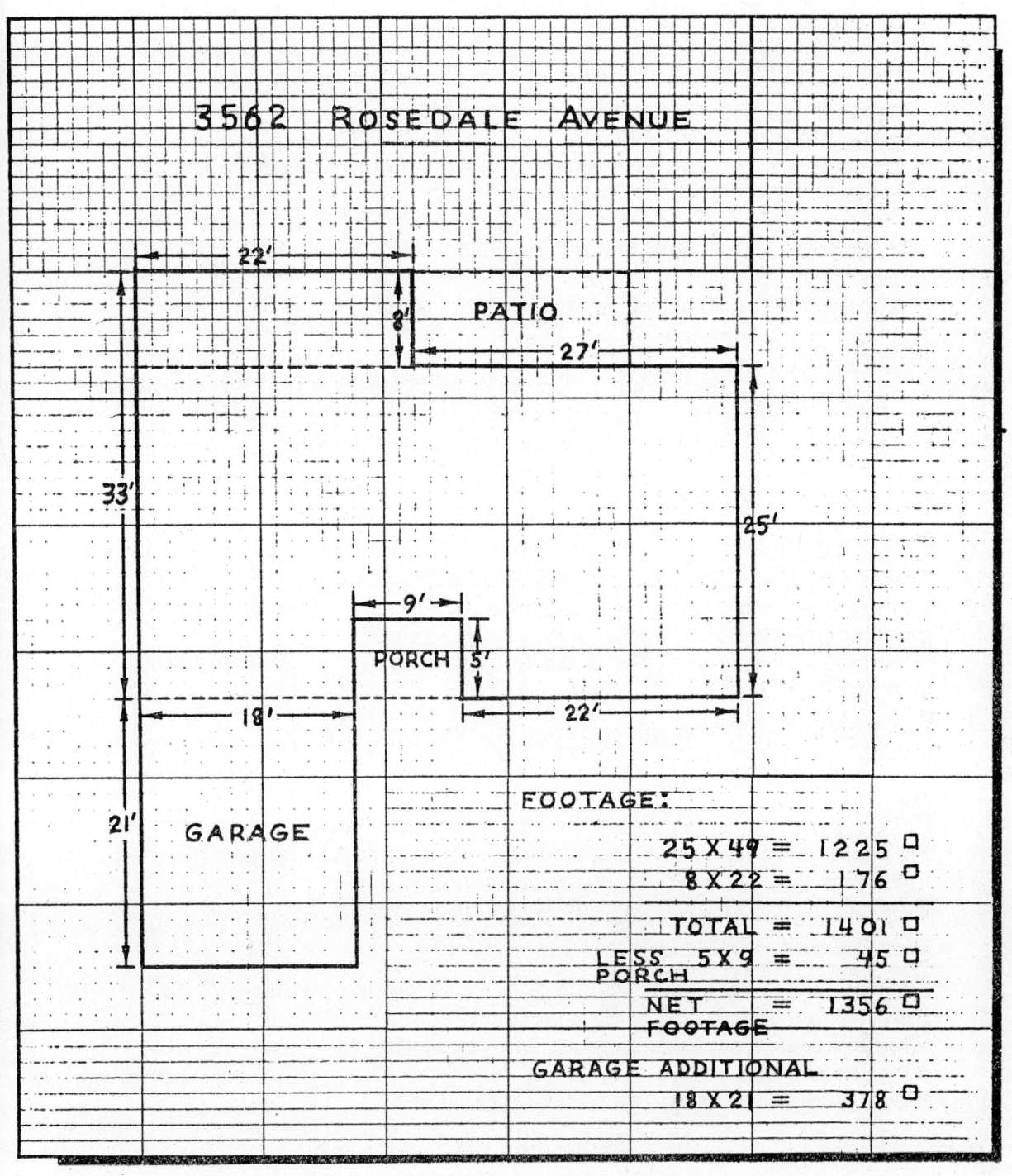

"No vanity in the baths"
"No dishwasher"
"No entry hall" etc.

Also, if you know the product they are buying, you can make observations like:

"I'm certain you will appreciate those double wardrobe closets in your new home, Mrs. Ervin."

"That modern, U-shaped kitchen with its electric appliances will certainly give you more room and convenience than this smaller pullman kitchen offers."

These observations and comments are part of the psychological conditioning used to help the seller realize the advantages of selling at a reasonable price in order to trade up to the better product they have selected. This is also a good time to ask questions which reveal the motives of the seller and help you determine the many hidden factors which must be uncovered before you make your presentation that evening.

CATEGORIES AND SAMPLE QUESTIONS

1. Questions to Determine Urgency

   "Have you and Mr. Ervin located another home yet?"
   "When will it be ready for your occupancy?"
   "When would you like to make the move?"
   "If we found a buyer for your home immediately, how soon could you give possession?"

2. Questions to Determine Experience

   "Have you and your husband owned other homes besides this one?"
   "Do you own other real estate?"
   "Before you decided to use our services, did you think about selling the home yourselves?" (This will sometimes uncover names of prospects they obtained while trying to sell it.)
   "How long have you lived here on Rosedale Drive?"

3. Questions to Ascertain Owner's Idea of Value

   "What improvements have you made since acquiring the home?"
   "Have you ever had your home appraised?"
   "What features are you looking for in your next home which this one does not have?"
   "How much insurance do you carry on the home?"

4. Questions to Uncover New Business in Area

   "Do your neighbors know that you plan to sell?"
   "I imagine you will be leaving behind a number of friends after living here for eight years, Mrs. Ervin!"

"Do you know of others nearby who may be marketing their homes at the same time yours is on the market?"
"Have any of your friends expressed interest in your home?"

5. <u>Questions to Uncover Neighborhood Benefits</u>

"Is this a quiet neighborhood?"
"Who lives in the lovely home next door?"
"Are there many children in the block?"
"Where is the nearest city bus line stop?"
"What school do your children attend?"
"Do you attend a nearby church? Who is the pastor?"

Many of these questions may not need asking if you already know the answers, but this general line of inquiry should be pursued in order to uncover the seller's personal reactions to these questions. You are looking for the motivations of this seller as well as reasons why new buyers might be interested in purchasing the home. <u>After asking a question, LISTEN!</u> Master salesmen know the importance of asking the right question and listening carefully for the full response to that question. Sometimes it is what the client does not say that provides the clue to motivations and facts about the proposed transfer. There is one question I always recommend asking, as it may uncover potential business. It is:

"Do you have any prospects from your own contacts who might be interested in purchasing your home?"

This question has uncovered many buyers for me in the past because a large number of sellers do try to make their own sale before contacting agents and often they have the names of people who expressed interest but whom they could not close without professional help. Some of these friends, relatives, or prospects may need professional service to locate other property. Always pursue any line of questioning which can lead to additional business since prospecting is a continual objective of the alert real estate salesman.

KEEP YOUR OBJECTIVES IN MIND

By now you may be concluding that this is a lot of trouble just to get one listing! It may be, but every bit of effort expended at this time will generally save you time and money later. <u>If there is any short cut to a sale it is in doing a competent and professional job when first listing the property.</u> It is essential to remember that you are doing more than just listing a piece of real estate! <u>You are also listing the people who own that real property!</u> Every question and answer helps you lay the foundation for the closing session a few days or weeks from now when you must sit with these owners and review an offer to purchase from a prospective buyer. If you have really absorbed the facts, uncovered the motivations, and won the confidence of your owners you will find your task of closing the sale relatively simple. Learn to be thorough and persistent in your real estate selling.

Once I nearly lost a listing because I failed to inspect the closets in the master bedroom. As I was passing through the living room I overheard the wife saying to her husband:

"I don't think this young man is very interested in our home. He didn't even look in the closets!"

Needless to say, I rectified that mistake and not only looked in the closets but even asked permission to look under the home and check the condition of the underpinning and plumbing. The point I wish to emphasize is simply this: <u>OWNERS WANT YOU TO DEMONSTRATE SINCERE AND COMPLETE INTEREST IN THEIR PROPERTIES BEFORE THEY ENTRUST THEM TO YOU!</u> After all they are going to be asked to pay a very sizable fee for your services, probably the largest single fee they will ever expend for any service ordered. They want and expect their money's worth. The salesman who fails to appreciate this fact will seldom be successful as a listing salesman.

You have now completed this informative tour of the home with Mrs. Ervin, and as you return to the living room you spread out the documents she has produced. From them you extract the following facts:

1. <u>Date the home was originally purchased by the Ervins</u>

    This can usually be found on the deed, title policy, or contract for purchase.

2. <u>The approximate amount paid for the home by the Ervins</u>

    This can be computed from the revenue stamps on the deed, or from the amount of the title policy, or from the purchase contract.

3. <u>The legal description of the property</u>

    This is always on the deed, and may also be in the original contract, or title policy. Sometimes a plot map of the parcel will be attached to the title policy or abstract of title. If it is a lengthy title description, ask the owner for permission to borrow the title policy in order to reproduce the information for your records.

4. <u>The mortgage indebtedness of the owners</u>

    This is a vital factor and should be carefully pinpointed. From payment books or loan papers ascertain the type and balance of the loan(s) as well as interest rate, mortgage lender, branch where paid, and loan number for reference. If possible, from the deed of trust or mortgage determine the prepayment penalty the seller will be expected to make if paid in full before the due date.

HOW TO OBTAIN AND SERVICE SALEABLE LISTINGS

A WORD OF CAUTION ABOUT PRICE

Most sellers have a habit of wanting to immediately know what price you believe should be asked for their properties, even before you have finished gathering and analyzing your facts. I believe it is basically unwise to commit yourself even in general terms on this subject until you can present your story completely and at the right time. If the owner asks this question, a good answer is:

"Mrs. Ervin, I would prefer not giving a 'horse-back' appraisal. I have many facts which I must relate in order to make a thorough analysis of your property. I am certain you will want me to reach a factual conclusion after a complete review of the information so I can help you realize the best possible price for your home."

It can be fatal to your listing presentation to state your opinion before you have completed your probing operation and laid the necessary groundwork to substantiate your viewpoint. It is certainly helpful to know what the sellers are thinking in terms of net price for their property, but this can be a stumbling block to later negotiations. No one likes to back down after he has taken a firm position, and sellers are tempted to support unrealistic prices they have quoted simply to justify their own egos and pride. You can determine possible price ranges acceptable to the seller by comparing original purchase price with time periods involved and the balance of present mortgages, as well as by the seller's reactions to your many questions. It is best to avoid direct questions on this subject until you have made your full listing presentation to both owners.

REVIEWING THE FACTS YOU HAVE GATHERED

With your work sheet filled with notes and your head with facts, you excuse yourself and remind Mrs. Ervin you will return at 7:00 this evening to discuss the listing with her and her husband. Now you return to the privacy of your office and review the data you have collected. You complete your "Property Description Form" (see page 64) or that portion of your listing contract which summarizes the details about the property. You also recheck your figures for square footage of the home as well as room dimensions. You are now ready to put the pieces of this listing puzzle together by mentally relating all of your known facts about the property and the owners. This is the appraisal process.

You know that the Ervins have lived in this 1356 square foot ranch home on Rosedale for four and one-half years. Mr. Ervin works for Modern Milk Company and was recently promoted to the position of assistant sales supervisor with a substantial raise in pay. This is one of the reasons for the move to a nicer home and neighborhood. Since moving here they have added two lovely children to their family and now need more room.

You have learned from the papers Mrs. Ervin gave you that they paid originally $16,750 for the property when they purchased it from the Dodson Construction Company with $1500 down and financed the balance

STONE & SCHULTE
STONE & SCHULTE, Inc.
PROPERTY DESCRIPTION FORM

EXCHANGE-A-PLAN — A NEW HOME FOR YOU

Owner KENNETH & SARAH ERVIN Phone EX. 7-3757 Show BY APPOINTMENT Key LOCK BOX
Renter OWNER Phone — Possession 10 DAYS C.O.E. Expires OCT 7, 19—
Listing No. Brochure

EXISTING FINANCING
First Loan $13,200 APPROX. as of OCT. 7 19— @ 5¼% $112.00 per mo./Type: F.H.A.
By KEYSTONE MORT. CO. Ln No. 431-186 incl. T&I YES Taxes $296.71 VE NONE
Second Loan $ NONE as of — 19 — @ — % — per mo./Type: —
By — assumable — assumption fee — Trust Fund Am't. $156.91
Other Loans or Assessments NONE

DESCRIPTION
LR 12'X17' DR 8'X9' FR NONE BDRMS (3) 12X13 MS, 11X10, 10X10
Baths 2 Showers 2 STALL Fixtures WHITE Tile KIT./BATH Vanities MASTER & HALLWAY
Breakfast Rm IN KITCHEN Kitchen Type PULLMAN Basement NONE Service Porch NONE
Fireplace L/R WORK Furnace CENTRAL/FA Floors HARDWOOD Foundation CONCRETE 220 IN KITCHEN
Roof SHAKE Fence 5'-REAR Patio C.C. 8'X13' BBQ NONE Sprinklers 13 HAND FRONT
Garage 18'X21' D/A Exterior RUSTIC & BRICK Style RANCH Stories ONE Sewer YES
Insulated CEILING 4" ROCK WOOL Weatherstripped DOORS, FRT. & REAR Windows ALUMINUM Sidewalks YES
Condition and quality GOOD ARCHITECTURE NEAT - WELL MAINTAINED

PERSONAL PROPERTY
Carpets W/W L/R & HALL Drapes L/R D/R Appliances ELEC. RANGE & H.W.
Other items T.V. ANTENNA

NEIGHBORHOOD FEATURES
Shopping MORELAND CENTER Bus: Type CITY LINES Where 2½ BLOCKS Frequency 30 MIN
Schools: Elem. BRACE ELEM 1-6TH Where 3 BLOCKS Jr. High MARKHAM Where 7 BLOCKS
High LEIGH - 10TH TO 12TH Where ½ MILE Parochial ST. LUKES ¾ MILE
Neighborhood characteristics TREE LINED STREET OF MODEST, NEAT HOMES

SUGGESTED FINANCING
Commitments: FHA COMING Ln Am't. 17,900 Seller Pts. 3 Term 30 YRS
Conventional: $ ABOVE EXISTING @ 5¼ % by KEYSTONE MORTGAGE for 21 yrs.
Secondary: $ 1500 OR LESS @ 6 % by SELLER IF NEEDED for 5 yrs.
Other Financing Notes RECOMMEND SECOND ON NEW - SELLER OR C/L

GENERAL NOTES
Reason for Selling: MOVING TO NEW HOME IN BIRCH HILLS ESTATES
Remarks: MANY SHRUBS AND FLOWERS, TALL PINE IN REAR YARD, FISH POND AND GRAVEL WALKS IN ORIENTAL GARDEN. COVERED PATIO WITH WISTERIA VINE.
Legal: Lot 114 Blk 2 Tract 1304 - ROSEDALE GARDENS Book 31 Pgs. 53
Lot size: 65' X 110' Square Footage 1356 FT Extra footage 423 FT Faces EAST
Salesman SAM SMITH Phone EY 7-3166 Branch CENTRAL Notes MLS

Cross Street:	Geo. Area	Map Key	City	Zoning	Down Payment — Terms
BLOSSOM AVE.	CBN	21-E-2	Y.T.	R-1	MINIMUM FHA or C/L

Address	Rms.	Bdrms.	Baths	Age	PRICE:
3562 ROSEDALE	6	3	2	4½ yrs	$18,950

The above information is acknowledged as to accuracy

Date: JULY 6TH 19—

Kenneth Ervin — Seller

Sarah Ervin — Seller

by a new FHA loan. Since they have now agreed to buy a custom home in the Blue Hills Estates subdivision from builder Joseph Quinn, subject to the sale of their home on Rosedale, they must complete a sale within 90 days. You have called Mr. Quinn and verified that the Ervins need $2500 to complete the down payment requirements on the new home.

Your figures reveal that the Ervins owe approximately $13,200 on the remaining balance of their 5 1/4% FHA loan, and there are apparently no other loans against the property.

APPRAISING AND PRICING THE PROPERTY

Now you carefully compare the property involved with those you viewed in the neighborhood from the information on your competitive property report form. One home, identical in size and floor plan, was sold last month for $18,250 at FHA value while several other plans recently sold from a low of $17,400 to a high of $18,950 in the past six months. From these facts you conclude that the home should sell in the general price range of $18,000 to $19,000. This is substantiated by your cost reproduction sheet:

Home = 1356 sq. ft. @ $9.00 per ft. construction =	$12,204.00
Lot = 65 x 110 compared to vacant lots for sale =	5,000.00
Garage = 378 sq. ft. @ $3.00 per ft. construction=	1,134.00
Patio, landscaping, etc. estimated value to property=	1,000.00
Total before depreciation allowance	$19,338.00
Depreciation on building and improvements only at local rate of 1 1/2% per year for 4 1/2 years =	- 968.00
	$18,370.00

Your competitive report and your cost reproduction estimates indicate a general value between $18,000 and $19,000 with a probable price of $18,500 as the most likely result.

COST REPLACEMENT APPRAISING

Of the three approaches to value used in real estate appraising, only two play a major part in residential evaluation when investment return is not a factor. These are:

1. Comparative Analysis or Market Data Method
2. Cost Replacement Method

The first is the result of gathering all the data about sales, listings, and so forth which we have now completed for this property. The second method, as just illustrated, is the result of determining reasonable replacement cost when a similar structure in today's market is built on a comparable lot and depreciated to present condition. The average real estate salesman is not expected to be an expert in cost replacement analysis, but he should be familiar enough with the technique and the estimated cost factors to compute values within a nominal margin of error.

Since you never depreciate the land (land nearly always appreciates) you must compute the building costs separately from land values and then add them together. The easiest and quickest way to become familiar with construction costs on a per foot basis is to contact a major builder or two in your area and have them show you the costs on a standard building typical of your market. There are varying qualities of construction, and each has its price range for replacement costs. Normally, you can approximate the per dollar per square foot costs by knowing the range of values offered by competing builders. You can also purchase appraisal handbooks published for various areas of the country which give tables and guides for computing replacement costs. When a property is quite old it is often impossible to use the cost replacement approach, since the very techniques and styles have long sinced been discontinued.

DETERMINING THE NET EQUITY

With the price of $18,500 in mind, you compute the possible net equity this would leave the Ervins after paying all normal selling expenses:

6% commission on sale of $18,500	$ 1,110.00
3% discount points on FHA loan of $17,700. . .	531.00
Policy of title insurance and escrow charges .	155.00
Revenue and tax stamps.	20.35
Proration of taxes 90 days from now.	137.50
Miscellaneous recording costs, etc.	25.00
Total costs to sell on new FHA basis . . .	1,978.85

Normally there would also be a prepayment penalty on the existing FHA loan equal to 1% of the original amount, but if a new sale was realized by means of refinancing under FHA terms this would be returned to the Ervins after close of escrow.[3] By adding these costs to the existing loan balance of $13,200 and deducting from the sales price of $18,500, you calculate that the owners will have about $3321 left from such a sale. If you located a buyer with a least $4000 or more to put down, the Ervins might carry a small second loan for the purchasers. On a sale which was entirely cash to loan, the Ervins might net as much as $3353 at a price of $18,000, since there would be no financing costs to meet.

It is important to understand the relationship of financing to selling prices when you are listing property. In most areas, financing is a major factor in the saleability of a property. The buyer who can pay all

---

[3] If the loan is over ten years old, the prepayment penalty under FHA financing is automatically waived.

cash does not expect to pay the "top price" which a "terms" buyer must pay. In evaluating property, you should do so from the standpoint of the average prospect such property will likely attract in your market area. This will vary by districts and communities, but the rule still applies. Ask yourself:

> What financing terms will the average buyer for this type of property need in order to consummate a sale? What price might the average buyer reasonably be expected to pay?

The terms affect the price one can realize from the sale of real estate, and you should learn to relate these factors as they apply to your vicinity. This is true primarily because financing costs money and those who need easy terms cannot expect to acquire property as cheaply as the "all cash" purchasers may. In most situations, the net result to the sellers is usually the same, regardless of financing, when the discount value of the financing used has been computed. The degree of fluctuation for financing terms will depend upon some or all of the following factors:

1. Demand and availability of similar type properties.
2. Competing terms offered by similar properties.
3. The varying costs experienced in the market for financing terms.
4. The average buyer's ability to meet the terms offered.

As a general rule, the more expensive residences, which are out of the medium priced market, will be sold on the equivalent of cash terms since the buyers in this price range generally do not need "easy terms." Homes in the middle class and lower income groups must usually be priced with competitive terms in mind to meet the average buyer's ability to acquire property. If you are operating in a market where there are many new subdivisions for sale, you should learn to equate your resale housing demand to the terms offered by builders.

THERE IS NO MAGIC IN PRICING REAL ESTATE

This brings us to another point you should understand: pricing real estate is not a true science. The actual price realized for any given property is what the buyer is willing to pay. To some buyers the same property will have a higher value than to others. One man's castle can be another man's white elephant! There is always the fluctuation of individual opinion and no real estate salesman can be expected to be so exact in his pricing that he can pinpoint the market every time he lists property. In fact, it is unwise to overlook the emotional factors which influence buyers, as they do play a major part in home selling. The tall tree in the back yard, an oriental garden, or an incomparable view are difficult amenities to price!

I have often told clients that selling real estate is a matter of looking for the "average" buyer for the type of property offered, unless the seller has no urgency to sell. To locate the unusual buyer who will pay more than anyone else is generally expensive, time-consuming, and difficult. There is always the top price such a buyer may pay, and on the other end of the scale is the low price which a distress sale might require; but normally we do best to price the property at the median level compared to similar offerings based on a normal exposure period.

HOW TO EVALUATE THE MARKETABILITY OF YOUR LISTING

Before making your listing presentation and determining your recommended price, you should carefully evaluate the major factors which control the saleability of any listing in the real estate business. Here are four such factors listed in the order of importance:

First: THE PRICE AND TERMS OFFERED
Second: THE URGENCY OF THE SELLER
Third: THE DEMAND FOR THIS TYPE OF PROPERTY
Fourth: THE COMPETITION OF SIMILAR PROPERTIES

Price, Urgency, Demand, and Competition: These four variables play the key role in weighing the relative merits of one listing over another. If all four points are rated highly, you have what we term a "hot listing." If you have only one, it had best be the "right price and terms" because when there is nothing else to motivate a sale, this is generally the only available drawing card.

Whenever you list a property the pressure is always to obtain, from the beginning the right price and terms. It certainly increases the chances of selling the listing and of serving the best interests of all parties involved. However, do not turn down a good listing just because the price is not exactly where you would peg it! It is possible to sell over-priced listings, providing you are willing to expend the extra effort to condition and negotiate which such properties require. If a listing has any two of the other major factors in its favor as indicated above, it is probably well worth taking and working to bring into line before sold. This is particularly true where the "urgency" of the seller is one of the factors involved, since this acts as a lever on price as the impending time period calls for action. Every effort should be made from the beginning to establish the best price and terms for your listing, but if you fail to do so, weigh the other factors before you reject the listing. I have generally found that when the seller has no reason or urgency to sell and is unrealistic about his price, it is wise to forego the listing rather than waste time and money trying to sell it. On the other hand, if there is a reason to sell and a demand for the type of property offered, it is often well worth the effort to condition the seller during the listing period rather than reject the opportunity to serve the client and lose the resulting commission. The important point to remember is that any over-priced listing is expensive to handle and carries with it a higher risk of expiring unsold, so every reasonable effort to do the job right in the first place should be exercised. If you do accept such a listing, be prepared to work constantly with the seller to bring the price into line as quickly as possible, and begin by telling the owner the truth about real estate values before accepting the listing.

THE LISTING PRESENTATION

With your preparation completed you arrive at the home of the Ervins in time for your 7:00 appointment. Since you have not previously met Mr. Ervin, you take time to get acquainted with him. This is vital in any selling activity. Always have the client's friendship and goodwill before you present your story. Talk about his job, hobbies, or home. Acknowledge the children, and where possible, find something about which to compliment your client. These are basic human relation techniques which always work, but too seldom are they used correctly.

After your brief introductory exchange, you ask permission to review your findings and recommendations with them at the kitchen table where there is good light and room to spread out your papers. Psychologically, it is helpful to be physically close to your clients in the closing stage of any transaction. When selecting a seat, try to locate yourself opposite both the husband and wife where you can control the interview and watch their expressions. Were you to place yourself between them, you would soon feel like an observer at a tennis match, turning your head first one way and then the other. You begin your listing presentation by making some complimentary observations about the Ervin's property. It has been said that any criticism should always be sandwiched between two compliments. Since you are going to have to tell the Ervins some facts which they may not be prepared to accept, it is wise to first acknowledge the good points about the home, including references to such things as good housekeeping, professional landscaping, and so on.

This stage of the listing presentation begins with the visual tools you have compiled for the occasion.

"Before I came to your lovely home this afternoon, I took the liberty of compiling a market report from our extensive office records" (You introduce the 'Competitive Properties Report Form') "You will note on this form that I have listed a number of properties which have experienced real estate activity during the past 12 months. Some of them sold, others failed to sell, and several are still for sale in the area.

"Now here is a home four doors away, formerly owned by Mr. and Mrs. Frank Jewel, which is almost identical to yours in floor plan and design. I believe it was built by the same developer, The Dodson Company. You will note that they listed five months ago for $19,450 and after four months sold for $18,250 on the basis of a new FHA loan. The buyers are Mr. and Mrs. Jenkins, whom possibly you know." (Pause for response)

"Another home in the next block, at 3693 Mardell Lane, sold after 63 days of exposure for $17,400 and was originally listed at $19,950. This home is the plan which is one bedroom smaller than yours."

"Now here you will note properties which did not sell even after a full 90 days of exposure, often because they were priced somewhat above the market. In this column, we have listed those which are still for sale and will be competing for the same buyer we will be hoping to attract in the next 90 days."

YOUR REVIEW WILL NEVER END.

In this manner you continue reviewing the list of actual sales and listings to emphasize the general price range of the market area. Then, while they are still digesting this information, you introduce the "Total Market Analysis Report" which summarizes the real estate activity for the entire community.

"Mr. Jenkins, here is an interesting report which our office produces monthly. It shows the volume and type of activity each of the neighborhoods of our city currently experiences. Since you live in the Cambrian area, you will be interested in the figures for this section. As of last Friday, this report shows there were 127 homes for sale in the district and only 39 sold last month while 37 expired unsold. Last year 837 homes were listed in this district and only 271 sold, which is 32% of those entering the market.

"One of the reasons this is true, Mr. and Mrs. Ervin, is because there are several new subdivisions operating on the fringe of this area, such as the one in which you are purchasing a home. Since most home buyers inspect many properties before making their choice, they will compare the advantages and values of the other properties available to those they finally select. Thus, competition does affect the marketability of your home. Since you have maintained the property attractively, it should fare well, if our price is in line with similar types."

At this point, Mrs. Ervin interrupts to point out the time and effort which went into the landscaping, building the patio, and planting the expensive flowers in the yards. "Certainly" she asserts, "these must add to the value of the home beyond what Mr. and Mrs. Jewel received for theirs."

You agree that it does but add: "You must remember, Mrs. Ervin, these factors do help you to compete more favorably with other properties, but they do not always add substantially to the actual price of the home since they are items which can depreciate rapidly if not maintained. I am certain we will be able to interest a buyer in the face of heavy competition because you have done such an excellent job of landscaping and maintaining your home."

At this point you produce your third exhibit, the worksheet on which you made your notes, and your cost analysis figures.

"When I inspected your home and measured it this afternoon, I computed the square footage of the liveable space as being approximately 1356 square feet. Using the accepted method of computing replacement costs, I estimate it would cost approximately $12,204 to build the home, $1134 for the garage, and $1000 for the landscaping, including the patio. Based on other vacant lots for sale, this one is worth at least $5000. Allowing a depreciation of 1 1/2% per year for the 4 1/2 years since construction, I show a net replacement value of approximately $18,370."

USE THE PRICE RANGE APPROACH

"Based on these figures and our competition from similar properties in the neighborhood, I believe the home should sell somewhere between $18,000 and $19,000."

At this point you pause and wait for the reaction. If there is none, you can proceed with reasonable assurance you have convinced them you are right. However, many sellers will resist your initial efforts to establish a price range, and if they do, don't panic. This is where you go to work! Your future sale can be lost right at this point, unless you make every effort to convince the seller to use good judgment in pricing the property. If selling were an easy task, there would be many more successful salesmen than there are. It requires patience, determination, understanding, and salesmanship to handle objections when they are presented. As expected, Mr. Ervin objects:

"We had expected at least $19,500 or more for our home. After all, we have spent nearly $2000 on improvements since we originally purchased the place, and the home is in much better condition than some of the others you mentioned. We do plan to leave the wall to wall carpets and the drapes and that should justify a price of $19,500, don't you think?"

You reply: "Mr. Ervin, I can certainly understand and appreciate your feelings in the matter. My responsibility as your agent is to help you obtain the very best price for your property, without permitting you to price it out of the market range of prospective customers. <u>My job is really to be your agent to the many other agents</u> who may have prospects for this type home. If we are to be realistic, Mr. Ervin, we must remember that the price you or I may want is not nearly as vital as the price the ultimate buyer will be willing to pay. I certainly like your home and can well appreciate your belief that it is worth $19,500, but, as any prospective buyer will have the opportunity to compare your property to the others for sale in this area, we must carefully consider their reactions. Once a prospect has mentally refused a property because of price, it is often difficult to stimulate his interest again, even if a reduction is eventually offered."

At this point Mrs. Ervin interrupts:

"But couldn't we start at the higher price, and come down? That is what many of our friends have done. Mr. and Mrs. Nelson did that very thing the other day."

You reply: "I realize, Mrs. Ervin, that approach to the problem does sound reasonable at first. But, the difficulty with it is simply this: it tends to discourage those buyers who are now in the market for a home like yours and since the first two weeks of the exposure period are most important it is generally unwise to over-price a home at the beginning. You see, every real estate salesman in this area has a few prospects with whom he is currently working. When your home first comes onto the market, it will be seen by many salesmen and if they feel the property is correctly priced for their prospective buyers, it will be immediately shown. Now, if either the salesmen or the prospects are discouraged by the price, no offers may be presented to you. Once we exhaust the buyers presently interested in purchasing, we must advertise for new ones and that often takes considerable time. Sometimes the lengthy process of looking for a buyer causes a property to become 'shopworn,' just like merchandise in the store that has been picked over several times. Salesmen and buyers should be most interested in showing and selling your home when it is first introduced to the market. For this reason, I strongly recommend a price of $18,500 or possibly $18,750!"

HOW TO TALK TERMS

At this point, you again refer to your worksheets and show Mr. Ervin that they would net about $3300 to $3500 selling at this price under the various terms outlined in your proposal. Mr. Ervin comments:

"You and your firm were highly recommended to us by the builder, Mr. Quinn, and you undoubtedly have done a thorough job of reviewing our property, but we must net at least $3800 in order to buy new rugs and drapes in the other home and so I wouldn't think of listing it with you for less than $19,000."

You reply: "I understand your desire, Mr. Ervin and let me assure you I will do all I can to help you realize that price. I would recommend that we price it at $18,950 which is psychologically more attractive to a purchaser. This $50 will not make that much difference to you, don't you agree?"

Mr. and Mrs. Ervin concur with your recommendation and you insert these figures in your previously prepared listing contract, obtaining their signatures in the proper spaces. You also ask them to acknowledge that the information on your property description form is correct so that your representations to other salesmen and buyers will be supported by the sellers' authorization. You point out that if an "all cash" buyer is found, the Ervins could sell for less and net the same dollars which the higher price would realize under refinancing terms.

PREPARE THE SELLERS FOR THE SELLING PROCESS

With a listing contract in hand, there is now a strong temptation to leave the scene without completing the smaller, but equally important details needed to properly service the listing. <u>The job is not over!</u>

The project of selling this property is a dual responsibility: <u>yours and the owners</u>. They must be told what to expect and how to assist you during the days and weeks ahead, until a sale is consummated. Here are some of the points to review with the sellers:

1. <u>The Repairs and Improvements Needed to Assure Saleability</u>

   "Mr. Ervin, when I was inspecting your home earlier today, a few items came to my attention which could be improved to help you realize the top dollar for your home. The hardware on the front door is corroded and should be retouched or replaced. Also, I noted that the grouting around some of the kitchen tiles has come loose, and should be filled and cleaned."

   Mr. Ervin readily agrees, and says he was planning to take care of these items anyway. You explain that it is often such little things which affect the buyer's interest in a property, and you would not want to prevent a sale for such small repairs.

2. <u>Explain the Things Which Will Happen Now</u>

   Since both sellers are relatively inexperienced in real estate activity, it is important to explain to them what to expect now that they have listed their property with you and your company. This includes:

   a. Caravan tours of the property by salesmen
   b. "For Sale" signs
   c. Choose your neighbor cards and other direct mail programs.
   d. Your need for two keys to the property and how they will be used
      1. Explain the controlled "Lock-Box" if you use one
      2. Key for the appraiser who will inspect for FHA

3. <u>Enlist Their Help in Properly Exposing the Property</u>

   You will now want to be sure the owners do all they can to help you and the other local salesmen who will represent the property to show it to advantage. You explain to Mrs. Ervin:

   "The task of selling your home is ours, but there are many ways in which you can assist us, Mrs. Ervin. During the pre-sale period, it will be helpful if you can arrange to continue the exceptional care you have already been giving your home. Two areas of the home which we find especially important to buyers are the bathrooms and kitchen. Any special attention you can give these rooms will be most helpful. The National Association of Real Estate Boards has prepared this pamphlet for home sellers which explains some of the other things you can do in connection with maintaining the home. [4]

---

[4] Copies of this pamphlet, entitled SHOWMANSHIP TIPS, are available from the National Association of Real Estate Boards, 36 Wabash Ave., Chicago, Illinois.

"One of the points covered in this leaflet is worth special mention. That is the matter of setting the stage for our salesman when he arrives with a prospect. Since most buyers are hesitant to enter someone else's home, and even more afraid to speak up in the presence of the owners, we highly recommend that there be as little distraction as possible when the buyers arrive.

"Television or hi-fi sets should be turned down or off so that the buyer can concentrate on the merits of your property. After the salesman introduces you to his prospect, it is wise to make yourself as inconspicuous as possible so the prospect will feel free to speak his mind, giving our salesman an opportunity to overcome the buyer's fears and objections, which might not otherwise be expressed. Some of our sellers have even conveniently arranged at this point to slip next door for a cup of coffee with a neighbor. I'm sure you can appreciate the importance of the proper environment in which the buyer can make a decision. Also, don't be surprised if you find our salesmen siding with the buyer instead of defending your property. This is an important psychology in selling, and is designed to win the buyer's confidence so we can help him buy your property or the one he should own."

4. Arrange For Loan Appraisals, FHA Commitments, etc.

Part of your job in obtaining a good listing is to arrange for necessary loan commitments and appraisals. In many areas, homes sell with terms created by the financing commitments. Immediate application for such appraisals is an important function of the listing salesman.

5. Explain Your Company's Advertising Policy

Each real estate organization has its own advertising program and policies. Whatever they may be, explain them to your seller! Most sellers, unless told to the contrary, automatically expect you to advertise their properties heavily. Unfortunately, this is a mistaken impression in many instances and should be corrected at the outset. I believe in the use of ads to make the phones ring and not to sell any particular listing. When you have a volume of listings, this is a sound approach. However, such programs need explanation in order to avoid later misunderstandings.

6. Final Check List Before Leaving

Now, before you depart, review once again all the things you should have covered and the points which must be reviewed with the owners before the marketing program begins. Have you asked about assessments and liens? Have you covered the matter of possession clearly, even if their new home is not ready when a sale is produced? Can the property be shown at all reasonable hours? Do you have a list of the personal property items they are willing to include or sell with the property? Have you discussed the possibility of the seller carrying part of the purchase price in secondary financing instruments?

A Good Rule to Remember: ASSUME NOTHING! People tend to hear only what they want to hear, and when you are in doubt about the receptiveness of your client always ask simple questions like:

"Do you understand that?"

"Do you have any questions about that point?"

Constant awareness of the inherent problems arising when two humans try to communicate will greatly increase your effectiveness as a real estate salesman.

POST SERVICING OF THE LISTING

Your initial job is done. You have a saleable listing and you have done a competent job of preparing your seller for the mutual responsibilities of selling the home. Now comes the daily task of supervising your listing and fulfilling the many little things connected with your listing responsibilities. Here is a check list of things to be done when you return to the office:

1. Lock-box and keys properly posted.
2. Double check the information on the contract and submit to the office secretary.
3. If listed on a multiple listing service, submit to the local MLS office within the allotted time period.
4. Arrange for caravan inspection tour by the other salesmen.
5. Put "For Sale" sign on the property.
6. Prepare a schedule of advertising.
7. Order the FHA commitment and other appraisals for loans.
8. Mail "Choose Your Neighbor Cards" or other direct mail pieces to area.
9. Schedule your regular weekly contacts with sellers to keep them informed.
10. Advise all the other salesmen in office about your listing and the merits of its value and saleability.
11. Take a picture of the property and insert it in your office records or display it on the bulletin board.
12. If you have a brochure program, make necessary arrangements to include this property in next issue.

The above are normal responsibilities of the listing salesman, but the most important one is to stay in constant contact with the owners during and after the sale. Communication prevents most problems - there is no substitute for contact in keeping your customers happy and your problems at a minimum. In the case of real estate sellers and buyers, no news is not good news! If you fail to stay in touch, your client will imagine the worst and assume you have lost interest. If several days, even weeks go by before you call the owners again, they will be sure you and your company do not care about their listing and are doing nothing to sell the property. If he calls you, before you call him, you are on the defensive immediately.

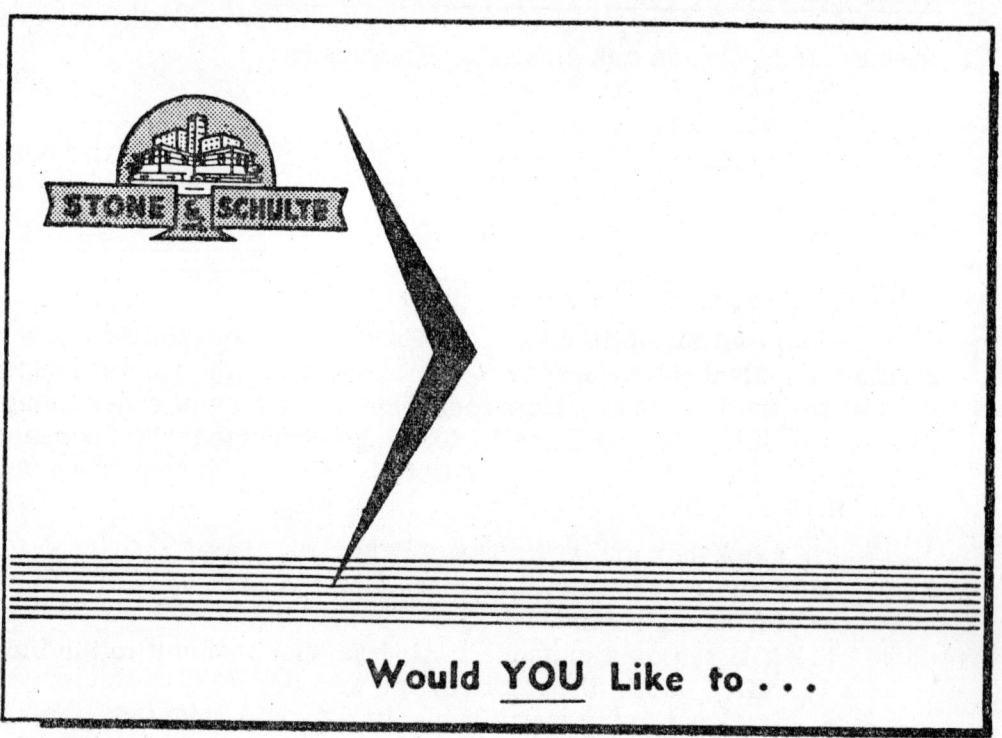

HOW TO OBTAIN AND SERVICE SALEABLE LISTINGS 77

STONE & SCHULTE

LISTING REPORT FORM - RESALES

(This form to be submitted with every listing for analysis of listing activity)

<u>Sam Smith</u>	<u>July 6TH, 19—</u>
Name of Listing Salesman	Date Listed
<u>3562 Rosedale Ave.</u>	<u>Oct. 7TH, 19—</u>
Property Address	Expires

<u>18,950 - Cash to Loan, New F.H.A. or Small Second</u>
Price and Terms

REASONS FOR SELLING <u>Buying New Home from Quinn in Blue Hills Estates</u>

Are you requesting any financing commitments? <u>YES — F.H.A.</u>

Is the seller prepared to carry any "Second Paper"? <u>$1500 or less if necessary</u>

Are you working with the seller on other property? <u>No — Already Purchased</u>

Have you put up a "FOR SALE" sign? <u>YES</u> Lock Box? <u>YES</u> Type Lock Box <u>MLS</u> SS <u>—</u>

Do you plan on mailing CHOOSE YOUR NEIGHBOR cards? <u>YES — 100</u>

How did Stone & Schulte obtain the listing? <u>Referral from Prospecting in Blue Hills Subdivision</u>

CHECK ONE OR MORE OF THE FOLLOWING:

Personal client referral	☒	Owner "For Sale" sign	☐
Phone call to office during floor time	☐	Referral from subdividion	☐
Result of Know Your Neighbor campaign	☐	Trade-in assignment	☐
Result of Stone & Schulte For Sale sign	☐	Result of S&S SOLD sign	☐
Personal door to door canvassing	☐	Friend or relative	☐
Result of "owner ad"	☐	Photo-Facts	☐

Other <u>Schedule for Caravan Tour July 10th</u>

Consider for the moment the time, money, and frustration which can be saved if you keep your client informed regularly. The seller wants to know what is happening and failure to advise him will produce visions of slovenly real estate salesmen who are unworthy of his listing. The professional salesman always calls first, at least once a week or more often, and reports on progress. If he has no news to report, he asks the client about the action from other salesmen. Before the seller can complain about lack of action, he puts the shoe on the seller's foot:

"You will recall, Mr. Ervin, I stressed the fact that the first two weeks were the most logical time to sell the property and if it did not sell quickly, we might require several weeks to locate the right buyer!" Stay close to your sellers and you will not only solve problems, you will build a continuous stream of referrals on which to help your career flourish!

TYPES OF LISTING CONTRACTS

Some discussion about the various kinds of listing agreements which are used in our profession is in order at this point. There are essentially four types involved:

1. <u>The Exclusive Right of Sale Listing</u>

This is the one commonly used by all real estate salesmen and recommended by any competent broker. It grants to the broker the exclusive right to represent that property for sale during the period identified in the contract and to be paid a full commission if a sale is consummated or a buyer produced who is ready, willing, and able to buy at the specified terms. If any other broker or the owner himself produces the buyer, the agent with the exclusive right of sale listing is still entitled to his commission.

2. <u>The Exclusive Agency Listing</u>

This listing contract makes the named agent the only broker who is entitled to show and sell the property for a commission, but still permits the owner to attempt to sell the property without paying a commission.

3. <u>The Open or Non-Exclusive Listing</u>

An open listing merely authorizes the broker to act as an agent for the sale of a particular parcel of property and to be paid a commission if he is the one who produces the ultimate buyer. However, the owner or any other broker can sell the property without obligating the owner for commissions to those holding open listings. These contracts are generally discouraged in most areas as they do not provide the broker with sufficient protection to warrant his professional attention and investment in procuring a buyer. Also, the danger exists that the seller will be quoting a lower price than the agent is authorized to represent. In my opinion,

HOW TO OBTAIN AND SERVICE SALEABLE LISTINGS

STONE & SCHULTE, Inc.
EXCLUSIVE LISTING AGREEMENT

In considering the services of STONE & SCHULTE, INC., licensed real estate brokers, I hereby list with Stone & Schulte, Inc., exclusively and irrevocably, for the period of time beginning July 6th 19— and ending October 7th 19— (Minimum period 90 days) all that real property known as: 3562 Rosedale Avenue

and legally described as: Lot 114 Blk. 2 Tract 1304 Rosedale Gardens as recorded in the County of Santa Clara California and as set forth in Book Number 21 at page(s) 53

And I hereby grant said broker the exclusive and irrevocable right to sell said property within said time for EIGHTEEN THOUSAND NINE HUNDRED FIFTY ($18,950.00) DOLLARS on terms of CASH TO EXISTING LOAN OR NEW FHA LOAN: SELLER MAY CARRY SECOND LOAN OF $1500 or LESS and to accept a deposit thereon.

I agree to pay Stone & Schulte, Inc. as commission 6 per cent of the selling price should, during the time set forth herein, said property be sold by said broker or by me or by another broker or through some other source or whether said property be withdrawn from sale, transferred, conveyed, or leased without approval of Stone & Schulte, Inc.

Should a sale be made within ninety (90) days after this authorization terminates to parties with whom Stone & Schulte, Inc. may negotiate during the term hereof and said broker notifies me of such negotiation, in writing, personally or by mail, during the term hereof within five (5) days after the termination hereof, then I agree to pay said commission to said broker.

In the event of sale or exchange of my property I agree to execute and deliver a deed, or such other instrument as may be required and to furnish a Policy of Title Insurance issued by a recognized Title Insurance Company of Broker's choice at my expense

In case a deposit is forfeited, one-half of same shall go to Stone & Schulte, Inc. as commission and one-half to me provided, however the agent's share shall not exceed the amount of the above named commission.

In consideration of the above employment, Stone & Schulte, Inc. agrees to use due diligence in procuring a purchaser and to include any of the specialized services listed below at the agent's discretion that will assist in satisfactorily consummating a transaction for and on behalf of the seller. Owner acknowledges receipt of a copy of this agreement.

Dated at YOURTOWN Signed _____ Owner
this 6th day of July 19—
by Sam Smith Signed Sarah Ervin Owner
   Salesman

STONE & SCHULTE SERVICES INCLUDE:

Exchange-A-Plan Trades	Escrow Processing	Insurance Counselling
Special Property Brochures	Mortgage Financing	Subdivision Lands
Nation-wide Exchanges	Professional Counselling	Investment Properties
Industry Contact Services	Merchandising Services	Home Developments

Ask about Exchange-A-Plan. It's the modern way to sell Real Estate. Exchange-A-Plan gives you:

1. **PEACE OF MIND:** You always know in advance the most and least you will receive for your home.
2. **MONEY:** You save many of the costs of selling and buying by combining them under one transaction.
3. **TIME:** Exchange-A-Plan relieves the uncertainties of moving dates, school registration, and employment deadlines.
4. **CONVENIENCE:** The management of the complex problems of real estate transfers are handled by experts.
5. **SECURITY:** With Exchange-A-Plan you know your valuable real estate is guarded from bargain hunting speculators.

there is little need to take open listings when a broker is prepared to perform a professional service for the sellers in his market area.

4. Net Listing

In a net listing, the compensation to be paid the broker is not definitely specified, since it is determined by all amounts in excess of the selling price established by the owner. The practice of using net listings is discouraged by many real estate boards and professional groups as there is a tendency to encourage "secret" or "exorbitant" profits by the broker, at the expense of buyers and sellers. If they are used, the full amount of the profit or commission made should be revealed to both buyers and sellers.

In addition to these four basic types of listing contracts, there is also the Multiple Listing Agreement which is normally just an "exclusive right of sale listing" with a special provision for circulating the information to "sub-agents" of the authorized broker through a particular multiple listing service. All other agents belonging to that association may then represent the property through the master agreement held by the listing office.

In most states, real estate law requires that every listing contract (except open listings) have a definite termination date in order to be valid. Further, failure to do so is cause for revocation or suspension of license in these same states. It is just good business practice to include specific dates of origination and termination in all listing agreements.

SUMMARY

A good listing worth taking requires effort and deserves attention. Sellers are the key to the real estate business and as a real estate salesman who wants to grow in this industry, you should concentrate your efforts on solving the problems of sellers. You will seldom spend more profitable time than that which you invest with sellers. But remember, when you accept a listing you accept a responsibility on the owner's behalf and failure to realize the obligations attendant with such assignments will lead to many painful problems and lost commissions.

You have obtained a signed, "exclusive right to sell" listing from Mr. and Mrs. Ervin for the home at 3562 Rosedale Avenue and you did so overcoming objections when they insisted on an unmarketable price. As a result, you have gained the respect of the owners and you can be proud of your craftmanship as a real estate counsellor. Like an attorney, doctor, or any other specialist you can take pride in the value of your talents and professional services.

If you are truly professional you will never have to resort to dishonesty or untruthfulness in order to render assistance to property owners. There is no excuse for falsehoods or insincerity when you are performing genuine service to people. If you try to help owners see the truths about real estate selling, you will win their confidence and support.

Finally, let me give you the advice a famous Realtor gave me. He said, "When you list a property always get both keys:
1. The Key to the Home
2. The Key to the Future Sale"

82   HOW TO OBTAIN AND SERVICE SALEABLE LISTINGS

QUESTIONS AND PROJECTS FOR CHAPTER FOUR

Questions:

1. Why should you do a thorough and professional job of listing a property?
2. Before leaving your office to inspect a potential listing, what research should you complete and from what sources?
3. Give three reasons why the two-visit plan for taking a listing is superior to a single visit.
4. When you are inspecting a neighborhood around a potential listing, what things should you observe and note?
5. If you need or want additional market data from present owners in a neighborhood, how can you obtain it? What questions can you properly ask? What questions should be avoided?
6. What are the four major factors you should always evaluate when determining the marketability of a particular property?
7. Recite the sequence of steps involved in taking a good listing, and review the reason for each step.
8. What relationship does the price of a property bear to the terms of sale under which it is offered? How should you weigh these factors when listing a property?
9. What are the three primary approaches to value used by real estate appraisers? Which is the most important to you when listing single family residences?
10. What are the advantages and reasons for using the "price range" approach to discuss the probable selling price with a seller?

Projects:

1. Make a listing kit for your personal use in presenting your services to sellers. Include all the visual aids you can use to demonstrate the value of your company's program and your own talents in handling property professionally.
2. On a sheet of paper, list all the known sources of appraisal data available to you in your office and area for use when listing property.
3. List four sources or ways you could determine how much a seller paid for his home without directly asking him that question. How would you use each, and which is the best one to obtain first?
4. To determine the age of a property without asking the seller, there are several good clues. List three and review which is the most practical for first attempts to secure this information.
5. Have your instructor assign you three properties to practice listing knowledge (or select your own) and then perform the following steps on each:
    a. Prepare a "competitive property report form" listing as many comparables as you can obtain from your records.

HOW TO OBTAIN AND SERVICE SALEABLE LISTINGS

    b. Inspect the property and tape the home, filling in your property description portion of the listing contract, and review all data available to complete your information.

    c. Tour the neighborhood and inspect at least three of the comparables or current listings which should play a part in determining the value of this property.

    d. Analyze your findings and submit a written report to your broker regarding your opinion on value and reasons for your conclusions.

6. Compute the following listing problems based on the normal costs and customs of your market area. Check your answers with your broker.
EXAMPLE DATA:

    An owner of property calls you to list his home at 220 Vine St., Yourtown, U.S.A. You do your usual preparation work, inspect neighborhood and listing, establishing the following facts:

    a. They owe a balance of $11,237.50 on an FHA loan of 4 1/2% whose original amount was $13,500 when they purchased the home 8 years ago for a purchase price of $15,950.

    b. There is an existing sewer assessment remaining due of $527.10 which must be paid by seller before closing an escrow.

    c. Based on comparable data, the home should be worth between $18,000 and $18,500 with an average for FHA appraisal at $18,250. The area involved usually brings approximate FHA price and terms.

    d. Current discount for FHA or VA financing in your area must be considered. Ask your broker, if the amount is unknown to you.

With the above information regarding this property, compute the owner's equity based on the following types of sales, always allowing the commission and closing costs which are common to your area. When completed, have your broker check your answers for accuracy.

    e. Compute the net equity to the seller if he sold at estimated FHA value on minimum down terms for a 30 year loan, buyer and seller each paying their normal closing costs.

    f. On the same property, determine the net equity of the seller on a cash to existing loan sale at $18,000.

    g. The property is refinanced to a new 80% loan for buyer from a savings and loan company, the seller paying half of the 1 1/2 points necessary to obtain the loan at a price of $18,250. What is the net equity of the seller?

    h. A buyer desiring a no-down G.I. loan applies for the property. What net equity would the seller realize?

7. Make a list of questions you can ask an owner to determine his motivations for selling and his urgency of decision. Also list questions you can use to help point out the obsolescence factors in the property they are selling.

8. The owner of the property described in project 6 has checked with more than one real estate firm and a competing broker has indicated the property might sell for $1000 more than your market data indicated possible. What would you do? Why?
9. List all of the post-servicing requirements used in your office, and prepare a check-list for handling your personal listings covering all these items and any other points you believe are essential to good follow through with your sellers.
10. Inspect at least 3 listings each day of this week, and try to analyze in each case the following:
    a. The owner's real reason for selling and the degree of urgency behind that sale.
    b. The owner's willingness to take terms other than those shown on the listing form submitted by the listing salesman.
    c. The value of the property based on competing merchandise.
    d. The various types of financing that could be used to sell the property and the effect these might have on the net equity or net price of the property.
    e. What new business is available in the area which can be obtained by asking the right questions.
11. Develop your own answers to the following common objections to listing property exclusively or on the terms recommended by a salesman:
    a. "I need a pad in my price.... I can always come down later."
    b. "We would like to try to sell it ourselves first."
    c. "A.B.C. Realty offered to list it for much more than that!"
    d. "I only want to list it for 30 days."
    e. "You are welcome to work on it, but I do not want to sign an exclusive listing."
    f. "Mrs. Jones up the street has her home listed for $20,000, and I know mine is worth more than hers."
12. Have your broker review with you all the things required by your office when submitting a listing for publication to the other salesmen.

5

HOW TO OBTAIN PROSPECTS FROM ADVERTISING

There is a recipe for rabbit stew which begins: "First, catch the rabbit. . . ." This is sound advice. To sell real estate, you must first locate potential buyers. Fortunately, this is not difficult in our profession since many prospects seek out the real estate agents whose offerings interest them. Most salesmen, in other selling fields, do not have such favorable customer reaction to their merchandise and as a result, they must cultivate every possible source to locate their clients.

Every real estate salesman should fully appreciate the opportunities his broker extends to him in providing advertising and floor-time privileges. When you associate with an agressive real estate office that receives unsolicited calls each day from interested buyers and sellers, your initial efforts to launch a career in real estate are greatly facilitated. If your broker has been in business for any length of time, he has undoubtedly spent thousands of dollars plus many long hours of effort to establish his reputation and his clientele. You are automatically a beneficiary of this investment when you are granted floor time assignments in your broker's offices. You are permitted to reap some of the fruits of his previous efforts and to enjoy the public acceptance attributed to a successful enterprise. In most real estate offices, the recommendations and referral from satisfied clients and friends are the most important source of new business. When a broker has a good community image, he receives a substantial number of such referrals from many sources. Such firms enjoy public confidence and when someone says: "What real estate firm would you use?" others will reply: "Contact A. B. C. Realty Company, they can solve your problem!" Thus, your activities within such organizations receive additional impetus from the climate of success in which you operate, and the manner in which you care for the business you receive will affect both your present and future income.

Many factors combine to bring business to a real estate office, and all are important to you. These include:

1. The general reputation and image of the firm.
2. The amount and type of daily classified advertising.

3. The number and type of "For Sale" signs displayed on property.
4. The personal referrals of the broker and his sales staff.
5. The impact of continuous direct mail campaigns.
6. The office appearance and the reactions of the public to both facilities and personnel.
7. The office location, since many customers shop in the neighborhoods where they intend to live.
8. The number, quality, and type of services offered by the real estate office.
9. The amount of institutional advertising including such media as television, radio, billboards, brochures, magazines, and newspapers.
10. The recommendations of brokers in other cities.

All of these things help to bring to your office a steady stream of prospect inquiries and referrals. Each media used tends to overlap the image-producing activities of the brokerage company, resulting in a total impact upon the market from which you benefit when they are all in good taste and proper balance. Consistent repetition of the company insignia, name, and identification has a sustaining effect on the creation of new business. The more "For Sale" signs your office has in a given neighborhood, the more business you will receive from that area. Every broker and salesman should do everything possible to increase the exposure of the company image in the markets they serve.

HOW TO HANDLE FLOOR TIME RESPONSIBILITIES

Each company has its own policies and procedures for rotating floor time assignments and caring for the business which its advertising has produced. You should be completely familiar with those which govern your organization and do your best to adhere to them faithfully. Brokerage companies must have rules of conduct in order to maintain normal business operations on a smooth, efficient basis. When you were employed, you were probably told what to expect in reference to major policies or given a policy manual to read. In any case, you should now be acquainted with the answers to the following questions in reference to floor time assignments in your company:

1. What hours are you expected to be on duty? Are there any variations?
2. What are your responsibilities regarding opening and closing the office?
3. If more than one salesman is to serve on floor days, what system of rotation is used to handle incoming calls?
4. What is the office definition of a floor call? Will you be responsible for:
    a. Rental inquiries?
    b. Broker calls?

       c. Commercial or investment inquiries?
       d. General information calls?
5. What is the office policy regarding handling personal inquiries or client referrals for other salesmen in the company?
6. Are you permitted to leave the office during floor time assignments in order to show properties, keep appointments, or obtain listings? If so, what is your obligation regarding finding a replacement?
7. If more than one client is calling, and everyone is busy, how are excess calls handled?
8. If an answering service is used, what coordination is required in relaying messages?
9. What rules of conduct does your broker expect concerning:
       a. Smoking?
       b. Eating in office?
       c. Drinking coffee in office?
       d. Handling clients?

Whatever the policies of your office may be, you have an obligation to observe and respect them as long as you work for that company. Even if there are no written policies on general office conduct, you should exercise good judgment in your performance of business activities and remember that any real estate office should be a place of business for professional people. Common courtesy dictates that we respect the rights of fellow salesmen and associates to carry on their business without undue interference or interruption. This does not mean there cannot be a general climate of good fellowship and cooperation in the office, as long as that does not result in horseplay, loud talking, boisterous laughter, and other disturbing activities. Since most real estate salesmen are really independent businessmen trying to earn a living from their chosen occupation, they should be given the opportunity of conducting their affairs in a reasonably business-like environment. A real estate office is not a place to loiter or pass the time of day. When you are within its walls you should be working. The rest of your time should be devoted to the development of business outside the office.

LEARN TO BE INDEPENDENT

To be successful in a real estate office where many salesmen are employed, it is best to stay on an even keel with your associates. Salesmen are basically competitors and for this reason you should be judicious in discussing your pending transactions with others. Also, you should learn to stand on your own two feet as quickly as possible and not depend on others to solve all your problems. Some salesmen develop the bad habit of leaning on others to do their thinking for them. This is unhealthy because it prevents them from becoming mature, professional salesmen. When you have completed your training period, you should be able to create listings and sales without constant supervision or assistance. By standing on your own two feet, you will learn to be an independent businessman working successfully within the framework of a well-managed real estate office.

PREPARING GOOD ADVERTISING COPY FOR CLASSIFIED ADS

Since classified advertising is still the major source of new business in most real estate offices, every salesman should know the basic principles involved in preparing, writing, and placing real estate ads, as well as the specific office policies his company follows regarding the advertising program. You should ascertain from your supervisor the following points:

1. What is the basic philosophy of your company in reference to real estate advertising?
2. Who is responsible for writing the ads? Who edits them? Who places them with the newspaper?
3. Does each salesman have an individual advertising budget or is there a collective one used by the entire staff? How is it computed?
4. Are salesmen permitted to use their own phone numbers? What rules apply to the basic format and content of ads?
5. What are the deadlines for submitting copy to the office for future insertion dates?

All real estate advertising is designed to make the phones ring! This is true regardless of the size of the real estate office involved, or the amount of advertising done. However, there is a difference in the approach to this objective by various real estate offices. Some advertise specific properties to obtain specific buyers for such properties, while others advertise a variety of listings to attract a variety of buyers who can be cross-fed to other properties. Both methods work if the advertising is well-planned and effective. I personally subscribe to the theory of collective advertising designed to attract the greatest number of buyers who can then be qualified for the properties best suited for their individual needs. My research indicates that only rarely is the home sold to the person who responded to the advertisement about that property. Most prospects must be carefully qualified and screened after they call and then shown properties which meet their requirements.

HOW PROSPECTS SELECT ADS

In order to understand how to write good ad copy, you should know how prospects make their selection of ads on which to call. Did you ever shop the classified columns of your local newspaper when you were looking for a home? Possibly, before you entered the real estate business, you did some house-hunting through the usual methods. If so, you may recall how you carefully scanned this section looking for ads which caught your attention and deleted all others. You may have been attracted by the "header" or "lead line" of those ads you marked which seemed by their wording to be exceptional values for the category of your primary interest. If you were average, you were looking for a "bargain" or real "value" and you may have even searched the "owner-for-sale" section on the mistaken assumption these might represent more reasonable offerings. Everyone would like to buy the home of his dreams at a fraction of its real value! That's why ads which emphasize value in relationship to amenities are often the most successful in obtaining customer response.

The important point to understand about this selection process is that buyers eliminate many ads before they select a few! It is a process of elimination rather than of selection which controls the effectiveness of our advertising campaigns. If the ads we write are the first to be eliminated, or cannot stand up with the other competitive ads for customer appeal, we are wasting our advertising dollars. The hastily conceived ad which is inserted at the last moment just to have something in the newspaper is one of the tragedies of our business. You might as well stand on the bank of a river and throw your money into the rushing stream as pour it uselessly into advertising which serves no purpose. To be effective, advertising must be planned, edited, and reviewed from the standpoint of maximum emotional appeal for the readers whose interest we are attempting to capture.

Why do people eliminate certain ads and respond to others? No one really knows all the answers to that question, but there are some proven facts which have been established to guide our thinking in this matter. First of all, most customers are looking for a bargain in the type of home desired. Secondly, their imaginations and motivations must be stimulated to some degree by the ads they read in order for action to be taken. Finally, each customer has one or two dominating requirements which must be satisfied in order to trigger his favorable response.

Thus, to be really effective, advertising must strike the motivating impulses of the reader before it can be expected to produce action! Study the following two examples. Both ads are written about the same property.

EXAMPLE 1

---

3 BEDROOMS — 2 BATHS

Near Almaden Hills we have listed a ranch home with 3 bedrooms, 2 baths, family room, and den. Has modern kitchen, covered patio, two fireplaces, and two tall pines in rear yard. $24,950. Call Ex 7-3100.

THOMPSON & SON, REALTORS

EXAMPLE 2

LANDSCAPED RETREAT !!

Towering pines and green lawns provide a restful backdrop for this 3 bedroom, 2 bath ranch home in Willow Park. From its vine covered patio and panelled family room you can view the Almaden Hills! Two fireplaces, a knotty pine den, and modern kitchen make this rustic retreat a real value at $24,950! Call Ex 7-3100.

THOMPSON & SON, REALTORS

Both of these ads contain the same essential facts, but one is aimed at the prospect's motivational urge to have privacy and beauty in a rustic retreat under towering pines. Which ad will bring the greatest number of calls? It is true that the second ad will cost a little more to run, but if it produces two or three times as many inquiries, isn't it worth the investment in an extra few lines?

THE IMPORTANCE OF HEADERS AND LEAD LINES

A traveler is reported to have once seen a farmer stopped beside a road with his donkey and cart and a big club in his two fists about to hit the donkey over the head. The tourist jumped out of his car and asked the local farmer what he was doing. "I'm trying to get my donkey back on the road!" he replied. The puzzled tourist asked, "But why are you going to hit him with that big club?" and the farmer replied: "Well, first I have to get his attention!"

The "lead line," "header" or "stopper" in any ad is primarily designed to get the reader's attention! If an advertisement is to be read, it must first arrest the reader's eye, and command his immediate attention! If the heading or lead line is uninspiring, the rest of the ad may never be read, despite the exciting things which may be included in the body of the copy. In preparing any ad, think seriously about the message you are attempting to convey and the dramatic emphasis the right words in the "stopper" can have in creating reader interest.

USE A THEME IN YOUR COPY

The header, or first line, in an ad is generally its theme, if properly presented. You have a story to tell or an idea to sell and the "theme" of the copy should quickly emphasize this point. What is it you are trying to convey...beauty?...privacy?...comfort?...prestige?...economy? These are just a few of the basic ideas used in theme material for good real estate copy. Each buyer has his own emotional "hot spots" and dominating interests. Your ads should be selected so as to cover the motivations of those buyers who would be most interested in what you have to offer. If you are featuring prestige (deluxe residential properties), your approach will emphasize an entirely different set of emotional factors than the real estate office which specializes in modest homes for the lower-income groups. <u>To plan good advertising copy, you must know what it is you are trying to sell!</u>

Every day new buyers enter the real estate market in your area. These will be people with different interests who can be classified in broad categories, based on motivational needs. By choosing your advertising copy very carefully, you can appeal to each of these groups with different ads. One can be designed to attract the "prestige" buyer while a different property is aimed at the "easy terms" buyer. To assist you in preparing good ads for the basic housing groups you serve, I have listed the following topics as major themes and given you a few suggested "ad headers" to go with them. Study these and then insert more good ad headers, or lead lines which will accent the emotional drives of the readers to whom you are trying to appeal.

<u>BASIC RESIDENTIAL MOTIVATION CATEGORIES</u> (alphabetically classified and not necessarily in the order of importance)

CATEGORY	Basic Motivations	Possible Headings For Ads
Animals	Children	"City Farmer"
	Country	"Bring Your Horse"
	Farms	"Raise Chickens"
	Freedom	"God's Half Acre"
	Large lots	"Paradise for Pets"
	Room	"Country Living"
	Rural	"Home for Horses"
Artists	Adventure	"Artists Hideaway"
	Architecture	"Secluded Bungalow"
	Beauty	"Unusual Charm"
	Creative	"Contemporary Model"
	Decor	"Dramatic Entry"
	Expression	"Creative Cottage"
	Individuality	"For Distinctive Tastes"

CATEGORY	Basic Motivations	Possible Headings For Ads
Beauty	Color	"View The Valley"
	Decor	"Architect's Dream"
	Design	"Simple Lines"
	Landscaping	"Sitting in a Garden"
	Pleasure	"Enjoy the Hills"
	Scenery	"Created to Enjoy"
Children	Education	"Walk to School"
	Environment	"Parkside Living"
	Pleasure	"Children's Playground"
	Rooms	"Room to Grow"
	Security	"Quiet Street"
	Space	"Bedrooms Galore"
	Welfare	"No Traffic"
Convenience	Close	"Walk to Work"
	Comfort	"Every Convenience"
	Easy	"Pleasant to Own"
	Modern	"Modern Design"
	Practical	"Wife-Saver Kitchen"
	Time-saving	"Close to Everything"
Couples	Convenient	"Neat as a Pin"
	Comfortable	"Cozy for Two"
	Low-Cost	"Budget Bargain"
	Retired	"Home for Life"
	Romantic	"Love Nest"
	Small	"Haven for Two"
Economy	Bargain	"Exceptional Value"
	Easy	"Easy to Own"
	Low-Cost	"$500 Down"
	Security	"Start Here"
	Shelter	"Move Right In"
	Small Investment	"$86 per Month"
Executives	Address	"University Avenue"
	Entertain	"Gracious Living"
	Expensive	"Colonial on Park Avenue"
	Luxurious	"Tradition and Beauty"

CATEGORY	Basic Motivations	Possible Headings For Ads
Executives	Prestige	"Rose Garden District"
	Recognition	"Live in Alameda Estates"
Families	Bedrooms	"Five for Five"
	Children	"Needs Children"
	Large	"Space to Grow"
	Room	"Room to Spare"
	Space	"Designed for Living"
	Value	"More for Less"
Handy-Man	Creative	"Creative Castle"
	Earn	"Earn Your Down Payment"
	Fix	"Paint and Putter"
	Imagination	"Use Your Imagination"
	Invest	"Elbow Grease Needed"
	Repair	"Weed it and Reap"
Hobbyist	Collect	"Collector's Item"
	Dens	"Hobby Hideaway"
	Garden	"Green Thumb Special"
	Privacy	"Putterer's Paradise"
	Space	"Hours to Invest"
	Workshop	"Hobby House"
Health	Climate	"Above the Smog"
	Convenience	"Close to Transportation"
	Easy	"Easy to Maintain"
	Facilities	"Restful Retreat"
	Relaxing	"Fountain of Youth"
	View	"Mountain Magic"
Investors	Opportunity	"Treasure Chest"
	Repair	"Watch it Grow"
	Return	"Tomorrow's Nest-egg"
	Security	"83 Dollars Per Month"

CATEGORY	Basic Motivations	Possible Headings For Ads
Investors	Speculation	"Only $1000"
	Yield	"Banker's Bargain"
Privacy	Beauty	"Landscaped Retreat"
	Freedom	"Private Paradise"
	Protected	"Nestled in a Valley"
	Quiet	"Restful Cottage"
	Seclusion	"Peaceful Haven"
	Shaded	"Under the Pines"
Recognition	Address	"Exclusive District"
	Area	"Banker's Home"
	Neighborhood	"Executive Estate"
	Prestige	"Elm Grove-5 Bedroom"
	Size	"10 Room Victorian"
	Tradition	"Colonial Mansion"
Recreation	Fishing	"Your Own Stream"
	Hiking	"Mountain Villa"
	Hunting	"Sportman's Hide-out"
	Golf	"Two Golf Courses"
	Playing	"Tennis Greens"
	Swimming	"Cool Pool"
Security	Investment	"Invest $650"
	Payments	"$90 Investment"
	Protection	"Safety and Security"
	Quality	"Finished to Perfection"
	Return	"Outstanding Value"
	Stability	"Built to Last"
Tenants	Easy Payments	"Easy to Own"
	Ownership	"Why Rent?"
	Savings	"Own for Less"
	Security	"Less than Rent"
	Small Down	"$299 Moves You In"
	Value	"Budget Bargain"

HOW TO OBTAIN PROSPECTS FROM ADVERTISING

CATEGORY	Basic Motivations	Possible Headings For Ads
Tradition	Architecture	"Classic Beauty"
	Beauty	"Decorator's Delight"
	Creative	"Restorable Retreat"
	Graciousness	"Elegant Age"
	Mellowed	"Old But Lovable"
	Seasoned	"Traditional Two Story"

These are but a few of the many topics for which you can index appropriate headings and themes. I have given you just enough to help you project the many possibilities for the listings you will represent. Homes are like people - they have personalities. When you start to write an ad for a listing, think about the people who might be interested in owning such a property. What would be their motivations and interests? How could you intrigue them with the possibilities of your listing? Just a little creative thought about the property and its potential owners will produce phrases and expressions needed to incite the reader's action. Once you have selected your theme, carry it from your heading to the body of advertising copy so the prospect's interest will be fanned into desire as he progresses.

TELL THEM ENOUGH, BUT NOT TOO MUCH

An ad can tell the prospect too much! If it answers all his questions, he has little reason to call, and if any of the facts presented are not completely satisfactory the reader's interest may be destroyed. Tell them enough to whet their appetite for more information but not so much you discourage further investigation. Three general categories should normally be covered in some fashion:

1. <u>The type, size, and style of home.</u>

   This means stating the number of rooms, bedrooms or space offered in this home, as well as the architectural style.

2. <u>The general location of the home.</u>

   Many buyers are looking for specific districts in which to live. If the home offers some advantage in area, give the general district involved.

3. <u>Price and terms offered.</u>

   Price and terms are both qualifying factors and should usually be included in the advertisement. Some buyers refuse to call on ads where they are omitted.

A TOWERING PINE

Provides cool shade in the big rear yard of this Los Gatos home! Nestled among trees and meandering lanes in the choice Los Gatos area, this 6 room home is within walking distance of town but is so secluded and peaceful that you feel like you are in another world! As you approach the home with its rambling fenced yard, you will know why the present owners hate to leave . . . but circumstances force them to! The enclosed summer room makes an ideal place to enjoy the warm days ahead. Priced at only $14,750, this is a real value! Call CY 7-3757 for more details.

Stone & Schulte
INC
1745 W. San Carlos   CY 7-3757

ROOM TO LIVE

On a large country lot out in the Campbell area we have a 7 room home about 8 years old that is ideal for a growing, active family! There are 2 full baths, a family room detached from the main house, extra large patio to extend living facilities, inside service porch, formal dining room, and extras like wall to wall carpeting. This country model will please the family that needs about 1700 square feet of house but whose budget limits them to $17,950! This home has hardwood floors, and custom construction features throughout. At this low price, you can own a large home cheaper than rent! Name your own terms! CY7-3757!

Stone & Schulte
1745 W. San Carlos   CY7-3757
(Open 8 A.M. To 8 P.M.)

COUNTRY GENTLEMAN!

That's what you'll be when you own this cutie-pie on the westside! It is a little gem on a BIG lot, with room to play, relax, and putter all in your own back yard! There is a covered lanai, separate workshop, 8 walnut trees, and a cross-fenced yard for privacy and beauty! Included in the price are carpets, drapes and other extras! Located on a street of fine homes this is a real buy for only $12,270 with as little as $500 down! Call CY7-3757 to see it first!

Stone & Schulte
INC
1745 W. San Carlos   CY7-3757
(Open 8 A.M. To 8 P.M.)

PLACE TO DREAM!

We have a perfect little home for the couple who would like a place to dream! It's a sparkling 2 bedroom home in Santa Clara with hardwood floors, big living room, pleasant kitchen and breakfast nook, and all on a nice landscaped lot with a hobby shop and shade trees. Full price $11,750, $500 down. CY7-3757.

Stone & Schulte
1745 W. San Carlos   CY7-3757
(Open 8AM To 8PM)

FRUSTRATED FARMER!

Near Sunnyvale we can offer you a 6-room home with 3 bedrooms and 2 baths going for a very low price! There is a country feeling about this one with its 13 apricot trees, 1 walnut and 2 peach trees. You can even raise chickens here and run a small ranch . . . if you're so inclined! The full price is only $10,995! Call now—CY 7-3757!

Stone & Schulte
1745 W. San Carlos   CY 7-3757
(Choose from over 1000 homes)

COLONIAL CHARM

Seldom do we have the opportunity to offer as fine a home as this Willow Glen beauty for $24,950! Listen: 2200 square feet, 3 bedrooms, 2 baths, separate family room, 2 fireplaces, service porch, formal dining room opening on magnificent rear yards shaded by tall trees and lined with terraced gardens! See it now by calling CY7-3757!

Stone & Schulte
INC
1745 W. San Carlos   CY7-3757
(Open 8 AM to 8 PM)

FIVE BY FIVE!

Five bedrooms are possible in this home that has 2 baths, 4 bedrooms, and large room convertible to a 5th bedroom! Located on a westside cul-de-sac lot with plenty of room for kids to play and including a big patio area for relaxed living, this is a top value at only $12,500! $800 will handle and make monthly payments under $100 per month! Ideal for a big family with a tight budget, don't delay! Call CY7-3757 today!

Stone & Schulte
1745 W. San Carlos   CY7-3757
(Open 8 a.m. to 8 p.m.)

BEGINNER'S BARGAIN

For the young couple who need a nice home but must watch the budget, we have a choice 3 bedroom home with hardwood floors, fireplace, family kitchen, patio, lawns, attached garage all in immaculate condition that can be purchased for $400 down and $97 per month! You'll love the neat, attractive arrangement and the view of the valley from the front yard. Call CY7-3757 for details.

Stone & Schulte
INC.
1745 W. San Carlos   CY7-3757
(Open 8 A.M. to 8 P.M.)

SATIN and PEARLS!

Rich red roses, satin and pearls go with this Saratoga beauty where gracious living is a way of life! The distinct custom finish both inside and outside this 7 room home sets it apart from the ordinary house! You step inside and immediately feel the warmth and charm of the living room with it's full wall fireplace, full wall windows, and covered portico extending into the patio. There is a separate family room, modern kitchen, service porch, 3 large bedrooms, 2½ baths, and an indoor BBQ. The plaster finish throughout the home is something to admire! Priced at $28,500, this is one of the best custom buys we can show you! CY 7-3757

Stone & Schulte
INC
1745 W. San Carlos   CY 7-3757
(Open 8 A.M. to 8 P.M.)

END OF THE LINE!

The sellers of this lovely westside home have come to the end of the line! They have moved to their new home in Morgan Hill and now must sell at any reasonable price the 6 room, 3 bedrm. 2 bath ranch type home they own here. It is truly a beauty with every desirable feature including G.E. kitchen, nice patio, large fenced yard, heavy shake roof and in all over 1500 square feet of livable space! The home is vacant now and ready for immediate occupancy. There is a large low interest loan to be assumed. NAME YOUR PRICE: CY7-3757!

Stone & Schulte
1745 W. San Carlos   CY7-3757
(Open 8 a.m. to 8 p.m.)

DON'T LOOK TWICE

There won't be time, as this little 2-bedroom custom home has so many fine features and is priced below market value that it will be bought by the smart investor or couple today! Hardwood floors, fireplace, covered patio, double garage, workshop area, and extra large lot are just a few of the reasons this is such a value at only $10,950! Try $500 down. Your payments could be as low as $71.77 including taxes and insurance!

Stone & Schulte
1745 W. San Carlos   CY7-3757
(Open 8 AM to 8 PM)

YOU FINISH IT!

The sellers of this large family home were just about half done with the new family room when the husband was transferred to Culver City! Now you can finish it and save a lot of money on the purchase price! There is almost 1800 square feet of living area in the home including a tremendous living room, 3 bedrooms, 2 baths, modern kitchen, and the partially completed family or rumpus room. Natural wood paneling finished with explicit care makes the home unique! There is even a separate workshop in back. Here's the amazing thing: all this space for the rock bottom price of $15,950 and with terms arranged for your pocketbook. Better hurry on this one! CY7-3757 Now!

Stone & Schulte
1745 W. San Carlos   CY7-3757
(Open 8AM To 8PM)

BRING $200 AND MOVE IN TODAY!

We have a 3 bedroom, 2 bath home that is top quality, insulated, weatherstripped, hardwood floors, all electric kitchen and brand new that is going to be sold at unheard of terms because of a divorce settlement. It must be sold today, so the owner is going to sell for only $200 down to his big low interest loan! A deal like this happens once in a lifetime! Call quickly: CY7-3757 and be there first!

Stone & Schulte
1745 W. San Carlos   CY7-3757
(Open 8 a.m. to 8 p.m.)

"BABY DOLL"

That's what this one is! A 2 bedroom gem surrounded by attractive patios shrubs, and fencing! The owners have spent hours of hard work putting in the extras . . . and now they have to leave the area! You'll love the indoor-outdoor living area of this contemporary bungalow. Price: $10,950! $500 down and payments of about $90 per month will handle! Call CY7-3757.

Stone & Schulte
1745 W. San Carlos   CY7-3757
(Open 8 A.M. to 8 P.M.)

COZY FOR A COUPLE

Right in the heart of Willow Glen on a lot that has a tall majestic fir tree in the front yard, is this English style custom residence with hospitality and warmth written all over it! The 5 rooms are just right for an elder couple who like the architecture and cozy comfort of English Tudor. It has hardwood floors, forced air heat, fireplace, dining room, and 2 large bedrooms. Full price: $13,975! Call now for an appointment: CY7-3757.

Stone & Schulte
1745 W. San Carlos   CY7-3757
(Open 8 a.m. to 8 p.m.)

MOUNTAIN RETREAT!

Nestled in the hills of Almaden just a few minutes drive from San Jose, is this rustic home on an acre of land with the perfect setting for relaxed, carefree living! Privacy is everywhere! Large rooms, family room, 2 baths, double patio, terraced gardens, green lawns, tall pine trees, and a view of the mountains from every room are just a few of the things that makes this one a truly unusual offering. There is room for raising horses or pets plus adding another home on one lot if desired. The bubbling stream can ull you to sleep at night! Priced at $18,500, it must be seen to be appreciated. Call CY7-3757 and let one of our professional home sales counselors show you this property!

Stone & Schulte

GARDEN OF THE GODS!

Once in a while a little home comes along that has all the charm and distinction of the really expensive residences, with choice landscaping and gardens given much personal attention by the sellers. We have just listed such a home! It has 3 bedrooms, fireplace and is just immaculate inside! But the beauty of it is the cozy garden with large shade trees, shrubs and a partially covered lanai in the patio area! You'll just have to see it to appreciate the value it represents at $13,450! Less than $1000 will finance with payments under $95 a month! Call CY7-3757 for the details.

Stone & Schulte
1745 W. San Carlos   CY7-3757
(Open 8 a.m. to 8 p.m.)

WHAT A CUTIE!

Here's a 2-bedroom home that literally is in a world of its own! Setting is that of a garden paradise with enclosed front patio, rock gardens, planters, trees and shrubs, making both indoors and outdoors one big living area! There is even a small hideaway den for the man of the house! Priced at $11,250, it can be owned for $350 down and monthly payments under $90! Hurry on this one! CY7-3757.

Stone & Schulte
1745 W. San Carlos   CY7-3757
(Open 8 A.M. to 8 P.M.)

KISS THE LANDLORD GOODBY

That's what you'll do when you see this cute 3 bedroom home that we have listed on the Eastside! It has hardwood floors, large fireplace, patio, fenced yards, and many fine features. $590 will buy it for you under FHA terms. Full price $13,250 and one of the best buys in the valley! CY7-3757.

Stone & Schulte
1745 W. San Carlos   CY7-3757
(Open 8 a.m. to 8 p.m.)

BRING $300 OWN FOR $10,000

Yes sir! We don't have buys like this very often! A cute little 2 bedroom home only 3 years old on a country sized lot with fruit trees and landscaping going for $300 down and $73 per month including taxes and insurance! If you have been waiting for that chance of a lifetime to own your own home — start with this bargain! Call now: CY7-3757.

Stone & Schulte
1745 W. San Carlos   CY7-3757
(Open 8 A.M. to 8 P.M.)

WEED PATCH!

Yes—the yards both front and back of this country home need a strong arm and back to clean them up! But with a little imagination they provide a wonderful place for kids and frustrated farmers! The home is only 6 years old and has nearly 1500 square ft. of modern space with 3 bedrooms, 2 baths, service porch and other features. There are loads of fruit trees on this big country lot and with a little work you'll have a fine home for only $13,500! Just $500 down will handle the financing! CY7-3757.

Stone & Schulte
1745 W. San Carlos   CY7-3757
(Open 8 A.M. to 8 P.M.)

BUDGET BEATER!

Beat the high cost of living with the low cost of monthly investments on the 3 bedroom sided home we have just listed located off The Alameda close to bus and shopping. It has 1400 square feet of living space, and includes such features as service porch, separate dining room and hardwood floors. The low price of $11,950 for this Spanish home represents a value and can make it possible for you to own a little home for very little each month. The house needs a little paint, but otherwise it's in fine shape. Call CY7-3757 and see for yourself.

Stone & Schulte
1745 W. San Carlos   CY7-3757
(Open 8 a.m. to 8 p.m.)

LIVE IN A GARDEN!

Have you ever wanted a home that made you feel like you were living on a tropical isle all by yourself? We have such a home with so many distinctive features words will not describe them. Among these are such things as three separate gardens, each with tropical flowers, ferns and shrubs, 2 patios, covered lanai, separate hobby shop, and tall shade trees that screen the world outside! The home itself is custom built and finished with plaster, natural woods, and choice decorating. When you come home from a long day of work, this haven of rest will truly make you feel like the king of a tropical isle! It can be yours for $850 down at the price of $15,950! Call CY7-3757 to see it!

Stone & Schulte
1745 W. San Carlos   CY7-3757
(Open 8 A.M. to 8 P.M.)

CAN YOU PAINT?

If so, this little value-packed home that needs painting, might be just the buy you have been looking for. It has 3 bedrooms, 1½ baths, formal dining room, service porch, and is a fine Spanish style stucco bungalow of pre-war vintage. Located just a block and a half off The Alameda close to buses, and shopping, it represents a real value for some one who can paint and putter a bit to put it in top shape. There is 1400 square feet of living space, hardwood floors, 220 wiring, and a new furnace all for the price of $11,950. Name your terms. CY7-3757.

Stone & Schulte
1745 W. San Carlos   CY7-3757
(Open 8 A.M. to 8 P.M.)

HOBBY HOUSE!

Out in the country with plenty of room and fresh air, is a big 7 room home that has 3 bedrooms, 2 baths, service porch, formal dining room, separate family room and a large patio! It is a perfect place to raise a big family.... and it will please the hobbyist too! The separate room behind the garage is ideal for the man or woman with hobbies! The 1790 feet of living area can be purchased for $17,950. Don't dismay if you are low on cash as we'll arrange the terms! CY7-3757.

Stone & Schulte
1745 W. San Carlos   CY7-3757
(Open 8 A.M. to 8 P.M.)

VIEW THE HILLS

Nestled in the hills of Monta Vista overlooking the valley is this country retreat where the owners raise chickens and dogs with complete rural freedom... yet only a few minutes from downtown San Jose! The 3 bedroom home is a perfect place for anyone who wants to be a country-land owner but has to work in the city. Full price: $12,950. A big G.I. loan can be assumed without qualifying: $71.50 per month including taxes and insurance. Call CY7-3757.

Stone & Schulte
1745 W. San Carlos   CY7-3757
(Open 8 a.m. to 8 p.m.)

PUTTERER'S PARADISE

We have just listed a custom built 7 room home with 3 bedrms., 1½ baths and every desirable feature, that is the perfect home for the man that loves to putter! There is a double detached garage with an adjoining workshop, den or hideout that the do-it-yourself fan will love! In addition there is a large covered lanai, dichondra lawns, sprinklers front and rear, fruit trees, and even an outside sink for the patio area. Full price $18,500! Easy terms! Call CY7-3757 to see it now!

Stone & Schulte
1745 W. San Carlos   CY7-3757
(Open 8 a.m. to 8 p.m.)

GEM ON A GREEN CARPET

The owners of this Saratoga beauty have spared no expense in designing and building their dream home! Now they are moving to larger quarters, and leaving this custom 3 bedroom, 2 bath residence to new owners. You will be enthralled by the scenic beauty of the distinctively landscaped yards as viewed from the picture windows of the spacious living room! Purple flowers, rock knolls, and flowering shrubs among winding paths provide a setting that cannot be duplicated. Your entrance into the tiled hallway will impress you with the rich decor of the interior! Priced at only $23,950, this can be owned for $3950 down to an FHA loan. Call CY7-3757.

Stone & Schulte
1745 W. San Carlos   CY7-3757

EXOTIC ACCENT'

Have you ever wanted a home that made you feel like you were living on a tropical isle all by yourself? We have such a home with so many distinctive features words will not describe them. Among these are such things as three separate gardens, each with tropical flowers, ferns, shrubs, 2 patios, a covered lanai, separate hobby shop nicely finished, tall shade trees to screen the world outside! The home itself is custom built and finished with quality materials like natural wood and genuine plaster. You'll love the knotty pine kitchen! When you come home from a long day of work to this haven of rest you'll truly feel like the king of a tropical isle! Price is $15,950 with only $750 down! Nowhere in the valley is there a better buy! Call CY7-3757.

Stone & Schulte
1745 W. San Carlos   CY7-3757
(Open 8 A.M. to 8 P.M.)

DECORATORS NIGHTMARE!

The interior of this 4 bedroom home needs complete redecorating to make it look like the real doll house it could be! But with a little paint and fixing, this big home with 2 full baths, living room with fireplace, screened in patio, outside workshop and hobby room, built-in air conditioning unit, and drapes and rugs, can be worth much more than the $14,250 which the seller is willing to take! $550 down and you can own this one with monthly investments including taxes and insurance of $108.26. Repaint this one and reap the benefits! CY7-3757.

Stone & Schulte
1745 W. San Carlos   CY7-3757
(Open 8 a.m. to 8 p.m.)

COZY COTTAGE $500

Just $500 down and you may own this cozy 3 bedroom family home located between Sunnyvale and Santa Clara. It is a spotless home that invites casual California living! The rear yards have been choicely landscaped and cared for! There are 2 patios, a BBQ with serving bars, playhouse with enclosed play area for the kids to romp, lots of fruit trees ready to use and enjoy. Payments are less than rent at the price of $13,950. Call CY7-3757 now.

Stone & Schulte
1745 W. San Carlos   CY7-3757

HANDY HOUSE!

Close to city bus lines, shopping, and Willow Glen schools, this custom 2 bedroom home with 1163 square feet is priced to sell at $12,750! $650 down and $95 per month will handle the financing! Call CY7-3757.

Stone & Schulte
INC.
1745 W. San Carlos   CY7-3757
(Open 8 AM to 8 PM)

BRING $350 WITH YOU

That's all you'll need including closing costs and without qualifying to purchase this new 3 bedroom, 2 bath Willow Glen home with hardwood floors, insulation, weatherstripping and many extras. The all electric kitchen will make really easy life for the wife! The big FHA loan can be assumed without qualifying problems. See this one today by calling CY7-3757.

Stone & Schulte
1745 W. San Carlos   CY7-3757
(Open 8 A.M. to 8 P.M.)

WANT TO INVEST $62

That's the total monthly payment including taxes and insurance on this westside value! It is a real doll house with hardwood floors, insulated ceiling, weatherstripping, lovely patio, and large landscaped yards with trees! The full price is only $10,950! Call now to see this one before someone else does. CY7-3757.

Stone & Schulte
1745 W. San Carlos   CY7-3757
(Open 8 a.m. to 8 p.m.)

YOU'LL HAVE TO BRUSH UP

And Also Down... to Repaint the interior of the 7 room country home we have just listed for sale. It has potential as a very comfortable and large family home with its big 3 bedroom, 2 baths (one with outside entrance), large living room with central fireplace flagged by patio doors, and a formal dining room. There is also a service porch, outside separate family room, hobby corners, large patio (which could make another room with some remodeling), and in all 1760 square feet of livable space. It needs paint and it needs you... and for as little as $1000 it can be yours! Name your price and terms! CY7-3757.

Stone & Schulte
1745 W. San Carlos   CY7-3757
(Open 8AM To 8PM)

A NEST FOR TWO!

On Bluebird Drive we have a love-nest for two that will delight any discriminating love-birds! This gem is on a big lot with room to play, relax, and putter! There is a covered lanai, separate workshop, 2 walnut trees, and a cross-fenced yard for privacy and beauty. $12,370 and $500 down. CY7-3757 to own this one for your canary!

Stone & Schulte
1745 W. San Carlos   CY7-3757
(Open 8 A.M. to 8 P.M.)

DO NOT USE ABBREVIATIONS

Real estate brokers seem to delight in finding new ways to abbreviate words! In an attempt to save advertising dollars, many firms resort to the use of shortened versions of common words. This is generally unwise as it increases the difficulty of the reader in trying to determine the author's meaning. Consider these examples:

CUSTOM BEAUTY

4 Bdrms, 2 bths, F.R., & Br. Firepl. 3 Blks to Sch. and Shp. Cent. Lg. Yd., Shrubs, Trees, & C.C. walks. $1,000 Dn. $125 p.m. Call Cl 8-9554.

JOHNSON REALTY

CUSTOM BEAUTY

This home has 4 bedrooms, 2 baths, family room, and brick fireplace. It is only 3 blocks from Evergreen School and Valley Fair Shopping Center. The large tree shaded yard is lined with green shrubs and concrete walks. Just $1,000 down and $125 per month will buy this classic beauty! Call Cl 8-9554.

JOHNSON REALTY

It is easy to see that the second ad is so much easier to read and more effective in creating customer interest. Abreviations are seldom worth the few dollars they save in comparison to the resulting lost calls.

USE EFFECTIVE LAYOUT

Each newspaper has its own method of arranging classified ads. Some permit pictures and signature cuts while others adhere to rigid rules regarding type and composition. Metropolitan newspapers will seldom permit variations other than size of type and spacing arrangements. Study your local situation and try to create a layout which will stand out when compared to other ads in the same section. If everyone is using small, tightly set copy, try using lots of white space, indentations, and contrasts. If your competitors are adhering to a particular format, try creating some variation that will give your ads distinction. This is not always easy to do. Once you find something which works, it will be copied and you will be forced to change again. However, it is possible to retain individuality by careful analysis of the composition pattern of your classified section and the changes which can be made to accent your offerings.

REPETITION HAS VALUE ALSO

Advertising experts assure us there is considerable value in repeating the type and style of our ads once we find a program that works. Repetition has a long range impact upon the reader. This is particularly true in using the company name or signature in ads! Buyers and sellers become increasingly aware of your advertising efforts when your company name and basic format are used in a recognizable fashion each day.

HONESTY AND TRUTHFULNESS IN ADVERTISING

In my opinion, there is never any reason to stoop to the unethical use of phrases and terms in your ads which cannot be substantiated by the facts regarding the property advertised. Always be completely honest in your advertising; it will win you both customers and friends. If you are advertising a dirty home, do not treat it as you would a clean one. If your listing is on a small lot, do not infer it is a large one. You may be surprised to learn that reverse psychology is occasionally beneficial in attracting buyers and sellers. When you admit your listing is not perfect, you make your entire advertising more believable! Consider the impact of the following ads:

WEED IT AND REAP

These owners have moved to New York and the lawns are in need of immediate attention! The price of this 3 bedroom, 2 bath westside home represents a real value to the customer who is willing to weed the yard and reap the benefits. Call Cy 7-3757 now!

BRIGHTON MANOR REALTORS

BRING A HAMMER AND PAINT BRUSH!

With some creative thought and energy, this older 2 story home near State College can be converted into a comfortable 8 room residence. However, restoring its original charm will require some work! That's why the price is only $15,750. Call now for details: Dr 5-2180.

BROWN & BROWN, REALTORS

HOW TO PLAN YOUR DAILY ADVERTISING

Each day a certain number of new buyers enter the market place and begin shopping for real estate. By running a variety of ads designed to appeal to the various segments of this market, you can attract the

102 HOW TO OBTAIN PROSPECTS FROM ADVERTISING

largest number of potential buyers. Very few firms could afford to advertise all of their listings every day, and the above selective method achieves the same result by bringing to your attention buyers for each of the listings you represent.

If you need assistance in preparing your ads, call on your local newspaper representative. He is an expert and will be more than glad to help you. You can also subscribe to real estate advertising services through your newspaper to give you fresh ideas each month.

WRITING AN AD FOR 3562 ROSEDALE

Now that you have learned the basic rules for writing good ads, let's try to compose one for your new listing on Rosedale Avenue! We will begin by first listing the important features of the property which might influence a prospective buyer:

1. It is a neat, clean, 4 1/2 year old ranch style home.
2. It has 3 bedrooms and 2 baths.
3. It has a covered patio, walks around rear yard, and fencing.
4. It is well maintained and has a yard which is filled with shrubs, flowers, and trees.
5. There are 1356 square feet of living space.
6. It is located in the Cambrian district, near the Rose Garden Park.
7. Only two blocks to city bus line and six blocks to the Valley Fair shopping center.
8. It is located on a quiet, tree lined street of modest homes.
9. Carpeting, drapes, and electric range are included in the price.
10. There are sprinklers in the front yard.

With these facts, you now ask yourself who is most likely to buy this kind of home. A retired couple? Young couple? Large family? You decide this home, due to location and size, is better suited for the retired couple than other possible groups. The quiet neighborhood and unusual charm of this home make it appealing to older people who want to be close to facilities but still enjoy the privacy afforded by its tree-shaded yards and covered patio. With these points in mind, you write two ads:

A ROSE GARDEN CHARMER

Here is a 3 bedroom, 2 bath, ranch home just 6 blocks from Valley Fair shopping and 2 from city bus lines. Manicured lawns, shrubs, and flowers set this one apart on a quiet, tree-lined street of modest homes. Inside and out it is a real charmer, priced at only $18,950. To see this today, call Cy 7-3757.

TEA FOR TWO!

Nestled among nice homes in a quiet, tree-lined district near the Rose Gardens, we have found a haven for two (or more) who would appreciate rustic charm close to Valley Fair shopping and bus. 3 bedrooms, 2 baths, and covered patio together with well trimmed lawns, shrubs, and flower beds combine to make this a cozy gem at $18,950. Call Cy 7-3757 today!

HOW TO HANDLE TELEPHONE INQUIRIES

The most effective ad is no better than the salesman who answers the inquiries it produces! I have shuddered at the careless answers given by salesmen in my office to the hard-earned phone calls we are fortunate to receive. Every phone call from a prospect is the result of conscious time and effort as well as money, and the ultimate objective of selling the caller a home may never be achieved if the salesman handling the phones does not understand how to convert the inquiry to an appointment.

The first rule of good telephone technique, is: <u>put yourself in the caller's shoes.</u> As you will recall, we reviewed the <u>process by which a</u> prospect selects the ads he wishes to call and eliminates those which do not interest him. When he picks up the phone to make the first call to a real estate office, he is <u>continuing</u> his <u>elimination process</u>! Since he has a number of other ads he has circled to call, he is really expecting to find some reason why he can terminate this inquiry and get on to the next one. It is important to understand the client's attitude and to be on guard against giving him any reason to hang up. You must retain his interest and keep him talking if you are to succeed in your basic objectives.

The second rule to remember about telephone calls is: <u>always control the interview.</u> Because the caller is the one seeking <u>information, he always begins by asking a question.</u> This is natural. However, the longer he asks questions and you give the answers, the less command you have of the situation. <u>The one asking the questions is always in control!</u> When you ask a question, you automatically place the other party in a defensive position. He must, of necessity, answer you. The prospect's one-track objective is to obtain more information about a specific property until he is sure it is not the one for him. Your task is to win the caller's confidence and arrange a face-to-face interview where you can properly counsel with him regarding his real estate needs. <u>Your goal cannot be realized unless you control the telephone interview!</u> How do you accomplish that? Well, when the prospect first calls, you should be ready to mentally disarm him. Like a Judo expert, throw your on-coming prospect off-balance so you can steer the conversation in the direction needed to achieve your pre-determined purpose.

104   HOW TO OBTAIN PROSPECTS FROM ADVERTISING

After all, you can only help this customer if you know his needs and abilities well enough to select the properties he should inspect. On the other hand, the prospect does not really understand what you can offer and he is intent on doing his house-hunting the wrong way! You and I know that only a fraction of the available listings are featured by any real estate company in one issue of the newspaper, and that the total inventory available for the potential buyer's review is much larger than he can imagine. In order to help him find the right house, you need to place him under your professional wing where you can properly counsel him about the real estate market as related to his needs. To do this you must stay on top of the conversation until you can arrange that appointment. One of the most effective ways of doing this is to answer a question with a question. If you give some information to your caller, do not let him get another question in before you can ask one. Finish your comment with another probing query which will force the prospect to give you information.

LIST COMPARABLES FOR EVERY AD

To be really effective, you must be prepared for your caller's inquiry. One of the recommended procedures is to always develop a good list of comparables for each advertisement featured in the daily newspaper. Beside each ad, list four or five other properties which are available and would be similar in nature to the ones advertised. To determine which comparables to use, study the theme of the ad as well as the price range involved and then look for listings which will fall into the same general category. With this list ready for use when the phone rings you can easily switch the conversation to other properties similar to the one your prospect identified and you can quickly justify to him the need of an appointment to review the relative merits of each offering mentioned. Note the example below of how your advertising sheet might look after preparing comparables for the day's featured listings.

Property Advertised:

18291 Highland Drive, San Jose

See Also:

7431 Ellis Street, San Jose
94321 Downey Brooke Ave., S. J.
5003 Glenbrook Drive, S. J.
53 Wainwright Road, S. J.

VIEW THE VALLEY

High above the valley in the majestic Eastern Foothills overlooking the Golf Course and all the panoramic beauty of our valley is this red, brick custom home. This 3 bedroom, 2 bath residence has everything! As you ascend the distinctive red brick staircase and enter the long living room, your eyes will be drawn to the Arizona Flagstone fireplace and then to the big, bay windows on one full wall opening before you, the magnificent sight. Let us tell you the rest. CL 8-9554.

Stone & Schulte

2521 Alum Rock Ave.   CL 8-9554
(Choose from over 1000 homes)

HOW TO OBTAIN PROSPECTS FROM ADVERTISING

USE A PROSPECT CARD TO RECORD THE FACTS

As you engage the prospect in conversation, you will want to make brief notes of the important facts he reveals about his needs. There are a number of prospect cards available and many real estate firms have designed their own. Select one which suits your needs and is approved by your broker, then follow a systematic program of gathering the facts from your prospects. (See the Prospect form, page 106.)

OBTAIN AND USE THE CALLER'S NAME

Use your prospect's name early and often in the conversation. It is good psychology. Here are some ways to achieve that objective:

1. Use Your Name to Force the Caller's Response

If you hold your name back just long enough to permit the caller to ask his first question, you can then use it to help extract his name. For example, when answering the phone you might identify only the company you represent and the department, but omit reference to your name until the first reply from the prospect.

"Smith & Smith, Realtors, Residential Department"; or "Residential Department, may I be of service to you?"

When the client responds, then use an approach like this: "I'm Tom Starr. With whom am I speaking?" or "This is Tom Starr. What is your name?"

2. Identify a Related Subject Which Can Lead to the Name

Sometimes you can extract the name by reference to related topics. For example, if in response to your question on where the husband works, the prospect names a business with which you are familiar, you can then ask the husband's name as a natural reaction to the answer. The same principle can apply to the prospect's identification of schools, areas, or other common interest topics which will permit you to probe for the name. When asking the area in which the caller lives, you might say:

"On what street do you live?"
"Coronado Drive."
"That's interesting! We just sold a home for Mrs. Smith at 234 Coronado near your home. You probably know them. What is your name?"

3. Try Pausing After Giving Your Name

If you pause right after giving your own name you will often find the caller will fill the void with the desired information about name and address. You can say:

STONE & SCHULTE

PROSPECT FORM

NAME _____ PHONE _____

ADDRESS _____ CITY _____

(Note: Be sure to tell them about your "HOME COUNSELING SERVICE" and explain that we have many other similar listings to choose from.)

I. Question: "How many are there in your family?" _____ Children _____ Ages

   Bedrooms _____ Baths _____ Sq. Ft. _____ Schools: ☐ Elem. ☐ Jr. Hi ☐ Sr. Hi.

   Notes: _____ ☐ College ☐ Par. ☐ Other

II. Question: "In what area do you prefer to live?" _____
    _____ City bus _____ Shopping _____

III. Question: "What special features do you desire?" _____
    ☐ Fm. Rm. ☐ Din. Rm. ☐ Fm. Kit. ☐ Built-ins ☐ Fireplace
    ☐ Dbl. Gar. ☐ Basement ☐ Ser. Por. ☐ Hdw. Flrs. ☐ F/A Heat
    ☐ Fenced   ☐ Landscaped ☐ Patio   ☐ Lot Size _____

IV. Question: "How soon must you move?" _____ Sell first _____ Trade _____ Rents

    Urgency _____
    Reason for buying _____

V. Question: "What is the most you feel you want to invest in a home?"

   Price _____ Down _____ Monthly _____ Notes _____

   ☐ Cash ☐ G.I. ☐ Cal Vet ☐ FHA ☐ Conv. ☐ Assume

VI. Question: "If new financing is required, we will need to know your approximate monthly or annual earnings..."

    Monthly _____ Annually _____ Type work _____ How long _____
    Where employed _____ Wife work? _____

APPOINTMENT RECORD: HOMES SHOWN:
_____   _____
_____   _____
_____   _____
_____   _____
_____   _____
_____   _____
_____   _____

STONE & SCHULTE

SALESMAN'S RECAP OF FLOOR CALLS

Salesman _____ Date _____

Weather & Day of Week _____ Floor shift time _____

ENTERED IN MASTER RECORD   CALLS POSTED IN AD BOOK

NO	AD HEADER CALLED ON	LETTER	PHONE	AD	SIGN	WALK IN	KN/CN	REFER.	PROPERTY ADDRESS	Appointment	Name & Number	General Information	Remarks
1.													
2.													
3.													
4.													
5.													
6.													
7.													
8.													
9.													
10.													
11.													
12.													
13.													
TOTALS													

"I am Tom Starr." (pause)
"This is Mrs. Cornell..."

4. <u>Create a Reason to Make a Return Call</u>

Any reason to call back can be helpful in obtaining the name and phone number of the customer. If you use answering services, switchboard girls or secretaries to handle calls, they can sometimes assist in this objective. The risk you take, is that the client may not give you the name and decide not to call back at all. If used, it should be carefully handled so as not to offend the client. For example:

"It will take me a few moments to obtain that information. To save your time may I call you back after I have looked it up?" or

"All of the phones in our office seem to be ringing at the same time. Would you mind if I called you right back?" or

"The salesman handling that property is on the other line at the moment. Can I have him call you as soon as he is finished?"

DEVELOP AN EFFECTIVE SERIES OF PROBING QUESTIONS

To obtain the most from your telephone interviews, you should be prepared with a list of proven questions which you can use at the appropriate moments in the conversations. The questions listed here have been used by my salesmen and myself thousands of times with great success, and you can undoubtedly think of similar ones which can achieve the same results.

1. <u>How Many in Your Family?</u>

In addition to identifying actual family composition, the replies to this question will often reveal the size home needed, the schools to be considered, the bedroom requirements and similar items of information.

2. <u>In What Area Do You Prefer to Live?</u>

Here you will receive clues as to the real estate districts preferred by the prospect and often learn what shopping or employment centers are important in relation to the housing area selected.

3. <u>How Soon Would You Like to Move?</u>

Answers to this one will give you some idea about the degree of urgency in the caller's plans. Urgency is a major factor in qualifying any prospect, and you should determine the need for action before you terminate your first conversation. A related question that works also is: "How long have you been looking for a home?" People that have been shopping for several months or years will be more difficult to handle than the client who is sitting in a motel with his bags packed!

HOW TO OBTAIN PROSPECTS FROM ADVERTISING

4. <u>What Special Features Do You Require in Your New Home?</u>

This is a broad question and is designed to bring to the surface the things considered most important by the prospect. You may receive your first clue as to the motivational hot spots which will later trigger a sale. Another question related to this is: "Have you seen any homes you particularly liked?" If they have been shopping with other brokers and located property reasonably close to their needs, you should know about it.

5. <u>How Much Had You Planned to Invest in This Home?</u>

The wording of this particular question will bring a variety of responses. The person who has only a nominal down payment will mention his cash investment in terms of down payment while the customer concerned with monthly payments or price will give you a different reaction. The use of the term "invest" is a more effective one than to say: "How much can you pay!"

You will note that all the questions above are encompassing enough to permit the customer to respond from the viewpoint most vital to him. This will help you determine what is really important to your caller and to evaluate how you can best serve his interests.

These questions are designed for use in a systematic manner each time the phone rings. They can be posted on a card beside the phone, where they are available as a constant reminder to use them. Each time a customer asks a question and you reply, one of these questions can be inserted before the prospect has time to think up another question for you to answer. In this manner, you remain in control of the telephone interview and eventually succeed in getting the name, number and counselling appointment you wanted from the beginning!

HOW TO USE THESE QUESTIONS IN AN ACTUAL INTERVIEW

Let us imagine you are assigned to floor duty shortly after the first ad you write for 3562 Rosedale Avenue has been featured. You receive a floor call from a prospect who has read your "Tea For Two" ad about that property. Your conversation might go like this:

You: "A.B.C. Realty, Residential Department. May I help you?"

Caller: "I was reading your ad in tonight's paper, the one that begins: 'Tea for Two.' What street in the Rose Garden district is that one on?"

(You recognize this trap and do not intend to give the street address over the phone)

You: "Yes, that ad has been receiving many inquiries. It is one of several similar properties we are currently featuring in that general area. This is Tom Starr. May I ask who is calling?"

HOW TO OBTAIN PROSPECTS FROM ADVERTISING

Caller: "This is Mrs. Carter. Does this home have a family room?"

You: "Mrs. Carter, there is a family kitchen which can serve this purpose. Is a family room important to you and your husband?"

(You have answered her question with a question and are back in control again).

Carter: "Not really, since there is only Mr. Carter and myself. Our only daughter was married earlier this year."

(As she momentarily pauses to think up a new question to ask, you jump to the opportunity and ask another one.)

You: "In what area do you and Mr. Carter prefer to live? You see we represent many properties in various parts of the city, some of which are very similar to the one on which you called!"

Carter: "Well, we would like to locate in the westside district reasonably close to my husband's office on the Alameda."

You: "Where does your husband work, Mrs. Carter?"

Carter: "At the Egyptian Museum! He is the Chief Administrator there."

You: "That is very interesting, Mrs. Carter. Although I have never met your husband, I feel I must know him as I have often admired those beautiful gardens around the museum. If you and your husband find a suitable home, how soon would you like to move?"

Carter: "We would have to sell our home first, so we are really just looking right now."

You: "Many people do that, Mrs. Carter and with our firm you have the advantage of our trade-in plan if I find you the right home. What special features do you require in your next home?"

Carter: "We want either 2 bedrooms and a den or 3 bedrooms, since we entertain our relatives frequently. My husband is particular about the yards since he enjoys landscaping and gardening. This ad says the home you featured has nice yards. That interests us. Could we arrange to see that one?"

You: "Certainly, Mrs. Carter! When would you and your husband be available to see it?"

(You are really trying to get an appointment to see the Carter's at their home first, but a positive reply is necessary to reach that objective.)

Carter: "Mr. Carter has tomorrow afternoon free. Could we make it then?"

You: "Mrs. Carter, I would be glad to arrange it for you. I will call for an appointment now. What is your telephone number?

HOW TO OBTAIN PROSPECTS FROM ADVERTISING

Carter: "Exbrook 2—7380."

You: "Will you and Mr. Carter be home this evening? I would like to see your present home and discuss various factors involved in the purchase of another property. I could be there about 7:00 p.m. Would that be satisfactory?"

(To make the decision easy, you are the one who suggests the time and place.)

Carter: "I guess it would be alright, but I would have to check with Mr. Carter first."

You: "I understand. Possibly you could check with him while I am arranging the appointment for seeing the property tomorrow. What is your address, Mrs. Carter?"

Carter: "1781 South 21st Street near San Carlos."

You: "Thank you Mrs. Carter. You will be hearing from me in about thirty minutes. Thank you for calling."

In this interview you achieved your three primary objectives:
1. Obtained the clients name, phone number and address.
2. Made an appointment to counsel and show property.
3. Determined the urgency of the customer's needs.

You did not use all the questions we suggested on pages 108 and 109, as some of them were not necessary for this particular conversation. You did use those which were most appropriate in helping you stay in control. If you practice this telephone technique and continue to improve your ability to handle prospect inquiries, your financial success in this business will be greatly accelerated.

IT'S A SMILE-A-PHONE!

Before we conclude this subject of telephone response, I would like to emphasize the matter of attitude and its effect on your voice. The human voice is a wonderful instrument of communication, but it is often misused and ineffective because the owner does not recognize how to control it properly. The tone and inflections of the voice play a major role in our efforts to communicate. These, in turn, are affected by our mental attitude at the time we speak. If you pick up a telephone immediately following some disagreeable incident, your voice will undoubtedly reflect the harsh, unpleasant attitude in your mind. The party on the other end of the line will not know why you are irritated or unfriendly. <u>He will just know that you are not interested in him at that moment.</u>

Practice developing a pleasant, friendly and sincere telephone voice which can attract the warm response of your callers. If you will try to put charm and enthusiasm into your voice, you will be greatly surprised at the increased warmth of the responses you receive. One way to insure a pleasant tone is to put a smile on your face before you answer. You cannot sound gruff while smiling! Use a tape recorder to practice your voice improvements and ask for comments from your broker, fellow salesmen, or wife. If you consciously work at putting enthusiasm into your voice, your effectiveness in handling telephone calls will greatly increase.

In this lesson we have covered the subject of writing good classified ads, handling floor time, and responding to prospect inquiries. These are all vital activities connected with your real estate career and I sincerely hope that from time to time you review the suggestions we have made regarding these topics. In the next chapter we are going to meet Mr. and Mrs. Carter, with whom you arranged a counselling appointment for this evening in preparation for the selection of properties to show these new prospects. If you perform your services well, you are on your way to a sale!

HOW TO OBTAIN PROSPECTS FROM ADVERTISING

QUESTIONS AND PROJECTS ON CHAPTER FIVE

Questions:

1. What are five factors which should be considered when advertising property for sale, and why are each important to you?
2. How do real estate buyers select the ads on which they call and how will that affect your advertising and handling of telephones?
3. What basic rule must be observed in order to control a telephone interview?
4. Why is the prospect's name important and how can you obtain it early in the telephone conversation?
5. What questions can you use to detect urgency and motivation over the phone?
6. How can you win your caller's confidence and help him to work with you in discussing his needs?
7. What factors and rules are important about each of the following advertising topics:
   a. "Headers" or "lead lines"
   b. "Themes"
   c. Abbreviations
   d. Motivational categories
   e. Truthfulness
   f. Repetition of company name
   g. Basic copy of the ad
8. What things should you do in preparation for your floor time assignments and how should your ad copy be arranged?
9. How can you use a prospect form to help you qualify a caller and control the telephone interview?
10. What part does your voice and manner play in helping you control the caller's interest?

Projects:

1. Select three different properties and write two ads each using the rules and suggestions made in this chapter. Review the results with your broker.
2. Taking current issues of magazines, list 12 good ad headers which are taken from the copy of well known products or services. Do the same thing for TV and radio advertising which is currently popular in your area.
3. Write two ads on the same property using a "reverse psychology approach" on one and then the usual "saleman's puff" on the other. Compare the effect on other readers.
4. Attach a tape recorder to your practice telephone (with your broker's permission) and rehearse sample calls to study your voice and your effectiveness in controlling telephone conversations.

5. Observe the various telephone responses and techniques of other salesmen and analyze how their approach would apply to your talents.
6. List six good questions you would use to control a telephone inquiry about real estate for sale, and then practice using these questions on calls received.
7. Study the current ads in the classified section of your newspaper and compare the techniques used by different real estate companies. Then, ask the office secretary for the records regarding the number of calls being received on the various ads featured by your firm. Study and compare the results.
8. Practice various ways of obtaining the caller's name in telephone interviews and then consciously learn to repeat them several times during conversations.
9. Listen to the various phonograph recordings available on telephone technique or have the telephone company send the material and services they offer on good telephone procedures.
10. Practice projecting and improving your voice over the telephone by use of tape recorders, monitors, or assistance from supervisor, wife, or friends.

6

KNOW YOUR PROSPECTS AND YOUR PROPERTIES

Before you can influence a man's thinking, you must understand his desires. A real estate salesman should know his prospects and his properties equally well if he hopes to succeed in his function of selling real estate to people. The ingredients in any real estate transaction are dominated by the personalities involved and the motivations of the participants. To have knowledge of property and none about the people who own it is like knowing the working parts of an automobile without the ability to drive it! <u>People are your business.</u> Only by appreciating and understanding the motivations of the various customers whom you will serve can you learn to bring properties and people together in happy unions. Many salesmen fail to qualify their prospects adequately before showing them properties, and this frequently results in lost time and unproductive effort. A thorough and professional interview with the potential buyer before showing property is an important aspect of good real estate selling procedures.

When you meet a customer on his own ground, you have the opportunity of observing him in a relaxed setting where he is king and you are guest. This permits him to speak freely and comfortably about his needs, wants, and aspirations. You are privileged to know him on a more informal basis than is possible in most other locations. Your relationship can begin on a plane of friendly interest in which you are able to create a climate of confidence between yourself and the customer, while probing for clues to his real motivations. You can study the surroundings in which he lives and observe the furnishings, decor and items of interest which he has collected. You can meet his children and establish an awareness of their relationship to the parents and how they will affect the selection of a new home. Frequently, you can even begin to judge which of the two mates will play the deciding role in the final decision to relocate, and whose interests will dominate that choice. All of these little things can be vital factors in the eventual showing and closing phases of your selling process.

This is why I heartily recommend that you make every effort to <u>visit the customer in his own home before you show any property.</u>

The hour or two spent in this fashion can save you many useless hours later and smooth the path to an easy sale. If your prospective buyer lives anywhere within reasonable driving distance, insist on the privilege of picking him up at his own home and meeting him there before the showing begins. Find an excuse to sit down with him first and ask the simple, direct questions that are so effective in uncovering motivational interests. Why does he want to move? When? Where? How? What type of home appeals to him and has he seen anything similar to these desired requirements? Can he afford the price range he envisions and what reserves does he command to assist in the acquisition of property? Can he make an immediate decision if the right home is found, or must his action await some other contingent approval or related event? These and other essential qualifying questions should be asked <u>before the showing begins!</u>

Have you ever visited a doctor when you were ill and asked his advice? If so, you can undoubtedly recall how he asked where you hurt, and how long you felt this way and many similar questions. He probably did not attempt to diagnose your case before he had asked numerous questions and probed for clues related to your illness! Even after completing the examination and prescribing the proper treatment to solve the problem, he undoubtedly took his time to reassure you about the situation and its outcome. Why? Because he also deals with people and is, in reality, a salesman of health! Before he can cure your body he must have the confidence of your mind. The most popular and successful physicians are usually those whose bedside manner has won for them the respect and trust of their many patients. Remember this point when you are asked to solve the problems of a homebuyer or seller of real estate. Before you offer a solution, be sure you know the problem and, more important, have the complete cooperation and confidence of the clients involved.

YOUR COUNSELLING SESSION WITH THE CARTERS

With these objectives well in mind, you arrive at the home of the Carters a few minutes before 7:00 prepared to conduct your first qualifying interview with your potential customers and to learn as much as possible about their housing needs. After a brief exchange of introductions, you are invited into the pleasantly furnished living room to review the Carters' proposed purchase of a new home. Your eyes scan the room for a quick impression of the French Provincial furniture and accessories which are tastefully arranged to accent the cathedral beamed ceiling and the imposing stone fireplace.

"This is a lovely home, Mr. and Mrs. Carter! I imagine you have enjoyed many pleasant years here."

Mr. Carter acknowledges your comment: "Yes, we have lived here 17 years now. I believe Mrs. Carter told you that our only daughter, Marianne, was married in April of this year and we decided we no longer needed such a large home since there are only two of us. Besides, this place is becoming a little difficult for my wife and me to maintain. We would like to find a smaller one which requires less care so we can spend some time traveling and enjoying life more."

"I can certainly appreciate that, Mr. Carter, and I am confident I can help you locate just the right home after learning something about your specific requirements. Our firm has a wide selection of exclusive listings from which to choose and to help save your time in reviewing all of them, I decided to visit with you and your wife this evening to ascertain your principal needs so as to relate them to our extensive inventory of available homes. Have either of you seen a particular home you liked?"

You have now launched your series of questions designed to extract the essential facts about the Carters' interests in making a decision to transfer. Have they been looking at property with other brokers? Is there a home which they have selected tentatively, while still shopping the market, or is this their very first endeavor to begin the house-hunting procedure? Are both Mr. and Mrs. Carter equally interested in making a move, or is it just Mrs. Carter alone? The answers to this line of interrogation will play a major role in your evaluation of the situation and the listings you elect to show.

From the answers to your questions you learn that the Carters have thought about making a move for some time, but until now they have done very little about it except drive around the neighborhoods where they might like to live, seeing an occasional "open house" or "For Sale" sign about which they inquired. They like the Rose Garden District as well as the area near Park Avenue, both of which are reasonably close to Mr. Carter's place of employment - the Egyptian Museum on The Alameda. At this point you ask permission to inspect their present home, since it must be sold before consummating the purchase of another property. Mr. Carter shows you through, while you continue your questioning in the same manner as used with Mrs. Ervin when obtaining the listing on Rosedale Avenue. During your tour of the premises you make mental observations about the age and condition of this two-story Victorian home, noting that there are a number of items which need repair or reconditioning before the home is marketable. You roughly estimate the home contains 1800 to 2000 square feet of living space plus a full sized basement which makes it ideal for a large family that appreciates the older style of architecture.

Since this is only a preliminary session and not a regular listing interview, you make your mental notes without discussing values with Mr. Carter. You silently estimate that the residence should bring $24,000 to $27,000, but decide not to make any comment regarding price until you have made a more thorough inspection and researched your comparable files at the office. You learn that the Carters owe approximately $15,000 on the mortgage with no other indebtedness and your mental calculations indicate they might have from $9,000 to $12,000 in gross equity. This could be used as a down payment on another home, after deducting selling expenses.

Back in the living room, you find occasion to compliment Mrs. Carter on her outstanding collection of demitasse cups which attracted your interest while inspecting the dining room. She immediately warms to your recognition of her hobby and begins telling you about several of the more cherished pieces in the set. <u>You are well aware of the importance of being interested in that which interests your customers!</u> Establishing common grounds of appreciation for the individual accomplishments of your prospects is one of the surest ways to build lasting friendships with them. During the next hour of your visit, you discuss with the Carters their interest in travel and photography, and Mrs. Carter's activities with the local children's welfare agency to which she contributes much time and effort. You talk about the fascinating museum Mr. Carter supervises for the city, and ask many questions concerning his interesting job in caring for these artifacts and historic documents. Later you steer the conversation to real estate opportunities, asking whether Mr. Carter has ever considered owning property as an income-producing investment. His reply indicates his possible interest in exploring future ownership of rental units in the area around State College.

With such background information well in hand, and a pleasant feeling of friendship developing, you redirect the conversation to the particular requirements they might desire when choosing a new home. You explore the points they like about their present home, which may be important in the next one, as well as the things they do not like and would improve, if possible. With each answer you listen for the little clues to the basic motivations which may be inferred from the replies. You are practicing good communication techniques!

A WORD ABOUT THE ART OF COMMUNICATION

It seems appropriate, at this point, to mention something about the importance of your communication techniques. All selling is, in truth, the communication of ideas from one human to another. The more effectively one communicates with the other person, the more obvious the results achieved. Whether you are interviewing a customer, showing him property, or closing the sale, you must rely on your ability to communicate with him to achieve your objectives. You are now trying to win the attention of the Carters, drawing them into your circle of satisfied clients and directing them to the right solution for their real estate problems. Your success or failure will depend directly upon your communication skills and how effectively they are utilized. Although this topic will be covered in other sections of this training manual, permit me to emphasize a few of the basic rules used in good communication techniques.

To control any conversation, always gain the other person's attention when you speak to him. You do this by using your voice and manners in a decisive, but pleasant fashion. Always look directly at your customer when speaking to him and <u>when he answers give him your undivided attention.</u> Speak clearly and when you want emphasis, speak slowly. To keep the conversation in your command, ask questions of the other party. <u>Then listen!</u> There is an old saying that God gave us two ears and one mouth, which means he intended us to do twice as much listening as talking. Most salesmen have this in reverse, to their own and the customer's disadvantage. To sell an idea you must know what the prospect is thinking and how your ideas will relate to his thoughts. How can you find out what those thoughts are if you do not completely listen to his responses, or give him an opportunity to be heard?

Another vital point in effective communication techniques is to be sincerely interested in those subjects which interest your customer. Nothing wins friends like genuine expressions of interest in the things which dominate the other person's attention. To be truly effective, however, such comments must spring from a sincere desire to know and understand the speaker's attitudes and ambitions. At the earliest possible moment in any conversation you should attempt to establish common grounds of understanding between yourself and the other person. Give him every chance to express himself and to demonstrate his knowledge and feelings on the subject at hand.

Finally, remember the rules we gave you when reviewing good telephone procedures. If you would keep the interest of your conversationalist and fully control the direction the discussion will take, always:

1. <u>AGREE WITH YOUR CUSTOMER</u> (even if qualified)
2. <u>CALL HIM BY NAME</u>
3. <u>AND ASK ANOTHER QUESTION:</u>

Whenever you use a person's name you immediately command his full attention, for this is the one sound in the world he knows better than any other. If you call a person by name you momentarily arrest his thoughts, giving you an opportunity to re-direct the conversation with an observation or a question. When you ask a question, the listener is drawn into your dominating sphere of influence because he feels compelled to respond in some manner to your demands. By agreeing with him when he makes a point, even if such agreement is qualified, you retain his favorable attention and his open frame of mind in which to continue your incisive direction of the discussion.

Powerful salesmen constantly improve their abilities to hold the reins of communication in well trained patterns of question and answer sequences. If you would become a master salesman, practice good communication techniques at every opportunity and become conscious of the effect your voice, manner, and questions have on the people with whom you do business.

<u>YOU ARE READY TO DISCUSS THE SHOWING OF PROPERTY</u>

Completing your list of questions about the Carters' requirements, you turn to Mr. Carter:

"When your wife called today she expressed interest in a property in the Rose Garden District which we advertised in today's paper. In evaluating your needs, I believe you should see this home since it does have some of the things for which you are looking. However, I have two or three other properties which I believe might be even more suitable and I would appreciate the opportunity of showing them to you."

Mr. Carter replies: "Well, you know we are not in a position to buy anything until we sell this home, so you might be just wasting your time showing us property. Wouldn't it be better if you gave us the addresses of these places so we could drive by and see them from the outside; then if we are interested, we can contact you?"

You are quick to pick up this challenge:

"I realize you must sell your home before we complete another transaction, but with our guaranteed trade-in program we can finalize a sale in a few days if we locate the right property. After all, unless we do find you a home you really want, there would be no need to sell your present home, would there, Mr. Carter? Here is a pamphlet explaining how our trade-in plan works, which you can review at your leisure. Essentially it is an "equity insurance plan" which eliminates the fears and problems usually attendant with your type of home transfer situation. As for seeing property, I feel it would be very unfair to both you and the sellers we represent to have you just look at the exteriors of the homes involved. After all, this is like judging a book by its cover, isn't it, Mr. Carter? The real value to most homes is the beauty and comfort they reflect inside and without a chance to properly see these features you might by-pass the very home you really want and need. Besides, all of these owners have entrusted their properties to us with the assurance we will show them only to qualified buyers, by appointment. I am certain you can appreciate the importance of this practice and will want the same courtesy when we list your home for sale."

Having clearly established the value of your services in showing property, the Carters finally agree to meet you at 2:00 p.m. tomorrow to see the homes you have selected for their viewing. You have achieved your basic objectives, obtained the answers to many important questions, and created a pleasant relationship with the Carters in which to conduct the next phase of your assignment.

OTHER POINTS TO REMEMBER ABOUT QUALIFYING INTERVIEWS

There are a few related topics I would like to cover before moving to our showing appointment. In each counselling session, the individual attitudes and needs of the customers will determine how you conduct the interview. You must learn to be flexible and adjust to the personalities of the people involved. Not all of them will give you an equal opportunity to explore their motivations, or cultivate their friendships. You should always attempt to obtain a favorable interview session, but be versatile in handling the qualifying session in the manner best suited for obtaining the facts. Sometimes, due to circumstances beyond your control, your counselling must be done in your office, car, motel lobby, or other improvised locations. Discretion and good judgment dictate how you should handle the introduction to your customer's needs.

The Carters did not have young children around the home, but had they, you would certainly have made it a point to get acquainted with them and demonstrate to the parents your interest in the children. In most families, children play a big part in the final choice of a home. Schools, neighborhoods, parks, security and safety are environmental factors which influence the selection of a family residence. Learn to include your customer's offspring in your qualifying sessions.

With completely inexperienced homebuyers, it is sometimes helpful, during the counselling process, to introduce the documents they will later be asked to sign when the right home is found. Reviewing and discussing these forms before showing property may eliminate some of the basic fears which the uninitiated exhibit concerning real estate transactions. Showing them the papers in the privacy of their home, and identifying the documents they will be approving when the right one is located, tends to overcome possible later objections which can be raised during the closing session.

HOW TO SELECT THE RIGHT PROPERTIES FOR SHOWINGS

When a baseball player steps up to the mound for his turn at bat, he is given three opportunities to hit the ball or strike out! Your experience in showing properties to buyers will be similar to those of a batter: <u>after a certain number of strikes - you're out!</u> Every time you show a prospect a wrong property, your batting average drops and eventually you lose the customer's interest as well as your own. Most salesmen do require one or two practice swings before they connect with a good hit, but it is generally vital to get the homerun early in the game because there is always the possibility you may not come to bat again! Selecting the right properties to show a prospect is just as important as conducting a successful qualifying interview before the showing begins. Customers who view too much property develop a disease we call <u>"House Indigestion."</u> When they contract this ailment they do not know what they have seen, what they want, or where to go next! Sometimes they give up in despair because they are just plain confused. This is caused by real estate salesmen who do not know how to control the prospects' interest by limiting the number of properties they are allowed to see and closing at the right time. Alert real estate salesmen recognize the symptoms and dangers of this malady and find ways to prevent its occurence. The best remedy is careful advance planning of the showing sequence after a thorough evaluation of the properties available that suit the buyer's basic needs and abilities.

It is true that some prospects require more conditioning and education about property values than others do. If your buyer has had very little exposure to the real estate market in your area, he may need to see several homes in order to convince himself the one he wants is worth the price asked. This often happens when people move into a new city with which they are completely unfamiliar. Real estate prices "back home" may seem a lot more reasonable than those offered in the new location. Obviously, when you have such a problem, your counselling session should include considerable education about values, terms, and prices of comparable real estate in your city so as to build a foundation of trust on which an ultimate decision can be based.

The degree of urgency in the prospect's time schedule for moving must also be considered. Those who are anxious to make an immediate transfer will be easier to sell than those who can afford to consume more time in the selection of a suitable property. <u>It is wisest, however, to always attempt to select the right properties the first time and close the sale the day they are shown!</u>

THE ROMANCE OF SELECTING A HOME

Choosing a home in which to live is something like selecting a marriage companion: there must be a certain amount of romance and excitement before consummation of a permanent contract. When picking a mate you can readily accept the idea that there may be hundreds of possible choices, but once the decision is finalized, all others are eliminated. Since your task as a real estate salesmen is to bring properties and people together in contractual unions, you must learn to set the stage for the proposals. It is your assignment to do for others what they find difficult to do for themselves, i.e., to make decisions about real estate ownership.

It is a proven fact that most people do not like to make decisions, and when there are too many options or possibilities, it becomes even more difficult to approve or reject any single offering. This is like seeing a long menu in a restaurant! It is extremely confusing to pick one entree from so many desirable dishes. You will face this same problem every time you show properties to prospective purchasers. There is so much from which to choose they will want to see them all before they make a final choice - <u>and even then they will not be sure!</u> Being afraid of making a mistake, they will often attempt to postpone the decision until later. The more choices they have, the more prominent will be the formidable obstacles of fear and indecision. Only as you are able to understand and cope with these natural decision-resisting barriers will you become a truly masterful and successful real estate salesmen. The first principle to remember in preventing buyer fears is:

DO NOT GIVE THE PROSPECT TOO MANY CHOICES

If you place before your prospect more than he can chew or digest, he may get up from your table without partaking at all. It is always easier for someone to make a decision when the alternatives are few and clear. It is extremely difficult to do so when they are many and complex. I have seen subdivision salesmen plagued with this problem when they were forced to offer too many options, extras, and alternatives for each floor plan shown. Clients, faced with such decisions would invariably say:

KNOW YOUR PROSPECTS AND YOUR PROPERTIES 123

"Let's go home and think it over before we decide which options we want!"

These people seldom come back! Thinking it over is an excuse for permanently postponing the decision. A residential resale salesman faces the same problem in terms of the size of the inventory he represents. It is not uncommon for a real estate company belonging to a multiple listing service in a metropolitan area to have 500, 1000 or more properties to show customers. Nobody, including the most capable real estate salesman, can remember or know 500 properties! It is extremely difficult to recall 100. Do you remember your first few days in this business when you started looking at listings? Didn't you find it difficult when you saw more than three or four in one day to remember any of them well? I know I did! As you become more proficient in your profession, you will find ways to help you remember a larger number of homes. Your prospects are not professional real estate people who are used to seeing many properties every day. That is why you should plan not to show more than three or four homes in any single session. When you violate this principle you often find your confused buyers working the next day with some other real estate office which is possibly smarter than you were about limiting the showings.

KEEP THE EMOTIONAL NEEDS OF THE BUYER IN MIND

Most selling is emotional rather than rational. Look at the clothes you have on at the moment. Why did you buy them? Because they were the longest wearing materials? Because they were made by the best machines? Certainly not! These items of quality may have influenced your choice but your real motive was based on a simple desire to satisfy your emotional needs: you liked them! Maybe the color, feel, cut, style or something else took your fancy, but your decision was based on the emotional satisfaction ownership would provide you personally! This is true because only robots and mechanical brains make decisions solely on the facts presented. The rest of us rely heavily on our "emotional hot spots."

Thus, your customer's desires will be more strongly influenced by his emotions than by the cold, logical truths you can reveal. You must learn to separate the decision-influencing emotions from the non-related facts he may give you. What a prospect tells you he wants and what he may ultimately buy are often entirely different. Why? Because even the customer does not really understand his own motivations well enough to define them for you, nor would he if he could! He tries to rationalize his ideas about the number of bedrooms, bathrooms, style, location and other important factors as he sees them. But when he is exposed to the property which triggers his hidden emotional responses, he unconsciously discards many of the previously conceived requirements and buys on the impulses of his emotional satisfaction. This is hard for real estate salesmen to accept or completely understand. When I first started in this business I could not appreciate why a customer who was looking for a one story, three bedroom home on the Westside would finally select a two story, four bedroom on the Eastside! <u>It took me some time to realize that most buyers do not know exactly what they want even if they tell you they do!</u> I had to learn to read between the lines and piece together the unrelated facts obtained in the counselling session to find the threads of emotional desire from which I could weave the fabric of the ultimate sale. These are the real "hot spots" which spring from our primary goals and aspirations in life. They are usually based on one or more of the following:

1. Love of family
2. Desire for personal security
3. Need for greater recognition
4. Need for more individual expression
5. Desire for privacy and peace of mind.
6. Need for stimulation and change.
7. Desire for comfort and convenience
8. Needs affecting personal health or well being
9. Desire for romance, love and excitement
10. And finally, financial security related to the above.

Thus, regardless of specific requirements handed to you by your prospects, learn to look for the underlying motivations which prompt their reactions to property. For the customer whose expressions indicate need for more recognition, you can sell the best neighborhoods and the ego-satisfying benefits of living in these areas. Those who want privacy and peace of mind should be shown restful retreats from the busy world. By probing the pattern of your client's past experiences and present desires you can often find the common motivating force which will produce the right emotional response for the proposed change. You may find yourself selling the tall pine tree in the back yard and throwing the house in for good measure; or selling the seclusion and beauty of a home while only incidentally treating the quality and design features.

MOST CUSTOMERS WANT MORE COMFORT AND CONVENIENCE

Whether we like it or not, we must recognize that we live in a "comfort-conditioned society." Everyone wants to own things which make life easier, better, more convenient than our previous experience afforded. We continue to be sold the advantages of new gadgets, luxuries and services which are designed to make our lives more pleasant. This same principle applies in the selection of a home. You must learn to weigh your customer's past housing advantages with those you propose to offer him. This is a relative task, since the people who live in a 600 square foot apartment unit with only one bedroom might be thrilled with a 1000 foot home with 2 bedrooms and one bath, while the owner of that property desires a larger unit with two baths and more conveniences.

KNOW YOUR PROSPECTS AND YOUR PROPERTIES

Learning to relate the present experiences of your buyers to their future property requirements will help you make the proper selection. <u>One man's cottage can be another man's castle!</u>

DO NOT BE INFLUENCED BY YOUR OWN PREFERENCES

Invariably the personal likes and dislikes of the real estate salesman are injected into the selling picture. This can be a hindrance to successful selling procedures, since the customer's desires and reactions will generally be different than those of the salesman. Many years ago, while I was a buyer for a California department store chain, I had to learn this lesson the hard way. Often I was tempted to buy the styles and designs I liked, only to learn my preferences were not always reflected by the buying public. Some real estate salesmen try to show their customers how intelligent they are by telling them everything they know about real estate. They even go so far as to tell the customer what they personally like or don't like:

"Now take this home, Mr. Smith. I wouldn't live in a two story if you gave it to me! All that running up and down stairs, etc., etc., etc.,"

<u>This is a prelude to a lost sale! What you want or think about property is not important to the buyer!</u> You are not going to live in every house you show or sell and your personal preferences are not necessarily those of your customer. To be effective, you must learn to evaluate your listings from your customer's point of view by placing yourself in his shoes and seeing the properties through his eyes. Be objective, not subjective!

THERE ARE NO PERFECT HOMES!

The perfect home has not yet been constructed! If you design a home for yourself and have an unlimited budget, you will find ways to improve it the moment you have moved in. This is so for every choice made by a customer. The one finally singled out will be a compromise in some manner from his original specifications - but a good compromise! It is often necessary to point this out to prospects when they fail to find all that they expect in the homes you show them. Some features in one home will be better than those in another, but the customer must decide which items are important and which expendable. If you have good insight to the driving forces of your client's personality, you can easily accent the key benefits which should influence his ultimate choice.

PRE-INSPECT THE HOMES YOU PLAN TO SHOW

The morning following your counselling session with the Carters, you arrive at your office early enough to begin reviewing your inventory for the selection of the best listings which they should see. You are convinced that both of them want a smaller, more convenient home than the one they now own, but it must be located in a choice neighborhood, well landscaped and tastefully decorated. Although they have indicated a desire for 3 bedrooms and a den, you do not believe this is a major factor if the basic home has the necessary amenities to appeal to the Carters' emotional needs. From your total list you earmark four homes which might qualify and you make arrangments to immediately inspect each of them before your showing appointment at 2:00 this afternoon. This permits you to refresh your knowledge of each home while establishing good relationships with the owners of the properties and determining their current attitudes regarding price, terms, and occupancy.

The re-inspection of property, before a showing appointment, is the soundest possible procedure to insure maintaining complete command of the situation when you do arrive with the prospective purchasers. <u>You cannot show property well if you do not know your merchandise!</u> How can you plan a sale if you do not know the present needs of the sellers and the terms they are prepared to accept? By calling on the sellers before showing new prospects you also impress the owners with your professional concern and interest. You set yourself apart from the average real estate salesman who does not bother to re-establish his knowledge of the product or the people who own it. If and when you bring an offer to these owners you will normally be afforded their fullest cooperation because of this extra consideration.

With this in mind, you call each of the owners of the selected properties and ask permission to see their homes this morning in preparation for a possible showing this afternoon. You then drive to the first one owned by Mr. and Mrs. Greybar at 461 Harrison Avenue and begin your inspection process.

"Good morning, Mrs. Greybar. I called you a few moments ago for permission to review your property before showing it to customers of mine this afternoon. If you can spare a few moments, I would appreciate your showing me your home as I am sure you must know it better than anyone else!"

It is always desirable to have the owner conduct these private inspection trips with you. It is not because you need their assistance in viewing or noting the features, but rather because it provides you with a good opportunity to establish personal acquaintaince with the sellers. This is particularly true when you are not the listing salesman of the property selected. The owner has the <u>key to the sale</u> and you want to determine how to use it at the right time with your buyer. Sixty days have passed since this listing on Harrison was submitted to your office and the chances are very good the motivations to sell or not to sell have been altered in the interim. Your questions will probe for the answers to the owners' present attitudes about selling, and the degree of urgency in their decision.

While touring the home with clipboard and notepaper, you ask Mrs. Greybar a series of questions and listen for the clues to your needed answers.

"Have you and Mr. Greybar located another home yet?"

She replies: "My husband and I are moving to Chicago to accept a promotion from his company. We haven't selected a home there, but his firm has arranged temporary facilities when we arrive to permit us to take our time in finding the right property in Chicago. I do wish we could sell this one soon and finalize everything!"

DON'T MISS OUT ON THE "WHY"

This is a vital piece of information which the listing salesman has neglected to cover on the printed listing sheet you received. The reason for selling should always be included in any listing, but often salesmen overlook this point and when they do, you must probe to uncover it.

"That's wonderful, Mrs. Greybar. I imagine you and your husband are thrilled at this opportunity. When do you plan to make the move?"

"Well, that is a little bit of a problem right now. Jack has to be in Chicago by the first of next month and if we haven't sold by then I may have to stay behind until we do sell."

You make a mental note of this important fact because it clearly indicates increasing urgency on the part of the Greybar's to make a sale of some type. While observing that Mrs. Greybar's tastes in furniture and decor are similar to those of Mrs. Carter, you ask another question:

"I note on the listing, Mrs. Greybar, you and your husband want "all cash" for your equity. Some buyers might be interested in a smaller down payment than that permits. Had you ever considered carrying part of your equity in a second note and deed of trust?"

She answers, "We have talked about it and would prefer not to do so, but I think Jack might consider handling part of our equity that way if it leaves us at least $2000 to pay expenses and move east!"

Her reply is another indication the price may be soft since any willingness to carry a note for part of the equity is generally a signal that the owner would take less for "all cash." Even if the Carters are not interested in this home, you now have information which can be helpful in selling it to someone else.

"Have you had any offers on your home yet, Mrs. Greybar?"

"Yes, right after we listed the home with your company some other real estate office brought us a low offer of only $19,000. We turned it down at the time although I'm not so sure we would do so again if it were available."

You have now uncovered your most important clue. This $21,500 listing may have softened to as low as $19,000 since it was originally introduced to the market. Obviously the listing salesman is asleep at the switch, but you know this is not uncommon in our business. Your questioning turns to things which might help you sell the home to the Carters.

128 KNOW YOUR PROSPECTS AND YOUR PROPERTIES

"Tell me about your neighbors, Mrs. Greybar. This looks like a nice neighborhood. Who lives next door and across the street?"

She replies, "Yes, this is a very pleasant neighborhood, and I'm going to miss my many friends here. Mrs. Fleming across the street is a very fine neighbor. Her husband works for the Brownston Electric Company as an executive of some kind. Next door on this side are Mr. and Mrs. Baxton. We play bridge with them every Tuesday night. He works for the Central Bank downtown as the Assistant Manager. The Partons are on the other side. They're a retired couple and very quiet. I see them working in their yard much of the time."

You pick up this line of thought: "I notice you and Mr. Greybar keep your own yards very neat and well trimmed. It is obvious you have spent considerable time in completing your landscaping. Tell me, Mrs. Greybar, are there many children in this neighborhood?"

She replies, "Actually there are very few young children. The Baxtons have two teenage daughters and I think the neighbor on the other side of them has a young son about 10, but other than that we seldom see children around. This is a section of mostly older families."

Your inspection trip about completed, you thank Mrs. Greybar for her kindness and promise to return at approximately 3:00 to 3:30 to show her home to the Carters. You suggest to her that it will be best to permit you to show the home without disturbance since the Carters might not feel free to make their comments in her presence. She says she understands and agrees to go next door after letting you and your customers into the home. As you drive away, you mentally review the facts you have gathered and decide this home is definitely one which should be shown to the Carters as it meets most of their requirements and should excite their basic interests. The garden room and superb landscaping will particularly appeal to Mr. Carter.

In the same manner, you thoroughly check the two other properties on Laurelei and Kingston Road and then swing by your own listing on Rosedale to advise Mrs. Ervin you plan to show her home also this afternoon. This excursion completed, you return to your office to evaluate your listings and establish the best manner in which to present them to the Carters.

PLAN THE SHOWING SEQUENCE FOR MAXIMUM EFFECT

The order of a showing session is often very important in conditioning the prospect's receptiveness to the listing you ultimately hope to sell them. Normally, it is wise to save the best until last, as this is like climbing a staircase to a sale: each property whetting the appetite of the purchaser and stimulating his emotional interest in the final one seen. However, there are those who like to show the right home first and then compare two or three others so as to return to the first one and close the sale. Both systems work, but your plan of action should be known to you in advance.

KNOW YOUR PROSPECTS AND YOUR PROPERTIES

When you are working with inexperienced homebuyers, it is often necessary to strongly emphasize values, prices and comparisons in order to sell the home you know they should own. This can be done by quoting prices of properties recently sold in the neighborhood near the listing you are showing, as well as underscoring the reasons for property values being at their present levels in this area. Another practical technique of conditioning is to make your first showing a property which you know is somewhat more expensive than desired but essentially of the right type. Then when you show a similar home or two for less, you have emphasized the relative values involved. Listing salesmen who encourage over-priced properties often find their listings are used as the conditioning tools for other sales, without benefiting the owners they represent.

Your inspection of these listings has revealed that the Jones's on Laurelei have cooled off about selling, since they have not yet found a new home they like, and unless a full price offer at $20,500 were submitted they will probably not sell. In your opinion, the home is at least $1000 or more over-priced. Your own listing on Rosedale is still a possibility, but it does not have a modern kitchen like the one on Harrison. The listing on Kingston Road is a little further out than you believe the Carters will want to live, but it is a deluxe home, with considerable privacy. Of these four, the listing on Harrison seems to be the best possible choice and you decide to put this one last in your showing sequence so as to properly emphasize its advantages to the Carters. The listing on Laurelie, will come first, followed by Rosedale, Kingston and finally the Harrison Avenue Property you hope to sell.

WHILE INSPECTING PROPERTY ALWAYS LOOK FOR NEW BUSINESS

Every time you inspect a property, whether it's your listing or someone else's, always be alert to new business which can be developed by asking the right questions! Certain questions produce results if asked often enough, and these should be memorized and used as frequently as possible. The owners of property are generally willing to be helpful when you ask for information about the neighborhood, other properties for sale, potential prospects, and similar business leads. I suggest you type the following questions on a 4" x 5" card and place it on the visor of your car where you can review it each time you are about to inspect a home. Ask these questions and you will uncover enough new business to justify their use.

Questions to Ask Owners When Inspecting Property

1. Do any of your neighbors plan to sell?
2. Before you listed your home did you attempt to sell it yourself?
3. If so, did you obtain any interested prospects? (Get names)
4. Has anyone stopped to inquire about your property?
5. Have you bought another home yet?
6. Have you considered additional real estate investments?

KNOW YOUR PROSPECTS AND YOUR PROPERTIES

7. Do you know anyone who plans to transfer?
8. Do you have friends who might be interested in buying or selling?

PREPARE FOR YOUR APPOINTMENT WITH THE CARTERS

It is now noon as you finalize your review of the properties selected to show your new customers. Your tour has refreshed your knowledge about each property involved and helped you uncover clues to the future sales they may unlock. In addition, you have cultivated better relationships with the owners of these homes and provided yourself with one or two new leads for business tomorrow. You now re-confirm your appointment with the Carters to make sure nothing has changed the schedule. After eating lunch and answering a few phone messages, you leave to pick up the Carters at their home. You are mentally alert, well dressed and prepared for your showings. You are confident of yourself because you have reinforced your salesmanship with knowledge of your properties and your owners. You know your prospects and your properties well, and you are ready to set the stage for Act Two of your role as chief negotiator for the Carters and the Greybars!

KNOW YOUR PROSPECTS AND YOUR PROPERTIES

QUESTIONS AND PROJECTS ON CHAPTER SIX

Questions:

1. What are the various advantages of qualifying a prospect in his own home?
2. What things should you try to visually observe and notice when in a prospect's home?
3. What are some of the questions and topics you can usually pursue to get the prospect to talk about himself and help you qualify his interests?
4. What are the three primary rules all good salesmen use to control any qualifying conversation?
5. What are some of the factors you should consider when selecting properties to show potential buyers?
6. Why is it dangerous or unwise to show a prospect too many properties?
7. What are "emotional hot spots" and what part do they play in the selection of residential property?
8. Why is it undesirable for a salesman to be strongly influenced by his own preferences in real estate?
9. What are some of the advantages of pre-inspecting homes before showing them to prospects and what questions should you ask when inspecting for showing purposes?
10. How can you determine financial ability and qualifying incomes of prospects?

Projects:

1. Ask a senior salesman for permission to go with him and listen to his next prospecting interview with a potential purchaser. (If he grants the privilege be sure to respect it by remaining quiet and courteous during the session)
2. Prepare a list of good questions you would use in conducting a qualifying interview in the prospect's home.
3. On your next showing appointment, determine to inspect the properties you plan to show in advance, and ask all the questions recommended in this lesson, noting the effect and response of your sellers.
4. Make a list of the basic subjects nearly all customers are interested in.
5. On your next showings, review the results obtained from proper qualification of neighborhood, showing sequence, and pre-inspection. Review, when you miss a sale, what effect, if any, the showing preparation and sequence might have on the lost transaction.
6. Write down your personal thoughts and observations on the following topics and review your answers with your broker:
   a. Order of showing sequence
   b. Number of properties a prospect should see in a given day
   c. Advantages of having the prospect in your own car

KNOW YOUR PROSPECTS AND YOUR PROPERTIES

    d. The route you select to approach the property you hope to sell
    e. The best methods of determining the seller's current attitudes on price and terms before showing a property
    f. The importance of selling the entire community, neighborhood and facilities related to the property you hope to sell
    g. The value of knowing as much as possible about competitive properties surrounding the listing you are showing as well as past sales activities

7. During the next week, observe your own ability to control conversations with your fellow salesmen, your employer, and your clients following the basic rules set forth on page 119. Practice also on your relatives, friends and acquaintances.
8. Read books which prepare you for dealing with people such as:

Sylvanus M. Duvall, *The Art and Skill of Getting Along with People*, (Englewood Cliffs, N.J.: Prentice - Hall, Inc.).
Dale Carnegie, *How to Win Friends and Influence People*
Vernon Howard, *Your Magic Power to Persuade and Command People*, (Englewood Cliffs, N.J.: Prentice - Hall, Inc.).
(Any others your broker may suggest or have in his library.)

7

SHOWING PROPERTIES TO BUYERS

Have you ever purchased a diamond ring? If so, you may recall how the jeweler presented it to you for viewing. Possibly he carefully placed it on a black velvet pad near a bright light and turned it gently to reflect exciting rays from each glittering facet! He certainly did not take it carelessly out of a box and unceremoniously drop it in your hands! Why? Because he knew the importance of showing his precious jewels to advantage where the romantic benefits of ownership could be dramatically emphasized for his potential buyers!

Presenting homes to prospective purchasers requires the same kind of showmanship any reputable jeweler would give his merchandise. The intrinsic amenities and benefits derived from the ownership of real property should be displayed against a background of emotion-producing actions designed to captivate the interest of the prospect. Possibly you are not one who believes showmanship is important in selling real estate. If so, take my word for it - it's very important! People respond when their imaginations and desires are stimulated. There can be no action until there is interest, and to obtain results you must set the stage for the favorable decision you hope to reach. You have probably heard some salesman say:

"Boy, did that buyer's eyes light up when he saw that home!" This is a simple expression of a basic truth. When people are excited by something, their eyes, expressions, and actions generally reveal their interest.

Selling real estate is essentially a four-part drama:

Act I	......	FINDING AND QUALIFYING THE PROSPECT
Act II	......	SHOWING PROPERTY TO THE PROSPECT
Act III	......	OBTAINING THE BUYER'S OFFER
Act IV	......	CLOSING THE SELLER

As in any well organized play, the stage must be set, the participants prepared and the audience conditioned before the curtain is raised. In this drama your role is that of "Chief Negotiator" for the buyer and seller, bringing them together for their mutual benefit. If you fail to provide the stimulating setting necessary for courtship, your show may "flop" and the critics who pan it will be the other sellers who decide to take their business elsewhere, since your ability to present their individual roles properly will be seriously questioned.

You are now on your way to begin Act II of this current drama which started yesterday with the Carters' inquiry about your listing on Rosedale. Your counselling session is over and because it was completed successfully, you can move to the next scene with confidence that you are in full control. You intend to skillfully execute your role of bringing the leading participants together under pre-arranged conditions, hoping that the property's dramatic appeal will have the right impact on your buyers' motivations. You plan to do all you can as a professional negotiator to help the Carters make a favorable decision. Arriving at their home promptly at 2:00, you find them waiting for you, and a few moments later you are on your way to the first property of your scheduled tour.

DRIVE COURTEOUSLY

Driving your prospects to a showing should not be similar to the experience of a New York first-nighter racing in a cab to be on time for the opening curtain! I have known salesmen whose driving antics would so unnerve a customer, it was impossible for the prospect to relax enough after arriving at the property to even give the offering due consideration. One lady complained by phone to me one day that my salesman had driven so fast and carelessly to a property, she refused to inspect any more homes unless I promised to give her a more courteous salesman with better driving manners! There is no excuse for racing to a showing appointment. This is the time to relax the buyer, set the stage for the showing and explore the mental reactions of your customers. Your tour to the home should be conducted to show the buyer the benefits of the surrounding areas through which you must pass to reach your destination, and to mentally prepare the purchaser so he will be receptive to the values you present.

WHAT TO TALK ABOUT

What should you talk about on the way to your first home? Well, for one thing, try not to talk about the property you intend to show except to condition the buyers for any obvious disadvantages they will see. I have found reverse psychology especially effective during this phase of the showing appointment. When you emphasize the few things about a home which may need attention or repair, you have the buyer's imagination working for you! Imagination is a powerful force! If you tell someone the home he will see needs painting and some reconditioning, he tends to picture a property in complete need of repair. If you say that the shrubs need trimming and the lawn deserves better care, your customer imagines a weed patch surrounded by scraggly shrubs ready to die. On the other hand, if you try to describe the home to them in glowing terms, they will invariably expect more than actually exists. If you state the home is charming and well decorated, your customer's imagination can transform this into an image of an exclusive custom model with the very finest decor. If you say the home is well landscaped, the buyer may envision an oriental garden with luxuriant ferns and waterfalls! No matter what you show him, he will generally have mentally conjured a more beautiful setting than the one which actually greets him. In other words, you can't win when you attempt to describe property in positive terms before showing, and you run the risk of spoiling for the client even the beauty which might otherwise have interested him. For this reason, I suggest that you never discuss the benefits of a property you are planning to sell <u>once you have the customers in your car!</u> Instead, use this time to prepare them for the worst things they may see, knowing they will be surprised to find it better than imagined. The tendency is then for the customer to defend the home once he sees it!

"Why, this is really not such a bad little home!"
"Just a little paint will fix this, easily"
"I thought you said the lawns were dead. Why, with a little care they will be green again in no time!"

When that happens, the customer is selling himself and nothing you will do or say can ever be as effective in closing the sale as when the buyer <u>defends the property</u> with his own statements.

With these points in mind, you begin conditioning the Carters to the first listing you plan to show on 2221 Laurelei:

"This first home I am going to show you, Mr. and Mrs. Carter, is about eleven years old and is not as modern as some, although it is in fair condition. You see, both Mr. and Mrs. Jones work every day and do not have time to maintain it as well as they would otherwise. However, it is in the general neighborhood in which you are interested in living and I believe it is well worth inspecting."

With that you drop the subject and point out the neighborhood features now being passed:

"There is the new Roosevelt High School just constructed last year. It is said to be one of the finest in our valley. Over here to your left, Mrs. Carter, are the famous Rose Gardens which have drawn so much local interest lately. You will note that most of the homes in this district are well maintained and range in value from $20,000 to $40,000. This one on your right just sold through our office to Mr. and Mrs. Woods for $27,950."

By discussing the schools, shopping facilities, parks and values of real estate in the neighborhood, you help to set the stage for the home they will see. Remember, <u>people do not buy homes!</u> They buy neighborhoods, environment, and related facilities. Recent research conducted by the National Association of Home Builders has verified that neighborhood amenities are just as important to a homebuyer as the property itself. Thus, when you have any area with features worth mentioning, be certain to discuss them with your prospects. Plan your route to the property so that these benefits will be seen. Drive by the nicer surrounding homes and whenever your personal knowledge permits, specifically point out the names, prices and facts about the people who have bought or sold in the district. This type of information can be easily accumulated when you concentrate most of your selling activities in limited real estate neighborhoods. Over a period of time you become an expert about the properties and people there.

During your trip to the property, you can also continue to ask probing questions if all the answers you need have not been gathered from your previous counselling appointment. Once in a while, due to circumstances beyond your control, your entire qualifying session may have to be conducted in the car on the way to a property. When this happens, be sure to use this time wisely and ask the many questions necessary to extract the vital statistics and basic motivations of your clients.

BE SURE IT IS THE RIGHT HOME BEFORE BEGINNING THE CLOSE

You have arrived at 2221 Laurelei and, shortly after entering the property with the Carters, it is obvious this one just does not interest them at all. You therefore, quickly finish the inspection and escort them back to the car. Mrs. Carter's lack of interest was evident as this home lacked the charm you knew she would expect. Since this is only the first of your four selected properties, you know there is no real difficulty with your other choices and you decide to proceed to the next one. <u>However, had you missed the reason for the lack of interest you should immediately start probing again - before continuing the showings.</u> If you are on the wrong track, find out why!

"Mr. and Mrs. Carter, permit me to apologize. I thought I knew what you wanted, but I missed something. Tell me, what was it you did not like about this home?" In this way, you at least avoid making the mistake of showing another wrong property and by honestly admitting you do not fully understand the customers' desires they will usually give you the information you need. If the first one is completely off-base and you do not know why - face it now rather than run the risk of losing a customer after showing three more incorrect selections.

At the Ervins' home on Rosedale, there is some interest by the Carters, but not enough to justify any closing efforts. As you return to the car, you hand Mr. and Mrs. Carter each a pad and pencil which you have kept at your dashboard for this purpose.

"Since we will be seeing several other properties, I thought you might like to make a few notes about each home to help you remember them later. I find that many of my customers like to make a few written observations about the highlights of the homes they inspect."

If possible, you note the items they record so as to weigh the degree of interest they have in this particular offering.

From here, you visit the listing on Kingston Road, which the Carters apparently like very well but they are genuinely concerned about the area and the distance to work. Now you return to the Rose Garden District and the listing at 461 Harrison where you are certain the Carters will appreciate the many features that this home contains.

YOU ARRIVE AT 461 HARRISON

As you approach this final listing, you do so from the opposite side of the street, parking where your customers have an unobstructed view of the street and homes surrounding the property. Getting out of the car with the prospects, you frame the home with your hands and say:

"There she is!"

Showing a home to advantage includes accenting its features against the background of adjacent homes, trees, lawns and scenery. Any home is automatically framed by its neighboring properties, and if these are beneficial to it, they should be emphasized. As you walk to the front door, preceding your customers, you observe the sprinklers by touching one with your toe and casting your eyes in the direction of the rest. You pause for a moment to give your prospects an opportunity to see the landscaping, lawns and shrubs. You know that it is not necessary to say anything about what they see as the view speaks for itself.

At the front door, you greet the owner, Mrs. Greybar, and introduce the Carters. As they enter the home, the seller takes your previous cue and excuses herself to visit a neighbor after she has turned off the television set and taken the children to the play area. You begin the tour through the home by leading the way down the hall to the sleeping quarters. Preceding your prospects to bedrooms and bathroom areas is wise because buyers can be embarrassed by opening doors and finding some unexpected situation. I had this happen to me once, and since then I have always led my guests through these private sections of the home.

DO NOT RUSH THROUGH A SHOWING

The process of showing a home should not be a hurried affair. Rather, it should be a relaxed tour with <u>both salesman and prospect viewing the property together</u>. You enjoy the <u>unfolding discovery of features together!</u> This keeps you on the <u>buyer's side</u> and he treats you as one of the family.

This is a very important rule in showing homes. You want the prospect to concentrate on the home he is seeing and not worry about you. You want him to think of you as being along side of him, helping him in his decisions about the property. As you take each turn of a doorknob or walk through a room, you and the customer <u>jointly discover the features</u> of this home. Every experience is shared and appreciated. You try to do nothing which might disturb the magic spell that is being woven. <u>Disinterested actions adversely affect your ability to close the sale!</u>

Reaching a bedroom, you first inspect the room to be sure all is in order, and then you invite the Carters inside, standing as far to one side as possible. A room always looks much smaller when you are standing in the middle of it obstructing the view than it does when you are off to one side blending in with the four walls. Try to stay away from creating a break in the visual impact of a room and, in really small ones, stand completely outside while your prospects are viewing it.

NEVER DEFEND THE PROPERTY

A used or resale home is just that: a used home! Everybody knows it, so do not apologize for it nor defend it! If you apologize, the customer will look for more things that are wrong. If you defend it against the customer's objections and comments, you will drive a wedge between yourself and the prospect. Nothing can be gained from argumentive defense of a home except a lost sale. Human nature being what it is, you should realize that it is more important at this stage to stay on the buyer's side of any issue than to defend the property against his views. If he offers objections, accept them in silence or agree with him. Most objections raised by a prospect are insincere. They may be said:

1. To break the silence.
2. To prevent an on-coming decision to purchase.
3. To obtain the salesman's reaction.

If they are sincere, you cannot overcome them by talking the client out of them at this point. If they are not, you can ignore them. The big danger in showing homes is the possibility of alienating the customer because of your over-anxious desire to sell the property to them. It's like trying to win an argument - nobody really does without losing a friend or a sale. You should be the buyer's "confidant" during this phase of a showing sequence and do all you can to build a relationship of trust in which your ultimate role can be achieved. Should the customer say:

"These closets are certainly small!"
Agree with him:
"Yes, they are a little small."

If then you feel compelled to qualify your statement by adding something, make sure it is a positive point and not a negative one.

"Yes, they are a little small, but did you notice this extra storage room under the window seats!"

Always agree with your prospect, because that keeps you on his side giving you opportunity to direct his attention to the positive features you want him to see and appreciate. Doing this, he may soon stop making objections, especially if he thinks you are not trying to force him to buy this particular property.

LISTEN

"Silence is golden!" That statement was never truer than when showing a home to a buyer. This is the time to be listening to the comments and watching the reactions of the customer. A sales manager once said to me: "This is the time when you keep your big ears open and your big mouth shut!" The little tape recorder in your brain should be storing the prospect's favorable comments for playback in the closing session! What do your clients like about the home? What do they dislike? Which objections must later be considered and which are meaningless? Are the customers beginning to imagine themselves in the home and can you detect signs of increasing interest? When you hear phrases like:

"John, I wonder if our kingsize bed would fit in this room?"

"Are those windows too big for the drapes that are in our living room?"

"Which room would we assign to the children?"

You know your buyers are selling themselves and you have your first "buying signals."

DEMONSTRATE BENEFITS

Personal demonstration of some features is helpful, providing it is kept in good taste. For example, you can use your finger to move wardrobe closet doors and note:

"Mrs. Carter, did you observe how easily these doors slide on their tracks?"

Or moving over to the light controls:

"Mr. Carter, try these silent light switches. They add a touch of luxury to the home."

Whatever you say, limit it to a few choice words or actions and spend the majority of your time concentrating on your clients' reactions and helping them set the mood for the favorable decision you want.

There is some value in giving your prospects a pleasant order or two.

When you say:

"Try this door, Mr. Carter" or

"Notice this view" or

"Open this closet, Mrs. Carter,"

you are beginning to subconsciously take control of your prospect's mind, developing an attitude of dependence upon your leadership. This should be done discreetly as it can be offensive if overdone or used on the wrong people. Salesmen who have developed a sensitivity to people often learn to use this technique to put themselves in full command of the buyers' attitudes and actions by the time the closing phase has arrived.

TEN GOOD RULES TO REMEMBER

Here are ten good rules to remember when showing property. Follow them and your effectiveness will automatically improve:

1. <u>REMEMBER</u> you are not going to show them the home. You are going to look at it together.
2. <u>LISTEN</u> for every clue dropped by your prospects which indicates interest or objections.
3. <u>INCLUDE</u> your clients in your comments by using such togetherness words as "we" and "ours." This puts you in the position of including yourself in the reactions experienced by your customers.
4. <u>PAUSE</u> whenever you reach a room you want the prospect to study. Use your eyes and gestures to draw their attention to special features.
5. <u>WATCH</u> the eyes and facial expressions of your customers. They will tell you much about their mental reactions.
6. <u>BECOME</u> the prospect's friend. Stay on his side and react as he reacts. This will reduce his fears and keep you in control.
7. <u>LET</u> your client absorb the details and features without distracting conversation. <u>Do not talk more than absolutely necessary.</u>
8. <u>LEAD</u> the customer's thinking by asking a few choice questions designed to stimulate the client's desire to own this property, and to obtain "yes" responses.
9. <u>DRAMATIZE</u> with <u>quiet</u> showmanship, every feature. As you open a door to a room, do so with almost an air of expectancy and reverence. Remember the jeweler and his diamond.
10. <u>IMAGINE</u> the family living here. See the home through your prospect's eyes and help him to develop desire for the property.

THE VALUE OF SHOWMANSHIP

The process of viewing a home with a customer should be one which is held in an atmosphere conducive to buying decision. For maximum effect, no distractions should be permitted. This includes children, television, hi-fi's, and talkative owners. It also means opening doors, demonstrating features and entering rooms as though it were the prelude to an exciting new adventure. After all, buying a home is a pleasant experience. Don't remove the fun from this singularly important shopping spree! People only buy and sell homes four to six times in their lives. Certainly these few occasions should be memorable events surrounded with projections of anticipated enjoyments.

DEVELOP EMPATHY

The dictionary defines empathy as:
"The process of entering fully through imagination into another's feelings or motives."

Empathy means putting yourself in the other person's shoes to see and feel what he sees and feels. If you can do this while showing property, you will be able to anticipate and appreciate your customer's reactions. You can achieve this effect by asking questions which help the customer to picture with you the benefits of living in the home. If, for example, you know the prospect's furnishings will blend well with the decor of a particular room, you might say:

"Mrs. Carter, do you think your French Provincial furniture will bring out the rich colors in this room?"

If you are right, she will probably visualize with you the furniture placement and its appearance in that area of the home. Once you have her picturing herself in the home you are on your way to a sale! You can plant the ideas of ownership in the minds of your customers by making selective comments, asking the right questions, and reacting with the buyers' responses.

THE DIFFERENCE BETWEEN NEW AND USED HOMES

A brief word should be offered here regarding the differences involved when new and resale homes are shown. New homes are something like new cars. They are represented by their manufacturers to have certain qualities, warranties and guarantees of performance. Pre-owned homes carry no such warranties, as they have obviously experienced the wear and tear of other occupants and been molded to fit the personalities of the previous families. In new homes, the builder's reputation, service agreements, and performance are important to the prospective buyer. Therefore, a new home salesman can and should speak with pride about each feature of the home because he represents the builder, knows the quality, and is authorized to make certain statements about the service which goes with purchase of the product. When selling resale properties, you seldom enjoy a similar position. You must sell what exists and cannot make claims about the property which will not be supported by the visible evidence. Buyers of used homes do not usually expect the service that new home purchasers demand, and they may distrust a salesman who makes unwarranted comments about the homes. <u>New home salesman can defend a new home while a resale salesman should never do so!</u>

PLAN YOUR TOUR THROUGH HOME TO ACCENT HOTSPOTS

Remember those emotional "hotspots" we talked about in the previous lesson? Well, now is the time to make them pay off. If, in your counselling, you have been able to uncover motivational interests which can be excited by the specific features of this home, you will want to accent those points that will bring the desired response. Plan your showing so as to spend time in these places and help your buyers visualize the related benefits.

Pausing at the den you say:

"Now here, Mr. Carter, is the real living room for the man of the house. A place for your favorite books, hi-fi and relaxing chair!" Then you see that he gets inside the room, sits down and contemplates from the big chair the future hours of quiet enjoyment within its four walls.

As you come to the kitchen where Mrs. Carter's eyes reflect interest you say:

"My, this room reminds me of grandma's kitchen - so cheerful and cozy! I can just taste one of those delicious apple pies she made!"

"Corny" you say? Maybe it is, but it works! Word pictures can be painted in a few brief moments which help to crystallize the thoughts of the prospect and increase the desire to experience the living pleasures contained in the home.

As you enter the patio area where Mr. Carter is obviously entranced you say:

"Mr. Carter, can you picture yourself under that magnificent oak tree on a warm summer day with a cool glass of lemonade in your hand? This would certainly be a pleasant place to relax, don't you think?"

As reviewed in the next chapter, such questions are "trial balloons" used to help obtain "yes" responses and measure the prospect's buying temperature. As you become increasingly aware of the rising interest shown by your customers in this property on Harrison Avenue you begin to steer them towards the decision to buy. Mrs. Carter's enthusiasm for the home is evident and you believe Mr. Carter is also warming to the idea. With that knowledge, you move into the final phase of your showing and prepare for Act III: "Obtaining the offer from the buyer."

SHOWING PROPERTIES TO BUYERS

QUESTIONS AND PROJECTS ON CHAPTER SEVEN

Questions:

1. Why is showmanship important in showing real estate to potential buyers?
2. What rules of good driving should you observe when driving prospects to property?
3. What should you talk about on the way to the property? What should you avoid discussing? Why?
4. How should the showing be conducted with the prospect and how can you best achieve your objectives?
5. When showing a property, what courtesies and good selling procedures should you follow regarding:
    a. Letting your prospect out of the car?
    b. Approaching the front door?
    c. Meeting the owner of the property with your prospects?
    d. Entering the property?
    e. Showing the sleeping quarters?
    f. Entering bathroom and bedroom areas?
    g. Showing a small room?
    h. Overcoming T.V., hi-fi, and noise problems?
6. Why is it unwise to defend a property to a prospect?
7. Why is listening one of the real keys to a successful showing?
8. How can you unobtrusively demonstrate the benefits of property by asking the right questions?
9. What is empathy? How can you use it to help you sell property to prospects?
10. Why is it important to be sure you have interest from a prospect before you begin to build a buying temperature or try to close?

Projects:

1. On your next showing, practice the various techniques presented in this chapter and note the response received from your prospects.
2. Review your thoughts and observations on the following points:
    a. Selling real estate is like a four-part drama.
    b. Your role is really that of negotiator.
    c. People are more important than property.
    d. Furnishings and decor can have a major effect on buyer's interest.
    e. Listening is important.
    f. Never defend a property to a buyer.
3. List the things you might do or say if you found you were showing the wrong kind of property to your buyer and you did not yet know their real desires.
4. Inspect three more properties each day this week and imagine you are going to bring a prospect through each of them. Ask yourself:

    a. How can I best show this home to advantage?
    b. Where is the focal point of interest for this property?
    c. What are the seller's motivations and how might they influence my showing?
    d. How can each of them be sold?

5. Visit your Chamber of Commerce and obtain the following information to have on hand when touring properties with buyers:
    a. Maps of the city.
    b. Pamphlets showing points of interest around city, including recreational areas, churches, and so forth.
    c. Statistical data about area including bank debits, building activity, tax rates, and employment facts. If your city has a list of industries and schedule of employment, obtain these also.
    d. Historical and factual data about your community that might interest a newcomer to the area. Most Chamber of Commerce groups have abundant material on such subjects.

6. Visit school district offices and obtain maps (or sketch your own map) of school boundaries for various districts and schools involved. Know the names of each school, the names of principals, and the things for which they are noted. Put this information into your personal working materials for reference when showing property.

7. Ascertain the tax rate for the basic areas you will work and what services are offered by the city and county involved which the tax rate covers.

8. Visit each of the recreational facilities in your city and know what they offer, how they can be used by your prospects, and the costs involved, if any.

9. Study the basic real estate districts served by your office, and know the general values and benefits each offers its owners. Determine what general class or type of customer will desire the various sections your office serves.

10. Study the employment centers which are major factors in your city, and determine from personnel officers or your broker what important points each industry group will probably consider when locating a home in your city.

8

OBTAINING THE OFFER

Instinctively you sense the Carters' growing interest in this Harrison Avenue listing, as evidenced by their comments and actions. The occasional nod of appreciation or passing observation between Mr. and Mrs. Carter supports your conclusion, and you decide it is time to kindle these sparks into a raging fire! You are alert to these signals, recognizing them as signposts along the road to a sale and your cue to begin steering the buyers toward the ultimate decision to purchase, which lies directly ahead. At this moment you know the Carters are going to buy this home! You also know it is your job to help them over the mental hurdles of fear and indecision which may arise before the sale is completed.

Until now, you have been careful to observe their reactions and wait for indications of their interest before trying to fan the emotional flames into a consuming desire to own this home. You did not want to risk insulting your customers' intelligence and alienate their friendship by trying to sell them something they did not want. The initial phases of your qualifying and showing activities with the Carters have been concentrated on building their trust in you and in setting the stage for your major role in this drama. Because you have carefully established the foundation to your customer relationship, you are now able to lead the Carters to the conclusion you clearly envision.

BUILDING THE BUYING TEMPERATURE

When there exists any basic interest in the merchandise offered, a salesman needs only to know how to intensify that desire until a positive action level is achieved. Some customers have "high sales resistance" while others are relatively easy to sell, but all prospects can be sold when their buying temperatures reach the individual levels necessary to overcome all the mental obstacles they can create. Once the ownership desire has been sufficiently kindled to attain or surpass this point where resistance crumbles, a salesman can close the transaction with relative

OBTAINING THE OFFER

ease, providing he knows how to close and is willing to assert his role in this decision-making process.

As most books on selling will emphasize, there are four essential steps to each of the selling phases. These are:

1. Attention
2. Interest
3. Desire
4. Action

Together, and in that order, they are the staircase to a sale:

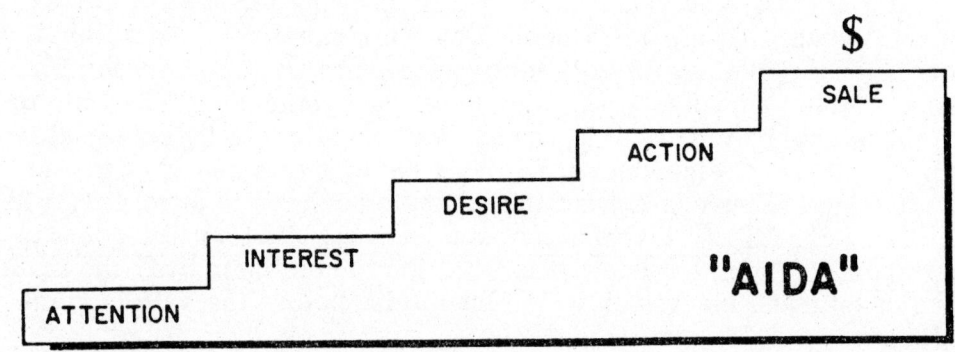

This "AIDA" formula works well in every portion of your four-act selling process, i.e., qualifying, showing, getting the offer, and closing the seller. During each of these stages, you must first gain the prospect's attention before you can arouse his interest, converting that interest into desire which leads to action and the ultimate sale. How can you constantly hold the customer's attention and build his interest into desire? The answer is: CONTROL THE CLIMATE OF THE CONVERSATION AND THE BUYER'S THOUGHTS WITH THESE FOUR RULES:

1. TO GET HIS ATTENTION: CALL HIM BY NAME
2. TO AROUSE HIS INTEREST: SHOW AND EXPLAIN
3. TO BUILD HIS DESIRE: BE ENTHUSIASTIC AND CONFIDENT
4. TO OBTAIN HIS ACTION: ASK QUESTIONS WITH A "YES" RESPONSE

A master salesman learns to guide his customer's mental reactions through each of these four steps and to maintain an attitude conducive to the favorable decision. As the prospect's interest increases, your enthusiasm should also increase. Your emotional processes should parallel or gently precede those of your client and provide an environment in which only positive actions can result. You set the stage and control the scenes so each line contributes to the total effect you are attempting to achieve. Your own attitudes and actions play a major role in helping your buyer to make the right decision.

OBTAINING THE OFFER

MASTER YOUR FEARS FIRST

Successful salesmen are good closers. They know how to control their buyers and can firmly direct them to desired objectives. They are people who <u>inspire confidence</u>. WHY? <u>Because they have learned to control their own fears and indecisions!</u> How can you ever help a prospect to overcome his fears when your own still dominate the scene? "If the blind lead the blind, they both fall in the ditch."

It is absolutely amazing to me how many salesmen will not take command of the closing situation simply because they are afraid! Afraid of what? That the buyer will say "no" or "yes?" I'm never really quite sure, although I am inclined to believe they are afraid of themselves! AFRAID TO FAIL! Some salesmen interpret a "no" answer as a personal failure rather than a professional challenge to continue selling. For this reason, many men prefer to prolong the agony of endless property showings rather than face the ordeal of the closing session.

There is only one way to become a top producer in the real estate business. You must have the <u>courage</u> to take command of your buyers' thought processes and lead them to the right decisions. If you lack the will to assume this responsibility you will fail yourself and your buyers! Customers frequently need a salesman's courage to inject confidence into their own decisions. Without that added strength, they may hesitate and miss the very opportunities they want and should have. How many sales have been lost because salesmen would not <u>help</u> their buyers take the necessary steps to real estate ownership? How many potential buyers have said:

"I want to think it over...."

and later found the properties they wanted sold to others? If you would serve your customers well, demonstrate the courage of your convictions and infuse your prospects' thoughts with the strength your confidence produces.

ASSUME THE SALE

I have never met a really successful salesman in any business who did not radiate an enthusiastic and positive attitude about his profession. People who believe they will succeed, usually do. Those who think they may fail, generally find their projections true. As Earl Nightingale emphatically states in his famous recording, "The Strangest Secret:"[1]

---

[1] This recording should be heard by every salesman. It can be purchased from Earl Nightingale, 469 E. Ohio Street, Chicago 11, Illinois.

OBTAINING THE OFFER

"We become what we think about."
Yes, you become exactly what you believe you will become, and you are the only one who determines the outcome! Enthusiasm is a contagious emotion which influences everyone around you and to really succeed in selling you should be enthusiastic and positive in all your attitudes and actions. If you would control your prospects' attitudes you must first learn to control your own. THINK SUCCESS! THINK POSITIVELY! THINK ENTHUSIASTICALLY! Your positive mental attitude will appeal to your customer and help him sell himself on the merits of your proposition. When you "assume the sale" you act and talk as though purchasing this home is a foregone conclusion. You know they are going to buy this property from you today! That confidence unconsciously infects your buyers' thoughts and, as a result, they develop increasing enthusiasm for your proposal.

As the sale progresses, you inject more warmth into your presentation and pleasant modulation into your voice designed to emphasize the positive benefits ownership of this property will bestow on your customers. Your enthusiasm need not be boisterous and overbearing. It is often more effective when evidenced as quiet confidence and reassuring conviction shown both in voice and manner. (This subject will be discussed in greater detail in Chapter 12.)

MAKE IT PAINLESS FOR YOUR CUSTOMER

Since most buyers do not like to make decisions and tend to resist situations which upset their mental security, you should try to reduce the painful aspects of the sale by making it easy for the customer to do business with you. You help him reach the big "yes" decision without having to say "yes" or think too hard about the pros and cons of your suggestions. You eliminate fears before they are expressed and overcome objections before they are major hurdles. The sale should be the automatic result of a smooth, pleasant series of minor agreements and events which you construct into an assumed closing. The conversation is kept on a plane of confidence, leading the customer from point to point without placing undue strain on his thinking processes. To retain this feeling, you never argue or disagree with your prospect! Instead, you always agree and turn each objection into an advantage by building value and stressing benefits.

OBTAIN "YES" RESPONSES

When a buyer has said "yes" many times within a short period, it is almost impossible for him to think "no!" The mind can be conditioned to a favorable decision by obtaining agreements on many minor points prior to the major question. Every nod, silent acceptance, or "yes" answer brings you one step closer to a signed purchase agreement. After many favorable responses, the buyer is usually helpless to reverse the trend when he is presented with that concluding "yes." When the Carters

OBTAINING THE OFFER

agree that the home has a cheerful kitchen, a superb view, an outstanding yard, and so on, they are unconsciously selling themselves on the merits of owning this property. You help them create a pattern of positive thinking in which to frame the picture of possession. Your questions are actually positive statements with a question mark injected to confirm the buyer's attitude:

"Mr. Carter, this garden shop would also make an ideal photography room, don't you think?"

"This is certainly a cheerful kitchen, isn't it, Mrs. Carter?"

"Mr. Carter, did you notice the exceptional view of the hills from our living room windows?"

These and similar questions give you an opportunity to mold the buyer's thoughts while serving as "trial balloons" to measure the level of the customer's buying temperature. After each one is released, you listen to their comments and observe their actions to determine how near you are to the closing.

USE "TIE-DOWNS!" You can always recognize a professional salesman, no matter what he is selling. He has developed a particular mannerism of speech which evidences his automatic closing techniques. If you listen to him carefully, you will observe that he always "ties his listener down" after making a positive statement. What is a "tie-down?" It is any question which forces the other person's agreement to what you are saying! Such phrases as the following are used to obtain mental agreement from the prospect:

Won't they?	Can't you?
Don't you agree?	Doesn't it?
Isn't that right?	Wouldn't it?
Don't you?	Don't you think?
Isn't it?	Wouldn't you?
Aren't you?	Aren't they?

That is the way to control a prospect, isn't it? You can force him to nod his head in agreement, can't you? And the result is a series of "yes" responses which lead to an easy closing, don't they? To develop an effective closing approach use this simple technique whenever you are engaged in any conversation which affords you an opportunity to practice "tying your listeners down!" Soon you will be doing it automatically, and increasing your power over others whom you want to influence.

CLOSING BY DEFENSIVE PERSUASION

Many years ago salesmen were taught to "pitch" their products with such thoroughness and finesse that customers would supposedly be "overwhelmed" with the advantages of ownership. Today, this concept of selling has been discarded by professional salesmen and replaced with a new technique known as defensive persuasion. It has literally revolutionized the thinking of many sales experts and today is taught to salesmen as the most effective way to close sales.

What is defensive persuasion? <u>It is the art of turning any question which is asked by the prospect into a closing tool.</u> If the customer says:

"Do the rugs and drapes go with the home?" instead of replying, "Yes, they do." you ask:

"Do you want the rugs and drapes to go with the home?" <u>If the customer says "yes," he has bought, hasn't he?</u> If he asks:

"Can I have possession in 30 days?" instead of replying with a positive statement, you ask:

"Do you want possession in 30 days?" <u>If he says "yes," he has purchased the home!</u> This easy rule of tossing it back to the customer with a question can reduce the problems of closing to a minimum and save hundreds of sales every day! Try it! It works!

OVERCOMING CLOSING OBJECTIONS

"To buy or not to buy, that is the question!"

As your prospects approach the impending conclusion to their house buying problems, they often unconsciously begin building resistance barriers to slow their own reactions. Genuine fear of making the wrong decision, plus normal fears resulting from any contemplated change, often dominate a buyer's thoughts as he is made increasingly aware of the oncoming answer.

At this point the prospect may introduce objections simply to give himself time to think and prevent an immediate decision. That is why many objections are insincere or defensive in nature. You must learn to handle these intelligently and weigh the importance of a given comment in relationship to the buyer's real attitudes. Those which are obviously insincere can either be ignored or treated lightly. Primary objections may require an answer, but one which is first qualified by your agreement:

"That is true, Mrs. Carter, but have you thought about this possibility?..."

"I can appreciate your point, Mr. Carter, but let me ask you a question: Wouldn't this area over here serve your purpose equally well?..." Again, use the basic rule:

1. ALWAYS AGREE
2. CALL THEM BY NAME
3. ASK ANOTHER QUESTION TO LEAD THEIR THINKING

Some objections will be genuine and these can be faced objectively. Remember, no home is perfect and you must help the buyer balance the advantages against the disadvantages and prove to him the scale is tipped in favor of the positive aspects. By emphasizing the features you know they like, you can overshadow the few things which may not meet their complete satisfaction.

THE FALLACY OF THE MAGIC MOMENT

Many sales books have been written about the art of closing and some of them leave the reader with the conclusion there is only one psychological moment when a sale should be closed. In my opinion, this belief is not founded on proven facts. It is true that good timing does help any salesman become a better closer, but closing a sale is not a single act in a transaction; rather, it is a series of steps which really begins when you greet your prospect for the first time. Thereafter, each activity is designed to increase the interest and arouse the desire, resulting in action. Once the buyer's desire for ownership has been raised sufficiently, there may be many opportunities to close - until he cools off again. Once cooled down, the buying temperature can usually be reheated with additional effort, but the risk of losing his interest also increases.

The first objective is to create a genuine and intense desire for ownership upon which you can use your talents to close the sale. Most sales are made because the salesman <u>assumes</u> from the beginning the buyer is going to buy, and they are eventually closed on "implied consent." The prospect has been in general agreement all along, nodding occasional assent as the salesman uses his talents to demonstrate and portray the benefits of owning a particular piece of property. The salesman is closing with everything he says and does, from the time he opens the front door until he has a signed purchase contract in hand.

There are, of course, many techniques you can use to aid your closing approach, and we will discuss several in this chapter. The important thing to remember is that closing is a sequence of agreements, explanations, and interest-arousing experiences during which you should be prepared to obtain the signatures of the customers whenever the opportunity presents itself.

WHERE TO CLOSE THE SALE

When the buyer is ready to buy, you should begin writing the offer, but this is not always possible. If the sellers of the home are present, you will have difficulty discussing terms and usually you must return to your car, office or some other location to complete the private negotiations. However, it is wise to request the freedom of the premises before your showing begins, so you can close on site if the buyer's interest matures sufficiently while you are there. If the seller hovers close by, do not try to obtain the offer because you will not be able to develop a free-flowing conversation with the prospects. Buyers are hesitant to discuss offers or review their personal financial requirements in the presence of the owners. When you must close in some other location, try to build the customer's interest and desire to a peak so that even if it decreases during the interval while reaching your car or office, you can maintain enough of the buying fever to assure a closing opportunity. If a choice must be made between returning to the prospect's own home or your office, always select your office as the best alternative. There you can remain in complete control while preparing the offer, and you have the psychological advantage over the customer. I have closed many sales in my automobile rather than risk losing the customer's interest during the trip to the office, and my best advice to you is to develop your own sense of timing on this matter as related to each customer and situation you handle.

MOMENTS WHEN SILENCE IS GOLDEN

To be a really successful closer you must know when to stop talking and start writing. If you have your mouth open and your ears shut, you may completely miss the signals which indicate the customer is sold and wants to buy. More sales are lost because salesmen refuse to give the customers a chance to sell themselves, than almost any other single reason. Do you want to make more sales? Then practice the art of listening and use your knowledge just enough to lead the customer's thinking, not enough to drown it. The truth is, most customers BUY, they are not SOLD. They help to convince themselves, with the leadership of a salesman, that they really want whatever it is they are being presented. If you do not give them the opportunity to "sell" themselves and express their opinions, you will close the prospect's mind and lose the sale. This is one of the most important things you can learn about selling! Here are eleven times when silence is truly golden and produces rich rewards to the salesmen smart enough to practice them:

1. When the client starts to agree with the sales talk, give him the floor - just listen. He will tell you himself what he likes about the property and really begin to reinforce his decision.

2. When the prospect goes the salesman one better in boosting the property, just nod in agreement, don't chatter; let him go on with his emphasis or let him pause and think about it.

3. When he says it will do the job or fill his needs, he is already sold - don't say another word, just close the transaction with your pen and pad.

4. When he says his family likes it, relax and let him talk about his family; this is the closest motivating force he has. Family love is behind most motivating purchasing in connection with homes. Don't tell him how much he will like it too - let him tell you.

5. When the customer says he's for it, just sit back and light up a smoke - don't keep selling. Let him sell himself.

6. When he starts to nod approval, be content to answer questions; don't go off on tangents and introduce strange subjects. Do not let the client nor yourself wander off into areas that will merely confuse - keep the thing on channel.

7. When he tries to get a word in edgewise, let him - don't be a conversation hog. One of the basic rules in selling is to listen to your client and let him express his inner feelings so he can make the decisions he needs to make.

8. When he asks a question, answer it but don't go on answering a lot of other questions you think he has in mind; introducing these subjects may, in actuality, destroy your closing climate. With the conclusion to your reply, ask another question designed to lead his thinking along the pathway to a sale.

9. When he and his wife start to discuss positive aspects of the prospective purchase, don't interrupt. Let them work it out between themselves. If the strong one is sold, leave them alone and that one will sell the other. Frequently they can sell each other.

10. Talk at the right time, just enough to lead the thinking. That time is when the client is receptive to the conversation about the property.

11. In other words, lead the thinking by statements which will let the client begin to sell himself. Do not continue to talk when you should be listening. The right questions and a few brief statements at key points can do a great deal towards helping the customer sell himself. When people are talking they are generally happy - <u>let them enjoy the purchase of the home and the conviction that this is the right decision.</u>

If you would learn to be a good closer, study when to speak and when to listen, becoming sensitive to the human relations techniques of making other people happy while guiding their thinking without their realizing you are doing so. The entire selling process, from beginning to end, is a matter of leading the client's thinking and permitting him to speak his mind so you can guide the conversation further along the paths you have chosen. <u>Remember, it is almost impossible to sell the prospect who refuses to speak, while it is relatively easy to sell the one who is willing to express himself.</u>

BACK TO THE CARTERS

Mr. and Mrs. Carter have completed their inspection of 461 Harrison, and nearly all of your "trial balloons" have received favorable responses. You know they are going to buy this property and you begin pressing for the offer, since you have the freedom of the home for the closing session.

You have already brought out the deposit receipt and laid it on the coffee table in front of you. You were prepared for this moment by having several contracts in a plastic folder in your coat along with blank checks, notes, and other necessary items. You know it is never wise to leave these things where you must return for them before completing the sale. Thus, you begin your major role in this drama:

"The owners of this home, Mr. and Mrs. Greybar, are planning to move to Chicago within two weeks as a result of an employment transfer and they must complete a sale within that time. Since you have a home to sell first, we could achieve the same result by trading yours for this one with our company's trade-in plan. I spoke to the Greybars about this earlier and they would be willing to accept such an arrangement with a 90-day delayed closing, if they had the assurance of a closing by that time."

Mr. Carter replies: "I'm not sure we are ready to make a move yet. After all, we are not certain how much your company will give us for our home!"

To allay his fears you continue: "Mr. Carter, that is the nice thing about our program. You are under no obligation whatsoever if we do not offer you an amount which is satisfactory to you and Mrs. Carter. In the meantime, at no cost to you, we can reserve this home for a period of three days while we are completing our arrangements with you. If, at the end of that time, we have not come to a mutual agreement on price and terms for your present home, our contracts will be cancelled without obligation to either party. However, our trade-in department is exceedingly fair, and I believe they can negotiate with you a price that will meet your approval."

NOW BEGIN WRITING PORTIONS OF YOUR PURCHASE AGREEMENT

At this point you begin writing portions of your purchase agreement.

"What is your full legal name, Mr. Carter?"

Mr. Carter unconsciously replies: "Edward Joseph Carter . . . but hold on a minute! We haven't agreed on a price yet! You said they were asking $21,500! That's a lot of money for this place. After all, Mary will want to redecorate the living room, and the home needs to be insulated. I think that's too much for the property and we would rather think it over tonight and give you an answer tomorrow."

You recognize this as a stall which Mr. Carter is injecting to slow down his increasing desire to buy this place and you are determined not to let it prevent the sale. On the other hand, you will never disagree so you reply:

"I appreciate that fact, Mr. Carter. A move of this type should be discussed and reviewed carefully, and it is a good idea to think it over." You have now temporarily allayed his fears about an impending closing and he begins to relax again while you consciously move forward to reach the decision you know is imminent.

"Before you leave here, let's put all the facts down on paper so you will have something to review later and on which you can base your decision." You now begin writing again.

ALWAYS PUT IT IN WRITING

A sale cannot be consummated until it has been reduced to writing! Further, a buyer cannot really make up his mind until he has specifics on which to base his choice. Writing a contract as part of the closing technique is important to both you and the buyer; it gives you a closing tool and the buyer a definite set of facts on which to make his decision. I have heard salesmen interpret the writing of contracts as "high pressure." Nothing could be further from the truth. High pressure results from asking a buyer to make up his mind when he has nothing on which to make a decision and nothing to sign when he has reached his decision. Reducing the facts to paper and reviewing the terms under which an offer can be completed is just as essential for the buyer as it is for the salesman. Remember that point and never shy away from a written contract. The worst that can happen is you will go through these exercises without making a sale, and that is part of your job. On the other hand, the odds are in your favor if there is any possibility at all that a sale will be finalized. Also, the buyer is in a better position to make a decision when faced with that opportunity in writing.

USE CLOSING QUESTIONS

"The order-blank close," as it is known in sales training circles, is the easiest and most effective of all closing techniques. It is easier because it provides a method of pinpointing and confirming the decision to purchase through a simple tool: the purchase agreement itself. Never be afraid to introduce the contract at an early point in your closing phase. In fact, carrying it in your hand ready for use is an accepted procedure by master salesmen.

When you want to close the sale, you ask a closing question. What is a closing question? It is any question, the answer to which can be entered on the purchase agreement. Such questions as the following are closing questions:

"What is your full name, Mr. Carter?" (That is a closing question when used this way.)
"Would you prefer possession in 30 or 60 days, Mr. Carter?"
"Shall I include the rugs and drapes in this agreement?"
"Shall we allow about 90 days to close the escrow, Mr. Carter?"

All of these questions confirm the sale, don't they? As you insert the answers in the deposit receipt or purchase agreement, you are closing the sale on the ASSUMPTIVE TECHNIQUE and using the written contract as the closing tool. The key to this approach is in asking closing questions and promptly writing them on the order blank. Professional salesmen know the power of this closing procedure.

WHAT DO THEY WANT TO THINK OVER?

When the Carters say they want to think it over, it is your obligation to ask them "what they want to think over." If they have genuine objections or questions, you should answer them. If this is a stall to prevent a purchase which they really want, but are afraid to face, your courage to force the issue is needed to help them over the hurdles of fear and indecision.

"Mr. Carter, are there any questions about the property which you would like to have answered before we leave here this afternoon?"

"Well, it is a nice home and seems to have many of the advantages we wanted, but it is such a big step to take that I would hesitate making a quick decision on the matter. We have lived on 21st Street for 17 years and, after that period of time, you grow accustomed to your surroundings, if you know what I mean!"

You quickly realize that Mr. Carter is using you as a sounding board to help crystallize his own thoughts and you are anxious to help him do so.

"I realize that fact, Mr. Carter, and I would not want you to do anything which was not in your best interests. The thing that impresses me about this home is that it matches your basic requirements so very well, don't you agree?"

FEED BACK THE POSITIVE COMMENTS

As you were touring the home you listened carefully for all the things which appealed to the Carters and you stored these away for use at this particular moment. By carefully playing these back you can help to reconstruct the very things the Carters liked about the residence, which should help to reinforce their desire to purchase it.

"You will recall, Mr. and Mrs. Carter, some of the specifications you gave me the other night when we reviewed your thoughts about a new home. This home has the comfort and convenience you desired, plus the ideal location for both of you. That modern kitchen, Mrs. Carter, will be so much more convenient than the one you have now, don't you agree?"

Mrs. Carter responds: "It is a lovely kitchen, and such a pleasant place to live!"

At this point you sense that Mrs. Carter, the more dominant personality in the matter, is really sold on the home. You decide to let her help sell Mr. Carter.

LET THEM TOUR THE HOME ALONE

When the wife is sold on a property, it is often very easy for her to help you sell the husband if you will give her a few moments alone with him. The woman is usually the major factor in the purchase of a residence and she can get her way when she really wants it. By permitting them to go through the house by themselves, she will have an opportunity to "put a word or two in his ear" and clinch the sale. The wife is one of the most effective salesmen you can ever enlist on your side and when she is in your corner let her go to work for you.

This is similar to what is known as "the puppy dog close" in other selling professions. The easiest way to sell a puppy dog is to let the customer take it home "overnight." Once the family sees it, they are unable to return it! Car dealers use this approach as a primary tool in selling new automobiles:

"Just drive it around for a day or so, Mr. Jones. There is no charge! Take it home to the wife and see how she likes it!"

When you let them go through the home privately and get the feel of owning the property for themselves, it will be easier to close them.

OBTAINING THE OFFER

Incidentally, while they are making this private tour, you have an excellent opportunity to bring out the deposit receipt and start writing. When they return, you are prepared for them.

Mrs. Carter takes your suggestion of touring the home again with her husband in order to remember all the points of interest, and you are certain she will plant a few ideas in favor of the move while you continue writing portions of the contract. After five or ten minutes, they return and you continue your presentation:

"While you were out, Mr. Carter, I was figuring how this transaction might be arranged for you. With the equity in your present home, you will not require more than $14,000 to finance the balance on this one. Your mortgage investment would be only $91.84 per month, plus taxes and insurance, when computed at 6% for 24 years. That should be fairly reasonable, don't you agree?"

Mr. Carter replies: "Well, that's not bad, but Mary and I have been talking it over and although we like this home, we don't think it is worth $21,000."

You quickly reply: "How much do you think it is worth, Mr. Carter?"

"Well, I'm not sure. . . but considering everything, I think we might be interested at $18,000. But I imagine the owners would not want to come down that far on their price."

TAKE THE CUSHION AWAY FROM THE BUYER'S OFFER

Many buyers try to offer prices which are completely unrealistic either in the hope that the owners will be desperate and accept them or that they can stall for time by negotiating the differences. This is a common practice in our profession, but it deserves extra effort by the salesman to eliminate the problems and disadvantages of low offers. The salesman's job is to negotiate all offers, but he should not accept the first one made without some effort to raise the buyer to the maximum amount he is prepared to pay before he submits it to the seller.

Low offers cause sellers to stand firm in their pricing because they resent the efforts of those who would "steal" their equities. To get the owner's cooperation, you should do all in your power to raise the buyer to his highest figure before presenting the contract. Also, you would much rather accomplish your assignment in one session with the seller than take two or three for the same results. Knowing this you continue working with Mr. Carter:

"That is a very low offer, Mr. Carter, but if it is your best one, I will present it to the Greybars since they are anxious to move to Chicago." (Again, you allay his fears and keep the door open for negotiations, then proceed:)

"However, let's talk about it for just a moment. You recognize, I am sure, that this home could not be reproduced for anything close to that figure. Consider that modern kitchen, the hand finished cabinets, and the expert workmanship in the flagstone wall fireplace. These are expensive features, don't you agree?

Mr. Carter gives you a half-hearted nod, and you move on with your argument:

"We have all agreed, I believe, that this home really suits your basic requirements and has the amenities which make it a very livable home. Mrs. Greybar tells me you will have very fine neighbors: Mr. and Mrs. Baxton, assistant manager for Central Bank on this side and Mr. and Mrs. Fleming, across the street. He is an executive with an electronics firm. The seller tells me this is a very quiet and pleasant neighborhood with respectable people who care for their properties. You could not duplicate the value of this home for even $20,000, Mr. Carter, so it should be worth at least $19,000, don't you think?"

Mr. Carter tries to play hard to get, and replies: "Well, I don't know. Why don't you present that offer to them and see what they say? After all, we can always come up later if they don't accept it!"

To show your good faith you continue writing portions of the contract, leaving the price open, but indicating a willingness to comply with the buyer's request.

"That may be possible, Mr. Carter and I am certainly willing to present any offer you give me. Since we are asking the Greybars to accept such a low price, it would be helpful to have a substantial deposit as evidence of our good faith. Ten percent of the sales price is customary and that would be $1,800. Will it be by check or some other form?"

ASK FOR AND OBTAIN LARGE DEPOSITS

The time to firmly cement a bargain is when everyone is still happy with it! This simple truth underlies the reason you should always try to obtain the largest possible deposit from your purchasers. The time to obtain it is when they are making the original offer. Salesmen frequently compromise on this important point because they are so glad to have any offer they are not concerned about the size of the earnest money deposit. Let me caution you on this and remind you that the only thing permanent is change - including customers who change their minds! Let me give you three good reasons for receiving that large deposit at the time the offer is made:

1. A large deposit takes the buyer out of the market place and discourages him from looking around after his offer is accepted.
2. The size of the deposit often influences the seller when he is unhappy with the price. Nothing talks as loud as cash!
3. If a forfeiture might result, consider the merits of having a sufficient amount to justify the inconvenience to the seller:
    a. He has taken his home off the market and possibly denied himself the opportunity of another sale during the interim.

OBTAINING THE OFFER

    b. He probably has made commitments and plans on which the security of his sale is pre**mis**ed.
    c. He may incur actual loss to meet the terms of this offer when vacancy, repairs, and other costs are considered if the sale is not completed as specified.
    d. He may accept a lower price than original listed price, which permanently places him on record as willing to sell for that figure and damages his position for future presentation.

An agent for the seller has an implied obligation to do everything within his power to protect the seller's interests. A large deposit is the best assurance that you can obtain in trying to make certain for the seller and yourself that the transaction will be closed!

Mr. Carter responds to your request:

"I don't have that much in my checking account at the moment, but I can give you $500. Will that do?"

"That's all right, Mr. Carter. While you are writing the check I will make out a note against the equity in your present home for the balance, since it is all subject to our trade-in arrangements on your present property."

THE NATURE OF THE EARNEST MONEY

If you cannot obtain cash, or a current dated personal check in the size you want, accept as much cash as you can obtain and take a personal note or some other suitable security for the balance. I would rather have an $1800 note secured by the equity in a home than a mere check for $100. The important thing to remember is that the size of the deposit has a strong psychological effect on both buyer and seller. If the buyer believes he is bound to the offer, your primary purpose in obtaining the deposit has been achieved. The seller is also easier to convince when the size of the deposit indicates good faith on the part of the buyer.

It is equally important to record on your purchase agreement the nature of the legal tender your buyer gives you. Under the law, you are responsible for the deposit monies you receive and also for proper identification of their nature. If you receive a check, be certain to specify that it is a check. The same holds true for personal notes, escrow assignments, and any other form of deposit. Failure to identify the deposit will be automatically interpreted as "all cash." When writing the receipt, do so just as you would a personal check, showing both the numerical and written amounts:

EIGHTEEN HUNDRED AND NO/100 DOLLARS ($1,800.00) consisting of $500.00 personal check and $1,300.00 by a personal note secured by the equity in 1781 South 21st St., Yourtown, U.S.A.

Mr. Carter writes his check and hands it to you, and as you take it you make another effort to obtain a higher offer.

"Mr. Carter, I've been thinking about the price you want to offer. I believe we will have a much better chance of getting an acceptance of your deal if we make that $19,000 rather than $18,000. If we make our offer too low we may create a mental resistance which could spoil your opportunity to obtain the property at less than listed price. You wouldn't want to lose this place for the difference, would you, Mr. Carter?"

Mrs. Carter comes to your rescue:

"John, I think he's right. $19,000 would be a fair price to pay!"

Mr. Carter pauses for a moment and finally says:

"Well, all right; but that's absolutely as high as I will go. If they don't want that, we will stay where we are!" (This is uttered to justify the face-saving change he has made and you recognize the natural reaction as being perfectly normal.)

With this authorization, you fill in the purchase price portion of the contract and complete the other details that are affected by that factor. Then you turn to the Carters:

"You will note I have shown the offering price as $19,000, and the terms as all cash to the seller, subject to the sale or trade of your home within the next three days with our company. With the equity in your home, we can arrange any loan necessary for the difference between the cash and the balance of the purchase price. You will also see that I have included the 8 x 12 oriental rug and the matching drapes you requested. You may approve this right here" (pointing to the large "X" you have placed beside the appropriate line on the contract).

Note that we recommend the use of the term <u>approve</u> instead of <u>sign</u>. It is a more pleasant term and generally less offensive to a sensitive buyer who is still debating his decisions.

Mr. Carter pauses for a moment, then takes up the pen and signs his name, handing it to his wife after doing so. He re-states the fact that he wants to be sure the price is right on his home before completing the sale, and you assure him this will be so.

BUYERS MUST JUSTIFY THEIR ACTION OR INACTION

A decision has been made and confirmed in writing. It does not matter that the Carters can still back out of the sale by refusing to cooperate with the trade-in negotiator, or possibly for other reasons. Mentally, at this point, most buyers will begin finding reasons why their action was the right one to take. Tonight, Mr. and Mrs. Carter will be planning the move to the new home and envisioning the enjoyments of living on Harrison Avenue. They will confirm their decision because it is human nature to always justify whatever action or inaction we take. All of us must have self respect in order to live with ourselves comfortably. The chances are very strong now that the Carters will reinforce their interest in this new property, despite normal doubts and fears which may intrude from time to time. Pride is on the side of the salesman who obtains positive action from a buyer.

OBTAINING THE OFFER

HANDLING AND PROCESSING DEPOSITS

Just as the law holds the real estate salesman and his broker responsible for the nature of the deposit, it also expects prudent care of the deposit itself. If you receipt for $1,000.00, you had better have it intact when the sale is consummated or rescinded, as well as maintained in a separate, neutral trustee account in the interim. Consider for a moment your liability if you receipt for a $1,000 personal check on a sale and carelessly keep it in your wallet two or three weeks before turning it over to your broker or title company. If, during that time, the maker should stop payment on the check, or withdraw his funds, you could very well be held responsible for the full amount, since you did not use due diligence in depositing and processing the funds on time. Do not make the mistake of taking lightly your legal and moral duties in this regard. Deposit monies belong to the sellers as security for performance, and it is your obligation to protect their interests.

WRITING VALID CONTRACTS

Before we leave this subject, a word or two should be offered about the nature of your real estate contracts. In most states in the union, a real estate salesman can draw the initial document or fill in standard contracts binding the buyer and seller to a purchase agreement, even if an attorney or someone else is required to finalize the arrangements. You should know the exact limits of your authority in this matter of preparing deposit receipts as identified by the laws of your state. It is equally important to understand the basic rudiments of preparing valid agreements on which sales can be readily consummated. At the outset of your career, determine to learn the fundamentals of legal, understandable real estate documents which you will be required to prepare in the performance of your professional services. Your broker can assist you in this matter and there are many courses given on the "legal aspects of real estate" by various colleges and universities.

This outline of essential fundamentals in writing valid deposit receipts or purchase agreements has been inserted here to help you review the basic points about contracts which every real estate salesmen should know. Your supervisor may have minor revisions based on customs used in your area, but the principles involved apply to most real estate transactions.

I. ESSENTIALS OF A CONTRACT
    A. Parties involved must be capable of contracting:
       1. Of legal age (be sure you know definition of a minor in your state)
       2. Not insane (of a sound mind)

B. There must be a consideration. This can include:
   1. Money or its equivalent
   2. Love and affection
   3. Exchange for other property
C. There must be a legal object or purpose. You cannot contract to perform any unlawful act.
D. There must be an offer from one party.
E. There must be an <u>unqualified acceptance</u> from the other party.
F. The agreement must be in writing if it involves real estate.
G. All parties must sign and receive copies of the contract.

II. <u>BASIC ITEMS CONTAINED IN MOST DEPOSIT RECEIPTS</u> (Earnest Money Receipts)

   A. <u>Date and place</u>: This starts the time running for the offer clause.
   B. <u>Purchasers' names</u>:
      1. Always use legal names
      2. Identify relationships of parties contracting:
         a. <u>Single</u> man or woman (never has been married)
         b. <u>Unmarried</u> man or woman (has been married and now is divorced or widowed)
         c. <u>Sole and separate property</u> (when taking title alone)
         d. <u>Married</u>: <u>his wife</u>, <u>her husband</u>.
      3. EXAMPLES:
         <u>Edward Joseph Carter and Mary Elizabeth Carter, his wife.</u>
         <u>Susan Anne Johnson, unmarried</u>
         <u>Betty Louise Parker, married but acquiring title as her sole and separate property.</u>
         Harry A. Smith, a single man
   C. <u>Receipt for the deposit or earnest money:</u>
      1. Write it out as you would a check:
         NINETEEN THOUSAND FIVE HUNDRED AND NO/100 DOLLARS
      2. Also show numerical value:
         ($19,500.00)
      3. Specify nature of the deposit whether cash, check, note, assignment or other legal tender.
   D. <u>Total purchase price</u>: write it out in full same as deposit.
   E. <u>Property description</u>
      1. Use legal description as shown on title or deed if possible.
      2. Street address can be used but should be further qualified to avoid mistakes and confusion.
      3. Identify by encumbrances such as mortgages.
      4. Identify by names of present owners: "now vested in..."

OBTAINING THE OFFER 163

  5. Attach exhibits such as plot maps and title papers, and refer to them as part of the contract for identification of the parcel.

F. Easement and encumbrances
   1. Some contracts contain a "blanket clause" covering these items, but the buyer is not necessarily bound by unusual items.
   2. Any unusual items should be noted in the contract to avoid later difficulties in the event there is disagreement.

G. Purchase Price Terms
   1. This section is the heart of the contract, and the one you must complete with your own deposit receipt language as a rule.
      a. Stipulates the amounts to be paid the seller and their source. Necessary financing arrangements are identified.
      b. Conditions of the sale often listed here, including any contingent events which must occur to complete transaction.
   2. Avoid any uncertainties in this section.
      a. To protect buyer: use "subject to" clauses on financing and other necessary items.
      b. To protect seller: use no ambiguous terms or phrases and place the burden of performance on the buyer.

H. Printed terms of the deposit receipt
(Certain standard clauses appear in most deposit or earnest money agreements. The major ones involved are discussed below.)
   1. Forfeiture clause
      a. Presumed valid, but court cases indicate broad interpretations applied. Actual damages can be more or less than amount on deposit.
      b. Seller or buyer have alternative remedies:
         1. Suit for specific performance
         2. Suit for damages
         3. Mutual recision
         4. Quiet title suit to clear clouds created by agreements.
   2. Marketability of seller's title
      a. Seller can convey no more title than he possesses.
      b. Seller is usually allowed 90 days to perfect any defective aspects. If unable to do so, the buyer may rescind his offer.
   3. Risk of loss clause
      a. Covers fire, condemnation, destruction by natural or unnatural elements.

       b. Places all risk upon the seller until title is transferred, even if the seller has granted the buyer possession prior to that date.
4. <u>Prorations</u>: Date of calculations established.
   a. <u>Taxes</u>
      1. If still owed by seller, charged to seller
      2. If paid in advance, credited to seller and charged to buyer.
   b. <u>Fire Insurance</u>
      1. If cancelled, seller receives rebate based on "short rate" return.
      2. If assumed, seller receives credit for remaining term.
   c. <u>Other items sometimes prorated:</u>
      1. Interest on mortgages.
      2. Rents from tenants
      3. Lease deposits from tenants
      4. Trust fund impounds
5. <u>Possession Clause</u>
   a. Unless otherwise specified, it is always close of escrow as established by courts.
   b. It is normal to grant a few days to the seller to move, but the seller does not have right to stay on unless specified in the contract.
   c. Unless a rent amount is specified for possession privileges, the buyer may not be able to collect from the seller for occupancy beyond the date of title transfer.
6. <u>Offer clause</u>
   a. Offer can be withdrawn until accepted and notified of acceptance.
   b. Offer is terminated by death or insanity.
   c. Original offer is voided if counter-offer made.
   d. To be valid, the acceptance must be <u>unqualified and absolute</u>.
   e. If offer accepted by seller after time period allowed has expired, contract may not be valid unless approved by buyer.
7. <u>Time is of the essence clause</u>
   a. Requires that no unreasonable delays can prevent transfer of title.
   b. Without this clause, interpretation of time periods may be left to discretion of parties or the courts.
8. <u>Extension of time clause</u>
   a. Provides for the extension of most of the elements of the contract where undue circumstances arise.

OBTAINING THE OFFER

      b. It may not apply to such items as date of acceptance or possession.
9. <u>Agent's signature</u>: Acts as a receipt, but has no binding effect upon the terms of the contract.
10. <u>Buyer's signature</u>
      a. Should sign as shown in printed portion of deposit receipt.
      b. Generally either a wife or husband can obligate to purchase but to be safe, obtain signatures of both.
11. <u>Commission Agreement</u>
      a. Recovery of commission is usually based on the original listing contract and not on the deposit receipt.
      b. This clause merely gives conclusive evidence that the listing agreement has been fulfilled with the acceptance of the seller.
12. <u>Sellers' signatures</u>
      a. In community property states, both husband and wife must sign to have a valid contract. This applies in some of the other states also.
      b. Either man or wife may obligate himself to pay a commission but cannot force the sale of jointly owned property if one of the parties refuses to sign.
      c. Copies of the agreement must be given all signers.

SUMMARY

Due to the many variations in customs, contracts, and title laws existing in individual areas of the United States, it is best to consult experts in your particular district for those regulations which will affect the conduct of your real estate business. The most important thing to remember is that the purchase agreement should be prepared carefully and with professional pride in serving the interests of both buyer and seller. The deposit receipt language, included on pages 162-165 will also assist you in eliminating misunderstandings which can develop when you use ambiguous phrases.

STANDARD PHRASEOLOGY FOR DEPOSIT RECEIPTS

Although there will be many acceptable variations of deposit agreement language, the phrases given here for standard transactions may be of some help to you when you are learning the business. Before using any of them, however, be sure to obtain the approval of your broker or supervisor, since local customs and procedures may alter some terminology.

OBTAINING THE OFFER

I. **ASSUMPTION OF EXISTING LOAN OR LOANS**
    A. Buyer agrees to assume the existing loan of approximately $_____ now payable at $_____ per month including interest at _____%.
    B. Buyer to pay the balance of the purchase price in cash, including the above receipted deposit, plus assumption fees and closing costs.

II. **ASSUMPTION OF EXISTING LOAN PLUS NEW SECOND LOAN TO SELLER**
    A. Buyer agrees to assume the existing loan of approximately $_____ now payable at $_____ per month including interest at _____%.
    B. Buyer agrees to execute second deed of trust (or mortgage) to the seller for $_____ payable at $_____ per month or more, including interest at _____% per annum. Said note to contain a _____ due date and an acceleration clause.
    C. Buyer to pay the balance of the purchase price in cash, including above receipted deposit plus assumption fees and normal buyer closing costs.

III. **REFINANCING WITH NEW LOANS**
    A. $_____ cash down payment, including the above receipted deposit plus closing costs and refinance charges.
    B. $_____ by a new (conventional, FHA, VA or other) loan on subject property for a term of _____ years with interest at _____% per annum.
    (If a second loan to seller is also involved add:)
    C. $_____ by a note secured by a second deed of trust (mortgage) executed by the buyer in favor of the seller, payable at $_____ per month or more, including interest at _____% per annum. Said note and deed of trust (mortgage) to have a _____ due date and an acceleration clause.

IV. **ALL CASH:** Clause merely states "All cash to seller."

V. **OTHER CLAUSES USED**
    A. Protection for buyer's qualification on new loans:
    "This agreement to purchase is made subject to the buyer qualifying for and obtaining above described loan."
    B. Trade-in or sale of another property:
    "This agreement to purchase is made subject to the sale or trade of the buyer's property at _____ within _____ days."
    C. Termite inspections
    "Buyer agrees to pay for the cost of a termite inspection and seller agrees to pay any costs of correction or repairs as recommended by a state licensed termite company, said work to be completed prior to close of escrow."

OBTAINING THE OFFER

D. <u>Possession and rental clauses</u>
   1. "Buyer to have possession on or before _____.
      Rent shall be fixed at _____ per (day or month) until
      close of escrow, payable in advance on the _____ day of
      each month. Said rent shall be pro-rated at close of escrow."
   2. "Seller to retain possession for _____ days after close of
      escrow at $_____ per (day or month), said rent to be
      paid to buyer _____ (state when due)."

E. <u>Inclusion of personal property in sale price</u>
   "Purchase price shall include the following personal property
   items for which the seller will deliver to buyer in escrow a
   bill of sale:
   1. (describe)
   2. (describe)

F. <u>Protecting seller for buyer's performance on loans</u>
   "Buyer agrees to apply for said loan within _____ days from
   the date of acceptance of this offer and to use due diligence in
   processing said loan."

A FEW SPECIAL NOTES ON CLOSING SALES

Although you will probably not have to use all of them in any one situation, you should know the basic closing techniques to use when they are required. We have already covered several, but others you may use are:

1. <u>Close on a minor point or alternative choice:</u>
   This one gives the buyer a small decision to make between two alternatives, either of which will automatically confirm the sale. For example:
   "The sellers can grant possession on June 1 or July 1, which would you prefer?"
   "Would you prefer to take title as tenants in common, or as joint tenants?"

2. <u>Create an impending or urgent event:</u>
   If we purchase now, we can take advantage of the low interest rates which are still in effect, but which may increase soon."
   "Several others have expressed interest in this property, and it may not be available tomorrow. Let's buy it today!"

3. <u>Introduce a third party story to dramatize:</u>
   Third party references are easy to accept as they are less personal and can be viewed more objectively. You should develop a series of true experiences involving your buyers and sellers which can effectively illustrate the various points you want to make. For example:

"This reminds me of a young couple I was working with the other day, Mr. and Mrs. Harold Parker. They were searching for a particular home and we found one they liked on Broadmore Avenue. Because it was their first home, they wanted to be extremely cautious and when I encouraged them to make an offer, they said they wanted to think it over. Nothing I could say changed their minds. The very next morning they called me and wanted to go ahead with the purchase, but I had to disappoint them because it was sold to the Harrisons the night before."

There are many other closing techniques which other books will provide in much greater detail. Review as many as you need, but never overlook the value of using your own personality, with all its natural talents, to the full. Be yourself at your very best!

THE PSYCHOLOGY OF THE CLOSING SESSION

One of the reasons people dislike making decisions is because most of us prefer to keep our minds at rest. We use them so little for major decisions and genuine thinking that when we are confronted with the necessity of making big decisions, we often feel very uncomfortable. Appreciating this fact, it is often advisable to force a final answer by taking advantage of this basic desire to have the mind back in its normal restful state. As long as the client is uncomfortable and struggling with a potential decision, there is a strong, subconscious desire to get it over and relax again. Your objective in the final phases of closing should be to keep the mental pressure at a peak until the decision is made in the affirmative, and then let the buyer relax while you confirm the wisdom of his choice.

It is a strange thing about human nature. As emphasized earlier, we always tend to justify and excuse whatever action or inaction we take. For example, if you let the buyer go home to think it over (as he says he wants), the chances are better than nine to one he will awake the next morning and say to himself:

"Boy, I'm glad I didn't let that real estate salesman sell me that home. The garage was too small, and that living room was too dark, and . . ."

Why does he do this? Because, during the night his indecision and inaction had to be justified and he created reasons to prove he made the right move by waiting. In his imagination, the driveway and garage grow smaller, the home decays with termites and his dollars go drifting away on the clouds. On the other hand, had you succeeded in obtaining his signature on a purchase agreement, he begins to find reasons why this was a very wise move and boasts about his choice to others. By morning he is sure he drove the best bargain in the world. Why?

Because it is important for humans to think well of themselves. We must live with ourselves every day and we will find excuses or reasons for all of our actions, right or wrong.

Have you ever met a man who just bought a new car who wasn't convinced he'd driven the best bargain and had the finest car his money could buy? I never have! Have you noticed how they even justify why they had to turn the old car in: "It was going to require a lot of fixing and would cost more than it was worth." This is just a natural reaction, but you should remember its impact on your profession and use it to reinforce the decisions your buyers and sellers should make. People seldom understand why they react as they do, since the emotional stimuli and subconscious desires are more deep-rooted than all the sound reasonings of mankind!

THE COURAGE TO MAKE OR BREAK THE SALE

There comes a time when working with a prospective buyer that the salesman must "take the bull by the horns" and either "make or break the sale" at that point. Some prospects would never make up their minds no matter how long or hard you worked with them, and you owe it to yourself and the customer to "go for broke" when you find the right property for your prospect. When the time comes to face the decision, you can say to yourself in all honesty: "This is the property my client should purchase. I have shown him everything that could meet his requirements and this is the best choice. I will either sell him this home or risk losing the customer, because I cannot be of service to him if he is not a genuine prospect!" <u>Being firm with yourself</u> will give you the courage to face the issues, and you will soon be surprised how often that attitude produces the extra push needed to do the right thing for you and your customer!

<u>Never forget that you came to close the sale!</u> Professional salesmen know that they are paid for their services only if they succeed in closing the sale! In order to succeed in the real estate business you must learn to control your customers, conquer their fears and indecisions, and force the positive action you know they want to take but which frequently they will not without your help. Most real estate sales are made within the first week of working with the customer, and often within the first two or three days. That's because the salesmen who actually make the sales realize they must stick with their customers until they are sold or drop them when they realize they cannot sell them. You are not paid for guided tours of your entire listing inventory! You are only paid when you render a service and close the sale. The weak never succeed in selling, because they have not mastered their own fears. That is a prime reason for the fact that 80% of all real estate sales are made by 20% of the salesmen! Which group will you be in?

WITH OFFER IN HAND

As you make the return trip to the Carter's home, you continue your selling because you realize there is always some uncertainty in the prospect's mind once the offer is made. You want them to relax and leave it in your capable hands, while picturing themselves living in the lovely new home they have chosen on Harrison Avenue. You sell the advantages of the property, the neighborhood, and the many amenities of this residence, while stressing that you will really be working hard for them to get the seller's approval of their offer. By your own enthusiasm for the transaction, you help to bolster the buyers' outlook and overshadow any remorse which might set in as the result of "after buying blues." As you deposit the Carters in front of their old home, you wave good bye and with your parting comment you cross your fingers and say "Wish me luck!" heading off to the sellers with your offer in hand.

OBTAINING THE OFFER 171

QUESTIONS AND PROJECTS ON CHAPTER EIGHT

Questions:

1. What are some of the major reactions you watch for when showing prospects a property?
2. How can you help to increase a buyer's desire to own a home when he first expresses some interest in the product?
3. What advantage can you gain by using the rule of "calling by name, asking a question, and agreeing" with your prospect?
4. What part does the salesman's attitude and actions play in helping to overcome buyer fears?
5. How can you "make it easy for a customer to do business with you" and why is it important to do so?
6. Give three standard buying objections and your answer for each.
7. Where is the best place to close a sale? Where is the worst place?
8. When is silence golden and how can you use your ears to make a sale?
9. Why should you always obtain a large deposit or earnest money amount when making a sale?
10. Why is it important to be able to write valid contracts? Name five things you believe most vital in a good deposit receipt or purchase agreement.

Projects:

1. List the four essential steps to any sale and then review the following points about each one:
   a. How can you establish and control each of the four steps?
   b. What questions can you ask to accelerate the buyer's interest and desire?
   c. What is the major method a salesman can use to gain and hold attention?
   d. How can you extract the action you want in closing a sale?
2. Develop various responses you might use to handle each of these standard buyer objections which often precede an impending closing:
   a. "I want to think it over first."
   b. "I want my uncle (aunt, father, etc.) to see it before we decide to buy."
   c. "We are not ready to make a decision yet."
   d. "We do not want to pay that much for a home."
   e. "We can't buy a home until we sell our present one."
   f. "I'm not sure now is a good time to buy. If we wait, prices may come down."
   g. "That's a lot of money to owe on a mortgage for 30 years."
   h. "It's a nice home, but we should see more before we decide."
   l. "I would like to talk it over with my lawyer (banker, doctor, etc.)"
   m. "I'm not sure we can handle the payments, especially if I lost my job or there was a depression again."

OBTAINING THE OFFER

3. Practice writing deposit receipts for the following types of sales:
   a. $18,500 sale, minimum down 30 year FHA loan, buyer and seller paying normal closing costs. Include termite clearance clause.
   b. $25,950 sale, cash to maximum available insurance loan at 5 1/2% interest, 25 years. Include a contingency for sale of buyer's home in 60 days or trade-in.
   c. $16,500 sale with a no down, veterans loan, 30 year term. Include an agreement to sell rugs and drapes for extra $750. Also, buyer's non-recurring closing costs to be limited to $200.
   d. $17,250 sale with $2000 down, assumption of existing loan which is in the approximate balance of $12,310 @ 4 1/2% interest (G. I.) and the seller to carry the difference on second loan for 7 years payable 1% of face amount per month with interest included at 6% per year.
   e. $20,000 sale with new first loan from a Savings and Loan Company equal to 80% of sales price for not more than 6 1/2% interest and a term not less than 24 years with cash down payment for the difference.
4. List the closing tools you should always have in your possession when working with a buyer.
5. Review the actual contract, deposit receipt, or earnest money receipt authorized by your broker and know the reason and importance for each clause it contains, as well as standard instructions your office desires followed when using it.
6. Rehearse examples of the following closing approaches:
   a. The assumptive close.
   b. The alternative choice on a minor point.
   c. Using an impending or urgent event.
   d. Using a third party example.
   e. Using the deposit receipt as a closing tool.
7. Discuss with experienced salesmen and your broker the psychology of the closing session and the various techniques different individuals use to build confidence in the buyer's decision-making processes.
8. Review your real estate licensing books and answer the following questions:
   a. What are the essential requirements of any real estate contract?
   b. What is valid consideration?
   c. When is an offer considered ratified?
   d. What is a legal description for real property?
   e. What is marketable title, and when may a buyer rescind an offer for failure of the seller to deliver marketable title?
   f. What remedies are available to buyer or seller when there is a failure by the other to perform according to contract terms?
   g. When can a buyer withdraw his offer with immunity?
   h. If there is an agent's extension clause in your contract, to what does it apply? What does it not cover?

OBTAINING THE OFFER

9. Discuss with fellow salesmen and your broker how you can use the deposit or earnest money agreement as a closing tool, and handle it in such a way as to remove the buyer's fears of closing.
10. What are your thoughts on the following subjects:
    a. Letting buyers go through a home by themselves after seeing it once with an agent.
    b. Putting the proposition in writing early in the closing situation rather than delaying until the buyer seems ready.
    c. Timing versus planning in determining when to close.
    d. The value of listening and feeding back the prospect's own comments to assist in building the closing phase.
    e. How hard a salesman should try to get the buyer to make his top offer rather than submit the first figure suggested.
    f. The size and type of deposit or earnest money you should try to obtain.
    g. When to take the position of "making or breaking a sale."

9

CLOSING THE SELLER

At the nearest pay phone you place an immediate call to the listing salesman, Joe Barber, advising him you have a purchase agreement on the Harrison Avenue property and requesting an early appointment with the Greybars to present your offer. You realize the importance of contacting the sellers as quickly as possible, since there is always the chance another salesman will introduce a sale ahead of yours, or that the buyers might withdraw their offer before its presentation. <u>Never delay presenting an offer to your sellers, even when the buyer has given you the right to take two or three days for that purpose!</u> This clause does not prevent your purchaser from cancelling his agreement before the expiration of that time period if you have not previously obtained full ratification and promptly communicated such acceptance to him!

<u>HOW TO PHONE THE SELLER</u>

You agree with Joe Barber that you should not be the one to place the call to the Greybars since it would give them an opportunity to ask questions about the terms of the Carter's offer. Discussing the contract by telephone risks everything while usually accomplishing very little. As one Realtor told me several years ago:

<u>"We owe it to the seller to protect him from his own impatience!"</u>

The owner will want to know the terms of your offer before it is presented to him, but seldom can he appreciate the full story without your personal selling efforts and knowledge. If he learns the terms of your offer before you can meet him face to face, he has time to build defensive reactions, often to his own disadvantage. Except in the case of out-of-town sellers where you may have no other alternative, you should avoid revealing your offers by phone, saving your presentation for a personal appearance with the owners, when your selling ability can be used to overcome objections and signatures obtained to confirm a positive decision.

One way to handle this problem is to have the office secretary or another salesman place the call. If the owners ask about the offer, the party calling can honestly claim lack of knowledge about such details, thus protecting you and the owner from any embarrassing exchanges.

"Hello, Mrs. Greybar? Your sales representative, Joe Barber, has just called the office to inform us he has an offer on your property. He would like to schedule an appointment to present it to you and your husband this evening. Would 6:30 be convenient?"

THINK IT THROUGH FIRST

It is sound advice to never go rushing off to a seller with a buyer's offer in hand without taking at least thirty minutes for quiet meditation to review your presentation. What do you think about?

1. Is this a reasonable offer?
2. Why should the Greybars accept it?
3. What is likely to happen if they reject or counter this offer?
4. How will the urgency of the seller's situation affect their decision?
5. What facts can you present to obtain a favorable decision?
6. How much activity and offers have these owners experienced since originally listing the property?

By mentally reviewing these important questions and analyzing the facts, you greatly assist yourself in handling the closing presentation with the sellers. The thirty minutes you take to think through the details of your buyer's proposal may well be the most important thirty minutes of the entire transaction. There is no substitute for preparation!

COOPERATING WITH LISTING SALESMEN

The listing salesman is always considered, and rightly so, the seller's agent. He is employed by the seller to represent the property to other salesmen, brokers and agents on the seller's behalf, and also to reach the ultimate purchasers through these representatives. The relationship between listing and selling salesmen should be fully appreciated by both. When you sell another salesman's listing, it is your responsibility to present your offer with the permission of the listing agent, and preferably in his presence. Most real estate offices have definite policies concerning this important topic. In general, these policies are designed to provide a cooperative working relationship between the various salesmen involved in a transaction. I personally believe the seller's agent should be present in most cases when an offer is presented. After all, he was hired for that purpose and if he hopes to ever cultivate future referral business from his client, he cannot afford to be absent during the vital closing session. Further, it is his responsibility as a professional salesman to protect the interests of his seller and assist in the details concerning the acceptance or rejection of an offer.

There is, however, an occasional problem in this regard. Some listing salesmen become almost "mother-hen protective" about their sellers, to the detriment of the owners and themselves. I would like to stress a very important point on this principle of agency:

NO REAL ESTATE SALESMAN SHOULD EVER PRE-EMPT THE SELLER'S PREROGATIVE TO DECIDE FOR HIMSELF WHAT HE WILL AND WILL NOT ACCEPT!

I once knew a salesman who had listed a home for approximately $35,000 and after it had been on the market nearly three months he presented them an offer for $31,500, which they rejected. Based on their decision, the listing salesman assumed the sellers would never reduce their price and when, sixty days later, an offer for $29,500 was presented to him for submission to his clients, he adamantly insisted there was no point in even taking it to the owners as it had no chance of being accepted. The selling salesman demanded his right to make the presentation regardless of the previous rejection of a higher offer, and so the contract was taken to the owners for their review. During the course of the session, the owner asked:

"If I accept this offer, how soon would I be able to obtain a check for my equity?"

Somewhat astonished, the listing salesman replied: "We can close the sale within 10 days, since it is an all cash offer and we already have a preliminary title report on your property."

Thereupon the owner signed the purchase agreement and handed it back to his agent. The salesman was baffled by this change of attitude and he could not resist asking why the seller had accepted such a low price when he had previously countered a much higher one two months earlier. The client replied:

"This offer comes to me at a time when I need money. If I can get $20,000 in my hands within the next two weeks, I can double it in a business venture I have been offered by one of my associates."

Thus, this salesman learned a major lesson: only the sellers of a property should have the final say on the acceptance or rejection of any offer, since their attitudes and needs change from day to day. In addition, the laws of agency require you to present all offers to the sellers of real estate, permitting them to exercise their own judgment in each case. This does not mean you should avoid making your own recommendations, but permit me to caution you about beclouding the issues in an attempt to demonstrate your knowledge.

EDUCATING THE SELLER

Before you reach the Greybars with your offer, let me warn you about another peculiar phenomenon of our business. Strange as it may seem, some sellers who have previously pleaded for action and demonstrated great anxiety about selling prior to receiving offers, suddenly become difficult and almost unapproachable when purchase agreements are actually brought to them. Your owner may act like a cat who hasn't eaten for several days but upon catching a mouse, prefers to play with it before satisfying his natural hunger! Most sellers do not understand the mechanics or nature of the real estate business and often presume they have the right to take all the time they want to consider, or change, a contract before signing the documents. You and I know this is not true, and it is our obligation to protect the seller's interests by emphasizing certain basic facts before permitting him to take an action that would be detrimental to his objectives. If the contract says the owner has three days in which to accept or reject the offer, he may be tempted to take that full time, without realizing that the law grants the buyer the complete freedom of withdrawing his offer to purchase at any time he so desires prior to receiving communication of an unqualified acceptance. You and I also know that the slightest change or pen mark on a deposit receipt is interpreted by law as a "counter offer" and gives the buyer the right to cancel the entire negotiation if he does not want to accept and initial this change. <u>Neither the seller nor yourself can return to the first offer unless the buyer wants to do so!</u> An offer to purchase must receive an unqualified and unconditional acceptance from the sellers in order to bind the one making the offer. Even real estate salesmen often make the mistake of assuming they have sufficient control of their buyers to permit counters on minor points in the contracts they prepare. When another salesman brings you an offer to present to one of your sellers, think twice before you recommend making any change on that offer, <u>even if the agreement is not written exactly as you would have prepared it.</u> Unless the change is absolutely essential to the transaction for the sellers' interests, do not risk losing the sale for the owners for the privilege of making minor pen notations on the deposit receipt. Before recommending a counter agreement, ask yourself these questions:

1. Is this change worth risking the loss of this sale should the buyer decide not to accept it?
2. Is there some other way to handle this item without affecting the contract?
3. Does the seller really appreciate that he is rejecting the buyer's offer when he makes any type of change on the original contract?

There will be many times when counter offers are both necessary and justified, particularly where the offering price and terms are entirely unsatisfactory. Your responsibility is to recommend to the sellers the course of action best designed to protect their interests and achieve the results they desire without jeopardizing their position. Always weigh the merits of your suggestions before making them to the owners.

WHO CARRIES THE BALL?

You are now ready to meet the Greybars and present the Carters' offer. Joe Barber and you have taken that vital thirty minutes to compare notes in preparation for the sales presentation you both know lies ahead. At the Greybars' home you exchange a few pleasantries and ask the sellers to permit you and Mr. Barber to sit at the kitchen table where there is good light and plenty of room to review the contract. You also know there is another good reason for this move, i.e., to be physically close to the sellers where you can watch their expressions and control their reactions. You are careful to seat yourself where you and Joe can maintain constant visual contact with the owners.

Joe opens by mentioning that he has just learned from you about the Greybars' decision to be in Chicago by the first of next month. Mr. Greybar acknowledges this and gives a little background for the company's insistence on the earlier date, but to make sure you know he still has the upper hand, he adds:

"But my wife is prepared to stay here as long as necessary in order to sell our home for a reasonable price!"

You had agreed in advance with Mr. Barber that, after he had set the stage, you would present your own story on behalf of the buyers and their offer. This is usually a very wise approach to the closing session. After all, you know more about your buyers and their personal circumstances than the listing salesman does, and therefore you can better relate your "fight" story about how you were able to obtain the offer you are presenting tonight. Effectively telling the sellers, in dramatic terms, how you convinced the buyers to purchase this home and obtained their highest offer will help you establish a relationship on which to win the sellers' confidence. After all, your buyers are just ordinary people who have problems and needs, and you want the sellers to understand this when you reveal the terms of their proposal. On the other hand, the listing salesman is normally in a better position to maintain control of the sellers, since he will usually be closer to their needs and desires. His personal strength may be needed in the final stages of this closing session in order to obtain the sellers' acceptance of your contract.

In this manner, each of you plays a part in this final act of your four-part drama. One party fills the "heavy role" while the other steps in from time to time to relieve tensions and take the seller's side of the issues, thus playing the "light role." This works very well when both salesmen understand their individual and mutual objectives. If the seller has to be "mad" at someone in order to vent his emotions, the salesman best suited for the task should play that part while letting the other one be the "good guy" who helps the seller reason with him the pros and cons of this particular offer. Before arriving at the seller's home these points should be thoroughly reviewed and a prior decision made as to which one will carry the ball across the goal line!

CLOSING THE SELLER

COVER CONTINGENCIES FIRST

A Realtor friend of mine from Whittier, California, always instruct his salesmen to work their offers "from the bottom up!" By this he means, cover all of the "subject-to" clauses and "contingencies" before discussing price and terms. If the offer is subject to a termite clearance certificate, a repair of a leaking roof, or inclusion of rugs and drapes, these points would be discussed before engaging the owner in the major hurdles involving the terms of sale. There are a number of good reasons why this approach is helpful:

1. Until the owner accepts a specific price, he is often willing to make concessions and extend his cooperation on minor points.

2. It also assists you in setting the stage for the major closing by obtaining a series of "yes" decisions on minor points. This is the same principle used with buyers.

3. It avoids the necessity, after obtaining the owners' approval on price, of re-opening the discussion due to these miscellaneous items.

"Mr. Greybar, have you ever had a termite report on your property?" Mr. Greybar replies:

"No, not since we originally purchased the home several years ago, but I'm sure we don't have any problem with them."

"That's fine! You will be willing to furnish our buyers with a termite clearance report from a state licensed inspector?"

"Why, yes."

"My clients noticed a loose step on the rear porch, probably something you had planned to repair. I'm sure you would want that fixed before we close the sale, wouldn't you, Mr. Greybar?"

"Yes... I had been meaning to get that done now for some time."

"If you receive a satisfactory price for your home, would you be willing to include that 8 x 12 oriental rug in your master bedroom with the matching drapes?"

Mrs. Greybar responds:

"Well, we hadn't really planned on it. What do you think, dear?"

Mr. Greybar turns to his wife and replies:

"Well, if it will help the sale, I guess we could leave it. After all, we would just have to pay freight on it to ship it east."

So far so good. You have covered most of your minor contingencies and now there is just one left.

"My buyers, Mr. and Mrs. Carter, own another home at 1781 South 21st Street and plan to sell or trade it before completing the purchase of your home. However, since we knew you would not want to take an offer subject to an indefinite sale, the buyers have agreed to use our trade-in plan to guarantee their equity and eliminate any risk to yourselves. We have allowed three days in the contract to complete those negotiations."

Mr. Greybar speaks up: "I've heard about your trade-in plan, and I guess it's all right, just so long as I do not have to be involved with the other home and will be certain of closing on time. You say it will only take three days?"

"No, Mr. Greybar, it may not take that long, but our agreement allows a maximum of three days. Often we can reach a decision within 24 hours or less. I have already alerted our Trade-In Department Manager and he is prepared to inspect this property tomorrow."

Mr. Greybar then says:

"As long as that's clearly understood, Mr. Barber, we will agree to those provisions, that is if they are submitting a reasonable offer. How much is their offer?"

Since you have now cleared the way by eliminating the contingencies, you are ready to hand the deposit receipt to the owners.

ALWAYS STAY CALM AND CONFIDENT

You place the contract in Mr. Greybar's hands, with the $1800 deposit attached for his personal observation. As he reads it, you just sit back and relax, waiting for his reaction. It isn't long in coming! Mr. Greybar spots the $19,000 offering price, and in a bellowing voice, reacts:

"This offer is ridiculous! Mr. Barber, you know that my wife and I previously rejected a similar offer! Why we wouldn't think of selling for $19,000! This home is worth much more than that. If you had told us over the phone, before you came here, what you were bringing, I would have saved you a trip tonight!"

At this point, all too many real estate salesmen are tempted to put their tails between their legs and run for cover, but permit me to assure you this is a perfectly normal reaction and one you will experience many times if you succeed in the real estate business. You must learn to stay calm, and help the seller over this emotional hurdle when he does not like something about an offer. Often the sellers just need to blow steam and unleash some of the emotional tension which develops from the uncertainties of selling real estate. If you keep your mental composure, you will be able to steer them to a reasonable discussion about the merits of your buyers' offer. I have come to accept the fact that neither buyer or seller are completely normal during any real estate transaction. The various frustrations involved in trying to buy or sell a piece of property, can and often do produce strong reactions over minor things which occur during this period.

Appreciating why the Greybars react as they do, you patiently let the air settle as Mrs. Greybar joins in to defend her husband's reaction:

"That is an awfully low price, Mr. Barber. After all, we've got a lot of money invested in this home. Just look at the way we have maintained this place! It just doesn't seem fair to have to take such a low price!"

You know that interrupting would be rude, so you just listen. It takes two to argue and you and Joe Barber do not intend being one of the two needed! Besides, it's much smarter to let them cool down before you graciously and professionally proceed with your closing presentation.

Once it's out in the open and the dust has had a chance to settle, you will have plenty of time to present the rest of your sales story. Never lose your professional dignity! By retaining your composure, you will win the confidence and respect of otherwise stubborn clients. At this point, Joe Barber speaks up:

"I'm sure, Mr. and Mrs. Greybar, you appreciate how hard we have been trying for more than two months to locate a buyer for your home - one who is ready, willing and able to purchase it! This is only the second offer we have received, <u>and both of them have been for $19,000.</u> This is true, despite the fact that your home has been shown to many prospective purchasers. Now I know our salesman here has done his very best to bring in the highest offer his buyers were prepared to make and we should seriously consider the merits of this offer."

REVIEW WHAT YOU HAVE DONE

Joe is using a very effective closing technique: <u>that of emphasizing the amount of activity and number of offers a property has received, which underscores the general reaction of the prospective buyers.</u> In his preconceived notion of value, the seller has difficulty accepting the fact that the price for real estate is primarily determined by the buyers. Carefully reviewing the history of activity related to a particular property will influence most owners to be more objective about the offers they are asked to consider. Joe now turns to you with that knowing look, which is your cue to pick up the ball and give your fight story.

"Mr. and Mrs. Greybar, I realize this offer may not be as much as you had hoped to receive, but I would like to point out that I had to spend considerable time with Mr. and Mrs. Carter to even obtain an offer of $19,000. They originally suggested a price of $18,000, but I convinced them they should raise their sights. You will note that this is an "all cash" offer which eliminates any question about financing your home or the buyer's ability to qualify for a new loan. When you accept this offer, you can start packing, because we will have a firm transaction we can close within a short period of time, once we confirm the trade-in terms on the Carters' existing home.

"You see, my buyers live by themselves now in a large home since their daughter married a young law student earlier this year. They want a smaller home in this general area, but they are a conservative couple who do not have to buy or sell and will want to be certain they are purchasing within their means. They believe they have made a reasonable offer considering their circumstances."

You are now employing human interest selling techniques to make the offer more palatable to the Greybars. When the buyers do not appear as speculative vultures waiting to snap up property from defenseless sellers, you will find less objections to the negotiations. You want your prospects to appear as the nice, elderly couple they really are and show the owners of this home that the new buyers will take pride in their purchase, since this is where they intend to spend their twilight years. Mr. Greybar responds:

"My wife and I do not question that you got the very best offer you could, but this is so much less than we are prepared to accept. We might consider a price of $20,000... but not $19,000."

Now the owners have committed themselves and you have a starting point from which to pin down the least they will accept for this home. You do not plan to leave here tonight empty handed, even if you must take a counter offer to your buyers. After all, a counter is better than a complete rejection because it gives your buyers a temporary option at a fixed price, and places the burden upon the sellers to notify you if they desire to withdraw before the expiration date allowed in the presentation clause. However, you are going to make every effort, with Mr. Barber's help, to get this offer accepted without qualification because you do not know whether or not you can raise the Carters' price again. Thus, you continue your selling efforts:

COVER ALL THE DETAILS

"I know this is less than you had planned to accept, but you realize it is our responsibility to bring to you any offer and let you make your own decision. We could not presume to reject a sale, especially since we do know that you want to complete a transaction and go on to Chicago. Somewhere between what the buyer wants to pay and your lowest price, we should be able to reach a meeting of the minds. Remember, we have finally located an "all cash" buyer who is completely qualified to buy your home and since you want to sell, we have the two most important ingredients for a sale, don't you agree, Mr. Greybar?" He nods his head half-heartedly, permitting you to continue:

"Now, Mr. and Mrs. Greybar, a real estate offer is somewhat like a streetcar. When it comes along, you can either take it or wait for the next one. However, we are never sure when the next one will arrive, if at all, and when it does, we are not able to assure you it will take you where you want to go. Since this offer is here now, we should seriously consider the possibility of accepting it, rather than risk waiting for the unknown buyer in the future. Don't you agree?"

You note that Mrs. Greybar seems more interested now and has nodded approval of your argument. Joe Barber senses the need to help the situation along and so he injects his comments at this point:

"I believe that is a very valid point, Mr. Greybar. We could possibly find another buyer even tomorrow, or we could wait another two, three, or four months before one came along. That's part of the real estate business we cannot control! I know you and Mrs. Greybar would love to make that trip east together, rather than be inconvenienced by separation for an indefinite time period. If you ratify this offer, we can close the details in time to permit both of you to leave for Chicago within

CLOSING THE SELLER

the next two weeks and there will be no worries left behind to plague the pleasures of your trip. That should be worth something to you, don't you think, Mrs. Greybar?"

Mrs. Greybar warms to this line of thinking and turns to her husband:

"It would be nice to make it at one time and not have to be separated for several weeks, John. What do you think?"

"Well, I don't know! I still think we ought to hold out for $20,000. Don't you think you could get your buyers up to that figure?"

You are now on the spot, and because you sense that Mr. Greybar is beginning to weaken in his determination to obtain that price, you decide to really emphasize the risk this approach will incur:

"They might, Mr. Greybar, but I certainly cannot assure you they will. I would hate to be the one who encouraged you to risk losing the entire transaction simply by countering **this** offer that I worked hard to obtain from the Carters. If you make any change on the contract, they are free to drop the entire matter if they wish. How much are we really talking about, Mr. Greybar? What is the very lowest offer you would consider?"

REDUCE TO SIMPLEST TERMS

You have now tossed it back into the seller's lap and you await his reply.

"Well, as I said before, I would be willing to sell for $20,000... maybe even $19,500... but $19,000 is just not enough for this home!"

Quickly you accept this $500 reduction and run with the ball:

"You say you will take $19,500. Is that right, Mr. Greybar?"

"Yes, I guess so..."

"Well, now, what are we talking about then between the Carters' offer and your price? Just $500. Let me ask you, Mrs. Greybar, would it be worth $500 to know you do not have to stay here alone for two or three months while your family is east? Wouldn't the peace of mind and freedom from worry, to say nothing of the long distance phone calls and other expenses, justify an investment of only $500? Just the relief of having this entire decision behind you, without the necessity of keeping house for strangers, should be worth something, don't you agree?"

You pause to give Mrs. Greybar a chance to help sell her husband. You know by her expressions that she does not want to stay behind, alone. She finally speaks to her husband:

"He certainly has a very good point, don't you think, John?"

Mr. Greybar is now wavering as he weighs the merits of your arguments and the affection for his wife's needs:

"I still say it's not enough, but I must admit you plead a good case. Joe, what do you think about this? What would you do if you were in my shoes?"

The listing salesman now uses his relationship to help the Greybars make this important decision. He knows that they should make it and that his assistance is required to complete the picture. However, he must stay on their side in order to continue his efforts if the first attempt fails, so he cautiously enters the arena:

"That's a very difficult question to answer, Mr. Greybar. After all, I'm not you and I'm not the one faced with the problem. However, I think our salesman has a real point in this matter of $500. I've been computing that $500 on paper, based on the life of a normal mortgage and I find it's only $3.66 per month, or 12 cents per day! It hardly seems worth while risking loss of a sale for such a small amount, considering the inconveniences and worries involved! I was also thinking about the fact that our next buyer might have to qualify for a new loan, and we never know for sure whether or not he can make it until the lender approves; that can take additional time. We do not have that problem with the Carters. If you decide to pass up this offer and wait for another one, you run the risk of maintaining a vacant home should Mrs. Greybar get lonely and decide to join you. These are some of the things I would carefully weigh before rejecting the offer, Mr. Greybar."

THE SELLER IS NOW A BUYER

After letting Joe Barber's comments sink in for a moment, you decide to use one of your strongest selling arguments to help close the case.

"Let me ask you a question, Mr. Greybar. Suppose I were to put you in my car tonight and drive you around the area looking for a home to buy. I pull up in front of this one and I ask you to buy it for $19,000. Would you do so on the "gamble" you might be able to make another $500 in two or three weeks or months?"

Mr. Greybar is confused by this unusual approach:

"What do you mean? I already own this home!"

"Not really, Mr. Greybar, because if you approve this contract, you have sold it to the Carters for $19,000; but if you do not you will have bought it back for that same price on the gamble you can make another $500 by waiting. Isn't that right?"

Mr. Greybar puzzles over your example for a moment and before he can object, Joe Barber adds:

"That's true, Mr. Greybar! At this moment you are only a signature away from not owning this home, and if you fail to sign this purchase agreement, you have actually bought your own home back from us for that price!"

You can tell that this line of reasoning is having a real effect on Mr. Greybar and since the wife seems sold, you are determined to put the finishing touches on your argument:

"Sixty-three days ago you employed our company to act as your agent in locating a purchaser for your home. During that time we have shown it to many prospects, and only two of them were even interested in making an offer. Both times that offer was for $19,000! Tonight, you are no longer a seller, but a BUYER! You have your choice because I hold here in one hand (you stretch out your hand) this home, and here in the other, $19,000 (you hold out your other hand with the purchase agreement). You can either buy back your home for $19,000 or take the $19,000 cash - whichever you see fit!"

Mr. Greybar looks at your imaginary house and the contract and suddenly says:

"Much as I hate to admit it, you both have some pretty sound arguments there. However, my wife and I would like to think this over until tomorrow."

HOW TO COMMAND THE "THINK IT OVER" REBUTTAL

You are once again faced with this "think it over" situation! You and Joe Barber know that permitting people to think things over will generally cause them to justify their actions and miss the opportunities they really want. Therefore, you determine not to let this happen!

"Mr. Greybar, I wish we could honestly give you the time to think it over, but that is not our prerogative. Despite the fact this deposit receipt does seem to indicate you can take three days to think about the offer, the truth is that this agreement is completely invalid without your signatures and may be withdrawn at any time by the Carters! If the Carters were to call us while we are sitting here tonight before you had signed the contract, and wanted to change their minds, we would be obliged to return the $1800 and the agreement to them. Nothing you could do or say at that point could change the decision! You see, you do not have even one second after I receive that call to accept the offer. Since the buyer has a right to change his mind, I believe it would be a serious mistake on your part to delay accepting their offer to purchase. Have we not reviewed everthing you would consider, even if you waited until tomorrow?"

At this point you have placed the contract again in front of Mr. Greybar with a pen close at hand and while waiting for him to sign, you relate a true story. You tell them about a couple who did stop to think it over and lost the sale as a result. These third-party true stories (and they should never be false) will lend great impact to any sales point you want to make. People can accept and laugh at the mistakes others make much easier than they can at their own.

The effect of your presentation and sound arguments has finally reached its mark, and Mr. Greybar picks up the pen and as he does so you say:

"You may approve the contract here," pointing to the "X" you placed on the appropriate line earlier in the evening. Then Mrs. Greybar signs, and you pick up the completed agreement.

YOUR CONTRACT IS CONFIRMED

As you hand the Greybars a copy of the agreement for their records, you congratulate them on the wisdom of their decision and express your hope that their move east will be pleasant. You assure them that upon completing the trade-in arrangements, you will immediately call and convey the information. You explain that if all goes well, they can probably sign final papers within 10 to 12 days.

Your sale was the result of careful and professional effort which utilized the very finest techniques in closing real estate contracts. Many sales will be much easier to make, a few somewhat more difficult, but all of them will deserve the same type of planning and preparation given this one tonight. Very few salesmen in this business can succeed today without exerting the refinements of professional salesmanship and knowledge!

OTHER CLOSING TECHNIQUES TO REMEMBER

Although you wielded many of the basic closing tools used by expert real estate salesmen, there are a few other ideas you might consider when needed. One of them is the use of "cash" attached to the purchase agreement, particularly when you can obtain substantial amounts. Nothing impresses a seller quite as much as large amounts of cash! I know of a sale made solely on the strength of the ten $1,000 bills which the real estate agent clipped to the deposit agreement. Once it was placed in the hands of the seller, she was unwilling to release it and had to sign the contract! If you need the power of money to help close, have your buyer permit you to exchange his check for cash before presenting the offer to the seller.

Once in a while, you will want to use the principle of letting one mate sell the other, the same as you will do with buyers. If one of the owners wants the sale, and the other is on the fence, let them have a moment by themselves to review the merits of your offer.

The competitive property report form (see page 52) has great value in convincing sellers to realize their true position as related to other homes and when needed, it should be prepared and used for the closing session, the same as it is for the listing session.

Reducing minor differences to their simplest terms when negotiating price variances can help to convince sellers they are being foolish to quibble over small amounts. A few hundred dollars spread over the life of a mortgage, or weighed against the advantages of a firm decision can frequently seem absurd, even to the owner. We used this principle tonight when showing the owner that $500 was only 12 cents per day over the life of a normal mortgage!

One of the strongest arguments you can use is that of relating the past enjoyments and pleasures of real estate ownership to the minor depreciation experienced upon selling. People will gladly accept as much as $1000 per year loss on the sale of an automobile simply for the pleasure of owning a new car with all its comfort and beauty. How much more should they be willing to take a small depreciation in the value of their homes when one considers the greater living pleasures and experiences connected with real property! You can relate examples of automobile depreciation to the minor variations in real estate values to accent the point and show how these small amounts are well worth the pleasures we have derived from our residences.

In some real estate markets, a substantial decrease in values has occurred for reasons no real estate salesman can control. When employment is low, or when several other factors combine to depress the demand for real estate, a salesman often needs very convincing arguments to show a seller why he must sell for much less than he paid for a property. Graphic charts showing the trends in the area, together with figures from the local and national offices where such data is compiled, are helpful in illustrating the situation to sellers. Such market conditions require extra effort and every bit of information you can compile, especially visual aids, to assist you in showing owners their true positions.

Of all the arguments which wield the greatest effect on sellers, none is more potent than the "peace of mind" benefits of making a decision. As explained earlier, people want things made easy for them and anything which can reduce the pain or uncertainty of life will generally be received with favor. When you stress the advantages of completing a transaction for the basic mental relief such decision will afford, you are striking a motivation every seller understands. It is difficult to keep a home spotless and open for inspection at all hours of the day. It is frustrating to have prospects pour through a property and never know when one of them will make an offer. It is disconcerting to not know when you can move or meet other obligations connected to your real estate sale. Knowing this, you have power to convince owners they should weigh the value of a decision against the uncertainties and inconvenience of indecision!

CONVEYING ACCEPTANCE TO THE BUYER

You now have a signed acceptance of the Carters' offer to purchase 461 Harrison Avenue for $19,000. But you are not through until you have conveyed that acceptance by phone or in person to your buyers! So while still at the Greybar's, you ask permission to use their telephone and promptly relay the good news to the Carters:

"Congratulations, Mrs. Carter! You and your husband have just bought a new home! I'll be by in the morning with our trade-in manager to confirm the arrangments we discussed regarding your present property. In the meantime, have a good night's sleep! I know you will be very happy with your new home!"

Never neglect this important detail! If you fail to convey the acceptance of the offer, your buyer may not be bound by the agreement should he later decide to withdraw his offer. Communication is an important part of real estate law! You should also give your purchasers a copy of the ratified agreement, exchanging it for the one you left them which did not have the sellers' signatures. This can be done by mail or in person, but should not be overlooked.

HANDLING COUNTER-OFFERS

Although this particular transaction did not require negotiating a counter-offer, many of those you handle will. For the sake of instruction, let's suppose the Greybars were unwilling to accept the $19,000 price after all your various selling arguments had been used to no avail. How should you handle the situation? Well, first of all, remember that you want some type of signature tonight, even if it is just a counter for full price, since this gives you one more opportunity to sell your buyers or re-negotiate another offer to the sellers.

"Mr. Greybar, this is your home and you certainly have the right to determine the price you will accept for it. I'm here to do exactly what you want me to and if you want me to tear up this agreement, I will. However, we do have a buyer who wants your home, and since we are only $500 apart on price, I would suggest that we counter his offer for that amount. Aside from the small difference in price, we are in complete agreement with the buyer, are we not?"

"You are aware, of course, that if we counter his offer, we are risking the entire transaction and may lose the buyer to some other property. However, if you are determined to take a chance of losing this sale, then let's do so by taking a positive action. Let's lose it by trying to improve it!"

These and other arguments can be used to extract a counter offer to your buyer, thus giving you another chance to make the sale. If you are successful, you would then promptly call the Carters to allay their fears and make an immediate appointment to see them. Your call might go something like this:

"Mr. Carter, will you be there for the next hour? I would like to drop by and discuss your new home!"

As in the case of the sellers, you never discuss the offer over the phone. When you arrive at the buyer's home, you want to treat the changes as though they are perfectly normal and nothing to discourage completion of the sale! Some of the ways you can handle this are as follows:

"Mr. and Mrs. Carter, the sellers felt they could not accept less than $19,500 for their home, but they have given you an exclusive option to purchase it for that figure! Just initial here, and it will be yours!"

If you meet resistance, you can use many selling arguments to convince them they should go ahead with the transaction. Sometimes you must go back over each step of your original closing techniques and re-emphasize the benefits, amenities and advantages this property will offer them. Here are some points you might make in the event you needed to re-sell them:

1. "Mr. and Mrs. Carter, are you going to buy this home for someone else? Right now you, the sellers and myself are the only ones who know they are willing to accept the figure they have granted to you as an option on their home. If you do not accept it, by tomorrow morning every real estate salesman in our office will know that the Greybars will take this much less for their home than the listed price. Someone else may own the property due to your efforts!"

2. "We could look through another hundred homes and not find one as well suited to your requirements as this one, don't you agree? Would you let the $500 involved prevent you from enjoying this fine residence?"

3. "Stop to consider what we are really talking about, Mr. Carter! Five hundred dollars! Why, do you realize that is only $3.66 per month over the life of the mortgage! Isn't it worth that small amount each month to enjoy the benefits this property can offer you and Mrs. Carter?"

4. "When we were reviewing your needs the other night, you informed me that the house you wanted had to have . . . (and you list their specifications). Now this home has these features, doesn't it? Let's end your house-hunting worries by accepting this contract from the Greybars!"

5. "You know we are really talking about a very small amount of money, Mr. Carter. Just $500! Let me ask you, when was the last time you bought a car?" (He replies and you continue.)
"You undoubtedly paid $3,000 or more for the car at that time, isn't that right?" (He nods.)
"Now, I'm sure you have experienced a loss of $500 or more, each year since then in sheer depreciation of your car! The reason you are willing to take that depreciation is because the car produces a certain amount of enjoyment and luxury in your life, don't you agree?" (Again, he nods.)
"Now, how much more so will that be of this home! Suppose you had to write off $500 a year on a home for the one you really wanted to enjoy. Wouldn't it be worth it if it were the right home? But you and I know we are not talking about losing $500, because this home is worth the price you are paying and probably will not depreciate more than the increased land value each year. But if it does, it will certainly not be $500 a year! You see, a home is more than an investment! It is part of your life and it brings joys which no dollar amount can truly measure.
"If you are willing to take a much bigger depreciation and decrease of your investment on other luxuries, isn't it reasonable to assume that owning a home should be valued on a similar basis?"

Finally, there is the third party story and other closing techniques which you might want to employ if required. In any event, remember that you treat a counter offer as a "partial confirmation of a sale" so that the buyer does not have to make the major decision again. <u>He has already agreed to buy.</u> Now it is only a question of approving the minor changes necessitated by the seller's situation. If approached with confidence, you can generally close any counter offer which is within reasonable limits of the original offer!

ALL CHANGES MUST BE INITIALED

To be valid, all changes on a contract must be initialed by the purchasers and returned to the other parties before the transaction is considered binding. The same rules about conveying acceptance on the initial offer apply to any counters made by buyer or seller. All parties must know that an "unconditional acceptance of the final contract" has been effected.

It is often advisable, after making several initialed changes and receiving ratification from the parties participating in the sale, to redraft the agreement and obtain new signatures as a method of eliminating any possible misinterpretation in the future. Your first contract will probably be valid, but the moment you get new contracts signed eliminating the messy items, you will have firmly bound the parties to the final agreement.

COUNTEROFFER

(Written on the reverse side of the deposit receipt or purchase agreement)

Date: July 10th, 19 -

We accept the offer on the reverse hereof with the following changes and modifications.

1. The purchase price shall be increased to $19,500.00.
2. The escrow on this sale must close by August 15, 19 -.

All other terms and conditions are to remain the same. This counteroffer shall remain in effect until 12:00 P.M. midnight July 12, 19 -.

Signed: John H. Greybar
Sally A. Greybar

Accepted by buyers this 11th day of July, 19 -.

Signed: Edward Joseph Carter
Mary Elizabeth Carter

YOUR NIGHT'S WORK IS DONE

As you head home, you can be justly proud of the contract you hold in your possession. The objectives of the Carters and the Greybars were achieved as a result of your persistance and thoroughness! Tomorrow, you will complete the trade-in arrangements and proceed to open escrow after confirming with the Greybars that everything has been settled. You know that this sale will close successfully because you have done your job completely! Act IV is just about over and now the stage hands, under your supervision, will move on the scene to clean up the details. You do not plan, however, to leave the theater until everyone has parted ways, content with the finale!

CLOSING THE SELLER

QUESTIONS AND PROJECTS ON CHAPTER NINE

Questions:

1. Why is it important to call for an immediate appointment to present a buyer's offer, and why should you work through the listing agent for this purpose?
2. How can you avoid discussing the amount or type of offer you have with the seller over the phone?
3. What are the advantages of thinking the offer through before presenting it to the seller?
4. What are your office policies regarding the presentation of offers on company exclusives? On other broker's exclusives? On multiple listings?
5. Why must all offers, regardless how ridiculous, be presented to a seller for his acceptance or rejection?
6. On what points must you be prepared to educate the seller about the real estate business when presenting a buyer's offer?
7. Who normally handles the initial phases of a presentation to the seller? When should the selling salesmen enter the picture? What should be his primary objective?
8. Why is it advantageous to cover contingencies in a contract before discussing the price and terms with the seller?
9. Why is it helpful to have the salesman stay calm and confident during the presentation? If the seller reacts adversely, what should you do? Why?
10. How would you handle each of the following closing objections:
    a. "We just can't accept such a low offer. We have more than that invested in our home!"
    b. "It isn't fair for us to have to consider such a low price. Your firm has only shown the property twice in 60 days!"
    c. "You shouldn't have wasted your time bringing us this offer!"
    d. "My neighbor, Bill Brown, sold for $1000 more than that offer, and his home isn't nearly as nice as ours!
    e. "Why don't you go back to your buyer and see if he will come up another $500 dollars?"
    f. "We want to think about it tonight. Call us tomorrow."
    g. "I want my lawyer (friend, etc.) to look this contract over before we sign it."
    H. "It's all right, but I want to change the possession date from Feb. 1 to March 1.

Projects:

1. When you obtain your next (or first) offer, ask your broker to go with you and observe the techniques he uses in closing the seller. Also ask permission to go with one of the senior salesmen in your office on a closing when the listing or selling salesman is not able to go and

CLOSING THE SELLER

then quietly listen to the closing procedures employed by the more experienced man. (Note: It is unwise for more than two to attend a closing, as the sellers may feel undue pressure is being placed on them and become uneasy about the entire matter.)

2. What are the six things you should review before presenting an offer? Review each of them and analyze their importance.
3. What are your office policies regarding the presentation of offers? How does your broker desire you to handle out-of-town owners?
4. When the next sale or two are closed in your office, ask the participating salesmen to relate how they handled the closing of the seller and their personal observations about the problems involved.
5. List your closing approaches with a seller under the following situations:
   a. Seller wants more money than your offer, but you know this offer is realistic based on market activity.
   b. Seller is not convinced your office has tried hard enough to sell the property, and wants to try longer to expose it to other buyers.
   c. The buyer's qualifications concern the seller and he does not want to take his property off the market for an unworkable transaction.
   d. The offer is based on a new FHA appraisal which has not yet been received, but seller does not want to sell for a price less than the one offered.
   e. Owner wants to review the terms of your contract with a banker friend before signing.
6. Discuss and review the following closing techniques:
   a. Reducing the amount involved to its simplest or most ridiculous terms.
   b. Showing the seller that he is now a buyer when the offer is presented.
   c. Emphasizing the peace of mind and personal benefits of making a decision now.
   d. Stressing the uncertainty of the real estate market and the shortage of buyers willing to make similar or better offers.
   e. Emphasizing the amount of activity received by the seller when this has not been extensive.
   f. Using a competitive property report form to educate the seller who believes his price is right when facts do not substantiate that conclusion.
   g. The use of third part examples to point out lost sales from delays or counter offers made by sellers.
7. Ask your instructor to review desired procedure in your office for preparing and handling counter-offers for sellers. Practice preparing counter-offer language on the back of deposit receipts.

8. Obtain factual market data about the average increase, decrease or market fluctuation of real estate values in your area, and graphically illustrate these in some form which can be used to demonstrate to sellers the truth about your current market. The U.S. Government has some statistics obtained from census reports and special surveys that may be of help. You can also check with the local representative for the Society of Residential Appraisers who will have source material to recommend.
9. How would you handle a counter offer when the buyer resisted attempts to close due to his "after buying fears?" List the various techniques you might use and review them with your broker or instructor.
10. Discuss with your broker how to utilize deposit amounts to assist you in closing the sale, and the merit of handing cash or large checks to the owner when presenting an offer lower than listed price.

10

HOW TO BUILD A PERSONAL REFERRAL BUSINESS

In one of the finest articles ever written about our real estate profession, Robert Brady in his book Real Estate, It's Wonderful[1] tells the story about a paper hanger he employed during the depression years while remodeling a home. Mr. Brady had allotted only 25¢ a roll for hanging wallpaper as it was an old home and one in which he could not afford extensive investment. When he returned to inspect the paper hanger's work, he was surprised and pleased to see the outstanding quality of work which had been done. Mr. Brady asked the paper hanger why he had gone to so much trouble to do a superior job when he was being paid so little! He replied:

"Mr. Brady, when I was just a little boy, my father impressed upon me that I could expect to get as my next job one no better than the last one I had done -- so I always try to do my very best!"

This paper hanger had learned one of the greatest lessons of life. If I could only tattoo that truth on the forehead of every real estate salesman I hire, both of us would be immeasurably richer. Someone once said:

"Doing little things well is the first step toward doing big things better." In the real estate business, nothing you do will have a more lasting effect on your success than the manner in which you service your clients, customers, sales, listings, and other business details. Whenever you obtain a listing or make a sale, your work has not ended -- it has only begun. It is how you take care of that listing or sale that will determine both your present and future success. How often have I seen salesmen complete a transaction and think their jobs were done, leaving all the vital clean-up work to others, or worse -- undone. Even if others are involved, the salesman should still be concerned with title reports, loan commitments, bank appraisals, mortgage processing, termite inspections, and escrow closings. You should look for ways to prevent errors, protect your clients, and speed the processing. Even

---

[1] Institute of Real Estate Brokers, National Association of Real Estate Boards, 39 Wabash Street, Chicago, Illinois.

if you are not required to do these things yourself, you should know that they are being done by someone, and be ready to assist when required.

SERVICING AFTER YOUR SALE

Possibly you have heard the saying:

"Why is it a man never has time to do a thing right the first time, but always time to do it over again?"

In this business, if you don't do it right the first time, you may not have a second chance. Many lost sales and unhappy clients have been buried under the good intentions of careless salesmen. Prompt and efficient attention to the obligations attendant with your new sale will prevent needless problems and potential disagreements in the future. You have sold Mr. and Mrs. Carter a home, but there are many things yet to do before you can collect your commission. Having delivered ratified copies of the agreement to buyers and sellers, your next duty is to see that the escrow is opened or the attorneys contacted who will handle the title transfer arrangements. In some brokerage firms, this obligation remains the responsibility of the listing or selling salesman, while in others the broker or escrow manager handles this task for the sales staff. In either case, the salesman is still responsible to deliver proper instructions and documents to the officer who will function in this capacity. I recommend the use of some type of deposit or escrow check list for your personal guidance in supervising these vital details.

CHECK LIST OF ESCROW DETAILS

Here is a list of things you should review when opening an escrow or submitting a sale for someone else to process.

1. Full names of sellers and the manner in which title is now vested.
2. Sellers' address and phone number.
3. Full names of buyers and instructions on how they want title vested.
4. Buyers' current address and phone number.
5. Address and legal description of property sold, together with copy of deed or other papers helpful to escrow holder.
6. Confirmation of exact sales price and all terms of sale necessary to complete the transaction.
7. The amount of the deposit held by the agent and its disposition.
8. The amount of additional cash needed to complete the escrow and dates when expected.

Note: On the above item, many purchases are started with token deposits, notes, or escrow assignments, and it is the salesman's duty to see that the buyer secures the balance as specified, including helping him obtain it, if necessary.

HOW TO BUILD A PERSONAL REFERRAL BUSINESS

9. The existing balance of any mortgage on subject property, together with the names and addresses of mortgagees or beneficiaries and loan numbers.
10. If termite or dryrot inspections are required, instructions on who is to order them and how costs will be handled.
11. Proration date to be used for taxes, insurance, interest, rents, and so on.
12. If there is an existing loan trust impound account, how is it to be handled? Normally, after prorations, it is returned to the seller.
13. Copies of existing fire insurance policies together with the name and address of present agent.
14. Instructions from the buyer on new fire insurance policies or assumption of existing amounts.
15. Possession date of the premises as understood by buyers and sellers, plus any instructions for collecting rents or executing occupancy agreements in escrow.
16. List of any additional liens, assessments, encumbrances, or bills which are to be paid from the sellers' proceeds.
17. Name of the title company, escrow company, or attorney to be used.
18. Name, address, and phone number of any cooperating broker involved.
19. Amount of commission to be paid and basis of distribution to cooperating brokers.
20. Definition of any special instructions for completing the purchase agreement.
21. Time limit for performance of the agreement and completion of the escrow.
22. List of personal property involved, including an inventory and requesting a bill of sale to the buyer.
23. If new financing for the buyer is involved, the following items must be arranged:
    a. Credit report and loan application.
    b. Verification documents for employment, deposit, and the like.
    c. Other papers necessary to satisfy the lender or government agency.

CLOSING THE ESCROW OR COMPLETING THE TRANSFER

I believe the salesman should always be present at the closing of the sales he originates. To build a referral business, you should render complete assistance in all phases of the transaction, including the final closing. If questions or disputes arise in these moments, you can settle them and calm the fears of those participating. Your concern for the buyer or seller will result in additional bonds for future business

DEPOSIT RECEIPT CHECK OFF LIST
(Please fill in completely and have all agents initial the commission split)

GENERAL DATA:
PROPERTY ADDRESS: _____
____/____ 19____ DATE SIGNED FOUR WAYS   M.L.S. # _____   S & S # _____
____/____ 19____ DATE SALE SUBMITTED TO OFFICE
_____ SELLER   ADDRESS _____ CITY _____
_____ STATE _____, Bus. Ph. _____ Res. Ph. _____
                       BUYER   ADDRESS _____ CITY _____
                       STATE _____, Bus. Ph. _____ Res. Ph. _____

LOAN & ESCROW DATA:

YES NO
☐   ☐   SOLD "SUBJECT-TO-SALE" of another property. ☐ Trade-Department notified.
☐   ☐   New Loan being obtained through: _____, Representative _____
☐   ☐   Present first loan held by: _____, Branch _____, Loan # _____
☐   ☐   Present second loan held by: _____, Address _____
☐   ☐   Bill of sale needed for: ☐ Items on D/R,   ☐ Items on attached list.
☐   ☐   Fire insurance to be prorated and assigned to buyer.   ☐ Policy attached hereto.
☐   ☐   Buyer taking new insurance from _____ Agents Phone # _____
☐   ☐   Termite report required: ☐ Ordered from _____, or, ☐ To be ordered by
         Escrow Dept. Inspection fee to be paid for by   ☐ Buyer, or   ☐ Seller
☐   ☐   Rental Agreement: ☐ Agreement included in terms of deposit receipt, or ☐ Rental
         agreement attached hereto, or ☐ to be drafted by Escrow Dept. on terms of $_____
         per ☐ day ☐ month; rent starting on _____ 19____ with $_____ payable in
         advance, and balance payable as follows: _____
☐   ☐   Trust fund to be ☐ assigned to purchaser, or ☐ returned to seller.
☐   ☐   Specific proration date (if any) _____ 19____ .
☐   ☐   Specific closing date (if any) _____ 19____ .
☐   ☐   FHA Valuation Statement attached.   ☐ Point slip attached.   ☐ Loan App. attached.
☐   ☐   Key for new buyer is located at _____
☐   ☐   Seller to be reimbursed for appraisal fee advanced for buyer.
☐   ☐ $25.00 attached by seperate check for appraisal fee.
☐   ☐   Escrow opened by Listing Office: Title Co. _____ Br. _____ Escrow # _____

         General Escrow Instructions: _____

COMMISSION DATA:			TRADE LISTING: ☐ YES ☐ NO	
GROSS COMMISSION	%____	$____	Trade Fee	%____ $____
LESS: Spec. Reduction	%____	$____	Photo Listing Fee	$____
Referral Fee	%____	$____	To:	____
Multiple Fee	%____	$____	Address:	____
Split to Co-op Broker	%____	$____	To:	____
NET COMMISSION (Divide)	%____	$____	Address:	____
Listing Agent	%____	$____	Agent ____	(initials) ____
Listing Agent	%____	$____	Agent ____	(initials) ____
Selling Agent	%____	$____	Agent ____	(initials) ____
Stone & Schulte	%____	$____	MGR ____	(initials) ____
Special (explain)	%____	$____	Explanation: ____	

STONE & SCHULTE, INC. PROCESSING CONTROL RECORD

RESL. DEPT.	JAN	FEB	MAR	APR	MAY	JUN	JUL	AUG	SEP	OCT	NOV	DEC
SUBD. DEPT.												
COML. DEPT.												

	Credit Application	Prelim. Reports	Loan Package	Credit Report	Subm. to Lender	Subm. to Gov't	Gov't Appraisal	Termite Report	Loan Papers	Funds Disb.	Property Appraisal	Trade Guaranty	Contract Contingency	Special (See Remarks)

PURCHASER: _____ PURCHASERS AGENT: _____

SELLER: _____ SELLERS AGENT: _____

LOT #: _____ DEVELOPMENT: _____ TRACT #: _____ UNIT #: _____ BUILDER: _____ PROPERTY ADDRESS: _____ CITY: _____

INVENTORY:
- M.L.S.# _____ EXCL. # _____
- DATE LISTED _____ 19__ DATE SOLD _____
- DATE EXPIRES _____ 19__ REPORTED TO M.L.S. _____
- DATE EXTENDED TO _____ 19__ DATE SALE D.F.T.'D _____
- DATE CANCELLED _____ 19__ D.F.T. REPTED TO M.L.S. _____
- LIST PRICE $_____ ☐ OFF INVENTORY ☐ OFF MASTER LOG
- REVISED LIST PRICE $_____ ☐ BULLETIN LIST ☐ CROSS REF. CDS.
- TYPE OF CONTRACT _____ ☐ KARDEX COMPLETED

☐ MASTER LOG ☐ TOUR SHEET
☐ INVENTORY ☐ S-S SEARCH
☐ TYPED ☐ DISTRIBUTED
☐ TO M.L.S. ☐ M.L.S. FEE LOG

ACCOUNTING:
DEPOSIT RECEIVED _____ 19__
POSTED TO SALES LOG _____ 19__
DEPOSIT AT: ☐ Ti. Co. ☐ Other Brk. _____

EXCHANGE-A-PLAN: TRADE # _____
PROPERTY: _____ CITY: _____
☐ DATE CONTINGENT LISTING EXPIRES _____ 19__
DATE OF PERFORMANCE ON GUARANTEE _____ 19__
DATE SOLD TO: _____
ESTIMATED CLOSING DATE _____

TRADER: _____ SERVICER: _____

ESCROW:
_____ OFFICER _____
CONTINUATION # _____ COMPANION # _____
TITLE CO. _____ BRANCH _____
PRELIMS ORDERED _____ 19__ Rec'd PREL. ____ C.C.&R's ____ RECIPIENT _____
I.D. STMT. REQ. _____ 19__
LN. PAYOFFS ORDERED _____ 19__
BRO. DEM'D TO TI. CO. _____ 19__
SALESMEN NOTIFIED _____ 19__
FUNDS DISBURSED _____ 19__ STONE & SCHULTE _____
ESCROW CANCELLED _____ 19__ TOTAL ORDERED _____

"PRELIMINARY REPORTS:

SPECIAL ESCROW COST DISTRIBUTION:
ITEM	AMOUNT	CHARGE	CREDIT
CREDIT REPORTS	$	$	$
APPRAISAL FEES	$	$	$
TERMITE INSPECTION	$	$	$
LOAN PACKAGING FEE	$	$	$

OCCUPANCY TERMS: $_____ PER DAY/MO. FROM _____ 19__

LOAN:
FNM# _____ CRV# _____
APPRAISAL ORDERED FROM: _____ 19__
APPRAISAL RECEIVED $_____ 19__ _____ YEARS
STANDARD LOAN APPLICATION RECEIVED _____ 19__ Rec'd ☐
CREDIT REPORT ORDERED FROM: _____ 19__
LOAN PACKAGE RECEIVED _____ 19__
LOAN SUBMITTED TO: _____ 19__
LENDER APPROVED AT _____ 19__ _____ % DISCOUNT
SUBM. TO GOVT _____ 19__ TO: _____
APPROVED BY GOVT _____ 19__ TO: _____
LOAN PAPERS REC'D _____ 19__ TO: _____
PAPERS TO TI. CO. _____ 19__

DEPOSIT RECEIPTS:

TERMITE INSPECTION: FROM: _____
ORDERED _____ 19__ RECEIVED _____ 19__
REMARKS:

TERMS OF SALE:
DOWN PAYMENT $_____
FIRST LOAN - TYPE: _____ $_____
SECOND LOAN - TYPE: _____ $_____
SALES PRICE - REMARKS: $_____

_____ 19__ PERFORMANCE DATE

PHOTO-COPY DISTRIBUTION: ☐ PURCHASERS AGENT ☐ SELLERS AGENT
☐ BUILDER ☐ SALES MGR — ☐ GEN'L ☐ INC ☐ RSL ☐ SUB

NOTES:

relations. The professional does not leave the scene until all the details have been satisfactorily solved and completed.

After the sale is closed, it is wise to personally deliver the check and closing statement to the seller or buyer. Any extra assistance you can render above the call of duty will stand out in sharp contrast to actions your customers may have expected. Such little things as helping your buyers arrange for gas, electric, water, and garbage service will be appreciated far beyond the minor investment in time and effort represented. You might even consider using a pre-printed list of instructions for purchasers with helpful tips on arranging the move to new quarters.

Do not overlook the matter of obtaining the keys from the sellers and delivering them to the buyers. Then after your purchasers have announced their possession date to you, arrange to notify the neighbors by direct mail of the new homeowners they will meet. The "Know Your Neighbor" Card (see page 201) is an effective means of achieving this goal. It is an excellent public relations tool, as well as advertising medium for your company, which usually leads to many new listings from the surrounding neighbors.

BUILDING A REFERRAL BUSINESS

A story is told about a young farmer boy from the Midwest who applied for a sales position with a major shoe company in St. Louis, Missouri. It seems this tall, lanky fellow walked into the sales manager's office responding to an advertisement they had featured for a traveling salesman. Being fresh off the farm, he did not look like a salesman, and the manager was being polite when he asked:

"Wilbur, what makes you think you can sell shoes?"

In his colloquial manner, the young man replied:

"Well, sir, I don't know much about selling shoes, but I do know how to plow, and one thing I learned in plowin' was to always plow straight to the end of my furrow!"

This answer impressed the sales manager, and after an extensive interview he decided to give young Wilbur Dawson a chance. A territory in the Ozarks had just been vacated by the previous representative who wired the main office in desperation:

"I resign! Nobody here wears shoes!"

Wilbur took over the assignment, and three weeks later wired the office:

"Wonderful territory: Everybody needs shoes!"

As it turned out, Wilbur did the impossible and sold shoes by the thousands, breaking all records and establishing himself as a hero of the company. The following year he was asked by his sales manager to relate his success story before the entire sales staff at their annual convention. Wilbur was no public speaker, and he accepted the request with reservations about his ability to address such a powerful group.

HOW TO BUILD A PERSONAL REFERRAL BUSINESS 201

Mr. & Mrs. Donald Hood
458 Harrison Avenue
San Jose, California

Would <u>YOU</u> Like to . . .

KNOW <u>YOUR</u> NEIGHBOR!

We have just recently sold to
Mr. & Mrs. Joseph Carter

461 Harrison Avenue

San Jose, California

The lovely home located near you at
461 Harrison Avenue

We feel certain that you will want to get acquainted with your new neighbor. They are another satisfied Stone & Schulte customer. Whenever we can be of service to YOU, please call on us.

Tom Stare
STONE & SCHULTE
PROFESSIONAL HOME SALES
COUNSELOR

To be sure he would not fail, he carefully memorized a ten minute speech on selling. When the day came for its delivery, he stepped before the audience and with his first look at the many faces, he promptly forgot every word he had planned to say. All he could do was just stare at them for what seemed an interminable period of time. Finally he gasped in whispered tones:

"See the people . . . see the people . . . see the people . . . !" Then he sat down. A hushed silence fell over the stunned audience and then to a man they stood and cheered -- for in one of the shortest sales speeches on record he had given them the real key to sales success: SEE THE PEOPLE!

I cannot vouch for the authenticity of this story, but I can attest to the truth of this simple formula "See the people." There is no better way to increase your effectiveness as a real estate salesman than to contact and cultivate people. There is no better way to build a referral business than to constantly be exposed to people, both those you served in the past as well as new ones you hope to serve in the future!

WHERE ARE YOU GOING?

Whenever I am interviewing a prospective salesman, I always ask him where he wants to be five years from now. His answers reveal much about his inner drives and motivations, while helping me to analyze his chances of succeeding in the real estate business. Let me ask you the same question: "Where do you want to be five years from now?"

Many salesmen have vague ideas about wanting more money, greater prestige, and more knowledge, but very few are willing to do those things which will automatically assure the attainment of their professed goals. Success is earned, not stolen! Great men have always realized this fact. Henry Wadsworth Longfellow phrased it well when he wrote:

> The heights by great men reached and kept,
> Were not attained by sudden flight -
> But they, while their companions slept,
> Were toiling upward in the night.

It is true that you can see big things with one eye closed, but little things are seen only with both eyes wide open. In business, as in life, the little things mark the great dividing line between success and failure. Let me ask you: what is the real difference between the professional real estate salesman and the average man? Is it not the fact that he has served his customers well and for this continues to merit their friendship and support? Is it not the fact that he has many satisfied clients because he took care of the little things which were important to his customers.

Henry Ford emphasized this point when he said:

" The great trouble today is that there are too many people looking for someone else to do something for them. The solution of most of our troubles is to be found in everyone doing something for himself! "

I sincerely believe this! If you will concentrate your efforts on doing the little things for yourself which improve your relations with others, you will be unable to prevent the flood of business such dedication will inspire! If you want to become a professional who enjoys the full rewards of his career and who wins the confidence of his clientele, channel your energies into taking care of the details which are important to those you represent. Your greatest security for tomorrow is in building a referral business today.

How do you build a referral business? Simply start by thinking about the people with whom you deal. Do you take a sincere interest in their problems and do you go out of your way to let them know you are concerned? The real professional builds a referral business because he never lets his customers forget him, and he never forgets his customers. Basic human relations techniques underly all real success in the selling world. If you want to be favorably remembered by someone, you must do something to help that person remember you. Thomas Wilson put it this way:

"Friendship is to be purchased only by friendship. A man may have authority over others, but he can never have their heart but by giving his own!"

Teddy Roosevelt once said:

"The most important single ingredient in the formula of success is knowing how to get along with people!"

WHAT ARE YOUR MOTIVES?

Some salesmen seem to have dollar signs for eyeballs! They cannot look beyond the commission dollars to see and understand the people who make their earnings possible. If your sole objective is making commission dollars, regardless of the cost, there is no way you can mask that greed from your clients. They will instinctively sense your insincere motives, and when they have no further need of your services they will shut the door on you. To cultivate and win friends, you must be motivated by a genuine desire to know, understand and assist people. When you demonstrate sincere interest in them, people respond and are drawn to you as iron is to a magnet!

This does not mean you should not value your time or maintain high financial goals. It does mean relating these objectives to the needs of your clients and striving to render your very best service to all who call upon you for advice and help. This you should do regardless of the financial, social, or racial status of the people involved. A customer who desires to rent should be given the same courteous treatment you would offer the wealthy client looking for a $50,000 home. Courtesy, friendliness, and sincere interest cost you nothing but a little effort. From such small investments come the greatest returns!

A MATTER OF MATHEMATICS

What do you see when you see a customer? Do you see one -- or many? The difference in the breadth and depth of your mental vision will directly affect your future referral business. Let me give you a brief lesson in mathematics. How many people do you think you know reasonably well? Fifty? One hundred? Two Hundred? Well, for the sake of argument, let's be ridiculous and say you only know ten people well enough to be in close confidence with them. Certainly any one of your customers will personally have that many in his own circle of influence.

Now, when you first begin your career, you will probably talk to at least two or three people a day about real estate. Many of these you will never meet, because they will be phone calls you did not control or customers you lost before you showed them homes. But out of that group, if you are average, you will have come in close personal contact with at least 14 of them every month, listing homes for 2 and selling 2 others, while losing 10 to other people or circumstances. You spent time with these 14, and should have developed prospect or client cards for personal follow-up programs. Using our rule of thumb above, each of these should know 10 people well, which means you have potentially 140 people within your sphere of influence after the first month's activity. Continuing that rate for one year, your exposure has grown to 1,680 people. Within two years it has climbed to 3,360 persons. Now, statistics indicate that at least 10% of our population moves each year in an average community. That means there will be 336 people in your sphere of influence who will transfer locations during the third year of your real estate career. Let's suppose that you could only reach 10% of these through your referral system, do you realize that you could enjoy 33 additional transactions that year without any cold turkey floor calls or personal canvassing efforts? At a conservative average of $400 per transaction to yourself, that would boost your income from referrals alone to $13,200. Impossible, you say! I can assure you it is not! I know this principle works and in this chapter I will give you examples of those who use this knowledge to earn substantial incomes and tell you how they do it.

THE CENTER OF INFLUENCE THEORY

The key to this mathematical formula for developing referral business is based on cultivating many individual "centers of influence," each working for you because you know how to help them do so. What is a center of influence? It is anyone who is able to help you extend your effective radius of activity to other people. Each satisfied customer becomes your entree to his friends, acquaintances and business associates. Some will be more valuable than others in this regard, but all are important to your continued success. In addition, you will cultivate some of your own from participation in lodges, civic groups, business associations, and other societies to which you devote a portion of your life.

How many centers of influence do you have now? Take several sheets of paper and list the names, addresses, and occupations of everyone you know or have met. Place these, upon completion, in some type of indexed referral file with notes on each card as to the nature of the contact and background information concerning your association. If you are just starting in the real estate business, send each of them a personal card or a formal announcement about your affiliation with a real estate office. You now have the beginning of a referral system which can literally become your personal gold mine!

WORKING YOUR GOLD MINE

Now let me tell you how to use your referral file to develop hundreds of future sales and listings. A Realtor friend of mine in Redwood City, California has perfected this system to unbelievable refinement and earned hundreds of thousands of dollars as a result. His name is Floyd W. Richardson, better known as "Rick," and he not only believes in a referral business, he has no time to handle anyone who is not referred to him! So effective has he found this consistent program, that he must channel new people to other salesmen and confine his efforts to his personal clientele.

When Rick first began in the real estate business as a salesman for a prominent office in his area, he made a promise to himself which he has sincerely tried to keep ever since. That promise was: "Every customer I meet will become my client for life!" This was certainly an ambitious goal, but Rick stuck with it and has built a fantastic following as a result. To start with, he set up a 3"x 5" card file index system, divided into two sections:
  1. Chronological, by months of the year
  2. Alphabetical, in sequence from "A" to "Z"

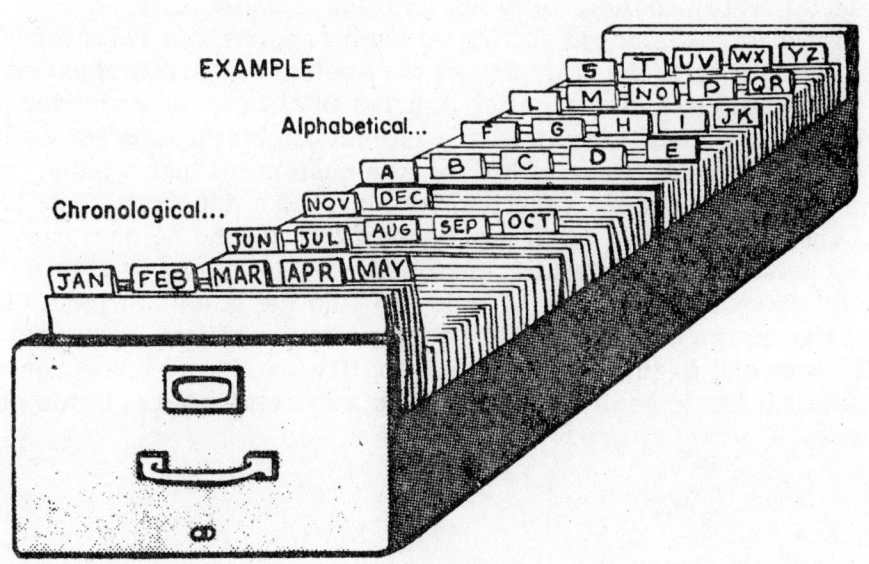

Into these alphabetical files, Rick inserted individual cards for everyone he knew when he first went to work, plus all those he met during each day of his real estate career. As he contacted buyers, showed properties, listed homes, canvassed for property, he added new cards for every person with whom he had established a basis of future relationships. On each card the following information appeared:

Name _____ Date _____

Address _____

Phone _____

Basic information: _____
_____

Notes _____
_____
_____

On the reverse side of the card, he maintained a follow-up record which provided for notes about all contacts, mailings, and other items of interest. This way he knew what had transpired in each case. The chronological cards were kept to remind Rick about the anniversaries of home purchases, birthdays, and other events which he wanted to use for future contacts.

In addition to this system, he also maintained a third record. This consisted of Polaroid pictures of each property he sold or listed pasted on the back of a listing sheet, where additional information about the buyers and sellers was added for reference. These were filed in a ring binder, alphabetically by street name, indexed for easy use when working with customers. By a visual presentation to his buyers and sellers of the many properties he personally sold or represented, he established greater confidence in his knowledge and ability.

However, it is not in setting up such records that referral volume is developed. It is in the daily use of the system to permit constant contact with the people involved. Rick carries in his pocket a slender notebook which is constantly used each day to note items of interest as they occur. If he learns that one of his former customers had a baby, recceived a promotion, took a vacation, or married a daughter -- <u>he jots it down</u>. When he receives a referral from a friend (and he has many every week) he notes who referred the customer and the names involved. Should he drive by a property he sold and find the home newly painted, he notes this in his book. When he returns to his office, he brings out his little book and begins mailing hand-written thank-you notes, or congratulation cards, to each of those he wants to remember. In his desk drawer he always has a complete selection of small cards in great variety, simple but in good taste. Some of the headings are:

"Congratulations on your New Home"
" Thank You"
" Thinking of You"
" It's Nice to Hear "
" So It's a New Baby "
" Congratulations"
... and many others.

Once each month he replenishes this supply by visiting the local stationery store, for he knows that the only way he can retain this program is by having the cards and the records at his finger tips when he wants to use them daily. That which you put off will seldom get done. To each of the people on his list he sends the appropriate card, <u>but never without first writing a personal, hand-written message inside or on the face of the card.</u> The friendly, sincere touch of personal interest has a great effect on his many friends. From his monthly contact file he extracts the names of those who bought or sold homes through him last year and he reminds them about the transaction.

> Congratulations on the anniversary of your home on Browning Avenue! I'll bet you forgot that it was a year ago this month you purchased your new home! How is everything with the Johnson Family?
>
> Your Realtor friend,
>
> Rick

People cannot resist the personal touch of those who take time to express interest and concern for others. When you add to this the spontaneous phone calls and personal contacts with these people from time to time, you have a good idea of the type of business one can build from such efforts. Treating people with the friendliness and respect for which they hunger, can only result in reciprocal interest in you and your business.

NEVER FORGET THEIR NAME

Throughout this manual, I have emphasized this one point, because it is so very important to your selling career and to life in general.

Remembering and properly using a man's name is the finest compliment you can pay him. It is difficult to do so without special effort, but the time required to master the techniques of remembering names will be well worth the invested hours. One salesman I employed mastered this business of handling people by phone, even when he could not remember their names immediately. Beside his desk was the referral file indexed as Rick Richardson suggests. When a client calls whom possibly he has not heard from in a year or more, he quickly pulls out the file card on all last names similar to the caller as given him by the office secretary. Flipping through them he brings out the appropriate ones. Then he might reply:

" Hello Mrs. Smith! How are you!" She then invariably drops some clue about their past association in the response and by then he has the right card at hand. She may be surprised to hear him say:

" Yes, Carol. It's nice to hear from you. How are Bill and your two daughters, Nancy and Susan? "

This unexpected response puts him in a class by himself and helps to build a solid referral business.

LOST SALES BUT NOT LOST CLIENTS

The first time a customer with whom you have been working tells you he bought a home from another salesman with a different company, you may be tempted to feel hurt or abused. Don't! Instead, now that a sale is lost, make up your mind to win a client for future business. Try saying something like this when he tells you about his new purchase:

" Congratulations! I'm so glad you found a home you like. Tell me all about it. Where is it located? May I stop by and see it? "

Then send them a " Congratulations on your new home " card, and put him in your personal referral file for regular contact. A year or two later, he won't even remember the fellow who sold him the home -- but he will remember you!

GIFTS AND REMEMBRANCES

Remembering a client _after_ a transaction has a more lasting effect than remembering him during it. Anything you do for him while you still have something to gain from his friendship will be considered normal, but when you no longer have any commission due and you stop by to wish him well in his new home -- you win a friend for life! It is appropriate to bring him some small token of your appreciation for his business. Such things as personalized door name plates, plastic document holders, barometers, plants, and similar items are always in good taste. Gold plated keys to the home or key cases make fine gifts. An evening out at some nice restaurant will be a special treat appreciated by your customers. To build an endless chain of referrals, always learn to thank people for their business.

DON'T NEGLECT PROBLEMS

Invariably, in the course of any business, you will incur some unhappy situations which you would have preferred to avoid. Unfortunately, they seldom go away if you ignore them. Neglecting a problem is the best way to create a bigger one. Like a wound left unattended, it will

fester and become more painful each day. Sellers and buyers become
angry, upset, and even mean when you fail to settle the problems for
which you are responsible. <u>The best, and simplest remedy is usually
direct action</u>. It is much easier to smooth out the little wrinkles in a
sale during the first few days after they originate than weeks or months
later. If some item arises which creates a misunderstanding between
buyer and seller, it is your obligation to negotiate the settlement and
calm the emotions of the parties concerned. You must be a counselor
and a buffer between buyers and sellers when they cannot handle the
difficulties which sometimes interfere with real estate transfers. You
should be willing to use the same tact and diplomacy which you demonstrated when making the sale in order to reduce or eliminate the minor
irritations of a transaction. Your thoughtfulness will frequently keep
the buyers and sellers in your camp and prevent an expensive and disagreeable deterioration of relationships.

ALWAYS KEEP EVERYONE INFORMED

Few things irritate a client more than for a real estate salesman
to forget to inform him about the processing of a sale, or the performance
of important details. Whenever you anticipate delays, immediately inform the buyers and sellers so everyone is posted about the problem. If
something must be done to expedite a case, do not assume someone else
will do it for you or that the participants know all about it. No one else
has a stronger motive than you have to build the right relations for future
business with your customers, or a greater interest in the current sale!

During the closing period, call your buyers and sellers at least
once each week, even if you have nothing to report except that everything
is on schedule. They want to hear from you and will feel better just to
know you are following the transaction closely. Stay in touch and you will
reinforce your client's trust in you and your company.

STAY ON TARGET

There is a story told about a hungry African lion who stalked the
grassy plains one evening, in search of a meal. Upon spotting a lumbering zebra, he darted across the fields towards his prey. As he was
almost there, a deer jumped from the reeds and crossed the lion's path,
causing him to quickly change his course in pursuit of this new game. A
moment later, a fat gazelle caught his eye, and he once again changed
directions to chase this potential meal. In rapid succession, the fickle
lion sped endlessly back and forth following a goat, a lamb, and hours
later, pursuing a white-tailed rabbit. The hopping bunny easily escaped
the exhausted king of beasts, leaving the monarch wiser and hungrier than
he was before.

Numerous real estate salesmen seem bent upon the same fruitless motions as this unfortunate lion! They never really know where to
turn for additional business, or how to take care of that which they have

in sight, and so they run aimlessly across the market place searching for prospects and clients without ever finding a satisfying source of business. Why? Because they are like the shepherd who drives the sheep in the front door of the barn while leaving the back door unlatched! They do not take care of the prospects they have and cannot settle on a course which will assure them of repeat repasts in the future.

I hope you are not one of those who fail to recognize the simple truths about real estate selling -- or any selling, for that matter. Take care of the business at hand and pursue one objective at a time if you would hope to dine well tomorrow. When you are blessed with a prospect who needs your services or a seller who commands professional help, render the talents and knowledge required without questioning the dollars attached. Be like my friend Rick, and upon finding a customer, make him "yours for life" by serving his interests well and remembering him even when commission dollars have been spent.

QUESTIONS AND PROJECTS FOR CHAPTER TEN

Questions:

1. Why is a substantial referral business extremely valuable to any salesman?
2. What is the principle underlying rule involved in developing a referral business?
3. What things can you do to help people remember you and be interested in you?
4. What part does personal motive play in helping you influence and cultivate a clientele?
5. What part does mathematics play in building a referral business?
6. How many people should you see or talk to each day in order to reach your goals in the real estate business?
7. What is a center of influence? How can you locate them? When you have developed one, how do you retain that center of influence as a force for your progress?
8. What are the merits of maintaining an adequate system of records for customer follow up?
9. How can you stay in touch with your customers and clients and make them feel you are more than just an average real estate salesman?
10. Why is the quality of professional workmanship an important part of your referral program? How can you assure yourself that you are doing a professional job?

Projects:

1. Buy an index file with 3" x 5" cards and begin developing a system of staying in contact with your prospects, sellers, and friends.
2. List all the people you have ever met, or known before you entered the real estate business, and put them in your referral file.

HOW TO BUILD A PERSONAL REFERRAL BUSINESS

3. Send each of those you have named some type of personal handwritten note to advise them you are in the real estate business and re-establish your contact.
4. Buy a quantity of small remembrance cards of various types and put them in your desk drawer where they will be quickly available for use when the occasion arises.
5. Consider designing some type of personal note pad or form which personalizes your own memos to clients and friends. Use them for the frequent handwritten notes you will send to various individuals.
6. Practice saying thank-you personally and in writing whenever anyone does something for you, such as referring a customer to you, or a listing contact.
7. Discuss with fellow salesmen and your broker various ways they have found successful to build a referral business.
8. Review your known centers of influence and ask yourself these questions:
    a. Am I staying in touch with each of them so that they will think of me when the next real estate deal comes along?
    b. Have I sent them written notes and messages to thank them for past business and expressed interest in their activities?
    c. Have I used gifts and other items to cement my personal relationships with these key people?
    d. Have I performed professional work that is worthy of their consideration?
9. Practice improving your memory for names and faces. This is a vital aspect of selling, and the more effective you are in recalling people's names, backgrounds, and interests, the easier your task of cultivating them will be. Memory courses are available in many areas, as well as excellent books on the subject. Ask the advice of those who seem to be able to do a superior job of remembering names how they achieve their proficiency in this area of personal performance.
10. List all the things you can personally do to improve the quality and excellence of your real estate activities. Nothing will bring you more business more quickly than the improvement of your professional services to the public.

11

FINANCING YOUR REAL ESTATE SALES

Financing is to a real estate transaction what a transfusion can be to a patient. It can put life into a sale which might not survive without it. For that reason, a working knowledge of financing is essential to any real estate salesman. Unfortunately, we can not possibly do justice to such a complex and vital subject as mortgage financing in the limited space we have allotted this chapter. However, I hope what we do say will stimulate your interest in this fascinating aspect of the real estate business, challenging your desire to learn more about creative ways to finance property.

Permit me to begin by reviewing a little of the history of the mortgage market in the United States. This country has done more to promote home ownership through liberal financing than any other nation in the world. Availability of mortgage credit is one of the reasons why, today, more than 60% of all American families own or are buying their own residences. Today's relaxed lending policies make it possible for almost anyone with good credit and a reasonable employment pattern to obtain a home with a very small cash investment. This has not always been true. As the following chart reveals, home ownership has grown consistently since 1890 when only 36.9% of American families had title to property. Now 62% or more enjoy the privileges and freedom afforded by owner occupancy.

FINANCING YOUR REAL ESTATE SALES

TABLE I[1]

Year	U.S. Population	Occupied Dwellings	Owner Occupied	Percentage Owned	Percentage Rented
1890	62,948,000	7,922,973	2,923,671	36.9	63.1
1900	76,094,000	10,274,127	3,556,809	34.6	65.4
1910	92,407,000	14,131,945	5,245,380	37.1	62.9
1920	106,466,000	17,600,472	7,041,238	40.0	60.0
1930	123,077,000	23,300,026	10,549,972	45.3	54.7
1940	131,954,000	27,747,973	11,413,036	41.1	58.9
1950	151,228,000	37,105,259	19,801,646	53.4	46.6
1955	164,607,000	42,280,000	24,100,000	57.0	43.0
1959	176,421,000	46,125,000	28,000,000	61.0	39.0
1963	181,310,000	49,212,000	32,511,400	62.0	38.0

[1] U.S. Department of Commerce, Bureau of the Census; Council of Economic Advisers; U.S. Savings and Loan League.

Most of the mortgage loans made prior to 1930 were non-amortized short term loans with due dates ranging from five to fifteen years. Buyers had to have substantial amounts of cash often (40% to 50%) in order to purchase homes. These high cash requirements made it extremely difficult for those with limited funds to acquire property. A young married couple could not expect to own their home until they had saved a sizable down payment. The following chart shows this trend by relating the number of homes free of mortgages in the years from 1890 to 1963.

TABLE II[2]

Year	Owner-occupied Dwelling Units	Percentage Free of mortgage	Percentage Mortgaged
1890	2,923,671	72.0	28.0
1900	3,566,809	68.0	32.0
1910	5,245,380	67.0	33.0
1920	7,041,283	60.0	40.0
1930	10,549,972	Not available	Not available
1940	11,413,036	55.0	45.0
1950	19,801,646	55.0	45.0
1959	28,000,000	44.0	56.0
1963	32,511,400	42.0	58.0

[2] U.S. Savings and Loan League.

The situation was dramatically changed after 1934, the year in which the Congress of the United States created the Federal Housing Administration by the enactment of the National Housing Act. The FHA was created to stimulate home ownership by insuring lending institutions against certain losses which might occur from making specific types of real estate and improvement loans. It made possible, by Federal law, the offering of insured loans with lower down payments, lower interest rates, and longer amortization periods; this decreased the monthly payments required to buy a home. The experience of FHA since that year has gradually convinced other lending agencies and institutions that most Americans can be trusted to meet their mortgage obligations, even when little or no cash has been invested, providing there is a reasonable credit control and employment pattern established for individual borrowers.

Today, as will be explained in this chapter, a home buyer can readily secure twenty to forty year financing of various types with low interest rates and relatively small down payments, providing his credit and income status show a reasonable relationship to the mortgage payments. As a result, home ownership is within the reach of more than 80% of all families in America. In this chapter, we will analyze the basic categories of real estate financing and discuss some of their advantages and disadvantages.

BASIC TYPES OF RESIDENTIAL FINANCING

Most residential financing can be divided into three categories:

1. Conventional financing
2. Insured or government financing
3. Private and secondary financing

Eliminating private and secondary financing for the moment, the next chart will clearly show that conventional financing has dominated the real estate market over the years, reaching its lowest points in 1947 and 1955. VA financing did not come into existence until 1944, following World War II.

TABLE III[3]

Percentage Distribution Home Mortgages

Year	Conventional	VA	FHA	Total
1940	81	--	19	100
1945	89	3	8	100
1950	66	19	15	100
1955	64	25	11	100
1956	68	22	10	100
1957	75	16	9	100
1958	76	7	17	100
1959	72	9	19	100
1963	79	8	13	100

[3] Housing and Home Finance Agency; U.S. Savings and Loan League.

1. CONVENTIONAL LOANS

On an average over these years, conventional lending has accounted for more than 70% of all residential loans, excluding any private financing. The term, conventional loans, is generally applied to those mortgages made by lending institutions without the benefit of government insurance or assistance. Conventional financing has been consistently dominated by savings and loan associations, with a marked increase since 1952, as shown by Table IV.

TABLE IV[4]

Mortgage Loan Recordings by Type of Lender

Year	Savings & Loan	Mutual Savings Banks	Commercial Banks	Insurance Companies	All Others	Total
1940	31.8%	4.2%	25.0%	8.3%	30.7%	100.0%
1945	35.8	3.8	19.4	4.4	36.6	100.0
1950	31.3	6.6	20.8	10.0	31.3	100.0
1955	36.7	6.5	19.7	6.8	30.3	100.0
1956	35.2	6.7	20.2	6.6	31.3	100.0
1957	38.0	5.9	17.6	6.1	32.4	100.0
1958	38.4	6.0	19.0	5.3	31.3	100.0
1959	40.6	5.5	18.1	4.7	31.1	100.0
1963	42.5	6.0	18.0	6.5	27.0	100.0

[4] Federal Home Loan Bank Board; U.S. Savings and Loan League.

Savings and loan associations are of two primary types: <u>Federal chartered</u> and <u>State chartered</u>. Federal savings and loan companies can always be easily identified as they must affix the word <u>Federal</u> to their public name. In California, as in a few other states, state chartered institutions dominate the local markets, while in the majority of states the Federals predominate. Revisions made by the government authority in 1961, under which Federal savings and loans operate, permit them to make a limited number of 90% loans for amortization periods not exceeding 30 years. Most of their conventional loans are limited, however, to a maximum of 80% of the appraised value. Secondary financing may be allowed on the 80% loans, while not being permitted on those in excess of this figure. Each state association operates under the laws passed by the local authorities, and therefore a variance of policies exists. Despite this fact, there is usually a basic similarity of regulations for both Federal and State chartered savings and loan institutions. For the specific facts about your area, consult with your local savings and loan companies.

<u>Lending Practices of Savings and Loans</u>

Because savings and loan companies must specialize in **real estate** financing, they are more liberal and flexible in their conventional lending policies. Interest rates will usually be slightly higher than banks or insurance companies, but appraisals and qualification requirements will often be considerably less stringent. The interest rates paid depositors bear a direct relationship to the ultimate charges made to mortgage borrowers. Currently, interest savings rates have been maintaining a range from 4% to almost 5% in some areas of the country, especially the West. Thus, rates to homebuyers for first mortgages will range from 5 1/2% to almost 7% interest on unpaid balances. Normally there must be a 1 1/2% to 2% difference between interest charged borrowers to rates paid investor depositors. Frequently, an additional charge will be made to originate the loan in order to increase the yield realized by the lending company. This may be as little as $50 to as much as three or more points.

It should be emphasized that although Federal and State regulatory agencies establish the maximum loan-to-value ratios, amortization periods, and other requirements, the individual policies of each savings and loan association will be determined within that broad framework by their board of directors. There is often considerable variance of policies between local companies operating under the same essential charter regulations. That is why you should personally ascertain the lending patterns of those institutions used by your real estate company, and relate such policies to the needs of your buyers and sellers.

Life Insurance Companies

Life insurance companies represent a small, but important, segment of the conventional loan market. Each insurance company throughout the United States operates its mortgage acquisition program based on:

1. The laws of the state in which it is chartered
2. The laws of the state in which it is lending
3. The policies of its board of directors or management
4. The availability of funds.

The state charters, under which insurance companies are authorized to make real estate loans, provide various statutory limitations imposed by state authorities. Insurance companies are generally required to be more selective in their mortgage programs than are savings and loan associations. Therefore, they are not as liberal as many local building and loan companies, but will offer lower interest rates with less origination charges for "prime loans." Insurance companies usually desire to make loans which have very little risk involved and where the down payment is at least 20% or more of the purchase price. By law, most insurance companies cannot make loans in excess of 75% of appraised value, which means a down payment substantially higher than required by savings and loans. However, the interest rate charged the mortgagor is often less than competing conventional sources. Currently, rates vary from 5 1/4% to 6% interest with only nominal origination fees of $50.00 to 1% of the loan amount. Prepayment penalties are usually less costly with insurance loans. Amortization periods will vary from 20 to 30 years, with the majority of them averaging 24 to 25 years.

For the qualified buyer who has 20% to 25% of the sale price as a down payment, an insurance loan will frequently be superior to other types of conventional financing, due to the lower interest rates and reduced charges involved. Most insurance companies use real estate brokers or loan correspondents to obtain and place their loans, as they cannot afford to maintain servicing offices in the hundreds of cities where they solicit business. These loan brokers represent the insurance companies (and other lenders), collecting fees for originating new loans.

Commercial Banks as Conventional Lenders

Commercial banks, both state and nationally chartered, are the second most important source of mortgage financing. Their lending patterns are similar to those of insurance companies, but occasionally more liberal in some markets. By law, they can seldom lend more than 75% of the appraised value for periods not in excess of 20 years. This limits them to "prime loans" where down payments and security are exceptionally high. They are generally more conservative than savings and loan companies since they are more tightly controlled by state and national laws and the Federal Reserve System. Banks have many outlets for their invested capital, most of which show a higher yield than do real estate mortgages. Nevertheless, banks frequently solicit real estate loans to balance their portfolios, and in recent years they have shown a more aggressive attitude in this field as they began to realize the importance of competing with other financial institutions for the mortgage business. Interest rates will be competitive with insurance companies, and sometimes lower, ranging now from 5 1/4 to 6%. Most banks have no additional service charge for originating a loan and frequently no prepayment penalty.

When you sell property to businessmen who have good credit at local banks, it may be to their advantage to place the loans with their own bankers. Banks are interested in protecting their relations with customers, even when they are not in the market to help new people. To determine what is available from your local banker, check with him about existing policies on mortgage loans.

Mutual Savings Banks

In the eastern states of this country, there are many large mutual savings banks whose functions are similar to those of the savings departments of commercial banks. They do buy and originate many mortgages annually, most of which are government insured FHA or VA loans. They do not play a substantial part in the conventional market. Like insurance companies, they usually work through mortgage brokers or loan correspondents.

2. INSURED OR GOVERNMENT LOANS

The Federal Housing Administration was the origination of government insured loans, as mentioned earlier. The FHA does not make any loans, nor does it build any homes. It is solely an insuring agency operating with government authority on a self-sustaining basis by means of the insurance premiums, (known as mutual mortgage insurance premiums) paid by each individual mortgagor in his monthly remittance, and which is based on the approximate annual rate of one-half of one per cent of the mortgage amount. Any approved lender (mortgagee) may make or buy an FHA insured loan for its portfolio, servicing it monthly under the terms of the Federal Housing Authority regulations. In order to qualify as an approved mortgagee, the lender must meet a number of requirements, including having liquid assets of $100,000 or more.

The FHA may insure any mortgage which is eligible for insurance, provided the total amount of all mortgages insured and outstanding at any one time does not exceed the maximum amount as established by Congress from time to time. In the event of default and foreclosure by the mortgagee, the FHA reimburses the lender with negotiable debentures from the Mutual Mortgage Insurance Fund, fully and unconditionally guaranteed as to principal and interest by the United States Government. These are normally 20 year debentures, bearing interest at the rate in effect when the loan was originally insured. Because of this high security, lenders will make many FHA loans. However, because the interest rate is fixed by law (despite varying market conditions affecting mortgage money) most lenders charge additional "points" or "discount" fees to offset the difference in yields expected from similar investments in the mortgage market. These discounts (except the 1% origination fee to the buyer) cannot be charged to the purchaser, thus forcing the seller to accept such costs if he desires to receive "all cash" for his equity by helping the buyer refinance through FHA. The same principle applies also to VA loans which are controlled by the Federal Government.

Under the FHA program, an individual buyer or property owner, or his agent, must work through an approved mortgagee in order to obtain an FHA loan. This mortgagee applies for the commitment to insure the loan once it is issued, and then, upon completing the government screening for credit and mortgage qualifications, funds the money if approved. After the transaction has "gone to record," the lender applies for the government insurance which is his protection against loss. Essentially, FHA loans are scientifically screened in order to reasonably determine that both buyers and properties involved meet the minimum standards established by the Federal Housing Administration.

The FHA Conditional Commitment

Normally when listing property for sale, the real estate salesman, who anticipates that a new FHA loan is the most logical method of refinancing the property for a buyer, will apply for an appraisal of the parcel by FHA on form #2004. This, together with a $25 fee,[5] are forwarded to the mortgagee, who, in turn, checks it and sends it on to the FHA district office. Shortly thereafter an appraiser reviews the property's qualifications on FHA standards, and a "conditional commitment to insure" is issued (if the property qualifies), with a statement of value indicating the amount on which the loan could be based. This is the maximum amount which FHA would insure a qualified buyer, providing the property was sold for the appraised value or more, and the buyer met all the requirements established by FHA for that loan amount. Later, when a purchaser is found, another form is completed setting forth the buyer's financial and credit history together with special documents to verify employment, cash on deposit, and other important factors needed to support the application for an FHA loan. Your mortgagee can discuss these forms with you and show you how to properly prepare them for submission to FHA.

There are many code sections under which FHA operates, but as a real estate salesman, you will be primarily concerned with the TITLE II loans -- Section 203B. These are loans made for residential property under the normal lending program. You may also be interested in TITLE I loans which provide funds for repairs and improvements on existing

---

[5] This fee may vary from area to area.

homes. At the time this book was published we obtained the most recent FHA loan eligibility limitations for single-family or multiple units, but since these may change from time to time, we suggest you verify current policies with your local FHA office or lending institutions.

REGULATIONS AND POLICIES GOVERNING FHA INSURED LOANS

I. FHA lends under Section 203B Title II
   A. Loans will be made to anyone of legal age meeting FHA and lenders' credit requirements.
   B. There is no limit to the maximum purchase price or sales price the buyer may pay, but the mortgagor must acknowledge the appraised values as established by an FHA appraiser before completing the sale.
   C. There can be no secondary financing prior to the recording of a new FHA, insured loan, and all obligations in connection with the transaction under penalty of perjury must be revealed.
   D. FHA does not lend money, it only insures loans made by qualified, approved financial institutions, known as mortgagees.
   E. There are maximum limits under which FHA operates for these residential loans. These maximum limits are currently as follows:[6]
      1. Single-family dwelling units
         a. Owner-occupied $30,000
         b. Non-owner-occupied   25,500
      2. Two or three-family units
         a. Owner-occupied $35,000
         b. Non-owner-occupied   29,700
      3. Four-family units
         a. Owner-occupied $37,500
         b. Non-owner occupied   31,800
   F. All insurable loans are based on an appraisal made by an FHA appraiser (or a fee appraiser hired by FHA). The basic cost for an FHA appraisal is $25.00, but various lenders normally charge an additional $5.00 or more for the cost of packaging and preparing the papers in connection with such appraisal.
      1. You should obtain a check for a conditional commitment from the seller of the property prior to obtaining a purchaser if you want to expedite the sale and the processing when a buyer is obtained. These commitment checks should be made out in the amount of $25 plus the lender's fee for processing.
      2. If no conditional commitment has been obtained, or if in the process of waiting for a conditional commitment to be returned a buyer is obtained, you may apply for a firm commitment based on both the property and the buyer.

---

[6] These are the amounts authorized under the Housing Act of 1964. For other charges consult your FHA district office.

FINANCING YOUR REAL ESTATE SALES

3. Conditional commitments may be renewed at the discretion of the district FHA office for a fee of $20.00 providing that the application for renewal is made within 60 days of the six months' expiration date.
4. A conditional commitment, due to expire on a processing loan, must be extended with an additional $20.00 fee or you may have an ineligible commitment at the time the case closes.

II. Insurable maximum loans are made on the following basis:

A. A single-family dwelling unit built under FHA inspection, or which is over one year old even though not built under FHA inspection, and which will be owner-occupied, the loan amount will be made as follows:
   1. Ninety-seven per cent of the first $15,000 of appraised valuation, or 3% down payment. (On $15,000 value the down payment = $450; loan = $14,550)
   2. Ninety per cent of the next $5,000 of appraised valuation, or 10% cash down payment. (On $20,000 value, the down payment = $1000; loan - $19,000)
   3. Seventy-five per cent of all excess over $20,000 to the maximum loan permitted, which is $30,000. (Maximum appraisal is $34,600 for loan of $35,000)

B. For a dwelling that is not built under FHA inspection, and which is less than one year old, for owner-occupied applicants the maximum insurable loan will be made as follows:
   1. Ninety per cent of the first $20,000 of appraised evaluation, or 10% cash down payment. (If the appraisal value = $20,000 - the down payment = $2000; loan $18,000)
   2. Seventy-five per cent of the excess to the maximum insurable loan, which is $30,000. (If appraisal is for $28,000, down payment = $4000; loan = $24,000)

C. If the borrower is not going to be the occupant of the property, then the loan cannot exceed 85% of the amount that would be available to an owner-occupant. (This would be issued for any investor qualifying for FHA financing)

D. At the present time, the interest rate for FHA loans is 5 1/4% of the unpaid balance per annum, plus the mutual mortgage insurance premium which is approximately 1/2% of the unpaid balance, although this is not on a true amortization schedule.

E. Maximum amortization periods of the new FHA loans may be either 30 or 35 years, depending upon whether the property was new or used and whether or not it was built under FHA. For a 35 year loan the property must have been built under FHA originally, or be a new home built under FHA currently. All others have a maximum insurable loan of 30 years. To establish maximum loan on used dwellings, the FHA uses a rule of thumb that the mortgage period should never be equal to more than 75% of the estimated remaining economic life of the dwelling. Thus it is possible to have FHA maximum loan periods of 15, 18, 20, or 25 years for properties which are not appraised for longer economic lives.

    F. When a new FHA loan is to be made in excess of $15,000, then, in determining the amount of loan, one must use multiples of the lowest $100. Under $15,000 they may be in multiples as low as $50. For example: if the FHA schedule indicates a loan amount of $17,385, you must reduce it to $17,300. If your figures would indicate the maximum loan to be $12,680, you drop it to $12,650.

III. Procedures for selling property under FHA terms

    A. The buyer must have the down payment in cash, or its equivalent, plus normal buyer's closing charges.

    B. The buyer may make a minimum cash down payment and pay his reoccurring closing costs. This means that the buyer legally must pay taxes, fire insurance, and mortgage insurance premiums in his closing costs. Additional closing costs will depend upon negotiations with the seller.

    C. Another way to obtain the legal down payment required by FHA is by using the security of another piece of property, the equity in a deed of trust, or some other asset which can be converted to cash, if required.

    D. It is also possible to accumulate the down payment from the excess in addition to basic rent which may be paid over a period of time for a piece of property. However, the FHA carefully controls these arrangements and basically, frowns upon them as there have been some flagrant violations of sound business procedures in connection with such plans. As a basic rule, FHA first wants to be certain that a reasonable rent is being paid, and that only the amounts in excess of that reasonable rent are used as credit towards the down payment when they are impounded in a neutral account.

    E. Painting, cleaning, labor, and other methods of establishing a down payment may be used, provided they have been approved by FHA. This is known as using "sweat equity" to establish a down payment. The procedures involving such "sweat equity," however, are too complicated to discuss in this chapter and we recommend that you contact your FHA district office or your mortgage lender for more details.

    F. A seller may accept as down payment for his property, under FHA, the equity in another property, in an automobile, a boat or any other material item providing it has a monetary value equal to or in excess of the required down payment.

FINANCING YOUR REAL ESTATE SALES

G. <u>Equity in other real estate</u> is frequently used as a down payment, as in the case of trade-in housing. However, it must be established that the equity exists and is being transferred to the property involved. Check with your mortgage lender or FHA office for further details.

H. It is also permissible under FHA regulations for one to borrow on his life insurance policies, savings accounts, stocks and bonds, or other assets to obtain the cash to meet a required down payment, providing he clearly sets forth the amount of any obligation to repay such borrowed amounts. If there is a repayment to be made, then this will be taken into consideration in determining his income eligibility to meet such excess payments.

I. A cash down payment may be furnished as a gift from a relative providing there is verification that the money is <u>solely a gift and does not have to be repaid</u>. This is frequently done with parents for their children where the gift is for love and affection and there is no obligation to repay it by the one receiving it. A <u>gift letter</u> must be furnished to FHA signed by the appropriate parties in order to establish this as a valid down payment.

IV. <u>Monthly installments of FHA loans depend upon:</u>

A. The amount of the loan
B. The amount of interest to be charged
C. The amortization period of the loan
D. The amount of taxes to be collected each month in the loan impound fund.
  1. This amount varies depending upon whether or not the purchaser or borrower is a veteran entitled to veterans' exemptions in some states, such as California.[7] (In the State of California, a veteran with assets not in excess of $10,000 or $20,000 under community property, is entitled to a maximum of $1,000 exemption on his assessed real estate tax valuation. However, in order to be eligible, the property must be recorded in the veteran's name prior to the first Monday of March of the year that he files for his exemption, and he must have, in turn, filed with the proper department by the first Monday in May.)
  2. An exception to this rule is possible where unrecorded sales contracts and contracts of sale are used. One should check with his tax assessing office to determine the application of this rule in his particular situation.

---

[7] Check with your broker on this matter for your state.

E. The amount of mutual mortgage insurance which is to be paid is equal to one-half of one percent of the unpaid balance of the loan, staircased on an annual rather than monthly basis. If the buyer is actively enlisted in the armed forces of the United States (wartime or not) he can obtain what is known as an FHA In Service loan, which means that he will not be charged the one-half of one per cent mutual mortgage insurance premium during the time that he is in the service. However, when he is discharged he will probably be required to pay the additional mutual mortgage insurance premium, from that date forward. To accomplish this, the buyer must obtain a military form DD802, authorized by the proper party from the base on which he is serving.

F. Insurance Payments
1. The type of insurance:
   a. Fire and extended coverage
   b. Fire and physical loss
   c. Homeowner's policy
   d. Others
2. Assumption of existing insurance:
   a. Fire and extended coverage or fire and physical loss may be transferred.
   b. Homeowner's policy is seldom transferable per insurance codes. New buyers generally have to get their own coverage.
3. For new loans, fire and physical loss policies are generally written with new insurance firms for the amount of the higher loan, since the FHA regulations require that the amount of insurance equal the amount of the remaining balance of the mortgage.

V. Methods and procedures for qualifying a prospective purchaser for an FHA loan

A. First establish that he has the correct amount of cash to pay for the down payment and closing costs as required for the particular loan involved, or the equivalent in equity or other assets.

B. Determine from the customer whether or not he has had any bad bills, gone through bankruptcy, or had any abstracts of judgments filed against him. If he has, these will definitely make it difficult for him to obtain FHA financing without full reports and elimination of the problems. Complete written explanations are necessary.

C. Determine your purchaser's annual income and divide it by 12 to establish the monthly income, then divide this by 5; this amount should be within a few dollars of the monthly installment

FINANCING YOUR REAL ESTATE SALES

that purchaser will be qualified to make. From the monthly installment, deduct any other installment payment that the purchaser will make so that you have his net monthly income divided by 5. Remember that this does not mean that he will qualify even with this rule of thumb, but it is a good start in obtaining a loan. Another fast way to qualify your purchaser is to take his annual income and multiply this amount by 2 1/2 times; this will show if he is trying to purchase too expensive a home for his means under normal conditions. Be certain to ask enough questions and probe deeply enough to find out everything you can about his character and financial reference in order to establish past credit history.[8]

D. Make sure he is employed in a field of work that he has been doing for the past two years. If he has been less than two years on that type of employment, he may have difficulty in establishing a pattern satisfactory to FHA. For example, if a man has been a painter all of his life, and then for the past three or four months has become a life insurance salesman or a real estate salesman, he is not considered (as a rule) a good risk for an FHA loan, since his pattern of work experience is too short to determine his degree of success, especially if it is a fully commissionable job. A person new to an area and new to his job may qualify, if he is in the same type of trade or business in which he was involved in a prior city. FHA desires to have a mortgagor who has been employed at least two years in the same line of work, or work closely related to his prior experience. One can change jobs or firms, but if he changes type of employment he may have difficulty in qualifying for FHA. This is only a rule of thumb again, and cannot be taken as final, since every case does stand on its own merits.

E. It is important to remember that FHA will search out all of the information they need in order to approve a purchaser for a home loan. Every case is evaluated on its own merit. The above suggestions and recommendations are only established in order to assist you in avoiding wasting time with unworkable transactions. Stability, credit, employment, and other factors play a major part in qualification standards.

F. Be sure you also carefully check the wife's income. It is sometimes allowable by the lender and the FHA depending upon the type of position and length of employment, the age, and whether or not it is a pattern of family life. Again check with your mortgage lender and FHA district office to establish to what degree the wife's income can be allowed.

---

[8] FHA does not use any rule of thumb nor have any special income-to-payment ratios.

G. If installment accounts, which are owed by the purchaser, can and will be cleared up within the sixty-day processing time, this should be determined and reported. FHA may then require, if it is a close approval, that these be paid off before the loan is granted. You should also carefully instruct your buyers in very strong terms <u>not to purchase any credit items prior to the approval of the loan and close of their escrow,</u> because there is generally at least one additional credit report made at the time the loan is funded just before FHA mortgage insurance is issued to the lender.

VI. <u>Here is an example of how you may determine the maximum amount of down payment a purchaser would need to qualify for a home under</u> FHA. If the sales price, for example, is $18,950 and the buyer wants the maximum loan, you determine the following facts:

    First: 97% of the first $15,000   = $450
    90% of the remaining $3,950   = $395
                                                                       $845

This would mean that the down payment might be $845 and the loan might be $18,105, <u>but remember that everything over $15,000 must be in lower multiples of even $100</u>; therefore, you must decrease the loan to $18,100 and add $5 to the down payment, making it in this case, $850 down to a maximum loan of $18,100 for an owner-occupant. If you are not selling to an owner-occupant, you would have to take 85% of this figure, which would mean that a non-owner-occupant could only obtain a maximum loan of $15,300.

Closing Costs Under FHA Loans

Because of the great differences in customs and procedures affecting closing costs in various sections of the United States, it is impossible here to furnish you with any standard instructions on escrow costs for buyers and sellers when FHA financing is used. One rule has already been stated and remains true, regardless of area: the buyer must pay his own re-occuring closing costs as already explained. Other than that, all other items (except discount costs for the loan) are a matter of negotiation between buyer and seller. By law, however, the seller is the only one who can pay the discount costs charged by a lender for originating an FHA (or VA) loan, except for the maximum 1% origination fee which the buyer can pay. Ask your local FHA office or mortgagee to explain local policies and procedures on closing costs to you so you can accurately quote these items to buyers and sellers.

Veterans Loans

In 1944 the Federal government passed the Serviceman's Readjustment Act, which included, among other veteran benefits, <u>special home loans for returning GI's.</u> Originally initiated by Congress to assist veterans in making the necessary readjustments from war life to civilian life, veteran home loans have played an important part in new home loans in the years since 1945. The benefits of the act have been extended several times by Congress, although at this time some of the benefits for original recipients have now expired. Korean War veterans are also eligible for benefits of the act, and they have a minimum of 15 years from the termination of their war experience to use their GI eligibility certificate for home loans. Your local veterans office will gladly furnish you with a current eligibility expiration date and a definition of benefits included under the act for your information. The basic eligiblity is based on having been honorably discharged from the armed services after a minimum of 90 days of active service during either World War II or the Korean War. If a veteran served in both World War II and the Korean War, he might have two eligibilities, provided he had used his first one prior to entering the Korean War.

Although the qualifying and processing procedures are similar to those used by FHA, they do have some special features that are different. For one thing, the veteran is prohibited from paying more for the property than the Veterans Administration appraisal establishes as a reasonable value.[9] The VA appraisal is known as a "Certificate of Reasonable Value" (C.R.V.). Under the veterans program, the mortgage lender is insured up to a maximum amount of $7,500 of the total loan. Any risk in excess of this amount must be borne by the mortgagee. For this reason, most lenders will not take VA loans much in excess of $21,000 or $22,000 based on their ratio of maximum loan to insurance although VA loans of $30,000 have been obtained. Currently the interest rates of VA loans are the same as FHA, namely 5 1/4%; this has not always been the case. Under VA loans there is no mutual mortgage insurance premium payable by the veteran, and therefore it is obviously less expensive on a monthly basis. The full cost of the administration of the program is borne by the federal government, out of tax funds, as a service to the veteran.

VA LOANS AND ELIGIBILITY

Requirements to Qualify for an Insurable Veterans Administration Loan:

    a. Anyone of legal age that has served in the United States Armed Forces during World War I, or World War II, and Korean Action. In service or with an honorable discharge.

---

[9] Except for personal property items such as rugs and drapes which can be priced separately.

b. The only requirement as far as price is that the sale price does not exceed the Veterans Administration's appraisal of the property, or commonly known as the C.R.V. which means Certificate of Reasonable Valuation. Cost to obtain a CRV is $25.00, usually payable by Veteran purchaser (or Seller may obtain a prior one).

c. Due to the fact that under a GI loan there is 100% financing and no required down payment there is no need for secondary financing. However, deals often fall through during a long closing process if buyer has made no deposit or down payment. Some type of security for performance should be received to protect seller.

d. In some remote cases a GI cannot find a lender that will lend in the area he has decided to purchase, and then he can obtain a direct loan from the Veterans Administration, a true government loan. Maximum loan, direct, to any veteran is $13,500.00.

e. There is no maximum limit placed on a VA loan, but the C.R.V. appraisal is the highest price a veteran can pay. This appraisal is made to assure the Veteran that he is not paying too high a price.

f. The current interest rate for a GI loan is 5 1/4% and the maximum term is 30 years.

g. With 100% financing there is no need for a down payment under GI (VA) loan, although it is desirable.

h. VA loans are made on single dwellings, duplex and, up to fourplex if borrower is to be an owner-occupant.

i. If for example the sale price on a home is $15,500.00 then the Veterans Administration appraiser inspected the property and the Veterans Administration issued a C.R.V. in the amount of $15,000 then a loan of $15,000 could be obtained.

j. There is no prepayment penalty on a VA loan, it can be paid off at any time, without additional costs.

k. A GI loan can be assumed by anyone just like an FHA loan, with a regular loan assumption fee, usually $15.00 which varies according to the demand of the lenders. However, original maker of note may still be liable if a deficiency occurs.

To Sell Under VA Conditions, the Cost to the Seller Is:

a. Discount points depend on money market, location, size of home, and pricing of home. During a tight money market sellers have paid as high as 14 pts. Example, on a $10,000 loan they paid $1,400.00. Currently discounts are about the same as FHA.

    b. If bonds are to be assumed the appraisal must exceed the sales price by the amount of the bonds.

Special State Veterans Programs

In addition to the Federal veterans home loan program, many individual states, following the war, initiated their own veterans programs to assist returning GI's. These state programs vary in many ways from one state to another, but in most cases the veteran has the advantage of using the superior credit of his state to provide a low interest home loan. In California the Cal-Vet program is in reality a contract of sale method of financing in which the title is vested in the state until the loan amount has been paid to them. The interest rate varies from 3% to 4%, which is obviously less than any other available financing in the State of California.

CALIFORNIA VETERANS ADMINISTRATION LOANS

I. Department of Veteran Affairs, State of California Farm and Home Purchase Program.

    A. In addition to having a good credit rating and a steady sufficient income or wage, to qualify for a Cal-Vet loan the Veteran must have been active for 90 days in World War I or II or in the Korean Action.

    B. Must be a "native son" of California or have been a bona fide resident of the State of California on entry into active service. This also applies to the widow of a State Veteran, that is, her husband must have been native born or a bona fide resident of the State at time of entry into the service actively, and has applied for his "Certificate of Eligibility" previous to his death. (If not, she is not eligible to receive any Cal-Vet real estate benefits.)

    C. The Veteran must have an honorable discharge or still be active in the Service.

    D. The State of California purchases the property and then sells it back to the Veteran on an Agreement of Sale or Contract of Sale. This means that the California Veteran does NOT get a Grant Deed until he has paid off the State.

    E. There are limits to the amount that the State of California will lend a Veteran, and they are:
       1. For single dwelling or 1 family unit $15,000.00
       2. For purchasing a farm $40,000.00

FINANCING YOUR REAL ESTATE SALES

- F. The home being purchased must be:
    1. Single family
    2. Home must be large enough to meet the needs of the Veteran and his family.
    3. In case of a farm purchase, the farm must be adequate to produce a living for a Veteran and his family.

- G. The top or maximum purchase price a California Veteran can pay for a home or a farm is as follows:
    1. Single family home $25,000.00
    2. Farm   no limit

- H. There can be no <u>secondary</u> financing <u>prior to</u> or <u>after</u> the close of escrow.

- I. The present day interest rate of a California Veterans loan is 4% (1962). However, this rate can be changed either up or down, but never higher than five (5%) percent.

- J. The term or length of a Cal-Vet loan or contract period is determined by the State Department of Veteran Affairs, in accordance with the amount of the Contract balance, age of property, condition of property. However, the usual term or length of contract is 25 years, but at the present, loans are being made for a maximum of 23 years.

- K. If the Contract is prepaid prior to two years from date of the Contract of Sale, the State charges a 2% pre-payment penalty of the original amount of the Contract of Sale.

- L. The Veteran must agree to reside on the property within 60 days from the date of the Contract of Sale.

II. Methods of Selling Under the California Veteran Affairs Program.

- A. Minimum down payment that is required:
    1. For single family home, owner occupancy, 5% of total sales price.
    2. For farms or ranches, owner occupancy and self productive, at least <u>10% cash down.</u>
    3. Sometimes the State <u>will,</u> or I should say, may waive the down payment if the appraisal of the property exceeds the amount to be loaned by at least five percent for a home and ten percent for a farm. This is very rare.

4. The California Veteran must apply and get a Certificate of Eligibility. When he has qualified, the State then gives him a certain period, to locate and submit a property that he wants. Then the Department will have the property appraised by a Cal-Vet appraiser. This appraisal is the figure on which the down payment of 5% is based. Any amount over this must also be paid in cash to the amount of loan the Department will make to the Veteran.

3. PRIVATE FINANCING

Private real estate financing includes many sources, exclusive of recognized institutional lenders. These are primarily the following:

1. The owners of property who retain part of their equity as a portion of the purchase price in the form of a mortgage or deed or trust
2. Private finance companies who deal primarily in the origination and purchase of second mortages or deeds of trust
3. Individual, private investors who buy and sell mortgages for their own investment portfolios
4. Pension and trust funds of various types
5. Investment syndicates which deal in real estate mortgages and acquisitions.

Of all those with which you will be concerned, no private source is more important than the owners of real estate who are willing to retain a part of their equities in the form of mortgage securities. Many sellers do not need (or want) all of their invested capital at the time they sell to new buyers. Indeed, for tax reasons, many cannot afford to take "all cash" and prefer installment sales, giving them an opportunity to defer the reporting of the income over a period of several years rather than in the year of sale. Secondary financing has long been an established and accepted method of assisting buyers and sellers to achieve their mutual objectives in the transfer of real property. When a seller wants "top" price for his property, or is in a highly competitive market, he can use his equity to assist the new purchaser by creating easy terms suited to the buyer's needs. In this fashion he avoids taking a substantial discount in the market place and makes possible an additional yield on his equity by charging a reasonable interest for the secondary financing. Salesmen who understand both the advantages and disadvantages of secondary mortgages can use them to help solve special problems while assisting the owners to achieve their sales objectives. Caution should be exercised never to encourage an owner to take a second mortgage when he does not fully understand the procedures and risks involved. While there are many situations which fully justify this approach to selling real estate, there are also many times when this method should not be pursued.

FINANCING YOUR REAL ESTATE SALES

Here are some of the situations when sellers can justifiably consider carrying all or part of their equity in first or second mortgages:

1. When the seller does not need all of his equity in cash, and would just as soon earn additional interest on the balance over a deferred period of time
2. When the competitive market of various property offerings makes it necessary to offer easier and more attractive terms to find buyers
3. When there is little or no demand for the type of property involved
4. When the monthly payments and down payments required under normal financing prevent the average available buyer from qualifying for housing

When you elect to recommend private, secondary financing to an owner, it is your obligation to explain both the risks and the benefits of such financing tools. Your concern should be to protect the seller from taking any equity instrument that will not provide adequate security for his investment. As a knowledgeable professional, the seller should be able to trust your judgment and business ethics. Failure to sufficiently protect the seller's interests by reasonably screening the buyer's credit qualifications, and inserting the necessary clauses to protect his interests, will place you in an embarrassing and possibly incriminating position at a later date. When sellers are asked to carry financing as part of the purchase price, the agent should exercise the same care any mortgage company would exert to protect it's investment. In reference to second mortgages, you should know and be able to explain the following special clauses used in such instruments (see Glossary):

1. Acceleration clause
2. Alienation clause
3. Subordination clause
4. Mortgage due date clause
5. Attorney's fee clause
6. Default clause

CREATIVE USE OF FINANCING INSTRUMENTS

When one understands that any mortgage instrument is a "security" which can be used to borrow additional funds, be hypothecated, or collateralized to assist in putting a transaction together, it is often possible to make many sales other real estate salesmen will miss. First, second, and even third mortgages are valid securities which can be traded or hypothecated to meet "cash flow" requirements in transactions. For example, a seller might not be willing to take a second mortgage from a buyer because it will not give him sufficient cash to complete another sale. If the salesman understands the various alternatives, he could recommend any of the following to achieve both the buyer's and seller's objectives:

1. Accept the second deed of trust on his present property and trade it in for face value (or discounted value) to the owner of the property being acquired by the seller.

2. Accept the second deed of trust and borrow against it (hypothecate) through an industrial bank or private lending company, assigning it for 50% borrowing capacity, until the funds are repaid.

3. Assign it to the bank or lending institution making the new loan on the property being acquired by the seller to secure an "overage" loan, and pledging it as an additional asset in consideration for making a larger loan than normal.

4. Discount the loan to a private lender or commercial source for the amount such securities usually bring in the local market.

5. Include it in the financial statement of the seller at face value to increase his assets so he can borrow at a lower rate of interest from a bank.

6. Use it as a down payment at face value for additional properties to be acquired for investment purposes, thus extending the "leverage" value of the instrument.

7. Assign it to the real estate company in part or whole for consideration of their commissionable efforts in the transaction.

8. Pledge it as security for making a sizeable loan on the existing property in order to create better cash flow for the seller, without penalizing his investment interests.

These are just a few of the ways mortgage instruments can be utilized to create additional sales. Your real estate broker can undoubtedly explain how these, and other ideas will profit you in negotiating difficult sales.

INSTRUMENTS USED IN MORTGAGE FINANCING

You should be familiar with the standard instruments used in mortgage financing and know their limitations and advantages. They include, first of all, the note signed by the borrower to secure any indebtedness and which may or may not be secured by mortgages or deeds of trust against real or personal property. These are essentially of two types:

1. <u>Straight, flat or non-amortized note:</u>
    This note is all due and payable in one lump sum at some future date (with the possible exception of interest.)

2. <u>Installment or amortized note:</u>
    This calls for regular payments at prescribed intervals, usually including interest and principal. This is the standard note for most real estate mortgages of a primary nature.

Every state has laws affecting the use of notes, minimum terms, and fees which can be charged for their origination, and restrictions on their endorsement and transfer. You must know these things in order to obtain your real estate license and should certainly be familiar with them to maintain a professional real estate practice in your state.

Endorsing a note or other negotiable instrument normally makes the endorser responsible for any secondary liability, unless it is qualified by the words: "without recourse." Most mortgage notes are transferred by "assignment" rather than endorsement, and the new owners receive them without qualification as to value of future security.

Discount financing is often difficult for real estate salesmen to understand and explain to others. The simple truth is that different security instruments are rated by:

1. Interest rate
2. Time of payoff
3. Risk
4. Discount

The investor who buys or originates a mortgage instrument is usually interested in computing his yield. Those wanting higher security take lower yields, and the investors willing to assume considerable risk demand higher discounts to increase yields. FHA and VA loans are fixed by law as to interest rate charges, and since the mortgage market fluctuates, as does the stock market, the cost for procuring such loans is based on current yields investors can receive for their money in comparable securities. The West Coast generally must pay a little more for mortgage money than the East Coast of the United States, due to the rapid growth experienced there and the limited supply of money to finance real estate sales.

QUALIFYING THE BUYER FOR FINANCING

The type of financing and the sources shown for its development are dependent upon the individual requirements of your various buyers and sellers. You should learn to evaluate the specific needs of each customer as determined by his financial abilities. A good "rule of thumb" used by many mortgage lenders is that a buyer can generally afford not more than 25% of his gross monthly income for housing expenses. This would include principal, interest, taxes and insurance, and possibly also general maintenance expenses. Thus, a person earning $600 per month, could probably afford not more than $150.00 for gross monthly housing expenses. There is another rule also commonly used, i.e., that a buyer should not purchase a home in excess of 2 1/2 times his gross annual income. A man earning $6,000 per year could purchase a home for $15,000 or less. FHA and VA qualification formulas follow a more liberal approach than these general guides, and such things as employment stability, indebtedness, and financial reserves may give any individual case merits for special consideration. Usually, in the lower price brackets, the ratio of monthly housing expenses to income will be greater than when clients with higher incomes are involved. Each home buyer should be given the benefit of your personal attention in reference to his mortgage requirements.

SUMMARY

We have included in this section a number of the instruments you will be using in connection with mortgage financing. You should make this material your own, based on the local policies of the lenders with whom you deal. You owe it to yourself to learn as much as possible about the financing market which is effective in your area of operation. You should be able to advise sellers, when listing property, on the best methods of financing, which ones will help to attract prospective buyers, and to clearly identify the probable costs the sellers may experience under the various methods selected. Likewise, when negotiating a buyer's offer, you must be able to recommend the logical type of financing for which both buyer and the property will qualify. You cannot divorce the buyer from the property when you are considering the financing program to be utilized. Many properties will not qualify for FHA or VA terms due to age, condition, obsolescence, location, or the general market. Insurance companies are selective in the properties acceptable to them for prime loans. All of these things must be related with your personal knowledge of the local mortgage market and the policies of the lenders with whom you will be dealing. Your broker, sales manager, or mortgage agent can give you the facts applicable to your real estate district.

Remember, also, there is nothing permanent about the terms offered in any mortgage market. Like other commodities, the price of money continues to fluctuate with the varying influences affecting supply and demand. Therefore, you should stay in touch with the market on a daily basis, by determining from your lenders the current quotations and probable changes that can be expected. In anticipating the cost to the seller of any financing required for the discounting of an FHA, VA, or other type of loan, be sure to plan ahead to the probable date of funding rather than the date of origination. The market may be 97 1/2 today but it could be 96 by the time your loan closes. If the seller is unprepared

LOAN APPLICATION — PERSONAL STATEMENT

To: .... Acct. No. ....

Deliver .... copies to Stone & Schulte.   Salesman ....

Deliver .... copies to lender

Property Address .... Phone .... Sales Price ....

Type loan .... Interest .... No. Years .... Loan Amount ....

IDENTITY

Husband's name .... Age ....
Wife's name .... Age ....
Address .... How long ....
Previous address .... How long ....
No. dependents other than wife .... Ages .... Yrs. married .... Single .... Widowed ....
Eligible for tax exemption .... Periods of Military service ....

PRESENT EMPLOYMENT

HUSBAND
Employer ....
Address ....
Type business .... Ph. ....
Position ....
How long ....

WIFE
Employer ....
Address ....
Type business .... Ph. ....
Position ....
How long ....

PRIOR EMPLOYMENT

HUSBAND
Employer ....
Address ....
Type business .... Ph. ....
Position ....
How long .... Monthly Inc. .... Hrly. ....

WIFE
Employer ....
Address ....
Type business .... Ph. ....
Position ....
How long .... Monthly Inc. .... Hrly. ....

INCOME

HUSBAND
Monthly gross $ .... Hrly. rate ....
Overtime ....
Other income ....
Total $ ....
Source of other income ....

WIFE
Monthly gross $ .... Hrly. rate ....
Overtime ....
Other income ....
Total $ ....
Source of other income ....

ASSETS

Bank .... Checking $ .... Auto/Yr. .... Make .... Val. $ ....
Branch .... Savings ....
.... Checking .... Dep. on the property $ ....
.... Savings .... Life Ins. Cash Val. $ ....
Stocks and bonds .... (Source of Dep., Dn. Pmt., Cl. Csts.)
Government bonds
                    Sub total $ ....   Total $ ....

REAL ESTATE

Type .... Address .... Value $ ....
Lender & Address .... Bal. ....
Total Mo. Payment $ .... P. & I. $ .... Taxes $ .... Ins. $ .... Gross Equity $ ....
Home: Sold .... Rented .... Leased .... To be sold ....

OBLIGATIONS

To whom	Address	Type loan	Balance	Mo. Paymt.
			$	$

(Include alimony and/or child support)

FIXED CHARGES / HOUSING EXPENSE

Annual fixed charges
Fed. Income Tax $ ....
Premiums of Life Ins. ....
Social Sec. & Ret. ....
Payments on install. accts. ....
Mortgage payments ....
                    Total $ ....

Annual housing expense
Mtge/rent payment $ ....
Taxes & insurance ....
Heat/water/elect. ....
Maintenance ....
Other ....
                    Total $ ....

CREDIT REFERENCES

NAME .... ADDRESS ....

LEGAL

	He	She
Divorced .... Date Final .... Sep.	Divorced .... Date Final .... Sep. ....
Have you ever filed bankruptcy? .... Yr. .... County, State ....
Have you had any suits, judgments, liens or repossessions? .... Explain briefly ....

PREVIOUS FHA LOAN TRANSACTIONS

1. Have you owned and sold any property within the last 6 months on which you had an FHA insured mortgage loan?
   ☐ YES ☐ NO. If answer is "Yes", please give the following information if known to you or available:
   (a) Name of purchaser ....
   (b) Did the purchaser intend to occupy the property as his home? ☐ YES ☐ NO ☐ UNKNOWN
   (c) Address of property ....
   (d) Original mortgage amount .... (e) Unpaid balance when sold .... (f) FHA case no. ....

2. Have you ever been obligated on a VA guaranteed home loan; an FHA insured mortgage; or an FHA insured property improvement loan on which default of payments resulted in judgment, foreclosure, or voluntary deed in lieu of foreclosure?
   ☐ YES ☐ NO. If answer is "Yes", please give:
   (a) Address of property ....
   (b) Name and address of mortgagee ....
   (c) FHA Case No. ....

Date ....   Signed ....

FINANCING YOUR REAL ESTATE SALES

for the additional 1 1/2 points, your sale may fall apart at the critical closing date.

Knowledge has been defined as being of two types: 1. Knowledge you possess which you can use and 2. Knowledge of where you can turn to find the answer if you do not know the specifics.

In mortgage financing, <u>to know where to go for the facts in any individual case</u> is just as important as knowing the basic factors about the market. The mortgage broker, loan correspondent, banker, insurance broker, savings and loan officer, secondary mortgage broker, and your fellow salesmen are valuable sources of loan information. Keep yourself posted on the mortgage market and learn to use all of the logical financing instruments in the appropriate situation. You cannot sell real estate without knowing financing. It is a basic tool which a professional real estate salesman uses effectively to benefit buyers and sellers he represents.

QUESTIONS AND PROJECTS FOR CHAPTER ELEVEN

Questions:

1. Why is financing such a vital and integral part of real estate selling?
2. Of all the institutional lenders, who plays the major role in real estate financing? Why?
3. Based on the policies of your state and area, answer the following questions:

   a. What is the maximum loan to value ratio for State chartered savings and loan companies? For Federally chartered associations?

   b. What is the current interest rate range charged in your area by the following lending institutions (based on conventional loans only)?

      1. Commercial banks?
      2. Savings and loans, State chartered?
      3. Savings and loans, Federally chartered?
      4. Insurance companies?
      5. Savings banks?
      6. Private lenders?

   c. What is the maximum loan that can be made by the groups listed in 3b?

   d. How much down payment or equity investment is the borrower expected to have for each of those listed in 3b?

   e. Which of those listed in 3b plays the dominant role in your area?

4. Why can most savings and loan companies take a more liberal approach to buyer and property qualifications than will insurance companies or commercial banks?

5. What costs will the buyer and seller each be expected to share with a loan of $18,000 on a residential property in your area, from the following sources:
   a. Insurance company?
   b. State savings and loan?
   c. Federal savings and loan?
   d. Commercial bank?
   e. Private lenders?
6. Describe the function the Federal Housing Administration has played in the mortgage market and its current impact in your area from its insured loans.
7. Describe the Veterans Loan and the advantages to a buyer who is eligible to receive one.
8. How can secondary financing in your local market assist you in making extra sales?
9. Discuss with your broker or supervisor how you can use the following financing tools in your area.
   a. Hypothecated second loans.
   b. Purchase money mortgages held by the seller.
   c. Commercial loans to secure down payment funds.
   d. Collateral from assets of the buyer to provide blanket loans, cash value deposits, or converted equities to complete a sale.
   e. Using secondary financing on one property as down payment on another.
   f. Equity in property to obtain maximum financing on new property or trade-in for necessary cash.
   g. Sweat equities for down payment where buyer does some authorized repairs to the property in order to earn the down payment and qualify for a loan.
10. Define the following clauses:
    a. Acceleration clause.
    b. Alienation clause.
    c. Subordination clause.
    d. Attorney's fee clause.

Projects:

1. Obtain an amortization schedule, mortgage yield guide, and other similar tools to help you compute mortgage amounts and terms. Have your broker show you how to use them.
2. Obtain a list of all lending institutions your company authorizes you to work with, noting the names of the representatives you should contact together with other pertinent information about their lending policies.

3. Contact one of your savings and loan companies and discuss with their officers the current policies under which they operate regarding real estate loan. Ask them for advice on how to utilize their services to your advantage.
4. From your local loan correspondent for an insurance company, determine current practices of insurance firms operating in your area and requirements they make for buyer and property qualifications.
5. From your banker, determine what types of real estate loans he is willing to make in the current market, and how such loans can be obtained.
6. Review FHA financing terms and regulations with your local FHA office or mortgage broker who serves your account. Ascertain the effective use of FHA commitments and appraisals in your market as related to actual selling prices and terms.
7. Determine what lenders in your area are prepared to make Veterans loans and the current discount for originating them.
8. Obtain a copy of the following instruments used in making loans on real property and review the language and terms involved in each:
   a. Mortgage or Deed of Trust
   b. Flat or Straight Note
   c. Amortized note
   d. Contract for Deed or Contract of Sale
   e. Chattel Mortgage
9. From the policies of your local area and the legal limitations fixed by State and Federal law, compute the loans available for the following situations:
   a. FHA sale at $21,250 on minimum down payment terms.
   b. $19,875 sale to maximum conventional loan from a savings and loan association in your area.
   c. $24,500 sale with maximum available insurance loan and cash for the difference.
   d. $15,950 sale with a commercial bank loan and the balance in cash. Buyer wants maximum loan available at bank rates.
10. Review the definitions of the following terms: (See Glossary if definition not clearly understood.)

   a. Amortization table
   b. Balloon payment
   c. Beneficiary
   d. Blanket mortgage
   e. Certificate of Eligibility
   f. Collateral security
   g. Deed of trust
   h. "Fanny Mae"
   i. Mortgagor, mortgagee
   j. Joint and several note
   k. Loan correspondent
   l. Modification agreement
   m. Mortgage banker
   n. Open end mortgage
   o. Partial release clause
   p. Payoff penalty
   q. Satisfaction of mortgage
   r. Secondary mortgage market
   s. Trustee
   t. Trustor
   u. Usury
   v. Verification of deposit
   w. Verification of employment
   x. Yield
   y. Yield guides

12

EXPANDING YOUR REAL ESTATE OPPORTUNITIES

Thus far in this training manual we have confined our discussions to the field of residential selling, since this activity plays a major role in most real estate careers, particularly in their initial years of development. However, it is appropriate that we give you a brief glimpse into the other phases of our business which may interest you as your career progresses, since you may desire to select one or more of these specializations as avenues for your personal achievement. Unfortunately, space does not permit us to cover these subjects in the manner they deserve, and it must be left to the student to do the additional research and study necessary to learn more about any particular topic that arouses his interest.[1]

SELLING INVESTMENT PROPERTIES

Listing and selling real estate investments is one of the most exciting and challenging aspects of our profession. Salesmen who learn how to present income producing properties to customers can create sales by demonstrating to their prospects the financial benefits ownership will produce for them To be successful in selling investment real estate, one must interpret the needs of a particular investor as related to a particular listing. All investors do not have the same needs or objectives although the financial return in one form or another will usually be the dominating factor. Before you present a property to a buyer you should ascertain his personal requirements related to real estate acquisition. Some of the questions you need to determine are:

1. Does he need <u>tax shelter</u> through depreciation, or does he require spendable income to supplement his current receipts?
2. Does he intend to work at his investment by expending <u>time</u>, <u>money</u>, and <u>energy</u> to improve his return, or does he want property with a minimum of maintenance which he can hold for future gain?

---

[1] The bibliography in the back of this manual lists many excellent reference books the reader can obtain for additional study. The author plans a sequel to this training manual covering the various aspects of real estate investment selling.

EXPANDING YOUR REAL ESTATE OPPORTUNITIES

3. Does he want long term capital gains, or immediate income?
4. Does he intend to use leverage to increase his yield, or does he want the security of unencumbered assets?
5. How much risk is he willing to take for speculative return?

These and many similar questions relating to the investor's objectives should be considered before presenting a given parcel to him for his analysis. As in all real estate selling, one should always thoroughly qualify his prospect as to abilities, needs and desires.

There is less emotional selling involved in the representation of investment properties to the public, since the financial facts are of primary importance to the buyers and sellers, rather than the individual appeal of properties. The decision to purchase or sell income producing properties is generally premised on the monetary impact of each transfer. Therefore, the salesman must be skilled in gathering and presenting the facts on which a decision can be based, and know how to interpret these items as related to the objectives of his investors. There is no substitute for preparation and knowledge when handling commercial real estate.

THE IMPORTANCE OF PROPERTY INFORMATION FORMS

It has been said that "the sale is made when the facts are correctly presented." This is certainly true with the representation of investment real estate. Half the battle is just to obtain, assemble, and interpret the various factors affecting the properties involved, and the other half is the logical presentation of these truths to the right investors. Unless you have the facts to begin with, you cannot effectively convince a buyer or seller that he should take action; if you have misinformation, your very career as a real estate specialist is in jeopardy! That is why the forms used to analyze investment properties and their net returns are vital to your success in this field. On pages 252 to 261 we have included forms used on different types of investment offerings for your review. You will note that each one provides space for identification of all the important factors affecting the net return realized by an owner. This is a vital aspect of your information gathering process. How much can a new buyer receive for his invested capital and in what manner will it be realized? Study these forms and you will learn much about the effective presentation of real estate investments.

THE FOUR TESTS OF AN INVESTMENT

When a man invests his money in a business venture, the stock market, or real estate, he is concerned with one or more of these four tests for his invested capital:

1. LIQUIDITY: How easily can it be re-converted to cash?
2. STABILITY. How much risk is involved and how secure is the investment?
3. APPRECIATION: How much gain in value will he realize over a given time?
4. YIELD: What will be his net return from his invested capital?

In order to convince an investor that he should acquire a property you represent, you must be able to relate the four tests of an investment as they apply to the needs of your buyer. Let's consider each of these factors and their effect on real estate investments.

Liquidity

Admittedly, real estate is not as liquid as some other forms of investment opportunities. Liquidity is measured by the ease with which the investment may be turned into cash, or sold to someone who will free the owner's equity. Government bonds and other stocks which are in high demand can be converted to cash by a mere phone call to your broker. Most real estate holdings require an extended time period of exposure to the market before a buyer can be found who will release the owner's investment, and thus, such invested capital is considered less liquid than similar offerings in other fields. However, it should be remembered that almost any piece of real estate can be quickly sold if the owner will take the market price, or a reduction below market. The stock market fluctuates greatly from day to day, and anyone desiring to sell his holdings must be willing to take the market price or he cannot sell. Because there are no market quotations for a given real estate investment, it is not often easy to convince an owner to accept the "C.M.V." or "Competitive Market Value" which his real estate will bring compared to similar products. If real estate salesmen will learn to think in terms of market value when representing merchandise to buyers and sellers, the liquidity of invested capital can be easily demonstrated to any owner.

Stability

The stability of any investment is a measure of its inherent ability to resist change and to remain secure against the risks affecting invested capital. The counterpart to stability is risk, and different investors will view these two factors from various viewpoints. Generally when there is high risk, there should be the opportunity for exceptionally high gain, if conditions develop as projected. When there is low risk, the return for invested amounts will usually be less, but more secure. The elements of supply and demand are the primary influences which control the stability of real estate investments. For example, an apartment house located in a convenient downtown area with all the amenities which renters desire will be far more secure than one built on the edge of town where there are no shopping facilities or conveniences to attract good tenants. In any downturning market, the apartment houses with the best locations will be filled at the expense of those whose placement does not meet similar advantages. The economic stability of a given real estate market is determined by the vitality and future of the community in which the property is located. Thus, real estate investments made in expanding cities of California will show greater stability and less risk than those made in areas of the country which are experiencing little growth or a trend towards increasing population

Appreciation

Appreciation is an increase in value from any number of causes. It is the opposite of depreciation. In real estate investments, appreciation plays a major role in attracting invested capital, since the fixed supply of land creates an automatic pressure for greater values as population and usage continue to exert increased demands. Every real estate investor hopes to improve his gain by receiving the benefits of appreciation over a given period of time. Often, a buyer will pay what appears to be top price for a property in today's market, and accept a low return in the interim, because he anticipates a substantial rise in value due to a change of land use or zoning that will create higher demand and increased appreciation of values. A real estate salesman must be able to correctly interpret these factors that control values and help his investors make the right real estate selections.

Yield

Of the four factors affecting investments, yield is by far the most important. What is yield? It is the "net return" realized by an investor in terms of "interest" on his money over a fixed period of time, usually measured annually; put another way, it is the percent of profit resulting from invested capital computed yearly. If you put money in a savings account, you will expect a "yield" of 3% to 4% annually. The same money invested in real estate can produce two, three, four, or more times this return, as proven by the experiences of millions of real estate buyers. The following is a comparison of yields realized on typical investment opportunities:

1. STOCK MARKET (Dow Jones Average). 3.6%
2. CORPORATE BONDS 4.5%
3. REAL ESTATE MORTGAGES 6.2%
4. APARTMENT HOUSES (From Calif. Survey. 1962) . 8.5%
5. TRAILER PARKS (From Calif. Survey, 1962). . . . 11.3%

It is easy to prove that most real estate investments show a higher yield for capital invested than other types of securities. The reason for this increased return is partly the "fixed supply" already discussed and partly the ease with which the investor can use "leverage" to increase his yield.

LEVERAGE

Someone once said:
"Give me a place to stand and a lever long enough, and I can move the world!" In real estate financing, leverage has become a principal

factor in prompting the acquisition and development of property. What is leverage? It is the use of "O.P.M." (Other People's Money) to increase the investment yield resulting from the gain on the total market value of real estate or its annual net income. Suppose I want to buy something with my dollar plus nine more you lend me to make the purchase, and later I sell the property acquired for fifteen dollars; I have then realized a net return or yield of <u>500% on my investment</u>. If this was held for a period of five years, the return on capital was 100% per year, providing there were no additional expenses for the borrowed money which were not covered by the income from the property.

By using your credit coupled with the security of the property, you can frequently borrow money at one rate of interest and realize a return on the total investment at a higher rate of interest, picking up the difference for yourself or your investor. <u>This is using leverage to advantage.</u> James C. Downs, Jr. noted Chicago investment analyst has said:

"What you owe today is what you will be worth tomorrow!"

He was speaking to real estate brokers and investors at the time, and he spoke an essential truth. Because of the various factors of appreciation, depreciation, leverage, and net income, it is possible to pay for a property out of its annual net receipts and build an estate from the amounts applied to principal and gained from increased value of the real estate owned. By borrowing capital against real estate acquisitions, an investor can:

1. own a larger number of properties and realize a gain on each;
2. increase his yield on the invested capital, gaining the difference between the amount paid for borrowed money and realized from the property itself;
3. enjoy the appreciation in value on the total investment while only having the minor portion of the purchase price secured by his own capital.

There are, of course, risks and dangers connected with the use of leverage in real estate transactions. The purchaser must be aware of these risks, accepting them as the reason for the potential gain being greater than from more secure investments. The sophisticated investor will understand this principle and will be attracted to real estate offerings which increase his yield by reducing his cash requirements. <u>The smaller the down payment, the greater the investment leverage and the more the potential profit!</u> Sellers who accept smaller down payments can obtain higher prices for their properties because they, too, can enjoy the benefits of leverage.

<u>ANALYZING EQUITY YIELDS</u>

Most real estate investors are interested in knowing their net yield based on the total cash input required to obtain and hold the property until sold. If you can learn to illustrate and prove the returns realized from owning various income producing properties, your success in the field of investment selling will be dramatically accelerated. A prospectus can be developed for a particular property setting forth all the known facts, including photographs, maps, and an "Equity Yield Analysis Report" which shows the prospect how his capital will work for him to increase his yield and build an estate for the future. (See the following examples.)

EQUITY YIELD ANALYSIS REPORT

PROPERTY ADDRESS:	736 Hudson Court, Yourtown, U.S.A. (5 unit Commercial Bldg.)	
PRICE		$ 125,000.00
FINANCING	First mortgage @ 6% for 25 years	85,000.00
DOWN PAYMENT REQUIRED		40,000.00
ACQUISITION COSTS (Loan fees, title, escrow, etc.)		1,850.00
TOTAL CASH INPUT		41,850.00
INCOME (see attached schedule)[2]	Monthly gross $1250 Annual gross	15,000.00
OPERATING EXPENSES: (see attached schedule)[2]	Estimate of annual taxes, insurance, utilities, license, etc.	2,500.00
RESERVES: (Estimate based on past and current experience)		
Vacancy factor: 5% of annual gross	$ 750.00	
Maintenance: 4% of annual gross	600.00	
Management: Fixed Fee	400.00	
Total		1,750.00
NET INCOME BEFORE DEBT SERVICE		10,750.00
DEBT RETIREMENT SERVICE: Loan installments 12 x 547.66		6,574.92
CASH FLOW: Monthly = $ 347.92 Annually		4,175.08
EQUITY GAIN: Principal reduction on borrowed capital (based on first year; increases thereafter)		1,496.12
TOTAL CASH FLOW AND EQUITY GAIN ANNUALLY		5,671.20
NET YIELD OR RETURN ON CASH INPUT:		13.55%

Suppose we were to take this same building and have the owner carry an additional $20,000 of the purchase price for 7 years at 6% interest. Then our yield would increase as follows:

---

[2] These items should always be substantiated by a detailed schedule so the customer can study them when considering the offer.

PRICE		$ 125,000.00
FINANCING	First mortgage @ 6% 25 yrs.	85,000.00
	Second Mortgage @ 6% 7 yrs. due	20,000.00
DOWN PAYMENT REQUIRED		20,000.00
ACQUISITION COSTS (Loan fees, title, escrow, etc.)		1,850.00
TOTAL CASH INPUT:		21,850.00
INCOME: .... (See attached schedule)[3]		15,000.00

OPERATING EXPENSES: (See attached schedule)[3]
        Estimate of annual taxes, insurance, utilities, license, etc.

RESERVES: (Estimate based on past and current experience)

Vacancy Factor: 5% of annual gross	$750.00	
Maintenance: 4% of annual gross	600.00	
Management: Fixed Fee	400.00	
Total		1,750.00
NET INCOME BEFORE DEBT SERVICE:		10,750.00

DEBT RETIREMENT SERVICE: Loan Installments:

1st... 12 x 547.66		6,574.92
2nd... 12 x 175.00		2,100.00
Total retired annually		8,674.92
CASH FLOW:		2,075.08

EQUITY GAIN: Principal reduction on borrowed capital.

1st	1,496.12	
2nd	825.00	
Total retired annually		2,321.12
TOTAL CASH FLOW AND EQUITY GAIN:		4,396.20
NET YIELD OR RETURN ON CASH INPUT:		20.7%

    In the previous examples you will note how the yield on invested capital was increased by using a second mortgage to the owner. When a prospect does not need spendable income and wants long term yields, this is a valid way of using his capital to advantage, permitting him to acquire more than one property and at the same time earn a return on the money invested by others besides himself. If you are to properly represent investment properties, you must know how to use leverage to assist your prospective buyer to achieve his financial objectives.

---

[3] These items should always be substantiated by a detailed schedule so the customer can study them when considering the offer.

TAX ADVANTAGES IN REAL ESTATE OWNERSHIP

One of the great attractions offered by investment real estate is its ability to provide a certain amount of "tax shelter" for the purchaser. The income tax laws of the United States provide special consideration for the real estate investor who desires to take advantage of allowable depreciation schedules, tax free exchanges, and other provisions contained in the internal revenue code. These make possible additional gains for the owners of real estate which would not be available without such protection. The real estate salesman must know enough about the tax law to correctly evaluate the buyer's needs related to a given acquisition, or refer him to a tax consultant for specific advice. The most important factor affecting tax benefits on real estate investments is the depreciation one can take for the building and other improvements acquired.

DEPRECIATION -- THE INVESTOR'S BENEFACTOR

Because any building or fixture will eventually have to be replaced due to normal obsolescence, wear and tear, and so forth, the investor is permitted to depreciate these items over their useful life. The useful life of property is not a matter of fixed determination, but rather of reasonable judgment. A fence might be depreciated on a 15 year rate, a separate garage at 18 years, and a main building at 25 years. The Internal Revenue Service has published a guide for estimating useful life, known as Bulletin F, <u>Estimated Useful Lives and Depreciation Rates</u>, which you can obtain from your local district office. Regardless of the life of the improvements being considered, the investor has a choice as to the method of depreciation he elects to use, and this can be an important factor in the net results to his income and return.

Straight-Line Depreciation

This is a simple method of calculating depreciation by dividing the useable life into the cost of the improvements, less a salvage value, and taking an equal amount each year.

Example:
Property cost	$25,000.00
Land value	5,000.00
Balance for improvements.	20,000.00
Salvage value @ 20 years	1,000.00
Balance to depreciate	19,000.00
Amount to take annually on 20 year life	950.00

Declining Balance Method

Under this approach to depreciation scheduling, the user does not consider any salvage value and he subtracts each year's depreciation before computing the next year's allowance on the rate of depreciation selected. In no case can the rate be greater than twice the amount allowed under simple straight-line depreciation. Using the same example as before, and with a 10% rate for straight line, we can use 20% rate for a declining balance schedule providing we have qualified for accelerated depreciation as explained later.

Example:

First Year:	Balance to depreciate over 20 years	$20,000
	Multiply by 20%	4,000 depreciation
Second Year:	Original amount	20,000
	Less first year depreciation	4,000
	New declined balance	16,000
	Multiply by 20%	3,200 depreciation
Third Year:	Second year balance	16,000
	Less second year depreciation	3,200
	New declined balance	12,800
	Multiply by 20%	2,560 depreciation

This approach is continued over the useful life of property or until sold to a new investor.

Sum of the Years-Digits Method

Under this method of depreciation you create a fraction in which the numerator is the years of useful life and the denominator is the sum of the numbers in the useful life. If the property had a useful life of 10 years and the basis was $21,000 less $1,000 salvage value, the balance would be multiplied by the fraction 10/55 to establish the first year's allowable depreciation.

$$10 = \text{years of useful life}$$
$$55 = \text{sum of 1 plus 2 plus 3 plus 4 to 10}$$

Each year the numerator is reduced by the years remaining. Thus in the second year the fraction would be 9/55 and in the third year 8/55, and so on.

ACCELERATED DEPRECIATION PROVISIONS

To qualify for maximum accelerated depreciation privileges, the applicant and property must meet certain requirements. They are that:

1. The property must have a useful life of 3 years or more, and
2. Must be purchased or constructed by the owner after December 31, 1953. (If the construction was partly prior and partly following that date, you can accelerate the depreciation on that portion completed after 12/31/53)

This second rule is known as the first user requirement. In order to obtain the maximum benefits of 200% declining balance, you must be the first owner and first user. If you cannot qualify under these terms, the maximum you may take for declining balance depreciation is a 150% rate, or 1 1/2 times the straight-line method. With our example, this would be 15% rate annually. For current and additional information, consult your tax authorities or internal revenue agent.

No matter which method of depreciation you or your investor elect to use, it always tends to increase the net profit when the property is sold. This is true because you are taxed (if not a dealer in real estate) on a capital gains basis equal to 25% of the gain or one-half your ordinary income rate, whichever is lower. Therefore, it generally is desirable to obtain the greatest amount of allowable depreciation as early as possible in the event you plan to sell the property before the conclusion of its economic life. (See example of tax shelter, page 250.)[4]

TAX-FREE EXCHANGES

The tax law says:

No gain or loss shall be recognized if property held for productive use in trade or business or for investment (not including . . . property held primarily for sale, nor stock, bonds, notes. . . .) is exchanged solely for property of a like kind, to be held either for productive use in trade or business or for investment.

Thus, when trading a piece of real estate for another property of "like kind" one can avoid paying income tax on the gain realized from the "sale" of the original parcel and carry forward to the new one the tax basis of the traded property. This is an extremely important provision for those sellers who have a low tax basis on existing property and who desire to acquire other income producing real estate in exchange for their present holdings. The matter of "like kind" has been seriously debated and reviewed, but up to this point the courts have been liberal in the interpretation of this clause. Apartment houses can be traded for vacant land, commercial buildings, and the like, so long as the purpose remains the same, namely: to realize income from the real estate holdings. This is a highly specialized subject, and I recommend that you consult with experts in the field if you desire further information.[5]

---

[4] New tax laws regarding accelerated depreciation became effective January 1, 1964 and provide for "recapture provisions" when sold under certain conditions.

[5] Institute for Business Planning, 2 West 13th Street, New York 11, N.Y., has excellent reference works and current publications covering this and related subjects on real estate taxation, law, and practice.

EXPANDING YOUR REAL ESTATE OPPORTUNITIES

INCOME TAX SHELTER EXAMPLE

	Cash Position	Tax Consequences
GROSS ANNUAL INCOME	$ 15,000.00	$ 15,000.00
Operating Expenses	4,250.00	4,250.00
NET INCOME before debt service	10,750.00	10,750.00

DEBT RETIREMENT SERVICE
$ 85,000.00 @ 547.66 per month @ 6%
Total annual installment $6,574.92
Amount applied to interest 5,078.80
Amortization of debt   1,496.12

Total annual installments	6,574.92	
Interest portion (tax deductible)		5,078.80
CASH FLOW	4,175.08	
TAXABLE CASH BEFORE DEPRECIATION		5,671.20

DEPRECIATION SCHEDULE
Total investment $125,000.00
Land value   30,000.00
Depreciable basis   95,000.00
Method used - 150% D/B
Depreciation rate: 25 yr. life - 6% per year
First year write-off   5,700.00

SPENDABLE CASH	4,175.08	
TAXABLE INCOME (net loss)		- 28.80

TAX SHELTER COMPUTATIONS:
(The amount by which depreciation exceeds amortization is <u>tax shelter</u>):
Depreciation (first year write-off) $ 5,700.00
Amortization of loan   1,496.12

Effective tax shelter		4,203.88
a. Cash flow	4,175.08	
b. Tax loss (added)	28.80	
c. Equal actual tax shelter		4,203.80

LISTING AND SELLING APARTMENT UNITS

It is very probable that your first venture into the investment selling field will involve a small apartment house of some kind, as this is the easiest step for a residential salesman to take. Duplexes, tri-plexes, **and** four-plexes are often sold to homebuyers or investors who are making their initial entry into real estate investments, frequently with nominal amounts of cash for down payments. Leverage can be readily used to increase the yield for apartment house buyers since many lending institutions will loan 75% to 90% of the cost of land and improvements to the builder or purchaser.

EXPANDING YOUR REAL ESTATE OPPORTUNITIES

With emphasis on convenience and economy, there is a noticeable trend, in most major cities, from suburbia back to central locations and apartment living. This has shown marked acceleration in the past ten years and seems to be increasing with each passing year. Thus, the opportunities for listing and selling residential income units are also improving. The first rule to remember is that nearly every apartment building is for sale -- if you can improve the owner's position by selling it. How do you list an apartment building? The same way you list a home -- by meeting the owners, asking questions and creating opportunities. Remember, however, that income selling requires emphasis on the financial benefits rather than the sentimental attachments commonly associated with home ownership. Show an owner of a multiple unit how he can improve his estate or personal income through buying or selling property, and he will readily work with you. Create a tax-free exchange for more profitable property or show him how his depreciation write-offs have now been exhausted and the property should be sold or traded, and you have the makings of a real estate transaction others overlooked.

Thoroughness in gathering the facts is just as essential, if not more so, than in home selling. This includes:

1. Interviewing the owner in detail for all pertinent information;
2. Inspecting the exterior of the building noting repairs needed;
3. Inspecting the interior of the building noting repairs needed;
4. Inspecting representative units occupied by tenants for condition and quality;
5. Interviewing the resident or property manager:
   a. Obtaining the rent schedule
   b. Obtaining itemized lists of expenses
   c. Obtaining accurate information on vacancy factors
   d. Verifying loan balances and other encumbrances
6. Projecting this information on apartment description forms, including analysis of yield related to price and terms available. (See forms on page 253)

There is a tendency for real estate salesmen to overlook such things as vacancy factors, maintenance, and management costs which should be considered when evaluating any income producing property. The typical broker's statement ignores these items, but no knowledgeable buyer will be fooled by this approach. It is much wiser to include reasonable reserves for these expenses rather than hide them from the public.

WHY DO PEOPLE BUY APARTMENTS?

There are many reasons why different buyers acquire residential income property, but most of them are financial. The advantage of ownership for one person may be simply in the tax shelter gained by depreciation and equity gain, while another may want spendable income. Apartment units seldom show as high a return as some other real estate investments will, but they are easier to acquire. Here, in my opinion, are the four major factors governing the motivations of apartment buyers in the order of their importance:

INVESTMENT LISTING AGREEMENT
DUPLEX and/or APARTMENT

Address_____ Cross Street_____ Units_____

Name_____ Furn_____

Style_____ Age_____ Lot_____ Dist_____

FLOORS													BASEMENT	PRICE
Entrance Hall													Gas Furnace	DOWN
Living Room													Oil Furnace	Month
Dining Room													Floor Furnace	1st Mtg.
Comb. L & D													Single Wall Furnace	Monthly
Kitchen													Dual Wall Furnace	Payable
Com. Kitchen													Gas Cir. Heater	2nd Mtg.
Breakfast Nook													Oil Circ. Heater	Monthly
Kitchenette													Electric Heater	Payable
Bed Rooms													A. E. Hot Water	Contract
Baths													Gas Hot Water	Monthly
Toilets													Gas Meter	Payable
Basin													Electric Meter	Total Payment
Shower													Wired Elec. Range	License
Den													Laundry Room	Taxes
Hwd.													Laundry Trays	Garbage
Pine													Washers	Insurance
Range													Driers	Heat
Refrigerator													Det. Garage	Electric
Fireplace													Att. Garage	Gas
Tile Kit Bath													Det. Carport	Water
H. K. Room													Att. Carport	Vacancy
Rentals													Parking Space	Miscellaneous
													Sewer	Total Expense
													Septic Tank	Gross Income
													Square Feet	Main Expense
														Net Income

Key Information_____ See Tenant_____

Legal Description: In County of_____, State of California_____

_____

Additional Information_____

_____
_____
_____
_____
_____

The above deemed reliable but carries no guaranty

In consideration of services to be rendered, I hereby give to_____
the_____ right to sell my property as listed above, for_____
(STATE IF EXCLUSIVE)
$_____ dollars and to accept the deposit thereon; for the _____ day period from
_____, 19____ to _____, 19____
and within _____ days thereafter to parties with whom said Broker negotiated during said period, provided said Broker notifies me in writing of said negotiation.
If a sale or exchange is effected _____ during their agency for the above described property, I agree to pay them _____ per cent of the selling price; as commission for their services, and to furnish satisfactory title to said property.
Owner acknowledges receipt of a copy of this listing.

DATED AT_____ SIGNED_____
                                                                    OWNER
THIS_____ DAY OF_____ 19____ _____
                                                                    OWNER
LISTED BY_____ ADDRESS_____
                        SALESMAN
ACCEPTED_____ PHONE_____
                        AGENT

EXPANDING YOUR REAL ESTATE OPPORTUNITIES

SUBMITTED BY: _____
PHONE NO. _____

STONE & SCHULTE

MULTIPLE DWELLING

NAME OF BUILDING _____ NO. APTS. _____
ADDRESS _____ PRICE $_____
CITY _____ DOWN $_____
TRADE FOR _____ EQUITY $_____

GROSS INC. $_____
EXPENSES $_____
PROFIT $_____
LOAN PMTS. $_____
SPENDABLE $_____

OWNER _____

ADD. _____

PHONE _____

MGR. _____

PHONE _____

HOW SHOWN _____

(Plot or Photo)

APT. NOS.	ROOMS	BRS.	FURN. UNF.	RENT MO.	EXPENSES (annual)		LOAN INFORMATION as of _____ 19__
				$____	TAXES	$____	1st $_____ $_____ mo.
				$____	INS.	$____	@ ___% Due ___ With ___
				$____	UTIL.	$____	2nd $_____ $_____ mo.
				$____	PHONE	$____	@ ___% Due ___ With ___
				$____	GARBAGE	$____	3rd $_____ $_____ mo.
				$____	SUPPLIES	$____	@ ___% Due ___ With ___
				$____	REPAIRS	$____	Other ___
				$____	WAGES	$____	
				$____		$____	Owner will carry $_____ @ ___%
				$____		$____	Payable $_____ per ___
				$____		$____	TOTAL FINANCING AVAILABLE $_____
TOTAL MONTHLY RENTALS $____					TOTAL	$____	TOTAL LOAN PAYMENTS $_____

CONSTRUCTION _____ STORIES _____ CONDITION _____ AGE _____ HEAT _____
ELEVATORS _____ FLOORS _____ BUILT-INS _____ TILE: KITCHEN _____ BATH _____
AIR COND. _____ CENT. HOT WATER _____ LAUNDRY EQUIP.: OWNED _____ RENTED _____
SWIMMING POOL _____ PATIOS _____ PARKING _____ LOT SIZE _____
REMARKS _____

BROKER Stone & Schulte, Inc. ADDRESS 745 W. San Carlos, San Jose
OFFICE PHONE CY 7-3757 LISTER _____ HOME PHONE _____

The information contained herein has either been given to us by the owner of the property or obtained from sources deemed reliable; however we do not guarantee its accuracy.

1. Tax shelter through depreciation while equity is building for the future
2. Appreciation in future value and equity accumulation
3. Spendable cash income
4. Ease of acquisition as first step in investment program

With any apartment building the most important single item of value is location. A careful study of the neighborhood and of the market from which tenants and future buyers will be found will indicate the quality of the apartment house site. To gather such information may require a door-to-door survey in the general area involved. Some of the things you will want to know to help your buyers and sellers are:

1. What level of rents are being charged for similar, competing buildings?
2. What is the current vacancy factor in this area and what impact is this likely to have on the units in question?
3. What services do competing owners offer their tenants that are not offered by your owner?
4. Are most units being rented furnished or unfurnished, and what type of tenants are available for each?
5. Are units leased or rented on month-to-month tenancy agreements?
6. What is the current turnover rate of tenants coming and going from competing units?
7. How many apartment buildings are for sale in the area of your survey?

DETERMINING THE PRICE

Each apartment building must be evaluated based on all the facts, with particular notice of competing offerings available to investors. The yield which can be reasonably expected by a new owner must be in line with similar properties and competing investments if the property is to be readily sold. The usual approach is to capitalize the net income by determining the expenses and deducting them from the gross income (sometimes less loan amortization amounts), multiplied by the return desired by the average apartment house investor as evidenced in the current market.

EXAMPLE:

PROPERTY: 892 Carver Boulevard, Yourtown, U.S.A.

NUMBER OF UNITS: 12 (8 one-bedroom; 4 two-bedroom)

LOT SIZE: (See plot map attached)

IMPROVEMENTS: (See attached detailed description and inventory)

INCOME:

8 units @ $115.00 per month	$ 920.00	
4 units @ $135.00 per month	540.00	
4 garages @ 3.50 per month	14.00	
Income from laundry facilities	15.00	
Total monthly income	$ 1,489.00	
Annual Gross Income		$ 17,868.00

EXPENSES:

Taxes	$ 1,680.00
Insurance	189.75
Electricity	611.55
Gas	529.32
Water	172.10
Garbage	187.50
Resident manager allowance ($75 pm)	900.00
Licenses and fees	44.80
	$ 4,315.02

RESERVES:

Management (5% of gross income)	$893.40
Maintenance (3% of gross income)	536.04
Vacancy Factor (5% of gross income)	893.40
	$ 2,322.84

ANNUAL NET INCOME: $ 11,230.14
CAPITALIZED AT 10% Building is valued at $112,300.00
CAPITALIZED AT 8% (net income X 100 divided by interest $140,377.00

In the above example, the items listed as <u>expenses</u> are those generally included in a <u>Broker's Net</u> and the ones marked <u>Reserves</u> are usually excluded from the listing information records. However, they are both valid costs and should be considered. Also, as already emphasized, the yield to the purchaser can be increased by financing the property and obtaining leverage value. If the owner assists in making this possible, the property can easily be sold for more than it would bring on an "all cash" basis and the price might be adjusted accordingly.[6]

MOTELS, HOTELS, TRAILER PARKS

With Americans on the move in increasing numbers, the importance of transient lodging has grown substantially since World War II. Trailer parks or mobile lodges have proven exceptionally popular in the West and

---

[6] Each broker has his own approach to the presentation of income producing properties and the reader should consult with his employer to ascertain the desired forms and procedures to be used in the office of his association.

are often among the more profitable investments available to real estate buyers. The salesman who involves himself in representing these properties must be willing to learn many details about their operation and know how to correctly interpret the information given by owners. Establishing the truth about income and expenses becomes a vital factor, as well as knowing the regulations of city, county and state agencies which control the lodging business. The forms on pages 257 to 258 will show you what information must be gathered to properly present a motel, hotel, or trailer park.

COMMERCIAL-INDUSTRIAL BUILDINGS AND LEASES

The selling and leasing of commercial or industrial real estate is a highly specialized field and can truly be recognized as the "big league" of our profession. Extensive knowledge is usually required before the salesman can properly handle large commercial or industrial offerings, but even the neophyte can practice on small units and gradually work up to the larger ones. Leasing professional units, shopping centers, and industrial buildings demands knowledge of the leasing provisions desired by owners and tenants, as well as the ability to arrange financing for both, if needed. Standard form leases seldom can be used in their entirety for any given situation, as each must be tailored to the specifications of lessor and lessee.

One of the more creative aspects of this field is the arranging of long term net lease-backs after selling the property to a new owner and permitting the tenant to remain in possession under a favorable lease. This is one of the more desirable real estate transactions, since it frees the present occupant's capital for use in his business, while permitting him to retain control and operation of the property for his enterprise. The new owner has a guaranteed income with a good net return and a lease he can even finance if he wants to increase his yield through leverage.

SELLING BUSINESS OPPORTUNITIES

In many states a special real estate license is required when one engages in the sale of businesses that are not incidental to the real estate. This again is a specialized field, requiring knowledge of accounting and business management. Selling restaurants, bars, grocery stores, service stations, and other places of business (when they are separate from the real property) demands a technical ability to interpret the business statistics and promote the enterprise to new operators. If you are interested, consult your broker for more information on selling business opportunities in your local area.

SELLING LAND, FARMS, RANCHES

Probably no aspect of our profession is more challenging than the sale and development of raw land. Truly, in this phase of real estate, the broker, builder, and developer have the greatest opportunities to create new wealth and new values. Raw land is just that -- until someone finds a use for it! Value in land is created and enhanced by the salesman, developer,

EXPANDING YOUR REAL ESTATE OPPORTUNITIES

STONE & SCHULTE

SUBMITTED BY: _____
PHONE NO. _____

MOTEL

NAME OF MOTEL _____ NO. UNITS _____
ADDRESS _____ PRICE $_____
CITY _____ HIGHWAY _____ DOWN $_____
TRADE FOR _____ EQUITY $_____

GROSS INC. $_____
EXPENSE $_____
PROFIT $_____
LOAN PMTS. $_____
SPENDABLE $_____

OWNER _____

ADD. _____
      _____

PHONE _____

MGR. _____

PHONE _____

HOW SHOWN _____

(Plot or Photo)

INCOME for 19___		EXPENSES (annual)		LOAN INFORMATION as of _____ 19___
JAN.	$_____	TAXES	$_____	1st $_____ $_____ mo.
FEB.	_____	INS.	_____	@____% Due _____ With _____
MAR.	_____	UTILITIES	_____	2nd $_____ $_____ mo.
APR.	_____	PHONE	_____	@____% Due _____ With _____
MAY	_____	RUBBISH	_____	3rd $_____ $_____ mo.
JUNE	_____	LINEN	_____	@____% Due _____ With _____
JULY	_____	SUPPLIES	_____	Other _____
AUG.	_____	SIGN	_____	
SEPT.	_____	TV's	_____	
OCT.	_____	GARDENING	_____	Owner will carry $_____ @____%
NOV.	_____	MAIDS	_____	Payable $_____ Per _____
DEC.	_____	MGR.	_____	
	$_____		_____	TOTAL FINANCING AVAILABLE $_____
	$_____		_____	TOTAL PAYMENTS, ALL LOANS $_____
TOTAL	$_____	TOTAL	$_____	

CONSTRUCTION _____ CONDITION _____ AGE _____ ROOF _____
ELEVATORS _____ NO. KITCHENS _____ TILE BATHS _____ SHOWER DOORS _____
HEAT _____ AIR COND. _____ TYPE _____ FLOORS _____
TV's ____ OWNED _____ LEASED _____ LINEN OWNED _____ LEASED _____ SEWER _____
OTHER BUILDINGS _____ LEASED? _____
LOBBY _____ SWITCHBOARD _____ COFFEE BAR _____ POOL _____ HEATED _____
OWNERS APT. (describe) _____
LOT SIZE _____ FRONT _____ BY _____ OR, _____
REMARKS _____

BROKER   Stone & Schulte, Inc. _____ ADDRESS 1745 W. San Carlos, San Jose
OFFICE PHONE CY 7-3757 _____ LISTER _____ HOME PHONE _____

The information contained herein has either been given to us by the owner of the property or obtained from sources deemed reliable; however we do not guarantee its accuracy.

MOBILE HOMES PARK

STONE & SCHULTE

SUBMITTED BY: _____
PHONE NO.: _____

NAME OF PARK _____ NO. SPACES _____
ADDRESS _____ PRICE $_____
CITY _____ HIGHWAY _____ DOWN $_____
TRADE FOR _____ EQUITY $_____

GROSS INC. $_____
EXPENSES $_____
PROFIT $_____
LOAN PMTS. $_____
SPENDABLE $_____

OWNER _____
ADD. _____

PHONE _____
MGR. _____
MGR. PHONE _____
HOW SHOWN _____

(Plot or Photo)

INCOME FOR 19___	EXPENSE (annual)	LOAN INFORMATION as of _____ 19___
RENT $_____	TAXES $_____	1st $_____ $_____ mo.
ELECT. $_____	INS. $_____	@ ___% Due _____ by _____
GAS $_____	ELECT. $_____	2nd $_____ $_____ mo.
STORAGE $_____	GAS $_____	@ ___% Due _____ by _____
LAUNDRY $_____	WATER $_____	3rd $_____ $_____ mo.
VENDING $_____	PHONE $_____	@ ___% Due _____ by _____
(other) $_____	RUBBISH $_____	Other _____
_____ $_____	SUPPLIES $_____	
_____ $_____	GARDEN $_____	Owner will carry $_____ @ ___%
_____ $_____	MANAGER $_____	Payable $_____ per _____
_____ $_____	LICENSE $_____	TOTAL FINANCING AVAILABLE $_____
_____ $_____	_____ $_____	TOTAL LOAN PAYMENTS $_____
_____ $_____	_____ $_____	
TOTAL $_____	TOTAL $_____	

Length Spaces	Rate per Mo.	Util. at Space
___ of ___ ft.	@ $___	Sewer ___
___ of ___ ft.	@ $___	Water ___
___ of ___ ft.	@ $___	Gas ___
___ of ___ ft.	@ $___	110v Elec. ___
___ of ___ ft.	@ $___	220v Elec. ___
___ of ___ ft.	@ $___	Phone ___
___ of ___ ft.	@ $___	TV Ant. ___

Rec. Room _____ Size _____ Pool _____
Play Ground _____ Laundry Room _____
No. Washers _____ No. Dryers _____ Owned _____
Leased _____ Workshop _____ Stg. Yard _____
Garages _____ Rest Rooms _____
Rental Buildings _____
Sewer _____ City Water _____ Own Well _____
Drives Paved _____ Landscaped _____
Lot Size _____ Zone _____
Owner's Home _____

REMARKS _____

BROKER Stone & Schulte, Inc. ADDRESS 1745 W. San Carlos, San Jose
OFFICE PHONE CY 7-3757 LISTER _____ HOME PHONE _____

The information contained herein has either been given to us by the owner of the property or obtained from sources deemed reliable, however we do not guarantee its accuracy.

EXPANDING YOUR REAL ESTATE OPPORTUNITIES

SUBMITTED BY: _____	STONE & SCHULTE	COMMERCIAL _____
PHONE NO. _____		INDUSTRIAL _____

NAME OR TYPE OR BLDG. _____ NO. RENTALS _____
ADDRESS _____ PRICE $_____
CITY _____ DISTRICT _____ DOWN $_____
TRADE FOR _____ EQUITY $_____

GROSS INCOME $_____
EXPENSES $_____
PROFIT $_____
LOAN PMTS. $_____
SPENDABLE $_____

OWNER _____

ADD. _____

_____

PHONE _____

MGR. _____

PHONE _____

HOW SHOWN _____

_____

(Plot or Photo)

Unit #	Size	Tenant	Rent Mo.

Loan Information as of _____ 19____
1st $_____ $_____ mo.
@____% Due _____ With _____
2nd $_____ $_____ mo.
@____% Due _____ With _____
OTHER _____

OWNER WILL CARRY $_____ @____%
PAYABLE $_____ PER _____
TOTAL FINANCING AVAILABLE $_____
TOTAL MONTHLY INCOME $_____ TOTAL PMTS. ALL LOANS $_____
ANNUAL INCOME $_____ OVERAGES $_____

EXPENSES (annual)   DESCRIPTION
TAXES $_____   CONSTRUCTION _____   CONDITION _____
FIRE INS. $_____   AGE _____   ROOF _____
LIAB. INS. $_____   BASEMENT _____   ELEVATORS _____
UTILITIES $_____   HEAT _____   POWER _____
JANITOR $_____   AIR CONDITIONING _____   TYPE _____
REPAIRS $_____   PARKING _____
_____ $_____   LOT SIZE _____   STREET FRONTAGE _____
_____ $_____   ZONE _____   PARKING DISTRICT _____
_____ $_____   REMARKS _____
_____ $_____   _____
_____ $_____   _____
TOTAL $_____

BROKER Stone & Schulte, Inc. ADDRESS 1745 W. San Carlos, San Jose,
OFFICE PHONE CY 7-3757   LISTER _____ HOME PHONE _____

The information contained herein has either been given to us by the owner of the property or obtained from sources deemed reliable; however, we do not guarantee its accuracy.

or entrepreneur who understands how to convert the natural assets into a project for public or private use. This is true even of the farmer or rancher who must learn how to extract a higher yield from the crops he plants or the animals he grazes.

As in the other specialities of investment selling, you must know as much as possible about the value and use of land you represent if you are to successfully sell it to someone. If you hope to sell it to a subdivider, there are many questions you should ask the owner and the other people concerned with this parcel before you ever present it to the developer. Here is a brief check list of some of the details any builder-developer would want to know before he purchased the property:

1. What is the exact size of the parcel in terms of acreage, not just an approximate figure?
2. What is the best land use pattern and what recommendations would an engineer make regarding its development?
3. What approximate costs of offsite and onsite improvements can the developer reasonably expect before arriving at finished lots or plots?
4. What are the tentative or firm zoning restrictions, and how does the master plan of the area conform to the proposed use?
5. What is the topography of the area, and how will this affect its development?
6. What is the nature of the soil? Is it stable? Is it productive? Will fill be required?
7. Obtain a location map and spot the following items for easy reference:

    a. All existing easements, their size and purpose
    b. Sanitary sewer outfall lines
    c. Storm sewer outfall lines
    d. Drainage directions indicated by red arrows.
    e. Existing water service lines and their sizes.
    f. Existing gas service lines.
    g. Existing electrical service lines.
    h. Any other offsite improvements to be considered.

8. Obtain letters from public utilities companies or governmental agencies stating the availability of facilities and projected services to this parcel.
9. Prepare a market analysis report setting forth your findings and recommendations for the development of this parcel.
10. Prepare a report on the competition the buyer will experience from similar properties and a comparison of values offered.

These facts properly included in a prospectus about the land you are representing can often create a sale that would not have been made were the many questions you answered left uncovered. There is never any reason why a salesman should not do a professional job when presenting real estate to buyers and sellers.

EXPANDING YOUR REAL ESTATE OPPORTUNITIES

SUBMITTED BY: _____

PHONE NO. _____

Stone & Schulte

RANCH AND ACREAGE

NAME OR TYPE OF RANCH _____ NO. ACRES _____
ADDRESS _____ MAJOR CROP _____
CITY _____ COUNTY _____ PRICE $ _____
TRADE FOR _____ DOWN $ _____
_____   EQUITY $ _____

GROSS INC. $ _____
EXPENSES $ _____
PROFIT $ _____
LOAN PMTS. $ _____
SPENDABLE $ _____

OWNER _____

ADD. _____

_____

PHONE _____

MGR. _____

PHONE _____

HOW SHOWN _____

(Plot or Photo)

1. CROPS or PASTURE
   _____ acres in: _____
   _____ acres in: _____
   _____ acres in: _____
   _____ acres in: _____

2. NUMBER OF HEAD _____
3. HOME: Rooms _____ Bedrooms _____ Dining Room _____ Breakfast Room _____
   Basement _____ Furnace _____ Flooring _____ Baths _____ Shower _____
   Fire Place _____ Exterior _____ Roof Type _____ Foundation _____
   Sewer _____ Age _____ Condition _____ Distance to High School _____
   Distance to Grammar School _____ Distance to Nearest Town _____

4. OTHER BLDGS: Garage _____ Barn size _____ Dairy Barn _____ Hay Barn _____
   Sheds _____ Poultry _____ Other _____
5. Well _____ Pump _____ Motor _____ GPM _____ Ground pipe _____
   Sprinkler system _____ Equipment _____
6. Taxes _____ Gross Income _____ Possession _____
   Terms _____
   _____
   _____
   _____
   _____

BROKER Stone & Schulte, Inc. _____ ADDRESS 1745 W. San Carlos, San Jose
OFFICE PHONE CY 7-3757 _____ LISTER _____ HOME PHONE _____

The information contained herein has either been given to us by the owner of the property or obtained from sources deemed reliable; however we do not guarantee its accuracy.

EXPANDING YOUR REAL ESTATE OPPORTUNITIES

If you are selling a farm or ranch, be sure you have all the facts about the productivity of the real estate and know how it can be used to increase the return to the owners. Know as much as possible about the farming practices of the current owners and the techniques of competing farmers. List all of the equipment, supplies, animals, and other items which will be sold with the property, and know the value attached to these things not connected with the real estate.

EXCHANGING -- THE CREATIVE TRANSFER OF PROPERTY

Because of tax laws and the personal financial requirements of property owners, the outright sale of real estate is not always the best answer to individual situations. Exchanging or trading one or more parcels for other real estate can serve many purposes, and is one of the more creative ways to produce real estate commissions. Exchanging is another specialized art and requires additional knowledge before one can attain any appreciable success. Essentially, it is a matter of finding owners with similar needs and arranging to transfer the equities with "cash" or "boot" differences used to adjust variations in the owners' interests. Since this subject is an extensive one with many aspects that command special attention, I recommend to you some of the publications on this topic [7] or attending one or more of the various courses given on exchanges. For an example of the type of form used to embody the exchange agreement and the points covered therein see pages 264-65.

PROPERTY MANAGEMENT

Wherever there is extensive development of commercial real estate, there is a need for professional property management. This is a function which realtors have been serving for many years, and most large real estate firms operate some type of property management department. Even small brokerage companies find themselves performing some of the duties of a property manager when they lease or sell income producing real estate, and it is not long before they consider establishing regular management service or assigning it to another brokerage company specializing in this field.

Although this is not one of the most profitable phases of our business, it is, nevertheless, a vital function of our profession. Property management requires a general background in both the selling and supervision of real estate investments, including accounting, maintenance, and leasing. If you are interested in this phase of business, write to NAREB, in care of Institute of Property Management, 36 Wabash St., Chicago, Ill.

APPRAISING

The real estate appraiser plays an important part in the sale and financing of real property. To become an experienced and qualified appraiser normally requires years of accumulated activity in the real estate business

---

[7] See Richard Reno's book on Exchanging (Prentice-Hall). Also write to the International Trader's Club, NAREB, 36 Wabash St., Chicago, Illinois.

EXPANDING YOUR REAL ESTATE OPPORTUNITIES

either as a salesman, broker, or mortgage representative. Appraising is a natural part of your activity as a real estate salesman, and as you progress in your career, you will learn to become more efficient in evaluating the factors affecting the properties you handle.

Appraising has been defined as:

"The gathering of factual data about property and the rendering of an opinion of value."

Every real estate salesman should take a course or two in appraising whether or not he intends to specialize in this activity, since he needs the basic knowledge in order to properly evaluate the listings he services and sells. On page 65 to 66, we have covered some of the fundamentals of appraising, but because of its importance we will review here other things you should know about the subject.

APPROACHES TO VALUE IN APPRAISING

There are three approaches to value used in most appraising. These are:

1. The Market Data or Comparable Approach

This is the gathering of information about competitive properties offered on the market; comparables of sales actually made; records of listings expiring unsold; appraisals of other parcels for loans or for sales; and a research of the neighborhood environmental factors which will influence values.[8]

2. The Replacement Cost Approach

This is a means of estimating value by determining the approximate costs incurred if the building and other improvements were replaced (not reproduced) with a product of equal or like utility. Per square foot cost guides can be used to assist in this estimate, together with a knowledge of raw land costs and depreciation factors.

3. The Income Approach

For investment properties, a third guide is used which is based on estimating the financial return and benefits which the property should reasonably produce for the owner now and in the future. This is generally done by capitalizing the income as explained on pages 254 and 255.

FACTORS OF DEPRECIATION CONSIDERED IN APPRAISING

Appraisers must be able to relate all the factors of depreciation which limit the value of real property. Depreciation has been defined as "loss of value for any cause at all." There are three primary causes to be considered:

---

[8] See the Competitive Property Report Form on page 52.

Exchange Agreement

....

hereinafter called first party, hereby offers to exchange the following described property, situated in ....
...., County of ...., California:

....

....

....

....

....

....

For the following described property of ....
.... hereinafter called second party, situated in
...., County of ...., California:

....

....

....

....

....

Terms and Conditions of Exchange:

....

....

....

....

....

....

....

....

....

....

The parties hereto shall execute and deliver, within .... days from the date this offer is accepted, all instruments, in writing, necessary to transfer title to said properties and complete and consummate this exchange. Each party shall supply Preliminary Title Reports for their respective properties Evidences of title shall be California Land Title Association standard coverage form policies of title insurance showing titles to be merchantable and free of all liens and encumbrances, except taxes and those liens and encumbrances as otherwise set forth herein. Each party shall pay for the policies of Title Insurance for the property to be acquired ☐ conveyed ☐.

If either party is unable to convey a marketable title, except as herein provided, within three months after acceptance hereof by second party, or if the improvements on any of the herein named properties be destroyed or materially damaged prior to transfer of title or delivery of agreement of sale, then this agreement shall be of no further effect, except as to payment of commissions and expenses incurred in connection with examination of title, unless the party acquiring the property so affected elects to accept the title the other party can convey or subject to the conditions of the improvements.

Taxes, insurance premiums (if policies be satisfactory to party acquiring the property affected thereby), rents interest and other expenses of said properties shall be pro-rated as of the date of transfer of title or delivery of agreement of sale, unless otherwise provided herein.

.... of .... Calif. ....
         Broker   *Address*   *Phone No.*

is hereby authorized to act as broker for all parties hereto and may accept commission therefrom. Should second party accept this offer, first party agrees to pay said broker commission for services rendered as follows:-

Should second party be unable to convey a marketable title to his property then first party shall be released from payment of any commission, unless he elects to accept the property subject thereto. First party agrees that broker may co-operate with other brokers and divide commissions in any manner satisfactory to them.

This offer shall be deemed revoked unless accepted in writing within .... days after date hereof, and such acceptance is communicated to first party within said period. Broker is hereby given the exclusive and irrevocable right to obtain acceptance of second party within said period.

Time is the essence of this contract, but Broker may, without notice, extend for a period of not to exceed one month the time for the performance of any act hereunder, except the time for the acceptance hereof by second party.

All words used herein in the singular shall include the plural and the present tense shall include the future and the masculine gender shall include the feminine and neuter.

Dated .... 19..........

ACCEPTANCE

Second party hereby accepts the foregoing offer upon the terms and conditions stated and agrees to pay commission for services rendered, to:-

.... of .... Calif. ....
         Broker   *Address*   *Phone No.*

as follows:- ....

Second party agrees that broker may act as broker for all parties hereto and may accept commission therefrom, and may co-operate with other brokers and divide commissions in any manner satisfactory to them.

Should first party be unable to convey a marketable title to his property then second party shall be released from payment of any commission, unless he elects to accept the property of first party subject thereto.

Dated .... 19..........

1. Physical Deterioration

This represents all items directly connected with the property, intrinsic to its nature, which have evidenced wear and tear or destruction due to natural causes. Such things as termites, rotting wood, peeling paint, and other damage, are items of physical deterioration. There are two categories: curable and incurable. The latter represents those depreciation factors which cannot be replaced without exceeding recoverable costs.

2. Functional Obsolescence

These are the items of depreciation inherent in the property resulting from design or usage and which limit its desirability in the market place today. Functional obsolescence is merely a reflection of the tastes and ideas of the buyers currently available to acquire a property. If the property does not meet competing standards, it is functionally obsolete in those areas.

3. Economic Obsolescence

These are the adverse influences outside of the property itself which affect the value or use of the property. Neighborhood influence, zoning, traffic patterns, and other external changes can seriously depreciate the value of a parcel of real estate. Misplaced or overimproved properties are affected by their environments and are said to be subject to economic obsolescence factors.

THE APPRAISER'S ROLE

None of the approaches to value or factors of depreciation are important by themselves and the appraiser's role is to correlate these various items to provide a reasonable estimate of value. If the appraiser works for a lending institution, he will appraise differently than were he to represent the real estate broker trying to establish the sales price, or the owner who is attempting to determine the value of his assets. At best, appraising is not an exact science since the opinion of the appraiser is subject to variations, and the buyers can pay more or less than the appraiser feels is reasonable. Any appraiser who can establish market value within a 3% to 5% margin of error is considered to be reasonably accurate.

Professional appraisers are usually well paid, especially those dealing in large parcels and who are experienced in court procedures to defend their opinions. If this field interests you, consult with your broker for further information, or write to the American Institute of Appraisers, NAREB, Chicago, Illinois.

MORTGAGE SPECIALITIES AVAILABLE

Many real estate salesmen graduate into mortgage financing as a profitable outgrowth of their real estate knowledge and experience. The procuring and arranging of mortgages for clients and brokers can be a very satisfying occupation. In most states, any licensed real estate salesman or broker can be paid a commission for arranging a loan for a customer or client, but generally this activity is performed by those who limit their duties to mortgage financing entirely. In addition to recognized lending institutions, there are three types of private mortgage functions usually served by real estate brokers or companies. They are:

1. Mortgage Brokers:

These are real estate brokers who "list" loans and then "place" them for a commission or fee. They seldom, if ever, use their own capital to buy and sell the mortgages they handle, but operate just as in real estate brokerage, listing and selling the securities they uncover. Their fees are usually paid by the lending company out of the "origination costs" paid by buyer, owner, or seller. Sometimes, however, the other parties agree to pay the broker for his help in procuring the desired financing.

2. Loan Correspondents

When a real estate broker obtains the representation of an exclusive account to which he presents mortgages for acquisition, he is said to be the "loan correspondent" for that particular lender. Insurance companies prefer the use of loan correspondents around the country rather than incur the costs of establishing branch offices and the overhead such operations would entail. Savings and Loans and other lenders occasionally make exclusive representation agreements with brokers in areas they cannot service alone.

3. Mortgage Bankers

Mortgage bankers are the entrepreneurs of the real estate financing field. They use their own capital or line of credit to buy and sell mortgages to other lenders and frequently retain the servicing of such loans for an additional fee. They deal primarily in FHA, VA, and similar loans, but also act as mortgage brokers for conventional loans. In the west they play a primary part in the origination and placement of government insured financing.

OTHER SPECIALIZATIONS IN REAL ESTATE

There are many other activities related to the real estate profession which could attract your interest as you continue in this industry. Detailed information about each can be obtained from other sources, since space here does not allow more extensive coverage. Review them and note those on which you desire more knowledge, then consult with your broker or other real estate friends about where to find the information you want.

1. Real Estate Insurance

   Insuring the real estate we sell has become an automatic partner to our basic business. Most offices operate some type of general insurance program to meet the needs of the buyers and sellers they represent, and in many cases, the insurance operation has grown to be an outstanding source of income and profit. Usually it must be supervised by one person who is completely responsible for its functions and who is licensed under the insurance laws of the state where operating.

2. Escrow and Title Work

   With the increasing popularity of Title Companies and Escrow Companies, many real estate people gravitate to positions of responsibility in these related enterprises. Normally, this type of work does not pay as well as real estate selling, but there are other compensating benefits.

3. Real Estate Counselling

   When you have qualified as an investment expert, it is possible to earn your living just advising buyers and sellers and their agents about the methods, procedures, and pitfalls of particular transactions. This is an "elite" group of real estate professionals, but one that will undoubtedly be expanded in the years to come.

4. Subdividing and Building

   Brokers and salesmen who learn real estate values and business management often turn their attentions to the acquisition and development of property for speculation or investment. Certainly this is one of the most lucrative aspects of our industry, but also one that takes capital, talent, and time to obtain profitable results. Be certain to review any thoughts you have about this subject with your broker, he probably has policies that will affect your activity in building or developing real estate.

5. Syndication

   Private syndicates of real estate investors are becoming increasingly popular due to the many advantages such diversified operations can offer their participants. The pooling of assets and knowledge makes possible the acquisition and development of real estate which few of the members could tackle alone. Some real estate brokers and salesmen become experts on organizing syndicates and then selling them properties as their exclusive agents, arranging all the financial details and collecting commissions for their efforts. It is practical to become a part of such syndication groups if you have the time and talent to dedicate to their growth. Most syndicates are limited partnerships with a general partner carrying the majority of responsibility. Corporations are usually discouraged because they do not provide the participants with the tax shelters of individual or partnership ventures, but some prefer the corporate structure due to its limited liability to stockholders. If you contemplate organizing any investment groups, consult your lawyer and your tax attorney for advice. Some of the sources of income to you or your broker might be:

1. Fees or commissions for brokerage, appraising, financing, or insuring the properties sold and acquired;
2. Participating as an investor by letting your commissions ride for a percentage interest in the venture;
3. Fees for managing the syndicate and its properties;
4. Opportunities to invest your own capital in the program;
5. Exposure to additional capital once you successfully organize and operate a syndicate.

CHART YOUR FUTURE WITH CARE

Before selecting any of these specialized phases of business for your personal emphasis, study your own market area carefully and weigh your natural interests and drives. Many salesmen are completely satisfied to make a career of residential selling, building a profitable business on their referrals and knowledge. If you elect to pursue one or more of these specialized fields, be sure you are mentally and financially prepared to make the transition. I am certain your broker will agree with me when I tell you it takes considerable "belt tightening" to become an investment property salesman. Be sure to take your sales manager or broker into your confidence before attempting a change as he can point out both the pitfalls and advantages as they apply to your individual talents. Residential selling is the "bread and butter" business which assures you a steady monthly income, wheras other activities often require many months of effort before returns are realized.

BE ACTIVE IN YOUR REAL ESTATE ASSOCIATION

It is my firm conviction every real estate salesman and broker owes it to himself and his industry to become an active member of the National Association of Real Estate Boards, through membership in the local affiliated boards. The principal advantage to you in such association is the opportunity to gain additional knowledge about your business and participate in the activities which benefit you and your industry. The California Real Estate Association, to which I belong, is an outstanding example of a well organized society of Realtors who contribute to the welfare of the real estate business. Hundreds of dedicated members give annually of their time and knowledge to conduct sales conferences, hold committe meetings, review legislation affecting real estate, and to bring together fellow members in an active program designed to raise the standards of the entire profession.

At the national level, the National Association of Real Estate Boards sponsors many activities that benefit realtors around the nation. Some of the divisions which will be of special interest to you are:

1. The Institute of Real Estate Brokers

   This group publishes four or more booklets each year about real estate which are of exceptional value in educating members regarding the techniques of the business. The annual fee is only $15.00 for those who hold membership in local boards.

2. The International Traders Club

   This division of the Brokers Institute specializes in exchanging and trade-ins and publishes a Trader's Journal that offers many helpful ideas on making extra sales through trading. Membership in this group is also only a nominal fee.

3. Institute of Property Management

   For those specializing in commercial property and property management, membership in this institute is highly desirable. A Property Management Journal is published regularly to further the education of members.

4. Institute of Real Estate Appraisers

   Connected with the National Association of Real Estate Boards is the institute for real estate appraisers, serving as an educational and qualifying board for those desiring to become professional appraisers.

5. Institute of Farm and Land Brokers

   This is another division of NAREB which has attained national recognition for its efforts to aid members in the representation of land and farms. It plays an active part in the development of land sales practices.

   At your local board level, you will find many additional functions and services which will be of direct value to you. Multiple listing services, training classes, weekly meetings, indoctrination courses, and caravans are typical functions of most real estate boards. Within the scope of your daily plans, you should try to include support of your Real Estate Board functions which are designed to help you become a professional among professionals.

DEVELOPING YOUR SALES PERSONALITY

Someone once said: "When you stop getting better, you stop being good." The sincere desire to constantly improve your sales personality, along with your professional knowledge, should be among your primary motivations as you pursue your daily real estate activities. Success in any business depends, to a great extent, on individual effort. As Benjamin Disraeli, the great English leader put it:

"The secret of success is constancy of purpose!"

Exposure and persistent activity is the surest way to more sales and higher earnings. Use every opportunity to tell people about your business, and distribute your business cards freely -- they are one of the least expensive investments you can make.

Charles Schwab, the outstanding sales manager and business administrator of United States Steel for many years, was reported once to have received the following telegram from one of his salesmen:

"Great news! Broke all sales records yesterday!"

Mr. Schwab promptly wired back this reply:

"What did you do today?"

With this brief message, he was accenting an important truth for this young salesman: <u>It is not what we have done that counts, but what we can still do!</u> During the early weeks of your real estate career, you will undoubtedly be filled with exciting enthusiasm for your new found energies and you may then experience some disappointments you had not anticipated. At that point many salesmen are tempted to lose sight of their objectives while others bounce right back with renewed vigor and confidence. The difference in reactions stems from those intangible qualities of character which combine to give men courage. The only difference between stumbling blocks and stepping stones is the way you use them.

Perhaps you have heard the story about the old fisherman who never failed to bring in his limit whenever he went fishing. Others, whose luck seemed less spectacular, were puzzled by his continued success. When asked how he accounted for this remarkable achievement, his only reply would be: <u>"I just keep fishing."</u> The willingness to "just keep fishing" is an important factor in overcoming the normal obstacles of life. When you consistently look for new business while caring for older clients, there is a tendency for such activity to produce results simply by the law of averages. If you are industrious, every day will be filled with opportunities you uncover and challenges you create. Do the things the average salesman doesn't like to do and you will make the extra sales and obtain the extra listings the average salesman misses. Industrious salesmen love people, work, and life, because they have a basic interest in seeing things done every day. They need and want new challenges to increase their zest for life and work.

USE YOUR KNOWLEDGE WISELY

Knowledge is power providing it is combined with the wisdom to direct it! A dictionary is full of many facts, but a dictionary is not capable of selling anything. As you learn more about your profession, increasing your interest in the specialities of real estate, do not overlook the equally important application of that knowledge. Your primary task as a real estate salesman is to communicate with people, helping them solve their real estate problems. The knowledge you possess should be used to help, not just to impress them. Your choice of words should be made with a view to making it easy for your clients to understand you. Simple words are often more powerful and effective, than complicated ones. As you absorb from experience and study the many facets of this exciting profession, develop the ability to relate this knowledge to the needs of those who call upon you for advice and assistance.

You will have many opportunities to pursue education about the real estate industry. Do not let them pass you by unnoticed! The vast majority of real estate sales people learn only enough to obtain their licenses and then cease searching for the basic truths which will help them in the years that follow. As you launch your career, plan to add to your knowledge regularly by taking evening courses at local colleges or reading books which expand your horizon of activities. Ask questions of those who have specialized information and search out the answers when you have particular problems. When sales clinics are sponsored by your real estate board, state association or other industry groups, take advantage of the privileges such meetings afford in increasing your knowledge about your business. As Henry Ford once said:

"If money is your only hope for independence, you will never have it. The only real security that a man can have in this world is a reserve of knowledge, experience and ability."

SINCERITY: A PRICELESS QUALITY

If there is one quality above all others which marks the truly great man, it is his sincerity of purpose. Sincerity is honesty, integrity and loyalty all rolled up in one dominating characteristic. Sincerity is not for sale. It's wellspring of existence is the basic conviction of the mind which trusts rather than condemns, believes rather than doubts. It prefers truth to falsehood. A man who is sincere will not be willing to sacrifice his integrity on an alter of greed and selfishness. The sincere individual will evidence loyalty to his principles, to his employer, to his clients, and most of all to his ideals. It has been well said that: "An ounce of loyalty is worth a pound of cleverness!"

HOW IS YOUR PERSONALITY?

When you meet someone new, do they normally like you? Are your attitudes and actions friendly? Do you radiate enthusiasm and personal warmth to others so that they are drawn to you? Or are you one of those unfortunate individuals who has never learned to appreciate people and who talks about himself instead of expressing interest in the needs of others? Your personality is the sum total of all your actions and reactions in the presence of others. Personality is what you are when others look at you. Character is what you are when you look at yourself. In a whole person, both are mirrors of each other.

Have you ever noticed how some people seem to radiate magnetic charm? When they enter a room everyone suddenly feels better just knowing they are around. What magic ingredients do they possess that others lack? Well, for one thing they are generally happy people who exude confidence and optimism. They make you feel comfortable because they have an enthusiasm for life which overrides the commonplace events and makes them seem like towering giants in a forest of shrubs. They love life, and the people who live it. How do they get that way? <u>By thinking right!</u>

The human mind is the most powerful force known to man. All the visible developments man has invented or created are only the projection of his thoughts; and this despite the fact that man uses less than 10% of his capabilities! Your mind can be likened to a river flowing toward the sea. If the river is permitted to take just a natural course, it accomplishes little more than cutting a winding path to the ocean, spending its energies in useless motion. However, if we harness that river with a mighty dam, the flow of water is controlled and the result is great power harnessed to produce beneficial goals. As thoughts flow through your mind, they may follow their natural course digging a winding rut or they may be harnessed by your superior will and channeled to generate great power. If your thoughts are positive, creative, happy, and imaginative, your personality will reflect these pleasant attitudes.

It has been said that "any human enterprise is only an extension of a man's personality." Examine the type and quality of business a man develops and you know what that man is like! On his eighty-first birthday, General MacArthur said:

"You do not grow old from years alone. Years may wrinkle the skin, but loss of enthusiasm wrinkles the soul."

Developing and maintaining the right mental attitude will do more to assist you in reaching your goals than anything else you may try. Every time you think a positive thought, you are putting money in your mental bank. The more positive thoughts you file away, the more you will have to draw out when you need them. Your mind will return to you only that which you have deposited within it, and as the Bible says:

"As a man thinketh in his heart, so is he!"

As you drive to meet a customer, show a property, or counsel with a seller, think positive thoughts that will condition you to the outcome you want and expect.

SMILE MORE OFTEN

The world always looks brighter from behind a smile! What a wonderful thing the human smile is! One small expression on a human face can warm the hearts of others. Scientists tell us it takes 43 muscles to frown and only 17 to smile, so why not smile more often? It's easier! A sincere smile is infectious and it lends strength to others whose mental burdens have weighted their lips in permanent frowns. I have also noticed that the best salesmen are usually in good humor, able to laugh at their own mistakes and freely showering their friends with pleasant anecdotes. As Charles Kingsley put it:

"The men whom I have seen succeed best in life have always been cheerful and hopeful men, who went about their business with a smile on their faces, and took the changes and chances of this mortal life like men, facing rough and smooth alike as it came."

LOOK AND ACT SUCCESSFUL

Others will have no more respect for you than you have for yourself. Look at yourself in the mirror. Do you dress and look like one who is successful? How do you walk, stand, talk, and act? Do you look and act as though you believe you are a successful and competent real estate salesman, or like a scared rabbit ready to run for the nearest hole? People can generally tell whether or not you have confidence in yourself and in what you are doing by the way you act.

Actions do influence our minds, and when we have difficulty thinking properly, we can produce actions which overcome our negative mental reactions. When you have doubts and fears about your success, you begin to destroy your effectiveness. Actually, you may even produce the very things you fear! Conversely, when you begin to act the way you would like to feel, you build your own confidence and assure your success. Dr. George W. Crane, phsycologist, says:

"Act the way you'd like to be, and soon you'll be the way you act." If you want people to accept your advice and listen to your sales presentations, you must dress and act the part. No salesman can afford to be without several good suits of clothes, even if he has to go into debt for them. When you dress poorly, your confidence and attitudes will be similarly affected. Next, practice standing erect and walking with a determined pace. I have long noticed that nearly all successful salesman walk faster and stand taller than the failures. There is a purpose in the way they walk! When you meet someone, do you look at him and shake his hand with firm enthusiasm? When you listen, do you really listen by watching the speaker's face and eyes? Little things? Yes, but mighty important!

The days when you are feeling your very best will be the days when you do your best work. When you are confident, happy and enthusiastic, one success will seem to follow the other almost without effort. Remember that fact and determine now to be your best more often. If you want others to like and respect you, you must learn to truly like and respect them. If you want people to be interested in you, you must be interested in them. When you meet someone, do you first look for his good points or for his weaknesses? Behind every man's surface reactions there is a genuine reason for his attitude, and sometimes understanding those reasons will unlock a lasting friendship. There are things to admire in all men and by looking for these traits, you can develop understanding and create interest. To influence your customers, you must first get in tune with them. This means meeting them on their own level and adapting yourself to their moods, interests, and thoughts. Different personalities do require different treatment. The timid little lady will not respond to the same approach used upon a bold, dynamic businessman. Adjust yourself to your client's wave length and you will more easily communicate with him; but remember that he must first accept and respect you before he will share his thoughts with you. Learn to project an image of confidence in the presence of others, and you will soon find your sphere of influence increasing in dimension.

APPROACH AND BE APPROACHABLE

Have you ever complained about someone being a "cold fish"? The chances are that person was just afraid and needed someone else to warm him up. It is a strange thing so many people find it hard to be the first to say "hello" or extend a friendly hand. Most people relish warmhearted enthusiasm and wish they had more themselves. They are often just timid about being the first to "break the ice." You'll discover new magic in your power to win friends and influence people when you begin extending your hand in warm welcomes before others do. Speak up and let the other person feel at home without demanding that he be the one to break the silence.

Along with this, learn also to be at ease in the presence of other people, and cultivate attitudes which make you one who is comfortable to be with. Avoid putting on airs of superiority or of humility. Be relaxed, and normal and let others be the same. Most important of all -- be a good listener. Of all the qualities you can use to advantage, the art of listening is high on the list. How can you train yourself to be a good listener? Well, the first rule is: do not talk about yourself. Instead, ask questions about the other person. The second rule is: keep your own mouth shut as often as possible and patiently listen with intense interest. People can tell whether or not you are really listening to them. If your eyes are wandering or your face is expressionless, they will sense that you do not care what they are saying. It is not alone in the ability to speak that you gain approval; it is also in the ability to listen. Let a man talk about his hobbies, avocations, interests, and joys and you let him relive his greatest pleasures, making him feel like a king. You may tell him nothing, but if you have truly listened to him, he will leave with a feeling of warm friendship for you.

YOU AND YOUR VOICE

Since everything you do centers around the processes involved in communicating ideas to others, the instrument of such expression deserves careful consideration. Learning to speak well is one of the skills every salesman needs to refine. The human voice is a marvelous creation. It can cover the entire gamut of human emotions, from singing to crying. With practice, we can improve the quality of our voices and our ability to use them more effectively. Voice teachers tell us there are four "P's" which control the range and impact of the human voice. Let's consider each:

1. Pitch

Although we cannot change the voice box or the sounding board that God gave us we can learn to use what we have to greater advantage. The pleasant voice is usually the lower, full, rich-toned voice. Low register notes are generally more pleasant to the ear than high ones. Most of us can lower our voice levels, regardless of present pitch, by practicing simple exercises. To prove my point, take the following sentence and repeat it in a singing voice about one octave above your basic speaking pitch: "Oh, it's a fine day today!" Now repeat this phrase twelve times, each time coming down one note lower on the scale. Continue as far as you can go with distinct pitch. Now try the same idea with your speaking voice by speaking lower and by consciously repeating your words several notes lower than your usual pitch. See what I mean? You can talk in a lower key if you work at it. As you drive to the office in the morning, give your voice a few simple exercises like this one to help you start the day right.

2. Pace

Most salesmen have a tendency to talk too fast. In their anxiety to convince a customer to take some action they get excited and permit one thought after another to tumble out before the previous ones have been absorbed by the listener. Except for a very few fast thinking individuals, such rapid fire delivery is difficult to follow. Speaking pace should be varied for colorful and interesting delivery, but generally it should remain in the slower categories for most effective listening. If you have a tendency to speak too fast, practice speaking at about one-half your normal pace and using the more relaxed delivery to develop emphasis and clarity in your tones.

3. Power

Power is the result of controlling volume and developing resonance in our voice. Whispered tones often carry greater impact than loud ones, especially when they are introduced in contrast to more intense preceding sounds. To develop real power for the voice, practice humming with your lips closed. This produces richness as well as fullness to the voice. Then put a cork between your teeth and read aloud as clearly as possible. Inflections of the voice can be greatly magnified when proper emphasis on the power behind each change is carefully directed.

In your daily conversations with others, learn to speak up with sufficient volume so that your message will be heard. If you do not, you should be listening instead of talking.

4. Pauses

There is a popular beverage with the slogan: "the pause that refreshes." They have accented a basic truth. In speaking, nearly all pauses refresh and add dimension to the speaker's words. When you pause, you give emphasis to the things that preceded and impact to that which follows. You make it possible for your listener to absorb the full meaning of what you have said while preparing him for the next point. A pause is a pleasant respite from the spoken word, soothing the listener's mind while deepening his impression of what has been said. In selling, pausing also gives your customer an opportunity to respond and give you vital clues as to his thoughts and motivations.

ENERGY AND HEALTH

To be an enthusiastic salesman who gets things done, you will need lots of energy. Human energy is both mental and physical, and to have the proper amounts of both we need excellent mental and physical health. You know how difficult it is to carry on any task well when you are feeling mentally low. People with physical handicaps frequently learn to release their limited energies more effectively than those who are in better physical condition but who do not properly channel their mental powers. As in everything else in life, you receive in proportion to your investment. If you want vitality and energy, you must first cultivate the attitudes which develop strong sources of mental energy. Confidence and energy are often directly related because daily inspiration springs from having a fair measure of both.

To keep your energy high at all times you should avoid abusing your body in any fashion. Moderation in all things is still the best rule! Always try to get a good night's sleep, rising refreshed in the morning, ready to face with confidence the challenges of a new day. Include in your schedule sufficient relaxation, the kind which stimulates and renews both mind and body. Allow time for your family, your church and your hobbies, so that your life is full, and well balanced. As a new salesman, there will be a tendency to drive yourself seven days a week because you are anxious to make a success. I can assure you this will only lead to mental and physical exhaustion created by sustained and unnatural strains. To sacrifice yourself and everything else for one extra sale is neither wise, nor profitable. The most successful salesmen lead a balanced life and are relaxed when they work with their customers, thus permitting them to control the the sequence of events.

Your daily and weekly plans should include time to meditate, energize and restore your mind and body. If you do not so organize your activities, you will soon find your energy decreased and your enthusiasm dimmed. If your company has no planned method of handling days off, find yourself another salesman willing to cooperate with you by covering alternate relief periods. The same principle works well when scheduling vacations.

LEARN TO KNOW YOURSELF

A wise man once said: "He who knows himself, knows others." There is a great truth in this saying. To know your weaknesses is to also know your strengths. No one knows himself perfectly, but the better he does, the more power he possesses in harnessing his life toward worthwhile goals. Self-evaluation should be part of your personal program for self-improvement. When you have a disappointing day, lose a sale, or feel mentally low, ask yourself why. When you have excellent days and achieve your purposes easily, also ask yourself why.

Humility and kindness are born from a recognition of one's own short-comings. It is always easier to understand another person's problems and feelings, once you have experienced a similar difficulty. Habit is a strong rope which ties us to the past, and often makes it painful for us to recognize our own failings. Grooves and ruts are closely related. A rut is just an open-ended grave we dig with our eyes shut! If you would be strong and influential with others, learn to evaluate your own failings and correct them before someone else must do it for you.

AIM FOR THE STARS

Most humans go through life only partially aware of the full scope of their abilities. Each of us has hidden potentials we have not developed simply because nothing has ever forced us to discover them. As we grow older, the tendency is to ignore interests we might have pursued in younger days, building walls around our thoughts and ideas in a kind of self-made imprisonment. And yet, experience teaches us that we should be able to do more as we mature, not less.

As you progress in the real estate business, there will be a strong temptation to be trapped by the congealing of your own ideas and the narrowing of your goals. You will remember when a certain property could be bought for half the price, so it couldn't be worth what they are asking now! Older salesmen will tell you why something can't be done, and while you listen, someone else will do it! Newer men will use the techniques that you knew so well, but somehow have lost, and their success may produce resentments you cannot understand. When you have gone a month or more without a sale, you may begin to think discouraging thoughts and blame others for your disappointing results. At such times, take a good look in the mirror and ask yourself who is to blame. If you would grow and attain new heights, keep your horizons and your vision wide. When you are tempted to complain, find fault or criticize, think about the effects you are producing within yourself, destroying the very energies you need to succeed. "It is always better to light a candle, than to curse the darkness."

There is no success that does not also court some failure. You will make mistakes, create problems, and endure disappointments as you forge ahead in the real estate profession. If you have your head up

EXPANDING YOUR REAL ESTATE OPPORTUNITIES

and mind clear, you will learn from these things more than your successes can ever teach.

John Burroughs said:

A man may fail many times, but he isn't a failure until he begins to blame somebody else!

The words of Daniel H. Burnham seem to best summarize this lesson and our training manual:

Make no little plans; they have no magic to stir men's blood and probably themselves will not be realized. Make big plans: aim high in hope and work, remembering that a noble, logical diagram once recorded will never die, but long after we are gone will be a living thing, asserting itself with ever-growing insistency. Remember that our sons and grandsons are going to do things that would stagger us. Let your watchword be order -- and your beacon, beauty!

QUESTIONS AND PROJECTS FOR CHAPTER TWELVE

Questions:

1. What specialties in the real estate field may interest you as you progress in your career? What reasons are behind your selection?
2. How can you improve your sales personality to more effectively control your success in selling real estate?
3. What do you think is the most important ingredient in successful selling?
4. What are the four "P's" of voice control and why is each important?
5. What does enthusiasm have to do with personal success? How does it manifest itself?
6. Why is membership in your local real estate board, state association and the National Association of Real Estate Boards beneficial to your progress in the real estate field?
7. What steps can you take immediately to increase your sales ability and the effectiveness you realize from your efforts? How do you plan to implement your objectives?
8. What education do you feel would be most helpful at this point of your career? Where can you obtain it? When will you start?
9. Having read this manual and possibly actively engaged in some real estate selling, do you believe sincerely that real estate is a challenging and personally rewarding career for you? (If your answer is doubtful, or indecisive, you may want to review the matter with your broker. No salesman can ever succeed when he does not believe wholeheartedly in what he is doing.)
10. What are your goals for tomorrow? next week? next year? How will you achieve them?

Projects:
1. On a piece of paper, list the major things you have learned from this manual and note how you intend to use them.
2. From your broker, ascertain what educational courses are available on real estate, and make plans to attend those which fit into your personal objectives.
3. Ask your broker how you can become a member of the local real estate board, state association and NAREB. Plan to do so as soon as possible.
4. To help you decide what aspect of the real estate business you may want to pursue in the future as well as determine the areas of greatest interest for the moment, gather the following information and analyze it for your area:
    a. How many new homes are constructed in your city or area in the past 12 months?
    b. What percentage of the population own homes as opposed to those who rent? (Available from U.S. Census figures of 1960.)
    c. How many used homes were sold in your area last year, and is the trend of real estate turnover increasing or decreasing?
    d. What was the total volume of recorded deed activity in your area in the past year? What percentage of this was residential? What percentage acreage? What percentage commercial or income property?
    e. What records of the real estate board are available to relate activity in your market? Obtain and review.
5. Ask for a private counselling session with your broker to review all of your basic objectives and your questions about your future. Ascertain for yourself what aspects of the real estate profession you want to pursue and then check with those who have more experience and knowledge in the business before finalizing your goals.
6. On a sheet of paper, list your strengths and your weaknesses as you see them. Then analyze these against your objectives in the real estate business.
7. Look over the list of books shown in the bibliography of this training manual, select those which appeal to the subjects of your greatest interest and order copies to read. Your real estate board probably has a library from which you can borrow many of these books, and others, on real estate topics of interest to you.
8. Ask your broker or manager his opinion of your talents and knowledge and his recommendations for your future success in real estate.
9. List the ways you can increase your exposure in the market place and the things you can do now to widen your circle of clients, properties, and prospects. Then set about to see that your desired coverage is obtained.
10. Resolve now to re-read this manual when you fall into your first major slump and need inspiration to put you back on the track. All of us need such guidance from time to time, and we must be big enough to seek it.

GLOSSARY OF REAL ESTATE TERMS

ABANDONMENT of Homestead: (See Declaration of Abandonment.)

ABEYANCE: A temporary suspension of action; an undetermined condition awaiting action.

ABSTRACT OF JUDGMENT: Record of a Court's judgment which creates a general lien upon all real estate and chattel property when recorded.

ABSTRACT OF TITLE: A digest or summary of documents or records affecting title to property.

ABUTTING OWNERS: Owners of real property whose lands touch or border highways or public owned lands.

ACCELERATION CLAUSE: A clause inserted in a note, mortgage, or deed of trust which requires immediate payment of the entire debt if certain conditions are violated during the normal term of the loan. Alienation of title is the standard violation involved, although failure to maintain the property, pay taxes, etc., are other factors generally included in this clause.

ACCEPTANCE: Consent to an offer or contract.

ACCESSIBILITY: Ease of access or approach to a property.

ACCESSION: The process of acquiring title to improvements made on your land without your approval before installation.

ACCRETION: The increase or acquisition of land by gradual action of natural forces such as water.

ACCRUED DEPRECIATION: The actual depreciation of property at any given date as contrasted to "book depreciation."

ACCOMMODATION: An obligation which is assumed without consideration.

ACKNOWLEDGMENT: A formal declaration before a duly authorized officer by a person who has executed an instrument that such was his act and deed.

ACQUISITION: The process of acquiring or purchasing a piece of property.

ACRE: An area of land measurement containing 43,560 square feet.

ACT OF GOD: Any disaster which is the result of natural causes, such as wind storms, lightning, floods, earthquakes, etc.

ADJUDICATION: The act or process of reaching a judicial decision. Adjudication in bankruptcy brings the entire estate of the bankrupt owner under the jurisdiction of the court at the date of filing the petition.

ADMINISTRATOR: A person appointed by a probate court to settle the estate of one who has died without leaving a will.

ADMINISTRATOR'S DEED: A deed given by one who is acting as the administrator of an estate.

ADULT: One who has reached legal age when the privileges of voting, contracting, and other similar privileges are attained.

GLOSSARY OF REAL ESTATE TERMS

AD VALOREM: Based upon or according to value. Property taxes are determined "ad valorem."

ADVANCE FEES: Fees or commissions charged in advance of the service rendered. Special controls now apply to those operating in the real estate industry on this basis.

ADVERSE POSSESSION: Open and notorious possession and occupation of real property under an evident claim to title which may, if uncontested for prescribed periods of time, result in actual title transfer to the offending parties.

AFFIANT: One who makes a sworn statement, such as an affidavit.

AFFIDAVIT: A written statement sworn to or affirmed before an officer authorized to administer oaths.

AFFIRMATION: A solemn declaration, usually made by one who is opposed to making oaths on religious grounds.

AGENCY: The act of serving as agent for a principal in the negotiations of business.

AGENT: Someone who is authorized to represent another individual.

AGREEMENT OF SALE: Any contract which established the terms of sale between a buyer and a seller. Deposit Receipts and Earnest Money Receipts are two forms used by real estate salesmen.

AIR RIGHTS: The rights involved in real estate ownership which control the use of air space within the vertical planes above the ground owned or leased by the holder of the estate.

ALIAS: A name assumed by an individual in place of his legal name.

ALIEN: A person living in one country who is a citizen of another.

ALIENATION: The process of transferring title to property from one person to another.

ALIENATION CLAUSE: A clause in a mortgage, note or deed of trust which accelerates the loan balance in the event title is transferred to a third party without the approval of the beneficiary.

ALIEN LAND LAW: A 1913 California Law which prohibited ownership of land by certain ineligible races, since declared unconstitutional.

ALLEGATION: The act of making a formal assertion or statement of fact in a pleading.

ALL INCLUSIVE DEED OF TRUST: A deed of trust which encompasses prior mortgage obligations known to trustor and beneficiary. It is similar to a contract of sale but with the advantages of a deed of trust concerning foreclosure rights.

ALLOTMENT: A plot of land which has been divided into small sections with or without improvements.

ALLUVION: The land which is added to property by the process of accretion. Such alluvion becomes the property of the owner of the land to which it is added.

AMENITIES: Those things which are marked by such qualities as pleasantness, comfortableness, and agreeableness. In appraising, the amenities of property are those qualities which increase the pleasure of ownership and are not necessarily related to monetary values.

AMORTIZATION: The process of paying off a debt by installments, normally by equal installments over a fixed period of time. A fully amortized loan has no "balloon" balance.

AMORTIZATION TABLE: A printed schedule of the monthly payments required to amortize a loan for specific interest rates and time periods. A book of amortization tables is standard equipment for real estate salesmen.

ANCHOR BOLT: A metal bolt imbedded in the foundation of a building to anchor the construction to the foundation.

ANCILLARY: A subordinate document or instrument normally attached to a prior document in a subservient position, designed to aid the principal one. An ancillary bill, suit, or attachment indicates the existence of another instrument with precedence.

ANNEXATION: The act or process of adding land to a basic unit, such as bringing land within the limits of a city or principality.

ANNUITY: The return from an investment of capital, with interest, in a series of yearly payments or other regular periods.

ANNULMENT: In marriage, the decree which cancels or nullifies the marriage contract and returns the parties to their prior state or relationship. Property is not ordinarily affected by a decree annulling a marriage unless the parties involved submit it as an issue.

ANTECEDENT: That which has gone before in the history of a person or thing. Antecedent events have preceded the current happenings.

ANTECEDENT DRAINAGE: (See Inconsequent Drainage.)

APPLICATION FOR DISCHARGE: The formal application of one who files bankruptcy papers seeking the "discharge" or release of all allowable and provable debts. If approved by the court, his debts will be "discharged" or cancelled.

APPRAISAL: A formal opinion or estimate of value by one who is qualified to evaluate factors of value. In real property appraisals, the purpose of the opinion may affect the type of report issued.

APPRAISAL INVENTORY: A list of all the individual items of property which were considered by the appraiser when preparing his appraisal report.

APPRAISAL SURPLUS: The difference between "book values" and "actual values" when the latter is in excess of the former as established by an appraisal.

APPRECIATION: The added value of property resulting from various market influences, whether of a temporary or permanent nature. The opposite of depreciation.

APPRECIATION RATE: The percentage figure used to compute the increase in value to real property based on future dates and various other conditions.

APPROACH TO VALUE: A principle method of computing values in appraisal techniques. The three commonly accepted approaches are: (1) Comparison, (2) Reproduction Cost, (3) Capitalization.

APPURTENANCE: That which is attached to land so as to become a part thereof. Buildings and improvements are typical appurtenances; a property right may also be considered one.

ARTICLES OF INCORPORATION: The formal statement made by those forming a corporation as to the nature of their corporate activities and basic business relationships as filed with the Division of Corporations.

ASSEMBLAGE: The process of estimating the cost of bringing two or more parcels of land under a single ownership, as compared to the costs or values of the parcels when owned individually.

GLOSSARY OF REAL ESTATE TERMS

ASSESSED VALUE: The value of real or personal property as established by an assessor for the purpose of levying taxes.

ASSESSMENT: A special charge placed against a particular property for some specific purpose, such as installation of sewers, sidewalks, or other improvements.

ASSESSOR: One who determines the value of property for tax purposes.

ASSETS: Those things owned by an individual or company which constitute its tangible or intangible value.

ASSIGNMENT: The transfer of an interest in some instrument, such as a mortgage, deed of trust, lease, bond.

ASSIGNOR: One who assigns or transfers a property or a right to another.

ASSIGNS; ASSIGNEES: Those to whom property or rights are transferred.

ASSUME: To accept the obligations of another party.

ASSUMPTION OF MORTGAGE: The process of assuming personal liability for the payment of existing loans for which property is the security.

A.T.A. POLICY: A broad coverage policy of title insurance issued by title companies to protect lenders for many items not included in the standard policy. Usually paid for by the purchaser to secure his loan.

ATRIUM: The entrance hall or open court of a Roman style home; a court.

ATTACHMENT: The legal seizure of the defendant's property as security for any judgment awarded by court to permit plaintiff to recover in the action. An attachment is a lien upon all real and personal property as a rule.

ATTORNEY-IN-FACT: A person to whom a power of attorney has been given by another to act for either specific or general purposes on behalf of the one granting the authority.

ATTORNEY'S FEE CLAUSE: A clause contained in many legal documents such as mortgages, leases, notes, requiring the maker to pay all costs incurred by the holder for attorney's fees, etc., in the event the maker defaults in performance of the contract or instrument.

ATTRACTION PRINCIPLE: The pulling force of a commercial business center due to one or more of the various merchandising factors existing.

AUCTION: The public sale of property to the highest bidder.

AUTHENTICATION: The certification of a document by the signature of an officer whose seal is usually affixed to validate the procedure.

AUTHORIZATION TO SELL: Another term for "listing."

AVULSION: The sudden removal of land from one property to that of another owner, usually by a change in the course of a river. By law the owner of the part removed can usually reclaim it within a limited period of time.

B

BALANCE SHEET: A financial statement setting forth the assets and liabilities of an individual or corporation to show current position of the parties involved.

BALLOON PAYMENT: An amount due when a note or mortgage becomes due which is in excess of normal installment payments.

BALUSTERS: The vertical members which support a hand railing along a stairway.

BANKRUPTCY: A legal proceeding under federal statutes whereby an insolvent debtor may be ruled incapable of meeting his obligations and his properties may be sold or distributed to satisfy his creditors. A petition in bankruptcy may be filed by either the debtor or the creditors.

BASE AND MERIDIAN: The survey lines established by U.S. Survey teams to divide the country into townships. Base lines run east and west; meridians run north and south.

BENCH MARKS: Permanent markers placed at strategic points by surveyors from which differences of elevation and topography are measured.

BENEVOLENT CORPORATION: Any corporation organized for charitable and non-profit purposes.

BENEFICIARY: One who receives income from a trust. Under a deed of trust the beneficiary is the lender.

BEQUEATH: To transfer property by will.

BEQUEST: The property which is transferred by will.

BETTERMENT: Substantial improvement made upon real property as differentiated from mere repairs.

BILATERAL CONTRACT: Any contract in which there is a mutual exchange of promises by two or more parties.

BILL OF SALE: The legal document used to transfer title to personal property.

BINDER: An agreement made preliminary to the actual contract to sell property, used as a temporary arrangement before entering into the formal deed or contract; usually requiring a cash deposit of some kind.

BLANKET MORTGAGE: A mortgage instrument which names as security two or more parcels of land.

BLIGHTED AREA: A real estate district where the conditions of property are below standard and productivity substantially reduced as a result.

BLUE SKY LAWS: Statutes regulating investment companies, the conduct of their business and the issuance and sale of their securities.

BOARD OF EQUALIZATION: The agency which determines the assessed value of public utility properties and controls county assessors as well as tax collectors to assure uniformity in tax assessment and collection practices.

BONA FIDE: In good faith; without fraud; qualified arrangements.

BOND: To encumber as with a mortgage; a certificate issued as security for the repayment of a loan out of future income or some designated fund.

BOOK DEPRECIATION: The amount set aside on the books of record to provide for the retirement or replacement of an asset.

BOOK VALUE: The total cost of a property less the total depreciation taken to date.

BOOM: An economic condition marked by rapid development of resources and population when unusually good profits can be realized.

BOOT: A profit gained in exchange of properties, not reflected by cash, upon which income tax is not deferred. Boot can be money or anything of monetary value used in an exchange to equalize equities.

BREACH: To break a law or a contract by failure or refusal to perform some act specifically required in the agreement.

BROKER: One who acts as an agent or negotiator for his principal when dealing with third parties on behalf of his client.

BROKER LOAN STATEMENT: A statement of charges and fees made in connection with a real estate loan which is furnished the buyer or mortgagor for his personal information.

BROKER'S DEMAND STATEMENT: A statement or letter issued to an escrow holder by the broker setting forth his instructions concerning the closing of escrow and disbursement of funds.

B.T.U.: A measure of heat known as a British Thermal Unit commonly used in determining the output of heating equipment, such as furnaces in a home.

BUILDING AND LOAN COMPANY: Same as Savings and Loan Company: an institution organized to make real estate loans with the funds received from depositors, paying interest to the latter for use of their money.

BUILDING CODE: The code or restrictions established by a government body, such as a city, county, or state, for regulating the construction of buildings of all types.

BUILDING CONTRACT: An agreement entered into between a contractor and an owner for the construction of a building.

BUILDING INSPECTOR: The authorized individual who reviews the various stages of building construction to verify conformance with the requirements of building codes.

BUILDING RESTRICTIONS: Same as building code. Also occasionally the restrictions contained within a deed or declaration of restrictions recorded to protect the usage of property by future owners.

BUILT-INS: The term applied to all appliances included in the construction of a property which become real property by nature of their installation.

BURDENSOME PROPERTY: Under bankruptcy laws the trustee is not required to take title to property which is unprofitable or subject to excessive liens and may obtain release from this property upon jurisdiction of the court.

BUSINESS AND PROFESSIONS CODE: That portion of state law which controls the activities of businesses and professions. Normally all real estate law is included in this section.

BUSINESS OPPORTUNITIES: In real estate terminology these are businesses in which real estate ownership factors are incidental to the businesses themselves and their leasehold rights. In California and some other states, special business opportunities licenses must be obtained from the Division of Real Estate before a broker or salesman can represent properties involving the sale of businesses.

BUTTERFLY ROOF: A type of roof characterized by two inverted wings, similar to those of a butterfly.

BUY AND SELL AGREEMENTS: Contracts between owners of a business executed to protect the surviving partner(s) in the event of death of one or more parties to the agreement, in which the survivor(s) has the right to acquire, at predetermined amounts, the interests of the deceased party.

BUY-BACK AGREEMENT: A term used for a special Trade-In Housing Contract which permits the one who accepted the trade-in to repurchase his property for a specified amount within a limited period of time at his option.

C

CAPACITY OF PARTIES: A term applied to the process of evaluating the qualifications of those who execute legal contracts. To be valid these parties must be of age and mentally sound, thus competent to enter into the obligations of a contract.

CAPITAL: The financial reserves available for investment and the production of additional wealth; also the funds originally invested to begin an enterprise plus the additions made from time to time by the partners or shareholders of the business.

CAPITAL CHARGES: The amounts needed to amortize the capital investment in business, plus the interest such capital would normally earn.

CAPITAL GAIN: (See Long Term Capital Gain.)

CAPITAL EXPENDITURES: The sums invested in a business or property which are considered a permanent contribution for the betterment of that asset. These are commonly such things as buildings, machinery, and necessary business equipment.

CAPITAL REQUIREMENTS: The sums of money needed to acquire or establish a business enterprise or investment, including working capital to maintain it.

CAPITAL SURPLUS: Sums of money or assets which are in excess of actual earned surplus normally resulting from increased evaluation of property, sale of stock, contributions of others, and other sources.

CAPITALIZATION: A method of appraising or determining value by using the net income and a reasonable rate of return.

CAPITALIZATION RATE: The percentage rate of return or interest used to compute the appraised value by the capitalization method. The amount used normally is chosen as that which is reasonable for the risk involved.

CAPITALIZING THE NET INCOME: The process of arriving at property value by the net income figures related to desired return. An apartment house earning $6000 per year after all expenses would be worth $100,000 if a return of 6% per year is considered reasonable by the investor. To determine value under this method, multiply the actual net income by the figure 100 and then divide by the rate of interest desired.

CAPTIVE MARKET: Business which is exclusively controlled by advantageous factors limited to the enterprises involved is said to have "captive markets." Typical situations are those created by air terminals, hotel shops, and similar environmental factors.

CARAVAN: As applied to real estate business, a tour of property by a group of real estate salesmen for the purpose of learning about new listings and appraising values.

CAR PORT: A covered area, opened in one or more sections used to protect the car in place of a normal garage.

CARRIAGE: A wood member on a staircase used to secure the treads and risers of the stairway.

CARRYING CHARGES: The various expenditures necessary to maintain a property from month to month, such as taxes, insurance, repairs.

CAVEAT EMPTOR: A Latin expression used in law to designate the buyer's responsibility to investigate before purchasing. Literally: "Let the buyer beware."

C.C. & R.'s: Abbreviation of "Conditions, covenants and restrictions" as applied to real property titles.

CEILING RATE: The maximum rent or fee that may be charged as established by any governmental agency.

CERTIFICATE OF CONFORMITY: A document which verifies that an acknowledgment made out of state meets the legal provisions of the state where executed and was acknowledged in accordance with the laws of the place where made.

CERTIFICATE OF ELIGIBILITY: The document which verifies the entitlement of an individual to the benefits of the Servicemen's Readjustment Act of 1944 by establishing his service record qualifications with the government agency.

CERTIFICATE OF REASONABLE VALUE: Commonly known as a C.R.V., this is the appraisal commitment of the Veterans Administration used to fix the value of a property being proposed for purchase by a veteran under the GI bill of rights. By law, the veteran cannot pay more for the property than the C.R.V. appraisal.

CERTIFICATE OF RECORDATION: A document verifying that an instrument has been duly recorded by the county recorder's office.

CERTIFICATE OF REVIVOR: The certificate issued by the franchise tax commissioner to verify that the corporation formally delinquent has made full payment of taxes due and which is generally recorded to lift a prior lien against property of that corporation.

CERTIFICATE OF SALE: Given by a sheriff at the foreclosure sale of a mortgaged property to the successful bidder. When the redemption period (one year) has expired, a sheriff's deed is issued in place of the certificate.

CERTIFICATE OF TITLE: A title examiner's opinion as to the condition of title for a particular parcel of real estate. Such certificate carries no guarantees and offers no protection to the purchaser against any hidden defects.

CERTIFIED COPY: A true copy of an original document, certified by any officer or qualified person.

CERTIFIED PROPERTY MANAGER: Commonly known as C.P.M., this identification is bestowed upon any property manager who has met the requirements of the Institute of Property Management operated under the auspices of the National Association of Real Estate Boards.

CHAIN: A measurement of distance. Engineer's chain is a series of 100 wire links each of which is one foot in length; a surveyor's chain is a series of wire links each of which is 7.92 inches long. The surveyor's chain has a total length equal to four rods or 66 feet. 10 square chains of land is one acre.

CHAIN OF TITLE: The history of a property as related to its various owners and encumbrances from the time of the original owner or patent or as far back as records are available for inspection.

CHAIN STORE: Any one of number of retail outlets operated by a single company under common ownership and with central management and common merchandise.

CHATTEL MORTGAGE: A mortgage or loan on personal property as contrasted to a mortgage on real property.

CHATTEL PERSONAL: Any personal property item that can be readily moved.

CHATTEL REAL: An estate related to real estate, such as a lease on real property or an interest in real property like the right of possession, use, or other personal privileges.

CIRCULATION PATTERNS: The flow of traffic through a property and the various effects design may have on such patterns.

CIVIL LAW: (See Common Law.)

CLEARANCE CERTIFICATE: A certificate indicating that performance of a requirement has been completed, such as completion of termite work.

CLEARANCE RECEIPT: A receipt issued by the Board of Equalization showing that the owner or seller of a business has accounted for his sales taxes.

CLIENT: The principal to a real estate transaction who employs the agent.

CLOSING STATEMENT: The settlement sheet which is a statement of debits and credits for the buyer or seller in summarizing the costs involved when selling property.

CLOUD ON THE TITLE: Any item affecting title transfer which prevents the buyer from receiving a "clear title." These are usually nuisance items requiring quit claim deeds or quiet title action.

CLUSTER HOUSING: A term used to describe housing which is grouped together to create more common areas between them and where normal setbacks and boundaries are sacrificed for the "open space" created by this arrangement.

COLLATERAL SECURITY: Items of value placed on record as additional security for the performance of any principal contract or note.

COLLUSION: An agreement between two or more people to defraud another of his legal rights or to obtain some object forbidden by law.

COLOR OF TITLE: A title which appears to be good on the surface, but is in fact not good title.

COMMERCIAL ACRE: That which remains of an acre of land after deducting the area needed for streets, sidewalks, curbs. It is a loose term applied to usable acreage when other needs have been met to service the area involved.

COMMERCIAL PAPER: Notes or bills of exchange used in the normal course of business enterprise.

COMMERCIAL PROPERTY: Any land suitable for use by business enterprise as zoned by city or county planning commissions or determined by normal usage. Commercial property is often valued by the front foot exposure to traffic.

COMMINGLING: The mixing of your own funds with that of your client's. General confusion of accounts in which there should be a fiduciary protection of other's interests.

COMMISSION: Compensation for services rendered or duties performed such as selling or leasing a property.

COMMITMENT: A promise to perform; in real estate, an agreement to loan a specified amount to a purchaser or seller in the event of title transfer or refinance arrangements.

COMMON LAW: A system of law resulting from past legal decisions or accepted traditions as begun in England and carried to most states of the United States.

COMMON PROPERTY: Property owned and used by the public or a group of people who live in an area. Common property is open to equal use by all those owning it, or having public interest in it.

COMMUNITY APARTMENTS: (See Cooperative Apartments.)

CO-MORTGAGOR: One who signs a mortgage or deed of trust as equally responsible for its repayment. The wife is usually co-mortgagor with the husband, although someone else might serve that purpose, such as a father.

COMPACTION: The process of compacting or tamping the ground to make it suitable for building purposes. Compaction tests are often required by building inspection authorities before authorizing construction.

COMPARATIVE ANALYSIS: The process of comparing the value of one lot or building with another to determine its reasonable evaluation. In appraising, this is one of the more important approaches to value.

COMPETITIVE PROPERTIES: Properties which are competing for the same market buyers at the same time. (See also Comparative Analysis.)

COMPETENT PARTIES: Those who are qualified or mentally competent to enter into a contract.

COMPOUND INTEREST: Interest paid on both principal and periodic computations of accumulated interest amounts.

CONDEMNATION: A ruling by a governmental body that a property must be altered or destroyed for reasons of public welfare. Also, the act of taking private property for public use by the right of eminent domain, such as for freeways.

CONDEMNATION GUARANTEE: A search made by a title company in lieu of a title policy when a property is undergoing a condemnation process.

CONDEMNATION PROCEEDINGS: The acts of government involved in the acquisition of land for public use by condemnation of private lands.

CONDITION: As used in real estate, a specific event or requirement which directly affects the instruments or documents involved in a transaction, and the performance or non-performance of which may terminate or alter the obligations of the contracts involved.

CONDITIONAL SALES CONTRACT: A contract to sell real estate to another upon completion of certain required acts, such as payment of specified sums, during the performance of which contract the title to the property remains vested in the seller until completely fulfilled.

CONDOMINIUM: An apartment house subdivided to give fee title to individual occupants by a description of the air and ground space involved for each unit. Condominiums have been in use for many years in other nations and are just now showing promise as a method of ownership in the United States.

CONFESSION OF JUDGMENT: An entry of judgment upon the admission or confession of the debtor without the formality, time, or expense involved in the usual proceedings.

CONGRESSIONAL GRANT: A grant of public owned lands to an individual, or other entity, by an act of Congress.

CONSENT: Voluntary agreement; an essential element of a contract. Consent of the parties to a contract must be free, communicated by each to the other.

CONSEQUENTIAL DAMAGE: A term used to define damage arising from the acts of public bodies or adjacent owners to a given parcel of land which impairs the value of that parcel without actually condemning its use in whole or part.

CONSIDERATION: The sums of money, valuables, promises, or acts which are given in exchange for the performance of a contract. In most states there must be a valuable consideration in any contract which transfers an interest to real property from one party to another.

CONSERVATOR: One who is appointed by a court to "conserve" the estate of another, such as an elderly or sick person who is unable to do so for himself. This is different from a "guardian" appointed for minors or incompetents, because no condition of minority or incompetency exists.

CONSERVATOR'S DEED: A deed to property given by a court appointed conservator when he executes his duties. His actions are subject to court confirmation, the same as in probate transactions.

CONSTANT PAYMENT: Any payment which recurs regularly and is a fixed amount which does not vary in any manner.

CONSTRUCTIVE FRAUD: Any breach of duty, which, without an actual fraudulent intent, gains an advantage for the person in fault; any act or omission as the law specifically declares to be fraudulent without respect to actual fraud.

CONSTRUCTIVE NOTICE: Notice given by public or recorded documents. The law presumes that everyone has the same knowledge of all instruments which are properly recorded and available for inspection by anyone.

CONTIGUOUS: Adjoining or bordering another parcel of land.

CONTINGENCY: Any requirement in a contract which must be completed before the contract can be considered ready for performance.

CONTINGENT FEES: Fees or commissions to be paid only if certain events or acts occur or specific results are obtained in the interim.

CONTINGENT LISTING (or trade-in): A listing on real property which is tied to the sale or purchase of another property, one of which cannot be acquired without the sale of the other.

CONTRACT: An agreement negotiated and entered into by two or more parties who exchange mutual promises to perform certain acts in accordance with the wishes of both parties.

CONTRACT FOR DEED: A purchase money instrument used to secure the remaining equity of the seller until the full purchase price has been received by the seller or substituted at some future date for another instrument, such as a mortgage or deed of trust. In law it is usually treated similarly to a mortgage, although fee title rests in the name of the original seller.

CONVERSION VALUE: The value in real estate created by changing the use of a property from one state to another, such as rezoning, or creating a higher and better use for the parcel.

CONVEYANCE: In real estate, a document transferring title to property from one party to another.

COOPERATIVE APARTMENT HOUSE: A community apartment house where each occupant receives an undivided interest in the ownership of the apartment he uses and a common interest in all other facilities. This is usually effected by forming a corporation with each owner receiving stock in the corporation equal to his investment. This is different from a condominium, where fee title is actually passed to individual owners of each unit.

CORNER INFLUENCE: The additional value attributed to a corner lot due to its various advantages for business uses.

CORPORATION SOLE: A corporation formed by the bishop, chief priest, presiding elder, or other presiding offer of any religious denomination society or church for the purpose of administering and managing the affairs and properties of that group. It has continuity of existence and may sell, convey, lease, mortgage, or otherwise deal in real and personal property the same as any natural person.

CORPOREAL: Having physical properties consisting of actual, tangible matter. In real estate corporeal hereditament is property of such a nature as to be cognizable by the senses and is connected with the land.

CO-SIGNER: One who accepts equal obligation for the performance of contract, note or other act by affixing his or her name to the documents involved.

COST BASIS: Usually the purchase price of property. As used in tax computations for capital gains purposes, it is the difference between the original cost basis and the adjusted cost basis on which the gain is determined and the tax paid.

COVENANT: An agreement entered into by two or more parties; a promise by which one binds himself to perform certain acts.

C.P.A.: Abbreviation for Certified Public Accountant.

C.P.M.: Abbreviation for Certified Property Manager.

C.R.E.A.: Abbreviation for California Real Estate Association.

CREDITOR'S POSITION: The part of real property market value which is represented by a first mortgage or which can be financed by a prime loan or mortgage.

CUBICAL CONTENT: The total space enclosed by the outside walls, roofs, and floors of a building measured in terms of cubic feet or cubic yards.

CUL-DE-SAC: A street with access from one end only and closed at the other with a curved, bulb-like enclosure.

CUMULATIVE ATTRACTION: A term used in describing the effect created in a shopping center site by the various influences each business has on the total attraction of business to the center.

CURATIVE ACT: A California law which cured all defects in acknowledgments recorded prior to July 29, 1926 and in all instruments thereafter that have been of record for one year, with minor exceptions.

CURTESY: The right which a husband has in a wife's estate at her death. States having community property laws have abolished the previous provisions of curtesy.

D

D.B.A.: Abbreviation for "doing business as" under a fictitious name.

GLOSSARY OF REAL ESTATE TERMS

DEALER (in real estate): A licensed real estate man or company who buys and sells for his own account as a principal instead of an agent.

DEBENTURES: Certificates issued to cover an obligation to pay certain amounts at a specified time under specified conditions bearing a fixed rate of interest.

DEBTOR'S POSITION: The excess amount above prime mortgages which evidences the equity of the borrower's position.

DECENTRALIZATION: A term used to define the outward growth of business centers away from the downtown cores or central business districts and the location of industry in areas away from commonly accepted centers.

DECIBEL: A measure of sound transmission or noise, commonly used in housing or apartment units to indicate effective controls on sound waves between rooms or floors.

DECLARATION OF ABANDONMENT: The document recorded to terminate a homestead.

DECLARATION OF HOMESTEAD: The document recorded to establish a homestead.

DECLARATION OF RESTRICTIONS: The document recorded by a subdivider or builder to establish deed restrictions concerning the use of land and improvements in the subdivision covered by them.

DECREE: A legal decision issued by a court or other authorized authorities.

DEDICATION: In real estate, the term applied to the required or voluntary transfer of interest in real estate or improvements to city, county, or state agencies such as the dedication of streets, sidewalks, curbs, and gutters to the city in which the subdivision is located.

DEED: A written instrument which conveys title to real property.

DEED OF TRUST: (See Trust Deed.)

DEFAULT: Failure to perform the acts or promises made, such as the default on a mortgage note when payment is not made on time.

DEFEASANCE: A provision in a deed or other instrument which, when violated, renders the document void.

DEFERRED MAINTENANCE: Repairs to a property which are required but not yet completed.

DEFERRED PAYMENTS: Payments which are to be made at some future time.

DEFICIENCY JUDGMENT: A judgment awarded by a court against a mortgagor or trustor when the security for the note was not sufficient to cover the obligation after it was sold to pay the balance of the loan.

DELINEATE: To outline, trace, or sketch pictorially for identification purposes.

DELIVERY: In real estate, the formal transmission of a deed to its new owner; once completed, there is no right to recall it.

DEMISE: In real estate: the conveyance or transfer of title to property for years, for life or at will; to lease property; to bestow by will.

DEPOSIT: An item of value or amount given in good faith to provide evidence of ability and willingness to complete the purchase or lease of real property.

DEPOSITION: A sworn statement taken from a witness to an event or act for the purposes of providing evidence as to the actual circumstances.

DEPOSIT RECEIPT: A common name for the purchase agreement between buyer and seller used to contract for the transfer of real estate.

DEPRECIATION: The gradual loss of value in property, personal or real, due to various factors, regardless of cause.

DEPRECIATION RATE: The annual percentage of change in property values resulting from depreciation.

DEPTH TABLE: A table used by real estate appraisers to determine the relative values in lots which have different depths from the fronting street.

DERELICTION: The gaining of additional land by the receding of water from the banks of a river, stream, lake, or ocean.

DESIST AND REFRAIN ORDER: A directive by a government, state, or city official to cease activity when it appears to that party that some law is being violated; such directive to remain in effect until an official hearing can be conducted.

DETERIORATION: One of the prime factors in depreciation evidenced by the loss in value due to wear and tear, destruction by the elements.

DEVISE: A gift of real property as the result of a bequeath in a will.

DEVISEE: One who inherits property by will.

DEVISOR: One who bequeaths real property by will.

D.F.T.: Abbreviation for a cancelled or non-completed sale meaning: "deal fell through."

DIRECT TRADE: A trade-in transaction in which title is passed immediately to the trade-in company, without benefit of improving the seller's position.

DISCHARGE: A discharge in bankruptcy releases a bankrupt from all of his provable debts, and a bankruptcy action is filed as an "application for discharge" to relieve debt obligations.

DISPOSSESS: To take legal action to remove an occupant from the premises of real property.

DISSOLUTION OF CORPORATION: The legal act of winding up a corporation for the purpose of dissolving its functions and assigning or selling its assets before final termination as a legal entity.

DOCUMENTARY STAMP: A revenue stamp attached to deeds, wills, and the like for payment of tax to the federal government due on such transactions.

DONEE: The one receiving a gift.

DONOR: The one giving the gift.

DOWER: The right which a wife has in her husband's estate upon his death, but which is negated by community property laws in those states having them.

DRY-ROT: A term used to describe fungus growth on wood and other materials created from water absorption by such items. It is a major cause of deterioration in older buildings and is often caused by leaking stall showers and water pipes.

DURESS: Unlawful forcing of one person to do an act which he would not have performed except when force is exercised.

E

EARNEST MONEY: A sum of money given to bind an agreement or an offer made to show good faith. (See also Deposit.)

EARNEST MONEY RECEIPT: (See Deposit Receipt.)

EASEMENT: The right or interest of one party to another person's land or property for a specific or general use, and which may be qualified in many ways.

ECONOMIC LIFE: The useful life of property improvements based on original intent and over which the structure is profitable to maintain.

ECONOMIC OBSOLESCENCE: Loss in value created by factors outside the property, such as changes in neighborhood factors. This is one of the principle considerations in depreciation.

ECONOMIC RENT: (See Ground Rent.)

EFFECTIVE GROSS REVENUE: Income received from the operation of a building before expenses but after vacancy and collection losses have been considered.

EGRESS: Means of leaving property without trespassing the property rights of other surrounding owners.

EMINENT DOMAIN: The right of government to take private property for public use when required for the general good. A just and proper compensation must be made at the time acquired by the government.

ENCROACHMENT: Illegal and unauthorized use of the property of another, usually by building or constructing something in part or whole on such property without permission.

ENCUMBRANCE: Anything that burdens the title to real property by limiting its totality. Mortgages, liens, easements, and restrictions are all various types of encumbrances.

ENDORSEMENT: Signing the back of a note or other transferrable document with a personal signature which authorizes payment or transfer to another.

ENDORSEMENT IN BLANK: Transferring by endorsement without qualification, which automatically makes the endorser equally responsible for the obligation involved.

ENDORSEMENT WITHOUT RECOURSE: A special endorsement which limits the responsibility of the endorser and does not guarantee future payment to holders of the instrument involved.

EQUITABLE ESTOPPEL: A doctrine in law which prevents an owner from stopping a sale of his property when he willingly permitted another to represent himself as owner and who knowingly permitted a sale to a purchaser through this representative.

EQUITABLE OWNER: An owner of real property who has hypothecated his property while retaining the rights of use and occupancy.

EQUITABLE REMEDY: In law, a remedy which is deemed by a court to be "equitable and fair." Specific performance of a contract might be an equitable remedy in some cases.

EQUITY: The interest one has in real property as an owner above all existing indebtedness.

EQUITY GUARANTEE: As used in trade-in housing programs, a guarantee to the owner of a certain specified sum within a specified time for all equities the owner might have above existing loan balances, in the event another buyer cannot be located in the interim willing to pay more than the guarantor.

EQUITY INSURANCE: Another term for trade-in guarantee loans or acquisitions.

EQUITY LOAN: A loan made in connection with trade-in housing which is based on the equity of the owner and calls for repayment on terms usually related to the performance contract established by the trade-in company.

EQUITY OF REDEMPTION: The right of an owner to redeem his property after a lien foreclosure sale. Under a mortgage foreclosure, this is usually a period of one year.

ERRORS AND OMISSIONS INSURANCE: An insurance policy available to real estate brokers and salesmen covering liability for errors and omissions in their contracts which might result in damages to clients or customers.

ESCALATOR CLAUSE: A clause contained in many leases which requires the increase in taxes, insurance, and other items to be passed on to the tenant under certain conditions.

ESCHEAT: The process by which the state acquires title to property when private ownership cannot be clearly established.

ESCROW: A depository for papers, funds, and instructions with a third party who is then obligated to carry out all instructions, providing they are in complete agreement.

ESCROW HOLDER: One who obligates himself to carry out all instructions of an escrow from all participants thereto.

ESTOPPEL: A bar which precludes a person, under law, from asserting rights in contravention to previous positions or representations he has made.

ESTOVERS: Wood which a lessee is permitted to use from the landlord's premises in order to provide minimum fuel, repairs, and tools for his necessary use.

ESTATE: Any right which is invested in real property. Any interest, share, equity, or ownership in real property is considered to be an "estate in real property." The same term may apply to personal property as well.

ESTATE AT SUFFERANCE: The status of a lease or occupancy when there has been an unlawful retention of possession after expiration of a lease of different nature.

ESTATE AT WILL: A lease or estate similar to periodic tenancy where no lease exists but permission for occupancy remains on the same basic terms as original lease, or at the will of either party.

ESTATE FOR LIFE: The right to use and occupy property during the life of the one owning the life estate; but after which it will revert to the original estate or others designated by recorded documents.

ESTATE FOR YEARS: Another expression for a lease or leasehold estate.

ESTATE IN REVERSION: That portion of an estate which remains when the other estates granted by the original owner have been terminated or fulfilled.

ESTATE OF INHERITANCE: An estate which may be inherited, but is not yet transferred.

ET AL: A Latin expression used in legal documents meaning: "and others."

ET UX: A Latin expression used in legal documents meaning: "and spouse."

EXCHANGE AGREEMENT: A contract which covers the understandings of two or more owners who agree to transfer their properties to each other with or without additional consideration.

EXCISE TAX: Federal, state, and local taxes which are imposed on purchases rather than on personal or real property.

EXCLUSIVE AGENCY LISTING: A listing for the sale or lease of real property which permits the owner to rent or sell without paying a commission but does not allow any other agent, except the one named in the contract, to act on behalf of the owner.

EXCLUSIVE RIGHT TO SELL LISTING: A listing on real property which permits the agent named to sell, lease or negotiate the transfer of title to real property exclusively. Even the owner cannot perform these functions under this agreement.

EXECUTE: To sign documents agreeing to carry out all understandings and commitments contained in such instruments.

EXECUTOR: The male named in a will to carry out the terms set forth in the document made by the deceased.

EXECUTOR'S DEED: A deed to property given by an executor to the new buyer.

EXECUTRIX: The female named in a will to dispose of an estate.

EXEMPT: To free or excuse from some burdensome obligation.

EXPROPRIATION: The act or process by which private property is condemned and taken for public use, such as by process of eminent domain.

EXTENDED COVERAGE POLICY: As pertains to title insurance policies, this covers specific risks not contained in a standard policy and for which a special policy is written with addition premium according to the risk involved.

F

"FANNY MAE": The nickname given to the Federal National Mortgage Association operated by the government as a secondary market for federally insured loans.

FEE: When applied to real estate: an inheritable right in real property. Also a commission or remuneration for services performed.

FEE SIMPLE ABSOLUTE: The maximum estate one can enjoy in real property

FEE SIMPLE LIMITED: An estate in fee granting fee rights to property as long as certain stipulated conditions are met, termination being governed by the occurrence of some event which has been prestated in the original establishment of the estate.

FEE TALL: An estate of inheritance in real property which is restricted to some particular heirs or a class of person to whom granted.

FICTITIOUS MORTGAGE: A mortgage on personal crops, property, or future realization of profits from their sale. Such mortgages are created to buy the materials necessary to plant and operate a farm.

FICTITIOUS NAME: An alias or name by which you are known for business purposes and which is not necessarily the same as your real name. People often conduct business under "D.B.A.'s" or fictitious business names.

FIDUCIARY RELATIONSHIP: The position of trust assumed by an agent or confidant when acting on behalf of a principal.

FINANCE GUARANTEE: In trade-in housing, an agreement to finance property at some future date in order to confirm a transaction at the time executed.

FINDER'S FEE: A fee paid to a person who has furnished information that is beneficial to the agent in arranging the sale, without a participation which requires a license.

FIXED CHARGES: The continuing costs which are required in order to maintain a property for the reimbursement of capital invested in the property

FLAT NOTE: (See Straight Note.)

F.M.V.: Abbreviation for "Fair Market Value" as established by recognized appraisers or by a government agency like FHA.

FORECLOSURE: The sale of property which has been pledged as security against the payment of a debt.

FORFEITURE: The loss of earnest money for failure to perform under the terms of a purchase contract.

FRACTIONAL DESCRIPTION: A description of real property which relates the parcel to the entire section of land involved.

FREEHOLDER: An owner of land in fee.

FRONT FOOT: The measure of a parcel of land, by feet, on the portion exposed to main traffic streets. This is used especially in commercial property pricing.

FRONT FOOT COST: The price of land expressed in terms of its footage on a main street. Business property might be priced at $1000.00 per front foot on a highly desirable business street.

FUNCTIONAL OBSOLESCENCE: A factor in depreciation of property caused by the inefficiency or decreased capacity of the property to serve the accepted needs of modern purchasers.

G

GENERAL INDEX: The index of general liens and judgments maintained by the recorder's office which do not apply to specific properties but all parcels owned by those involved.

GIFT LETTER: A letter prepared for a mortgagee or government agency which verifies that the sums of money being used to acquire a parcel of property were a gift from a relative, made without obligation of repayment.

GIFT TAX: A state tax made on gifts received by an individual.

GI LOANS: (See Veterans Loans.)

GOOD CONSIDERATION: In real estate, a consideration for the transfer of real estate other than valuable property; commonly, love and affection.

GOOD WILL: The general reputation and business enjoyed by a company based on its name and past services. This is a purchasable commodity in the sale of business opportunities.

GRADUATED LEASE: A lease for real property which requires varying amounts of rents over the term of the lease.

GRANT DEED: A deed to real property which carries implied warranties, and the most commonly used instrument to convey title in California.

GRANTEE: One who acquires title to property by deed.

GRANTOR: One who conveys title to property by deed.

GROSS EARNINGS: Total revenue from all operating sources before deducting any expenses for collecting such revenue.

GROSS INCOME: Total revenue accrued before deduction of expenses.

GROSS LEASE: A lease for real property in which the owner-lessor is responsible for all charges to the property which are normal, regular costs of ownership.

GROSS MULTIPLIER: A number which is used to determine approximate selling price for income property by multiplying the gross income times this number: (income x multiplier = selling price).

GROSS PROFITS: Profits accrued before the deduction of general expenses and taxes.

GLOSSARY OF REAL ESTATE TERMS

GROUND RENT: The profit or net rent paid for the use of unimproved land or that amount of the rent which should be properly credited to the land rather than to the buildings upon it.

GROSS REVENUE: (See Gross Income.)

GROSS SALES: The total invoiced sales before adjusting returns, credits, etc.

GUARDIAN: One appointed by a court to manage the affairs of minors or incompetents.

GUARANTEE OF TITLE: An opinion rendered regarding the condition of title based upon a review of the official records and backed by a fund to compensate those damaged by negligence.

GUARANTEED MORTGAGE: A mortgage acquired or negotiated by a mortgage company and sold to an investor with a written guarantee that all payments of principal and interest shall be made or the mortgage company will reimburse the investor from its own funds.

GUARANTEED SALES CONTRACT: Another term for a guaranteed trade-in sale.

GUARANTEED TRADE-IN: A contract to purchase real property executed by a trade-in company, builder, or dealer with the seller in which a set time is allotted for the performance of the guarantee and during which the seller may sell to someone else for more money than the trade-in company guaranteed.

H

HABENDUM: The common name for the clause "to have and to hold" which is often inserted in deeds.

HEAD OF FAMILY: One who is responsible for dependents. Does not have to be male nor married in order to qualify.

HEIRS: Those who obtain property from the estate of a deceased person.

HIGHEST AND BEST USE: A term used in appraising real property to describe how a parcel of land can be used to generate the maximum return.

HOLDER IN DUE COURSE: One who receives in the course of business and in good faith a note for value without prior knowledge of any defects.

HOLOGRAPHIC WILL: A handwritten will signed by the testator.

HOMEOWNER'S POLICY: An insurance policy for real property which offers coverage for many things not insured under a standard fire policy.

HOMESTEAD: A home for which a Declaration of Homestead has been recorded and which thereby is given certain protection against future judgments.

HUNDRED PER CENT LOCATION: The best location in a community for a commercial business enterprise.

HYPOTHECATE: To pledge property as security for money borrowed or repayment of a debt but with the continued right of ownership and use.

I

IMPLIED: Not expressly stated or written but understood to be included.

IMPLIED WARRANTY: A warranty assumed by law to exist in an instrument, although it may not be specifically stated.

IMPOUND ACCOUNT: (See Trust Fund.)

IMPROVEMENT ACTS: Laws which authorize installation of street and other improvements which may then be assessed directly to the properties involved.

IMPROVEMENT BOND: A bond issued by a district, city, or state for the installation of improvements such as highways, streets, etc., and which is then sold to investors to finance the projects covered.

INCOMPETENT: One who is unable to manage his own property and affairs due to insanity, senility, or mental disability.

INCONSEQUENT DRAINAGE: Drainage established prior to the deformation of the drained section and continuing after a change in the earth's surface.

INCREMENT: An increase of some type. Used often to refer to the increase in the value of land resulting from population growth and additional growth.

INCUMBRANCE: (See Encumbrance.)

INDEMNITY: Any guarantee against possible loss, such as an insurance policy.

INDENTURE: A deed or contract entered into by two or more persons, each of whom obligates himself to perform certain things set forth in the indenture.

INDEPENDENT CONTRACTOR: One who operates his business separate from the other enterprises with which he may be associated. Real estate salesmen are often considered independent contractors rather than employees.

INDUSTRIAL PROPERTY: All the real and personal property, together with tangible and intangible assets, which comprise the total value of a manufacturing enterprise; also, the specific property on which such businesses can locate their operations.

INDUSTRIAL BANK: A lending company with broad lending powers, including the right to lend money on second mortgages.

INGRESS: An entrance to property which does not trespass over the property rights of others.

INHERIT: To obtain property as an heir.

INJUNCTION: An order of court requiring the performance or non-performance of some act.

INSOLVENT: The condition of having more liabilities than assets.

INSTALLMENT NOTE: (See Amortized Note.)

INSTITUTE OF REAL ESTATE BROKERS: A division of the National Association of Real Estate Boards which furnishes educational material to members. Every real estate broker and salesman should subscribe to this service.

INSTITUTIONAL LENDER: A recognized mortgage company or bank which is authorized to make real estate loans as well as purchase government insured loans. Banks, savings and loans, insurance companies, mutual savings banks are the principal ones involved.

INSTRUMENT: In law, any document by which the acts and agreements of the executors are made known to others.

INTANGIBLE PROPERTY: Those things which do not have physical properties but represent values, such as good will, ownership rights, etc.

INTER-CITY: Between cities. Today there are networks of real estate brokers working on an "inter-city" basis to handle the transfer of property.

INTERIM OCCUPANCY AGREEMENT: (See Occupancy Agreement.)

GLOSSARY OF REAL ESTATE TERMS

INTERLOCUTORY DECREE: A decree issued by a court which is not final, but is binding upon the involved parties until finalized. Commonly used in divorce proceedings.

INTERNATIONAL TRADERS CLUB: A committee of the National Association Of Real Estate Boards which is devoted to increasing knowledge and interest in the exchanging of real property. Anyone interested in this phase of the real estate business should become a member.

INTESTATE: Death without leaving a valid will.

INTER-STATE: Between different states.

INTRASTATE: Within a particular state.

INTRINSIC VALUE: True value, or actual value.

INURE: To serve to the use or benefit of someone.

INVOLUNTARY LIEN: A lien on real property which is imposed without the owner's authorization, such as taxes.

IRREVOCABLE: Without the right to cancel or void the act involved.

IRRIGATION DISTRICT: Special areas or districts created by law to furnish water to the lands involved and assessing the members thereof if necessary.

J

JOINDER: Acting jointly with one or more persons; joining.

JOINT NOTE: A note signed by more than one person, each with equal responsibility for payment, who must be sued together if action is necessary.

JOINT AND SEVERAL NOTE: The same as a joint note, except makers may be sued together or individually in the event of a default.

JOINT TENANCY: Equal ownership in property by two or more persons with the four "unities" of joint tenancy assured to all: time, title, interest and possession, plus the right of survivorship to the remaining tenants when one dies.

JUDGMENT: A final determination or order of a court of law that sets forth the decision of the judge in a lawsuit.

JUNIOR LIEN: Any lien which is subordinate to another lien that has prior claim on the security. Second mortgages and trust deeds are typical junior liens.

K

KEY LOT: A lot which is located in such a manner that one side adjoins the rear of another lot.

L

LACHES: Inexcusable delay in asserting your rights. Literally "sleeping on your rights."

LAND CONTRACT: The sale of real estate by means of an installment agreement during which title remains vested in the original seller until the predetermined terms of sale are satisfied.

LAND GRANT: (See Congressional Land Grant.)

LANDS, TENEMENTS, AND HEREDITAMENTS: A phrase used in early English law to express all kinds of property of the immovable classifications. It is, in essence, real estate with all fixed improvements thereon.

LAND TRUST CERTIFICATE: A certificate which verifies a beneficial interest in real estate while title is held in trust by a trustee, who issues this proof of interest.

LATENT: That which is concealed, hidden. A defect in property or title may be "latent."

LEASE: An agreement by which real estate is rented for a fixed period of time; an estate for years or leasehold estate.

LEASEBACK AGREEMENT: A device used to secure the right of occupancy under a lease as a condition of the sale terms on real property. Shopping center owners, and other businesses often develop their own land and then free the cash investment by selling the property with a "lease back" provision for themselves.

LEASED FEE: Land which is leased to others while the fee owner retains the rights to ground rentals and the further right of repossession when the allotted time has expired.

LEASEHOLD ESTATE: A less than freehold estate; a lease, or estate for years.

LEGAL DESCRIPTION: A description of property which can be recognized by law and by which the property in question can be definitely located by reference to recorded maps.

LEGAL RATE OF INTEREST: A fair rate of interest as recognized by courts where no rate is specified. In California it is 7% and in other states as low as 6%.

LEGATEE: One who receives personal property by will.

LESSEE: One who contracts to rent property from the owner, or master tenant.

LESSOR: One who rents property to another; a landlord.

LESS THAN FREEHOLD: Another term for a leasehold estate.

LEVY: To seize or attach property for payment of a debt.

LIEN: An encumbrance against property which becomes the security for the obligation. Typical liens are mortgages, trust deeds, taxes, assessments.

LIEU LANDS: Property which the state can substitute for lands granted it by the U.S. government when such lands are of equal area to original grants.

LIMITED PARTNERSHIP: A business association in which the party so designated has only limited liability for the venture while the general partner carries the major responsibilities under the law. This form of partnership is often used in syndicated ventures to acquire and develop real estate.

LINE FENCE: The fence which separates the boundaries of two or more parcels of land.

LIQUID ASSETS: Any property or valuable securities which can be readily converted to cash. Real estate is seldom considered a liquid asset.

LIQUIDATE: To sell property at its cash value in order to generate funds.

LIQUIDATED DAMAGES: A specific sum of money to be paid under a contract in the event of a breach of the contract's terms.

LIS PENDENS: A notice recorded to advise all interested parties that a law suit is pending against certain defendants and their property.

LISTING: A contract with a real estate broker authorizing the payment of a fee for the performance of specified services in connection with the property identified.

LITTORAL: Property which borders a large body of water, such as a lake, ocean, or sea is said to be littoral property.

LIVERY OF SEIZIN: The ancient English term for delivering possession of the land from one party to another, originally done by handling the new owner a handful of dirt from the land he was buying.

LOAN BROKER LAW: A law covering the obligations and responsibilities of real estate brokers who negotiate the origination and sale of mortgages.

LOAN CORRESPONDENT: One who acts as the exclusive agent for a lending institution in a defined market area for the purpose of procuring loans.

LONG TERM CAPITAL GAIN: An increase in the value of an asset occurring over a period of at least six months' duration and on which the owner can claim special tax privileges when the property is ultimately sold.

M

MARGINAL RELEASE: A notation on the margin of the recorder's books showing that a mortgage has been satisfied. This system is not used very often, having been replaced with the recording of "Satisfaction of Mortgage."

M.A.I.: Abbreviation for "Member of Appraisers Institute," a highly skilled and elite group of appraisers who have met certain rigid standards.

MAINTENANCE RESERVE: An amount of money set aside during the operation of a building to meet expected repairs and maintenance expenses.

MAJORITY: The age at which a youth becomes legally an adult able to vote and own property.

MARK: The signature of one who does not know how to write. It must be witnessed by two or more persons to permit valid recordation.

MARKETABLE TITLE: Title to property which can be conveyed without inherent defects or clouds which would impair its value to the new owner.

MARKET ANALYSIS: A report on the various factors and conditions which affect a given market and which will be influential in any decisions made regarding a business venture.

MARKET PRICE: The price a property should bring based on comparable sales of similar properties within recent months.

MARKET VALUE: The price a property should bring from a fully informed buyer when he is under no pressure to buy and the seller is under no pressure to sell.

MASTER PLAN: A guide to the use of property within a community as established by a planning commission to project the desired future growth and nature of the area covered.

MASTER'S DEED: (See Sheriff's Deed.)

MATERIAL FACT: Any information which, if revealed, might affect the decisions and judgments of those involved in a transaction.

MECHANICS LIEN: A lien which protects the interests of those performing work upon property when they have not been paid or when there is material furnished for which the builder or owner have not paid. The law provides specific remedies for such liens.

GLOSSARY OF REAL ESTATE TERMS

MENACE: In law, the use of threats or violence to induce one to sign a contract.

MERIDIAN LINE: The U.S. Government Survey lines running from north to south, used to establish township boundaries.

MESNE PROFITS: Profits extracted from a property during the interim period when such property was illegally withheld from its rightful owner.

METES AND BOUNDS: A method of describing real property by boundary markers and lines.

MINOR: Any child who has not attained legal age.

MISDEMEANOR: A crime of lesser consequences which is subject to minor jail terms, fines, or both.

MISPLACEMENT: Construction of a building on a property which causes depreciation in value from misuse.

MISREPRESENTATION: Falsely representing property to buyers, or facts about such property, or concealing important truths about the transaction from the participants.

M.L.S.: Abbreviation for "Multiple Listing Service."

MODIFICATION AGREEMENT: A written change to a document which modifies the original terms by mutual agreement of all parties. This is commonly used to alter the terms of a mortgage.

MONTH TO MONTH TENANCY: (See Periodic Tenancy.)

MONUMENT: An object placed at a fixed point by surveyors to establish their survey lines.

MORATORIUM: The suspension of liability for a debt during certain emergency periods when the government or lending institutions consider this step necessary for the public welfare.

MORTGAGE: A legal instrument used to make real property or personal property the security for payment of a loan. Mortgagor has one year for redemption after foreclosure and may maintain possession in the interim.

MORTGAGE BANKER: One who deals in mortgages, usually with his own capital or line of credit, selling such loans to other investors at more favorable prices and retaining the servicing responsibility for an additional fee.

MORTGAGE BROKER: One who negotiates the placing of loans but does not use his own capital for that purpose.

MORTGAGE CERTIFICATE: An instrument used to signify partial ownership of a mortgage when there are many persons with a beneficial right to the mortgage, each with an undivided interest.

MORTGAGEE: The one who lends money secured by a mortgage. In its broader sense, any lender dealing in real property securities.

MORTGAGEE'S STATEMENT: A statement issued by a mortgage lender as to the condition of the loan, amount due, and other information.

MORTGAGE INSURANCE: Life insurance written to cover the amount of a mortgage on real property and paid in full in the event the mortgagor dies before the balance on the loan has been fully retired.

MORTGAGE MARKET: The general condition of the lending sources which are available at any given time to acquire and hold mortgages or trust deeds on property.

MORTGAGE PARTICIPATION: The assignment of a partial interest in a portfolio of loans to other lenders in order to recover capital and reinvest it for higher returns. This is a common practice among savings and loan associations, as well as some other lending institutions.

MORTGAGOR: The one borrowing the money secured by a mortgage.
MORTGAGOR'S STATEMENT: The loan application form filed by a proposed borrower with the lending institution setting forth his assets, liabilities, income and credit history for the review of the lending company.
M.P.S.: Abbreviation for "Minimum Property Standards," an expression used in connection with FHA insured loans and also VA loans.
MUNIMENTS OF TITLE: Title deeds and documents showing the chain of title on a property.
MUTUAL CONSENT: The complete agreement of all parties to a contract regarding the terms of that contract.
MUTUAL WATER COMPANY: A non-profit company formed to provide water to its stockholders who control its operation for their joint benefit.

N

N.A.R.E.B.: Abbreviation for "National Association of Real Estate Boards."
NATURALIZED CITIZEN: A person who has been made a citizen of the United States under an act of Congress.
NEGOTIABLE INSTRUMENT: A promissory note or check which can be transferred by endorsement and meets certain legal requirements.
NET EARNINGS: Receipts from operating sources after deducting direct expenses but before depreciation, mortgage retirement, and financing charges.
NET INCOME: (See Net Earnings.)
NET LEASE: A lease wherein the landlord pays all expenses directly chargeable to the property, such as taxes and insurance.
NET LISTING: A listing agreement with a broker whose fee is determined by the amount he can obtain in excess of the seller's net figure. These listings have many problems and are frowned upon by many real estate boards and companies.
NET-NET-NET LEASE: A lease where the lessee pays his pro-rata share of direct expenses, such as taxes and insurance, and the lessor is assured of receiving a fixed income.
NOTARY PUBLIC: A person authorized by law to take acknowledgments and oaths from individuals.
NOTE: (See Promissory Note.)
NOTICE OF ABANDONMENT: The notice which is filed when work is discontinued on an unfinished building job.
NOTICE OF APPEAL: A notice filed to indicate that a court decision will be appealed to a higher court.
NOTICE OF CESSATION: Same as notice of abandonment.
NOTICE OF COMPLETION: Notice filed when all work has been completed upon a building according to contract specifications.
NOTICE OF INTENDED SALE: A notice recorded when a business is sold, to give public and creditors knowledge of the transaction.
NOTICE OF NON-RESPONSIBILITY: A notice, which, when properly recorded and posted on the property, relieves the owner from the effect of mechanics' liens, under certain specified conditions.
NOTICE TO QUIT: A three day notice required by law before a tenant delinquent in rental payments can be evicted by suit.

NOTICE OF DEFAULT: A notice filed by a lender or trustee advising the borrower he is in default, and which starts the time running for foreclosure proceedings.

O

OBSOLESCENCE: (See Depreciation, Functional Obsolescence, and Social Obsolescence.)

OCCUPANCY AGREEMENT: An interim agreement with a buyer to permit occupancy of the premises until the escrow can be closed and on specific terms and conditions.

OFF-SALE LICENSE: A liquor license permitting the sale of packaged goods which must be taken off the premises.

OFFSET STATEMENT: A statement from a lender or lien holder as to the status of the lien, the balance due, and any other requirements.

OFF-SITE IMPROVEMENTS: In reference to subdivisions, these are improvements other than those physically on the lots involved and include streets, sewers, storm drains, and the like.

ON-SALE LICENSE: A liquor license permitting consumption of such on location such as a bar or cocktail lounge.

OPEN END MORTGAGE: A mortgage which permits the borrower to make improvements and obtain additional amounts to cover them without drawing new mortgages or creating additional costs.

OPEN LISTING: A non-exclusive listing given to one or more real estate agents, each of which can sell the property if he procures the buyer accepted by the owner, but under which the owner can also find his own buyer without paying any commission.

OPTION: A written contract granting a proposed buyer or lessee a specific period of time in which to complete the agreement or forfeit the option deposit.

OPTIONEE: The one obtaining the option right.

OPTIONOR: The one granting the option to another.

OUTLAWED CLAIM: A claim which is nullified because the one making it waited beyond the legal limits provided for exercising his claim.

OVERBUILDING: The construction of too many properties of a similar nature in a given market area, creating a surplus condition or reducing the value of all properties as a result.

OVER-IMPROVED: A property which has received greater investment than its surrounding neighbors, when such cannot be easily regained upon sale, is considered an over-improvement.

P

PAROL CONTRACT: A verbal contract or oral agreement.

PARTIAL RELEASE CLAUSE: A clause in a land purchase contract and subsequent mortgage instruments which provides for the release of a parcel of land from the blanket mortgage when a specified, pro-rata sum has been paid to the holder of the mortgage or land owner. Subdividers use this procedure in order to develop land in sections while owner still holds an interest in the mortgage on the balance of the land involved.

GLOSSARY OF REAL ESTATE TERMS

PARTIAL RECONVEYANCE: Same as partial release clause.
PARTITION: The dividing of an estate among its common owners.
PARTY WALL: A dividing wall which separates two or more properties and to which each abutting owner has equal rights of use.
PAR VALUE: Market value. In reference to loan discount, no costs involved when quoted at "par" since this is 100¢ on the dollar.
PATENT: An original conveyance of real estate from the Federal Government to a private owner.
PAYEE: The one receiving the sum due on a note.
PAYOR: The one paying the sum due on a note.
PAYMENT GUARANTEE: In trade-in housing programs, a guarantee to advance monthly payments and holding costs for a property owned by a buyer in order to give him time to sell and complete his other purchase.
PAYOFF PENALTY: (See Prepayment Penalty.)
PEDESTRIAN COUNT: A tally of the number of persons passing a given location used for appraising business property.
PERCENTAGE LEASE: A lease which fixes the tenant's rent as a percentage of his gross monthly or annual business receipts.
PERCENTAGE LEASE: A lease which fixes the tenant's rent as a percentage of his gross monthly or annual business receipts.
PERFECT ESCROW: The status of an escrow when all the monies, documents, and instructions necessary to close the transaction have been received by the escrow holder.
PERIODIC TENANCY: Tenancy of property for an indefinite period which can be terminated by either party with property notice.
PERSONAL PROPERTY: That which is essentially moveable, or not affixed to real property. Chattel.
PETITION: An instrument presented to a court or legal body requesting action on a matter.
PHYSICAL DEPRECIATION: Any loss to property values caused by normal wear and tear or usage. Also includes such things as termite damage, dry rot, and the like.
PISCARY RIGHTS: The right to fish in the waters where such rights exist.
PLAINTIFF: The one commencing a lawsuit.
PLANNING COMMISSION: A government agency of city, town, or county which recommends certain zoning and property use for the benefit of the local citizens and whose actions are subject to the approval of elected officials as a rule.
PLAT: A map or plan of a subdivision.
PLEDGE: A deposit of personal property used to secure a debt.
PLEDGEE: The one who receives the pledge.
PLEDGOR: The one making or giving the pledge.
PLOTTAGE VALUE: The increased value enjoyed by a parcel when it can be acquired or utilized in connection with adjacent parcels.
POINTS: A term used to describe loan discounts collected by mortgage lenders as a means of increasing their yield on real estate loans.
POLICE POWER: The power vested in a State Government to enact and enforce laws that are for the public welfare.

GLOSSARY OF REAL ESTATE TERMS

POTENTIAL VALUE: A value based on possible future circumstances which must occur before the value exists.

POWER OF ATTORNEY: The instrument used to make a person an attorney-in-fact for another individual.

POWER OF SALE: The right of a trustee or mortgagee to sell a property when the terms of the loan have not been met.

PRE-EMPTION: The act of buying something before another person can do so.

PRELIMINARY TITLE REPORT: A brief title report issued quickly to disclose any defects or problems which may exist before completing the transaction.

PREPAYMENT PENALTY: The penalty inflicted on mortgagors when they elect to pay the balance of the loan before it is due. Such payoff penalties vary greatly from one loan to another and should be checked before determining any given situation.

PRESCRIPTION: Obtaining an easement on the property of another by adverse use for a number of years.

PRIMA FACIE: Literally "on its face," or evident by its contents.

PRINCIPAL: One who employs an agent or becomes a participant in a real estate transaction as owner, buyer, etc.

PRIVITY: Mutuality of relationship or closeness.

PROBATE COURT: A court which has authority over the property of deceased persons and others incapable of managing their properties.

PROCURING CAUSE: The person responsible for bringing the property and buyers together or introducing the facts to those who ultimately act upon them.

PROFIT-SHARING GUARANTEE: In trade-in housing, a contract which permits the seller and the guarantee company to share the profit generated above a certain fixed figure if more can be obtained.

PROMISSORY NOTE: A written promise to pay a certain sum of money at a definite date in the future.

PROPERTY MANAGEMENT: A real estate specialty which includes the care, leasing and maintenance of property for a fee. Property management is becoming an increasingly important service in all metropolitan areas.

PROPERTY SETTLEMENT AGREEMENT: Agreements between divorcing man and wife as to the disposition of property which they jointly own.

PRORATION: To divide proportionately among the parties involved based on a fixed date of computations.

PUBLICATION DATE: In foreclosure proceedings, the date when the notice of sale was first published as prescribed by law.

PUBLIC REPORT: As pertains to subdivisions, a report issued by the Real Estate Commissioner (or his equivalent) setting forth the known facts about a proposed subdivision, which report must be given to each buyer before he signs a purchase agreement.

P.U.E.: Abbreviation for "Public Utilities Easements."

PURCHASE MONEY MORTGAGE: Any mortgage originated with the sale of property as part of the purchase price, or in some states, any mortgage held by the seller of property as part of the purchase price.

Q

QUASI: As, as if, or of similar nature to.

QUIET TITLE: An action taken to remove clouds from a title by lawsuit, or to determine true status of title.

QUIT CLAIM DEED: A deed by which the grantor transfers any interest in a parcel of real estate he might have but without any warranties.

R

RANGE: A strip of land running north and south, six miles wide, as established by U.S. Government survey.

RATIFICATION: Unqualified acceptance of a contract or agreement.

REAL ESTATE BOARD: An organization of realtors and their associate salesmen operating to improve their knowledge and professional conduct of the real estate business.

REAL PROPERTY: Land and everything that is attached thereto.

REALTOR: The name applied to one who is a member in good standing of the National Association of Real Estate Boards, who exclusively own the rights to this title.

RECEIVER: One appointed to manage and dispose of the property of a bankrupt.

RECISSION OF CONTRACT: The nullifying of a contract by mutual consent or court decision.

RECONVEYANCE: To return to the original owner, as in the case of a trust deed which has been satisfied; the trustee signs a "deed of conveyance."

RECAPTURE CLAUSE: A clause in an agreement which permits the lessor to recover possession.

RECOVERY FUND: A fund established from the proceeds of licensing fees in some states for paying the claims of investors who have been injured by the acts of real estate men.

REDEMPTION: The reacquiring of foreclosed property by the original owner during the prescribed time period.

RELEASE CLAUSE: (See Partial Release Clause.)

RELICTION: The gaining of land by the gradual receding of water from the usual water mark.

REMAINDER: The right to future possession after the termination of a life estate.

REMAINDERMAN: The one receiving the remainder.

REPRODUCTION APPRAISAL: A method of appraising based on computing the costs to reproduce a structure plus the value of the land involved.

REQUEST FOR NOTICE OF DEFAULT: An instrument anyone can file to request notification of any foreclosure action by a specific lien holder.

RESERVATION: The temporary withholding of a property from the market to one buyer until he can confirm his decision.

RESIDENT MANAGER: One who lives on the premises of an income producing building and manages the units in a limited fashion.

RESTRICTION: A limitation on the use of property imposed by the previous grantor or subdivider.

RETAINER: An amount paid to retain the services of any professional man, such as a lawyer.

REVENUE STAMPS: The government documentary stamps which are affixed to all deeds and transfer documents to verify payment of tax.

REVERSE FINANCE GUARANTEE: A trade-in tool used to assure the seller of property that the funds necessary to liquidate the buyer's property will be available at a specified time.

REVERSE TRADE-IN GUARANTEE: In trade-in housing, the transferring of a trade-in property to the seller of the first property with a back up guarantee from the trade-in company to assure sale of said parcel.

REVERSIONARY INTEREST: The remaining right to an estate or the residue when the life estate is terminated.

RIGHT OF SURVIVORSHIP: The right contained in a joint tenancy deed for the surviving tenants to acquire the interest of the deceased tenant.

RIGHT OF WAY: An easement which grants to its receiver the right to pass over or maintain use of a parcel of property belonging to another.

RIPARIAN RIGHTS: The rights of an owner to use the water which is on, under or adjacent to his land.

RUNNING WITH THE LAND: An expression used to identify any right in property which continues despite the sequence of ownership.

S

SALE AND LEASEBACK AGREEMENT: (See Leaseback Agreement.)

SALES AND USE TAX: A levy on retail sales collected from the vendor by the state or city in which he operates.

SANDWICH LEASE: The remaining interest of the original lessee after real estate has been subleased to another tenant.

SATISFACTION OF MORTGAGE: An instrument recorded to verify that the mortgagor has satisfied his debt.

SEAL: The legal identification of corporations and political entities used to attest to their actions.

SECTION: Pertaining to land, a standard measurement containing 640 acres and being one square mile.

SECONDARY FINANCING: Junior liens created to help finance the acquisition of property or secure additional indebtedness.

SECONDARY MORTGAGE MARKET: The outlet for primary mortgages to those who buy them for investment after the original lender has completed his purchase of the loans. Fanny Mae is a prime factor in the secondary mortgage market.

SECURITY: Any stock, note, treasury stock, debenture, or other evidence of indebtedness which can be used to "secure" the interest named.

SEND OUT SLIP: Used in business opportunity transactions as evidence that a prospective buyer was introduced to a property by a certain broker, the prospect signing the slip before inspecting the property.

SEPARATE PROPERTY: Property of either spouse which is not part of the community estate.

SEVERANCE DAMAGE: The loss in value to a property as the result of a partial condemnation or acquisition by another for a part of the original parcel and which should be then compensated for the lowered remaining value after severance.

SETBACK LINE: The building line established by local authorities who control where buildings may be placed on a given lot.

SHERIFF'S DEED: A deed given when property is sold by order of the court for payment of a debt.

SINKING FUND: A method of handling depreciation by setting aside certain amounts from the income of the property to offset the replacement costs when they are needed.

SITE ECONOMICS: The analysis of a given building site for commercial purposes which relates cost to productivity and the efficiency of the site in terms of related amenities.

SOCIAL OBSOLESCENCE: Depreciation in value due to external rather than internal influences, such as a change in the neighborhood, and similar factors.

SPECIAL ASSESSMENT: A levy against property for improvements which are designed to benefit that property particularly.

SPECIFIC LIEN: A lien which is applicable to one property in particular versus a general lien which applies to all property of the individual involved.

SPECIFIC PERFORMANCE: A court order requiring a person to do what he has previously agreed to do.

SPECIFIC RISK GUARANTEE: In trade-in housing, a guarantee which obligates someone to carry a specific amount of any loss which might result from the trade.

SPENDABLE INCOME: Money left over after paying mortgages, taxes, and other expenses, from the proceeds of rent which gives the owner funds he can use for other purposes.

SQUATTER'S RIGHTS: The right to occupy land by virtue of undisputed and undisturbed usage, but without legal title to such property. (See Adverse Possession.)

S.R.A.: Abbreviation for "Society of Residential Appraisers."

STANDARD TITLE POLICY: The title policy usually issued to a buyer of real property which insures against all defects of record, but excludes physical inspection of the premises and other important items. (See A.T.A. Policy.)

STATEMENT OF CONDITIONS: (See Mortgagee's Statement.)

STATEMENT OF IDENTITY: A questionnaire used by title companies to help identify a person when the records indicate confusion due to many persons having similar names.

STATUTE OF LIMITATIONS: State law limiting the time in which certain actions may be introduced in a court of law. When expired, the action is said to have outlawed.

STATUTE OF FRAUDS: Law which requires certain types of contracts to be in writing.

STATUTORY DEDICATION: The enforced granting to city, state, county, etc. of land by an individual for certain specific uses, such as streets. Subdividers must frequently dedicate their completed streets to the municipality in which they subdivide.

STAYBONDS: A bond issued to cover a judgment while such is on appeal to a higher court.

STEP-UP LEASE: A lease which provides for increased amounts of rent over succeeding periods.

STRAIGHT LINE DEPRECIATION: Setting aside or allowing a fixed sum of money each year to offset replacement or improvements when needed.

STRAIGHT NOTE: A non-amortized note which is all due and payable at one time in one sum.

SUBCONTRACTOR: One who accepts an assignment of work from another contractor, who is known as the general contractor.

SUBDIVISION: Definition of a subdivision varies by state. In many, it is any parcel divided into 5 or more parcels for sale or lease. A subdivision map is usually required for filing within the county recorders office of the area where project is located.

"SUBJECT TO" CLAUSES: In real estate contracts such clauses acknowledge a condition or debt but do not necessarily make the purchaser liable for them. Also, any "subject to" condition of a contract becomes a contingency, which makes the entire contract void if not completed according to written terms.

SUBLEASE: The letting of property to another under the terms of an existing primary lease.

SUBORDINATION CLAUSE: A clause in a mortgage or trust deed which provides that this debt and security be secondary to other obligations which the mortgagor intends to incur and which are usually specified in the agreement to subordinate.

SUBPOENA: A judicial writ requiring a person to appear in court at a particular time and for a particular matter.

SUBROGATION: The act of substituting one person in the place of another with reference to a claim or right.

SUCCESSION: The process of receiving property as the result of some subsequent event, such as the death of a wife, or husband.

SUCCESSOR'S LIABILITY: The liability of the new owner of a business for the unpaid taxes of the former owner if they have not been satisfied.

SURETY BOND: A bond guaranteeing performance of a specified act or payment of the amount required to complete that act.

SURFACE WATER RIGHTS: The right to use the water which is on the surface of the ground.

SWEAT EQUITY: Obtaining title to property or earning the down payment to purchase property by performing certain items of work for a predetermined value.

T

TANGIBLE PROPERTY: That which has material existence and is susceptible to the senses. In general, land, buildings, furnishings, etc.

TAX ABATEMENT: A reduction or deduction in taxes generally resulting from an appeal to the Board of Equalization when one feels he has been unfairly taxed.

TAXABLE VALUE: (See Assessed Value.)

TAX DEED: The deed given when property is sold for a tax delinquency.

TAX PENALTY: A levy for failure to pay taxes on time.

TAX SALE: The sale of property by the state at auction to settle delinquent taxes.

TAX SERVICE FEE: A fee paid to an independent company for searching the tax records annually to assure the lender that the taxes and other assessments are current or report any delinquencies.

GLOSSARY OF REAL ESTATE TERMS

TENANCY: An estate less than freehold. A leasehold estate.

TENANCY AT SUFFERANCE: The continued occupancy of a property by a tenant after the lease has expired, with the owner permitting this arrangement on a temporary basis.

TENANCY IN COMMON: Ownership by two or more persons who hold undivided interests, not necessarily equal, without any right to survivorship.

TENDER: An unconditional offer of payment of a debt or an offer of performance.

TENEMENTS: All rights in land which are conveyed when the land is conveyed.

TENTATIVE MAP: The map produced by a subdivider for submission to governmental agencies and bodies for approval before finalization.

TENURE IN LAND: The manner and nature in which land is held. Also, a period of time.

TESTAMENT: A will.

TESTATE: Leaving a will upon death.

TESTATOR: Man who makes a will.

TESTATRIX: Woman who makes a will.

TIDE LANDS: Property covered from time to time (if not permanently) by ocean or lake waters.

"TIME IS OF THE ESSENCE" CLAUSE: A clause which specifies that time is an essential ingredient in the contract concerned and that failure to meet time for performance will be considered a violation of the contract.

TITLES: Evidences of ownership and lawful possession to property.

TITLE INSURANCE: Protection to a property owner against loss through special insurance purchased when property is acquired or financed.

TOPOGRAPHY: The general nature of the surface of land.

TORRENS CERTIFICATE: A document issued by the public registrar to indicate to whom the property in question currently belongs.

TORRENS TITLE: A system of land registration used in some states, but discontinued in most.

TORT: A wrongful or harmful act which violates legal rights.

TOWNSHIP: A unit of land six miles square (36 square miles) which is established by government survey.

TRUST DEED: A form of mortgage instrument used in lieu of a mortgage in many states. There are three parties to a trust deed: the trustor (borrower), the trustee (interim title holder), and the beneficiary (the lender). It has many advantages to both lender and borrower and is gaining in popularity for that reason.

TRUSTEE: A person or corporation which holds title in trust until a debt has been repaid or a service performed. Under trust deeds, he holds title for the beneficiary until obligation is paid.

TRUSTOR: The one who borrows money under a deed of trust.

TRUST FUND: A fund or impound collected from the mortgagor to meet his tax and insurance payments when due. Many lenders require this monthly collection in order to assure having sufficient amounts on hand when obligations are due.

U

UNBALANCED IMPROVEMENTS: An improvement to real property which is not the best one suited for the site on which it is placed.

UNDER-IMPROVEMENT: Construction of improvements on land which is less expensive and smaller than required for that land to produce highest use.

UNDIVIDED INTEREST: An interest which cannot be separated from the interests in that property which others may have and which gives the holder an equal right to the use of the premises.

UNDUE INFLUENCE: Taking any advantage of another by playing on his weaknesses or distress.

UNILATERAL CONTRACT: A contract which imposes an obligation on only one party to the contract.

UNIMPROVED LAND: Land upon which no buildings have been constructed.

UNITIES: The essentials to a joint tenancy deed which are the unities of time, title, interest, and possession.

UNLAWFUL DETAINER ACTION: A legal action to lawfully remove a tenant from a building after he has defaulted and been notified to move.

UNMARRIED: The status of one who has been married but is now divorced or widowed.

UNSECURED: Not protected by assets, or security instruments.

URBAN PROPERTY: Property located within the core of a city.

URBAN RENEWAL: Program to improve substandard areas and buildings in metropolitan cities.

USE TAX: A sales tax on goods purchased out of state.

USURY: Charging a higher rate of interest than the law allows.

V

VA: Abbreviation for Veterans Administration.

VACANCY FACTOR: The percentage of non-occupancies in a building or a type of unit as related to the total available.

VALID: Legally enforceable; binding.

VALUATION: An estimate of worth or price.

VEHICULAR TRAFFIC: The number of cars or vehicles which pass a given point.

VENDEE: The buyer.

VENDOR: The seller.

VENUE: The place where an acknowledgment is taken, or an action held.

VERIFICATION: A confirmation of the facts as sworn by written statement.

VERIFICATION OF DEPOSIT: A document used by FHA and VA to verify the amount of cash assets held by the buyer or his trustees for the performance of the purchase agreement.

VERIFICATION OF EMPLOYMENT: A document used by FHA and VA to verify the current and past history of employment for an applicant for a loan.

VETERAN'S EXEMPTION: In some states veteran property owners are given a tax exemption on a portion of their tax bill. In California they are entitled to $1000 in exemption on valuation if assets are not in excess of $5000.

VEST: To bestow upon or grant, as title to property.

VOID: Not valid at law; not binding.

VOIDABLE: Something that may be declared void in the future but which is not actually void until so judged by a court of law.

VOLUNTARY LIEN: A lien placed on the property with the consent of the owner, such as a mortgage.

W

WAIVE: To abandon, forego, or relinquish a right.

WARRANTY DEED: A deed that recites certain specified warranties, commonly used in most states except California where the Grant Deed has replaced it.

WATER TABLE: The depth underground of the natural waters as measured from the surface.

WASTE: In real estate, the abuse of property by a tenant or someone having a temporary interest in the property, resulting in loss to the owner.

WRIT OF EXECUTION: A court order that property must be sold to pay a debt.

Y

YIELD: The return for invested money which is anticipated by the investor. It is computed based on three factors: interest, term, and discount.

YIELD GUIDES: Tables for computing the various yields one can receive from investments, such as mortgages, second deeds of trust, etc.

Z

ZONING: The control of land usage by city, county, or state authorities with power to limit the property use to these standards.

BIBLIOGRAPHY

A Selected List of Books, Periodicals, and
Publications Available on Related Real Estate Topics

The real estate salesman who desires to become a professional in his chosen career, will always accept every opportunity to further his education about the real estate business. For the reader's benefit, I have compiled a list of books, magazines, and pamphlets available on many of the specialized phases of our industry.

ADVERTISING AND PUBLIC RELATIONS

California Real Estate Association. The Realtor's Public Relations Guide, Los Angeles, Calif.: California Real Estate Assoc., 1960.
Barton, Roger. Advertising Handbook, Englewood Cliffs, N.J.: Prentice-Hall, Inc., 1950.
Berge & Herrold. Real Estate Advertising.
National Institute of Real Estate Brokers. Real Estate Advertising, Chicago: National Assn. of R.E. Boards, 1955.
McDonald. How to Use Classified Advertising to Sell More Real Estate, Englewood Cliffs, N.J.: Prentice-Hall, Inc., 1957.
McKay. Real Estate Advertising That Clicks Now.
Stark, Jack. Successful Publicity and Public Relations in Real Estate, Englewood Cliffs, N.J.: Prentice-Hall, Inc., 1958.
Woessner, Charles. How to Get Profitable Real Estate Listings Through Newspaper Advertising, Englewood Cliffs, N.J.: Prentice-Hall, Inc., 1952.

APPRAISAL AND EVALUATION

American Institute of Real Estate Appraisers: The Appraisal of Real Estate, 1951.
    Appraisal Terminology and Handbook, 1954.
    Case-Study Appraisal Reports, 3 Vols., 1957.
    152 Problems in Real Estate Appraisal with Suggested Solutions, Robert L. Free, 1956.
    101 Rural Appraisal Problems with Suggested Solutions, Walter F. Willmette, 1958.
    Real Estate Appraisal Practice, 1958.
    Selected Readings in Real Estate Appraisal, 1953.

BIBLIOGRAPHY

Chicago, Ill.: American Institute of Real Estate Appraisers. See also their monthly publication, The Appraisal Journal.

American Institute of Architects. Building Cost Manual, Chicago Chapter of Institute and Chicago Real Estate Board, New York: Wiley, 1957.

Babcock, Frederick M. The Valuation of Real Estate, New York: McGraw-Hill, 1932.

Crouse, Earl F. and Everett, Charles H. Rural Appraisals, Englewood Cliffs, N.J.: Prentice-Hall, Inc., 1956.

Elwood, L.W. Ellwood Tables for Real Estate Appraising and Financing, Ridgewood, N.J.: Published by Author, 1959.

Friedman, Edith J. Encyclopedia of Real Estate Appraising, Englewood Cliffs, N.J.: Prentice-Hall, Inc., 1959.

Financial Publishing Co. Financial Compound Interest and Annuity Tables, Boston: Financial Publishing Co., 1942.

Grant, Eugene L. and Norton, Paul T. Depreciation, New York: Ronald Press, 1955.

Husband, William H. and Anderson, Frank Ray. Real Estate Analysis, Homewood, Ill.: Richard D. Irwin.

Knowles, Jerome, Jr. and Pervear, John E. Real Estate Appraisal Manual, Northeast Harbor, Maine: Published by Author, 1957.

May, Arthur A. The Valuation of Residential Real Estate, Englewood Cliffs, N.J.: Prentice-Hall, Inc., 1953.

McMichael, Stanley L. McMichael's Appraising Manual, Englewood Cliffs, N.J.: Prentice-Hall, Inc., 1951.

Medici, Giuseppe. Principles of Appraisal, Ames, Iowa: Iowa State College Press, 1953.

Murray, William G. Farm Appraisal, Ames, Iowa: Iowa State Collage Press, 1954.

Orgel, Lewis. Valuation Under the Law of Eminent Domain, 2 Vols., Charlottesville, Va.: The Michie Co., 1953.

Schmutz, George L. Capitalization Tables with Problems, Los Angeles: Published by Author, 1936.

———— Condemnation Appraisal Handbook, Rev. by E. Rams, Englewood Cliffs, N.J.: Prentice-Hall, Inc., 1949.

———— The Appraisal Process, Englewood Cliffs, N.J.: Prentice-Hall, Inc.

Stevens, Marshall and Stevens Company. Residential Cost Handbook, Published by Marshall and Stevens Company.

Techmeyer. How to Value Real Estate, Englewood Cliffs, N.J.: Prentice-Hall, Inc.

Thorson, Ivan A. Simplified Appraisal System - Land Economics, Los Angeles, Calif.: Realty Research Bureau, Inc., 1951.

U.S. Federal Housing Administration. Underwriting Manual, Washington, D.C.: U.S. Fed. Housing Adm., 1958.

U.S. Army Corps of Engineers. Real Property Appraisers' Handbook, Washington, D.C.: U.S. Army Corps of Engineers, 1956. Order from Superintendent of Documents.

Wendt, Paul F. Real Estate Appraisal, New York: Holt, 1956.

Wenzlick, Roy and Company. Residential Appraisal Manual, St. Louis, Mo.: The Company, 1957.

BIBLIOGRAPHY

BUILDING AND CONSTRUCTION

Abel, Joseph H. and Severud, Fred N. Apartment Houses, New York: Reinhold, 1947.

Architectural Forum. Building, U.S.A., Editors of Architectural Forum, New York: McGraw-Hill, 1957.

Baker, Geoffrey, and Funaro, Bruno. Motels, New York: Reinhold, 1955.

Beyer, Mackesey, and Montgomery. Houses Are For People: A Study of Home Buyer Motivations, Ithaca, N.Y.: Housing Research Center, Cornell University, 1955.

Colean, Miles L. and Newcomb, Robinson, Stabilizing Construction: The Record and Potential, New York: McGraw-Hill, 1952.

Dietz, Albert G. Dwelling House Construction, Princeton, N.J.: D. Van Nostrand, 1954.

Jones, A. Quincy and Emmons, Frederick E. Builders' Homes for Better Living, New York: Reinhold, 1957.

Johnstone, B. Kenneth and Joern, Charles E. The Business of Home Building, New York: McGraw-Hill, 1950.

Ketchum, Morris, Jr. Shops and Stores, New York: Reinhold, 1957.

McMichael, Stanley L. Real Estate Subdivisions, Englewood Cliffs, N.J.: Prentice-Hall, Inc., 1949.

National Association of Home Builders. Home Builders' for Land Development, Washington, D.C.: N.A.H.B., 1958.

United States Gypsum Co. A Blueprint for Profit. Operative Remodeling.

Wehrly, Max S. and McKeever, J. Ross. The Community Builders Handbook, Washington, D.C.: Urban Land Institute, 1956.

COMMERCIAL AND INVESTMENT PROPERTIES

Cadwallader, Clyde T. How to Buy Real Estate for Profit, Englewood Cliffs, N.J.: Prentice-Hall, Inc., 1958.

    How to Deal in Real Estate, Englewood Cliffs, N.J.: Prentice-Hall, Inc., 1955.

Casey, William J. Real Estate Investments and How to Make Them, New York: Institute for Business Planning, Inc., 1958.

    Real Estate Forms, Etc., Institute of Business Planning, Inc.

    Note: Also see the monthly service provided by Institute of Business Planning.

ARCHITECTURAL RECORDS

Baker, Geoffrey and Funaro, Bruno. Shopping Centers - Design and Operation, New York: Reinhold, 1951.

California Real Estate Association. Creative Real Estate Investment, Los Angeles, Calif.: C.R.E.A., 1962.

    Real Estate Investment, Los Angeles, Calif.: C.R.E.A., 1963.

Grebler, Leo. Experience in Urban Real Estate Investment, New York: Columbia University Press, 1955.

Greenfield, Harvey and Griesinger, Frank. Sale-Leasebacks and Leasing in Real Estate and Equipment Transactions, New York: McGraw-Hill, 1958.

McKeever, J. Ross. *Shopping Centers Re-Studied*, Washington, D.C.: Urban Land Institute, 1957.
National Institute of Real Estate Brokers. *Make Your Estate Real Estate*, Chicago, Ill.: N.A.R.E.B., 1963.
Nelson, Richard Lawrence. *The Selection of Retail Locations*, New York: F.W. Dodge, Corp., 1958.
Nickerson, William. *How I Turned $1000 into a Million in Real Estate*, New York: Simon and Schuster, 1959.
Parnes, Dr. Louis. *Planning Stores that Pay*, New York: F.W. Dodge, Corp., 1957.
Schultz, Robert E. *Life Insurance Housing Projects*, Homewood, Ill.: Richard D. Irwin, 1956.
Snider, Harold Wayne. *Life Insurance Investment in Commercial Real Estate*, Homewood, Ill.: Richard D. Irwin, 1956.
University of California Extension Program. *Commercial and Investment Properties*, Berkeley, Calif.: U. of C., 1955.
Winnick, Louis. *Rental Housing: Opportunities for Private Investment*, New York: McGraw-Hill, 1958.
———. *Commercial Buildings*, New York: F.W. Dodge Corp.
———. *Design for Modern Merchandising*, New York: F.W. Dodge Corp.
———. *Motels, Hotels, Restaurants and Bars*, New York: F.W. Dodge Corp.

EXCHANGING REAL ESTATE

International Traders Club. *The Monthly Trader*, Monthly publication of I.T.C., 36 Wabash St., Chicago, Ill, Only Realtor members eligible for subscriptions.
Mitchell, Harold. *From Rags to Riches Trading Real Estate*, San Francisco, Calif.: Dolores Press, 1958.
National Institute of Real Estate Brokers. *Real Estate Exchanges*, Chicago, Ill.: N.A.R.E.B., 1951.
———. *Real Estate Trader's Handbook*, Chicago, Ill.: N.A.R.E.B., 1956.
Reno, Richard R. *Profitable Real Estate Exchanging*, Englewood Cliffs, N.J.: Prentice-Hall, Inc., 1956.

FINANCING REAL ESTATE

American Institute of Banking. *Home Mortgage Lending*, New York, N.Y.: by the Institute.
Bryant, Willis R. *Mortgage Lending, Fundamentals and Practices*, New York: McGraw-Hill, 1956.
Conway, Lawrence V. *Mortgage Lending*, Chicago, Ill.: American Savings and Loan Institute Press, 1960.
DeHuszar, William I. *Mortgage Servicing*, New York: McGraw-Hill, 1954.
Fisher, Ernest McKinley. *Urban Real Estate Markets: Characteristics and Financing*, New York: National Bureau of Economic Research, 1951.
Hoagland, Henry E. *Real Estate Finance*, Homewood, Ill.: Richard D. Irwin, 1954.
McMichael, Stanley L. and O'Keefe, Paul T. *How to Finance Real Estate*, Englewood Cliffs, N.J.: Prentice-Hall, Inc., 1953.

Morton, J.E. *Urban Mortgage Lending*, Princeton, N.J.: Princeton University Press, 1956.
Pease, Robert H. and Cherrington, Homer V. *Mortgage Banking*, New York: McGraw-Hill, 1953.
Ratcliff, Richard U., and associates. *Residential Finance*, New York: Wiley, 1957.
Saulnier, R.J. and associates. *Federal Lending and Loan Insurance*, Princeton, N.J.: Princeton University Press, 1958.
―――― *Urban Mortgage Lending by Life Insurance Companies*, New York: National Bureau of Economic Research, 1950.

HOUSING AND HOUSING PROBLEMS

California Department of Veterans Affairs. *Farms and Homes for California Veterans*, Sacramento: State of Calif., 1958.
Carter, Deane F. and Hinchcliff, Keith H. *Family Housing*, New York: Wiley, 1949.
Dean, John P. *Home Ownership, Is It Sound?* New York: Harper, 1945.
Graff, Raymond K. *The Prefabricated House*, New York: Doubleday, 1947.
Greenwald, William I. *Buy or Rent*, New York: Twayne Publishers, 1958.
Kaufman, Gerald Lyton. *Homeseekers' Handbook*, New York: George W. Stewart, 1947.
Meredith, L. Douglas. *How to Buy a House*, New York: Harper, 1947.
Mock, Elizabeth B. *If You Want to Build a House*, New York: The Museum of Modern Art, Simon and Schuster, 1946.
Moral, Herbert R. *Buying Country Property*, New York: Macmillan, 1947.
Paxton, Edward T. *What People Want When They Buy a House*, Washington, D.C.: U.S. Dept. Commerce, 1955.
Rossi, Peter H. *Why Families Move*, Glencoe, Ill.: The Free Press, 1955.
U.S. Veterans Administration. *Questions and Answers on Guaranteed and Direct Loans for Veterans*, Washington, D.C.: U.S. Dept. Veterans Administration; V.A. Pamphlet 4A - 1.
―――― *Pointers for the Veteran Homeowner*, Washington, D.C.: U.S. Dept. Veterans Administration, V.A. Pamphlet 4A - 14.
―――― *To the Home-Buying Veteran - A Guide for Veterans Planning to Buy or Build Homes with a G.I. Loan*, Washington, D.C.: U.S. Dept. Veterans Administration, V.A. Pamphlet 4A - 10.

INSURANCE IN REAL ESTATE

Huebner, S.S. and Black, Kenneth, Jr. *Property Insurance*, New York: Appleton-Century-Crofts, 1957.
Magee, John H. *Property Insurance*, Homewood, Ill.: Richard D. Irwin, 1955.
Mowbray, Albert H. and Blanchard, Ralph H. *Insurance - Its Theory and Practice in the United States*, New York: McGraw-Hill, 1955.
Riegel, Robert and Miller, Jerome S. *Insurance - Principles and Practices*, Englewood Cliffs, N.J.: Prentice-Hall, Inc., 1947.
Schultz, Robert E. and Bardwell, Edward G. *Property Insurance*, New York: Rinehart, 1959.

LAND ECONOMICS

Alexanderson, Gunnar. The Industrial Structure of American Cities, Lincoln, Neb.: University of Nebraska Press, 1956.
Baker, Geoffrey and Funaro, Bruno. Parking, New York: Reinhold, 1958.
Barlowe, Raleigh. Land Resource Economics, Englewood Cliffs, N.J.: Prentice-Hall, Inc., 1958.
Bartholomew, Harland. Land Uses in American Cities, Cambridge, Mass.: Harvard University Press, 1955.
Calef, Wesley C. and Daoust, Charles. What Will New Industry Mean to My Town? Washington, D.C.: U.S. Office of Technical Services, 1955.
Colean, Miles L. Renewing Our Cities, New York: The Twentieth Century Fund, 1953.
Ely, Richard T. and Wehrwein, George S. Land Economics, New York: Macmillan, 1940.
Fisher, Ernest M. and Fisher, Robert M. Urban Real Estate, New York: Holt, 1954.
Forth, Milburn L. and McKeever, J. Ross. Planned Industrial Districts: Their Organization and Development, Washington, D.C.: Urban Land Institute, 1952.
Hoyt, Homer. One Hundred Years of Land Values in Chicago, Chicago: Uni-University of Chicago Press, 1933.
The Structure and Growth of Residential Neighborhoods in American Cities, Washington, D.C.: U.S. Federal Housing Admin., 1939.
Jonassen, C.J. The Shopping Center Versus Downtown, Columbus, Ohio: Bureau of Business Research, Ohio State University, 1955.
Kelley, Eugene J. Shopping Centers: Locating Controlled Regional Centers, Saugatuck, Conn.: The Eno Foundation for Highway Traffic Control, 1956.
Mitchell, Robert B. Urban Traffic: A Function of Land Use, New York: Columbia University Press, 1954.
Nelson, Richard L. and Aschman, Frederick T. Real Estate and City Planning, Englewood Cliffs, N.J.: Prentice-Hall, Inc., 1957.
Pasma, Theodore K. Organized Industrial Districts: A Tool for Community Development, Washington, D.C.: Department of Commerce, 1954.
Ratcliff, Richard U. Urban Land Economics, New York: McGraw-Hill, 1949.
Renne, Roland R. Land Economics, New York: Harper, 1958.
Rowlands, David T. Urban Real Estate Research, Washington, D.C.: Urban Land Institute, 1959.

LEGAL ASPECTS OF REAL ESTATE

Bigelow, Harry A. Introduction to the Law of Real Property, St. Paul, Minn.: West Publishing Co., 1945.
Bowman, Arthur G. Real Estate Law in California, Englewood Cliffs, N.J.: Prentice-Hall, Inc., 1958.
Dunham, Allison. Modern Real Estate Transactions - Cases and Materials, Brooklyn, N.Y.: The Foundation Press, 1958.
Dykstra, Gerald O. and Dykstra, Lillian G. The Business Law of Real Estate, New York: Macmillan, 1956.
Friedman, Edith J. Handbook of Real Estate Forms, Englewood Cliffs, N.J.: Prentice-Hall, Inc., 1957.

Gordon, Saul. Standard Annotated Real Estate Forms, Englewood Cliffs, N.J.: Prentice-Hall, Inc., 1946.
Grange, William J. Real Estate, New York: The Ronald Press, 1940.
Horack, Frank E. and Nolan, Val, Jr. Land Use Controls, St. Paul, Minn.: West Publishing Co., 1955.
Kratovil, Robert. Real Estate Law, Englewood Cliffs, N.J.: Prentice-Hall, Inc., 1958.
Lusk, Harold F. The Law of the Real Estate Business, Homewood, Ill.: Richard D. Irwin, 1958.
Metzenbaum, James. The Law of Zoning, New York: Baker, Voorhis, and Co., 1955, 3 vols.
Nussbaum, Louis M. Law for the Homeowner, Real Estate Operator and Broker, New York: Oceana Publications, 1956.
Ogden, Melvin B. Ogden's California Real Property Law, Los Angeles, Calif.: Parker and Son, 1956.
Rathkopf, Charles A. and Rathkopf, Arden H. The Law of Zoning and Planning, New York: Clark Boardman Co., 1956. 2 vols.
Semenow, Robert W. Questions and Answers on Real Estate, Englewood Cliffs, N.J.: Prentice-Hall, Inc., 1957.
Stumpf, Felix, Horwitz, Wilma and Deal, Betty. Legal Aspects of Real Estate Transactions, Berkeley, Calif.: University of Calif., 1956.
Thorson, Ivan A. Essentials of California Real Estate Law and Practice, Los Angeles, Calif.: Realty Research Bureau, 1958.
Van Buren, De Witt. Real Estate Brokerage and Commissions - Law and Practice, Englewood Cliffs, N.J.: Prentice-Hall, Inc., 1948.
Wescott, R.D. Real Estate Primer, San Gabriel, Calif.: Primer Publishers, 1963.

PERSONAL DEVELOPMENT

Bettger, Frank. Benjamin Franklin's Secret of Success and What It Did for Me, Englewood Cliffs, N.J.: Prentice-Hall, Inc., 1960.
Duvall, Sylvanus M. The Art and Skill of Getting Along with People, Englewood Cliffs, N.J.: Prentice-Hall, Inc., 1961.
Funk, Wilfred. Vocabulary Power and Culture, New York: Wilfred Funk Publishers, 1954.
Howard, Vernon. Your Magic Power to Persuade and Command People, Englewood Cliffs, N.J.: Prentice-Hall, Inc., 1962.
Keyes, Kenneth S. How to Develop Your Thinking Ability, New York: McGraw-Hill, 1950.
Latham, James L. Human Relations in Business, Columbus, Ohio: C.E. Merrill, 1964.
Nichols, R., and Stevens, L.A. Are You Listening?, New York: McGraw-Hill, 1957.
Peale, Norman Vincent. The Amazing Results of Positive Thinking, Englewood Cliffs, N.J.: Prentice-Hall, Inc., 1959.
_____ The Tough-Minded Optimist, Englewood Cliffs, N.J.: Prentice-Hall, Inc., 1961.
_____ The Power of Positive Thinking, Englewood Cliffs, N.J.: Prentice-Hall, Inc.

BIBLIOGRAPHY

Schindler, John A. *How to Live 365 Days a Year*, Englewood Cliffs, N.J.: Prentice-Hall, Inc., 1956.
Serif, Med. *How to Manage Yourself*, Cities Service Oil Co., Business Research and Education Dept., 60 Wall St., New York, N.Y.
Uris, Auren. *Developing Your Executive Skills*, New York: McGraw-Hill, 1955.
White, Milton W. *The Power of Self Knowledge*, New York: The Julian Press, 1957.
Wright, Milton. *Managing Yourself*, 2nd ed., New York: McGraw-Hill, 1949.

PROPERTY MANAGEMENT

Bliss, Howard L. and Sill, Charles H. *Real Estate Management*, Englewood Cliffs, N.J.: Prentice-Hall, Inc., 1953.
Building Manager's Assn. of Chicago. *The Percentage Lease*, Chicago: The Association, 1955.
Cowgill, Clinton H. *Building for Investment*, New York: Reinhold, 1951.
Downs, James C. *Principles of Real Estate Management*, Chicago, Ill.: Institute of Real Estate Management, 1957.
Eckert, Fred W. *The Hotel Lease*, Chicago, Ill.: The Hotel Monthly Press, 1947.
Geer, Mary Warren. *How to Profit by Rehabilitating Real Estate*, Englewood Cliffs, N.J.: Prentice-Hall, Inc., 1957.
Institute of Real Estate Management. *Cooperative Apartments: Their Organization and Profitable Operation*, Chicago, Ill.: Institute N.A.R.E.B., 1956.
⎯⎯⎯ *Practical Real Estate Management*, Chicago, Ill.: Institute N.A.R.E.B., 1958. 2 vols.
⎯⎯⎯ *Rehabilitation as a Business*, Chicago, Ill.: Institute and Build America Better Council, N.A.R.E.B., 1952.
McMichael, Stanley L. *Leases - Percentage, Short and Long Term*, Englewood Cliffs, N.J.: Prentice-Hall, Inc., 1947.
National Institute of Real Estate Brokers. *Percentage Leases*, Chicago, Ill.: National Institute of Real Estate Brokers, 1957.
⎯⎯⎯ *Journal of Property Management*, See quarterly publication by Institute.

REAL ESTATE OFFICE MANAGEMENT

Black, Nelms. *How to Organize and Manage a Small Business*, Norman, Okla.: University of Oklahoma Press, 1950.
California Real Estate Association. *Real Estate Office Administration*, Los Angeles, Calif.: C.R.E.A., 1962.
⎯⎯⎯ *Real Estate Office Management*, Los Angeles, Calif.: C.R.E.A., 1961.
⎯⎯⎯ *Real Estate Office Policies and Procedures*, Los Angeles, Calif.: C.R.E.A., 1959.
⎯⎯⎯ *Modern Concept of Real Estate Administration*, Los Angeles, Calif.: C.R.E.A., 1958.
⎯⎯⎯ *Selecting, Training and Reducing Turnover of Real Estate Sales Personnel*, Los Angeles, Calif.: C.R.E.A., 1958.

Doris, Lillian. Real Estate Office Secretary's Handbook, Englewood Cliffs, N.J.: Prentice-Hall, Inc., 1953.
Hefti, Wilma C. How to Keep Real Estate Office Records, Englewood Cliffs, N.J.: Prentice-Hall, Inc., 1954.
Kelley, Pearce C. and Lawyer, Kenneth. How to Organize and Operate a Small Business, Englewood Cliffs, N.J.: Prentice-Hall, Inc., 1955.
Lasser, J.K. How to Run a Small Business, New York: McGraw-Hill, 1955.
McMichael, Stanley L. How to Operate a Real Estate Business, Englewood Cliffs, N.J.: Prentice-Hall, Inc., 1947.
National Institute of Real Estate Brokers. Office Policies and Procedures, Chicago, Ill.: National Institute of Real Estate Brokers, 1959.
U.S. Department of Commerce. Establishing and Operating a Real Estate and Insurance Brokerage Business, Washington, D.C.: U.S. Dept. of Commerce, 1946.

REAL ESTATE PRACTICE

Benson, Philip, North, Nelson, and Ring, Alfred. Real Estate Principles and Practices, Englewood Cliffs, N.J.: Prentice-Hall, Inc., 1954.
California Division of Real Estate. Real Estate Reference Book, Sacramento, Calif.: Division of R.E., 1962.
California Real Estate Association. You and Your Real Estate Business, Los Angeles, Calif.: C.R.E.A., 1957.
_____ Knowledge Makes the Difference, Los Angeles, Calif.: C.R.E.A., 1956.
Case, Frederick E. Modern Real Estate Practice, New York: Allyn and Bacon, 1956.
Davies, Pearl Janet. Real Estate in American History, Washington, D.C.: Public Affairs Press, 1958.
Downs, James C. Inflation and Real Estate, Chicago, Ill.: Institute of R.E. Brokers, 1961.
Hoagland, Henry E. Real Estate Principles, New York: McGraw-Hill, 1955.
Holmes, Lawrence Gilbert. The Real Estate Handbook, Englewood Cliffs, N.J.: Prentice-Hall, Inc., 1948.
Husband, William H. and Anderson, Frank Ray. Real Estate, Homewood, Ill.: Richard D. Irwin, 1954.
Martin, Preston. Real Estate Principles and Practices, New York: Macmillan, 1959.
Prentice-Hall Staff. Encyclopedic Dictionary of Real Estate Practice, Englewood Cliffs, N.J.: Prentice-Hall, Inc., 1955.
_____ Prentice-Hall Real Estate Service, Englewood Cliffs, N.J.: Prentice-Hall, Inc.,
Reynolds, Welden. This Business of Real Estate, Chicago, Ill.: The National Assn. of R.E. Boards, 1949. 2 vols.
Ring, Alfred A. Real Estate Questions and Practice Problems, Englewood Cliffs, N.J.: Prentice-Hall, Inc., 1955.
Smith, James, Martin, Howard, and Abercrombie, Roland. Real Estate in California, San Francisco, Calif.: General Educational Pub., 1958.
Spilker, John B. Real Estate Business as a Profession, Cincinnati, Ohio: John S. Kidd, 1949.

Unger, Maurice A. Real Estate, Cincinnati, Ohio: South-Western Pub. Co., 1959.
Weimer, Arthur M. and Hoyt, Homer. Principles of Real Estate, New York: Ronald Press, 1954.

SELLING REAL ESTATE

Arnold, Ray H. How to Close in Selling Homes, Englewood Cliffs, N.J.: Prentice-Hall, Inc., 1953.
———— How to Overcome Objections in Selling Real Estate, Englewood Cliffs, N.J.: Prentice-Hall, Inc., 1955.
California Real Estate Association. Blueprint for Selling Real Estate, Los Angeles, Calif.: C.R.E.A., 1957.
———— How to List and Sell Real Estate in a Competitive Market, Los Angeles, Calif.: C.R.E.A., 1964.
———— The Keys to Selling Single Family Homes, Los Angeles, Calif.: C.R.E.A., 1963.
———— This is Your Life, Real Estate Salesman, Los Angeles, Calif.: C.R.E.A., 1962.
Cook, G. Hall. How to Sell Real Estate by the Sell-An-Idea Technique, Englewood Cliffs, N.J.: Prentice-Hall, Inc., 1957.
Garn, Roy. The Magic Power of Emotional Appeal, Englewood Cliffs, N.J.: Prentice-Hall, Inc., 1960.
Geer, Mary Warren. Selling Home Property, Englewood Cliffs, N.J.: Prentice-Hall, Inc., 1951.
Ivey, Paul W. (Revised by Walter Horvath). Successful Salesmanship, Englewood Cliffs, N.J.: Prentice-Hall, Inc., 1953.
King, A. Rowden. Realtors' Guide to Architecture: How to Identify and Sell Every Kind of Home, Englewood Cliffs, N.J.: Prentice-Hall, Inc., 1954.
Leterman, Elmer G. Personal Power Through Creative Selling, New York: Harper, 1955.
Lewis, Charles W. Essentials of Selling, Englewood Cliffs, N.J.: Prentice-Hall, Inc., 1952.
McMichael, Stanley L. Selling Real Estate, Englewood Cliffs, N.J.: Prentice-Hall, Inc., 1950.
Meloan, Taylor and Rathmell, John. Selling: Its Broader Dimensions, New York: The Macmillan Co., 1960.
National Institute of Real Estate Brokers. Better Ways to Obtain Profitable Listings, Chicago, Ill.: National Institute of Real Estate Brokers, 1950.
———— Real Estate Salesman's Handbook, Chicago, Ill.: National Institute of Real Estate Brokers, 1950.
———— Sales Ideas That Click, Chicago, Ill.: National Institute of Real Estate Brokers, 1958.
———— Salesmen's Success Stories, Chicago, Ill.: National Institute of Real Estate Brokers, 1963.
National Association of Homebuilders. New Home Salesman's Handbook, Washington, D.C.: National Assn. of Homebuilders, 1959.
Prentice-Hall Staff. Successful Real Estate Ideas, Englewood Cliffs, N.J.: Prentice-Hall, Inc., 1951.

Prevette, Earl. How I Sell, Englewood Cliffs, N.J.: Prentice-Hall, Inc., 1960.
Russell, Frederic A. and Beach, Frank H. Textbook of Salesmanship, New York: McGraw-Hill, 1959.
Sherman, Arthur B. Selling Business Real Estate, Englewood Cliffs, N.J.: Prentice-Hall, Inc., 1955.
Teckemer, Earl B. The "How" of Selling Real Estate, Englewood Cliffs, N.J.: Prentice-Hall, Inc., 1954.
————— How to Value Real Estate: The Foremost Factor in Selling, Englewood Cliffs, N.J.: Prentice-Hall, Inc., 1956.
Tralins, S. Robert. How To Be A Power Closer in Selling, Englewood Cliffs, N.J.: Prentice-Hall, Inc., 1960.
Vogel, Lois T. How to Help Your Real Estate Salesmen Produce More Business, Englewood Cliffs, N.J.: Prentice-Hall, Inc., 1957.
Wheeler, Elmer. Selling Dangerously, Englewood Cliffs, N.J.: Prentice-Hall, Inc., 1956.
————— How to Make Your Sales Sizzle in 17 Days, Englewood Cliffs, N.J.: Prentice-Hall, Inc.
————— Tested Sentences That Sell, Englewood Cliffs, N.J.: Prentice-Hall, Inc.

TAXES AND TAX PLANNING IN REAL ESTATE

Atlas, Martin. Tax Aspects of Real Estate Transactions, Washington, D.C.: Bureau of National Affairs, 1956.
Brown, Harry Gunnison, and associates. Land Value Taxation Around the World, New York: Robert Schalkenbach Foundation, 1955.
Casey, William J. Tax Shelter in Real Estate, New York: Institute for Business Planning, 1957.
Haber, Paul and Kotkin, Bernard. Tax Opportunities in Real Estate, Los Angeles: Tax Publishers, 1955.
Lasser, J.K. Tax Planning for Real Estate, New York: Reinhold, 1955.
Morton, Walter A. Housing Taxation, Madison, Wis.: University of Wisconsin Press, 1955.
Weir, Robert A. A Supplement to Advantages in Taxes.

TRADE-IN HOUSING PROGRAMS

Hess, John M. Trade-In Housing Management, Palo Alto, Calif.: Stanford Research Press, 1959.
Stone, David. How to Operate a Real Estate Trade-In Program, Englewood Cliffs, N.J.: Prentice-Hall, Inc., 1962.

URBAN LAND USE AND PLANNING CITIES, ETC.

Aronovici, Carol. Community Building: Science, Technique, Art, New York: Doubleday, 1956.
Breese, Gerald and Whiteman, Dorothy E. An Approach to Urban Planning, Princeton; N.J.: Princeton University Press, 1953.
Burton, Hal. The City Fights Back, New York: The Citadel Press, 1954.
Chamber of Commerce, U.S. Urban Development Guidebook, Washington, D.C.: U.S. Chamber of Commerce, 1955.

BIBLIOGRAPHY

Chapin, F. Stuart, Jr. Urban Land Use Planning, New York: Harper, 1957.
Churchill, Henry S. The City Is The People, New York: Reynal and Hitchcock, 1945.
Dahir, James, Communities for Better Living, New York: Harper, 1950.
Fisher, Robert Moore. Metropolis in Modern Life, New York: Doubleday, 1955.
Gallion, Arthur B. The Urban Pattern - City Planning and Design, New York: D. Van Nostrand Co., 1950.
Giedion, Sigfried. Space, Time and Architecture, Cambridge, Mass.: Harvard University Press, 1954.
Gist, Noel P. and Halbert, L.A. Urban Society, New York: Crowell, 1956.
Greer, Guy. Your City Tomorrow, New York: Macmillan, 1947.
Hatt, Paul K. and Reiss, Albert J., Jr. Cities and Society, Glencoe, Ill.: The Free Press, 1957.
Hallenbeck, Wilbur C. American Urban Communities, New York: Harper, 1951.
Lee, Rose Hum. The City: Urbanism and Urbanization in Major World Regions, Philadelphia, Pa.: J.B. Lippincott, 1955.
Marx, Herbert L., Jr. Community Planning, New York: H.W. Wilson Co., 1956.
Millspaugh, Martin and Breckenfeld, Gurney, The Human Side of Urban Renewal, Baltimore, Md.: Fight-Blight, Inc., 1958.
Mumford, Lewis. The Culture of Cities, New York: Harcourt Brace, 1938.
Owen, Wilfred. Cities in the Motor Age, New York: Viking, 1959.
Rannells, John. The Core of the City, New York: Columbia University Press, 1956.
Robson, William A. Great Cities of the World: Their Government, Politics and Planning, London: Allen and Unwin, 1956; New York: Macmillan, 1957.
Sert, Jose L. Can Our Cities Survive? Cambridge, Mass.: Harvard University Press, 1942.
Stein, Clarence S. Toward New Towns for America, New York: Reinhold, 1957.
Tunnard, Christopher and Reed, Henry Hope, Jr. American Skyline, Boston, Mass.: Houghton Mifflin, 1955.
Weiss, Shirley F. The Central Business District in Transition, Chapel Hill, N.C.: University of North Carolina, Department of City Planning, 1957.
Woodbury, Coleman. Urban Redevelopment: Problems and Practices, Chicago, Ill.: University of Chicago Press, 1953.

INDEX

A

Abbreviations, use of, in ads, 100
Acceptance, conveyance of, 187-88
Action, inciting the client to, 146
Advertisements:
. classified, copy for, 88-101
. layout of, 100-1
. listing comparables for, 104
. as source of listings, 30-31, 33, 34, 35
Advertising:
. ethics of, 101
. planning of daily, 101-2
Advertising policy, 74
Advertising privileges, 85
Agency, the principle of, 176
Agent, salesman as seller's, 175
AIDA formula, the, defined, 146
Amenities:
. neighborhood, 135
. of touring a home, 137-38, 141-42
Amortization tables, 16
Apartment units, sale of, 250-55
Appearance, salesman's personal, 14-15
Appointment book, the, 15
Appointments, listing, 49-52
Appraisal methods, 57-60, 65-66, 262-67
Appraisal records, 51-53
Appreciation:
. of investment, 241, 243
. of land, 66
Approachability, 275
Associations, professional, 269-70
Assumptions of the sale, 147-48
Assumption of the sale, 147-48
Attention, securing the client's, 146
Attitude, 3, 5, 12-14, 138
Attorneys as listings source, 37
Automobile, the salesman's, 13-14
. etiquette of, 134

B

Banks:
. commercial, lending practices of, 217-18
. as listings sources, 37
. savings, lending practices of, 218
Benefits, demonstration of, 139, 141-42
Births, and real estate transfer, 4
Brief case, the salesman's, 15
Brokerage, mortgage, 267
Building and loan associations as source of listings, 37
Building permits as listings lead, 39
Business, building a referral, 200-2
Business contacts as listings source, 35, 37 38
Business transfer notices, 35
Buyers (see also Clients):
. actions of, justification for, 160
. attraction of, 21
. emotional needs of, 123-24
. as source of listings, 39
Buying temperature, building the, 145-46

C

California veteran's loans, 229-31
Canvass:
. door-to-door, 23-26
. telephone, 28-33
Canvass area:
. development of, 26-28
. selection of, 23-24
Card index of listings, 15
Center of influence theory, the, 204-5
Classified ads (see Advertisements)
Clergy, as listings source, 39
Clients:
. self-selling, 135
. understanding one's, 115-16

INDEX

Clients (continued):
. deportment with, 86-87, 134
. emotional needs of, 123-24
. informing the, 209
. as listings source, 38-39
. responsiveness toward, 139
Close, beginning the, 136-37
Closing:
. costs of, 226-27, 228-29
. objections to, 150
Closing session, the:
. presence of salesmen at, 197-200
. psychology of, 168-69
. site of, 151-52
Closing techniques, 167, 186-87
Comfort as motivation, 124-25
Commercial banks (see Banks)
Commissions, payment of, 21
Communication, 13, 118-19
Company policy manual, the, 16
Comparative analysis appraisal, 65
Competition:
. analyzing the, 55
. and marketability, 68
Competitive Properties Report Form, the, 52
Conduct with clients, 86-87, 134
Contractors as listings source, 35
Contracts:
. alterations on, 190-91
. confirmation of, 186
. contents of, 161-65
. listing, types of, 78-80
. protective clauses in, 166-67
. validity of, 161
Conversation:
. guiding the, 134-36, 146, 148-49
. rules of, 152-53
Copy, classified ad, 88-101
Cost replacement appraisal, 65-66
Costs, closing, 226-27, 228-29
Counselling, 268
Counselling session, the, 116-18
Counter-offers:
. cushioned, 157-58
. legal form for, 190
. negotiation of, 188-90
Courage, 169-70
Courtesies, extension of, 31-32
Creativity in salesmanship, 2
Cushion, buyer's, 157-58

D

Daily Work Plan, the, 10
Day, planning one's, 9-12
Deaths and real estate transfer, 3
Dedication to goals, 16-17
Defensiveness, 138
. as persuasive device, 149-50
Demand and marketability, 68
Deportment with clients, 86-87, 134
Deposit monies:
. disposition of, 159
. legal aspects of, 159
. receipts for, 162-67, 198
Deposits, size of, 158-59
Depreciation, 263-66
. accelerated, 248-49
. calculation of, 247
. declining balance method, 247-48
. factors of, 56-57
. straight-line method, 247
. sum of the years-digits method, 248
Descriptions, legal property, 62
Desire, building the client's, 146
Desk, the salesman's, 14
Deterioration, factors of, 56, 266
Development, land, 268
Direct mail programs, 34
Directories, reverse telephone, 23
Divorce, and real estate transfer, 3-5
Divorce notices as listings lead, 35
Documents (see Records)
Door-opening gambits, 24-26
Driving courtesy, 134

E

Earnest money:
. defined, 159-60
. receipts for, 162-65
Economic obsolescence, 266
. defined, 56-57
Effort, concentration of, 26-28
Eligibility (see Qualification)
Emotional factor, the, 122, 123-24
Empathy, development of, 140-41
Employers, sellers as, 20
Employment, and real estate transfer, 4
Energy, maintenance of, 277
Enthusiasm, cultivation of, 17-18
Equity:
. determination of net, 66-67
. yields on, 244-46

Equity Yield Analysis Report, the, 245-46
Escrow:
. review of, 196-97
. transfer of, 197-200
Ethics, advertising, 101
Etiquette:
. of driving, 134
. of touring homes, 137-38, 141-42
Exclusive agency listing, the, 78
Exclusive Listing Agreement Form, the, 79
Exclusive right of sale listing, the, 78
Experience, determination of, 60
Exposure, the mathematics of, 204

F

Failure, the fear of, 147
Fears, mastery of, 18, 147
Federal Housing Administration (FHA), the, 218-19
. regulations and policies of, 220-27
FHA Conditional Commitment, the, 219-20
Feedback, conversational, 156
Fees, title policy, 16
Filing box, the, 15
Financial pressures and real estate transfer, 4
Financing:
. instruments used in, 233-34
. private, 231-32
. qualification of buyer for, 233-35
. residential, types of, 214-16
. terms of, 67
Floor Call Recap Form, the, 107
Floor plans, 58-59
Floor time responsibilities, 86-87
Forfeiture clauses, 16
Format, basic ad, 101
"For Sale by Owner" ads, 30-31, 33, 34
"Free land" concept, the, 1
Functional obsolescence, 56, 266
"Furniture-For-Sale" ads, 35
Future, planning one's, 202-3

G

Gifts, 208
GI loans (see Veteran's loans)
Goals, career:
. dedication to one's, 16-17, 209-10, 278-79
. establishment of, 7-8
Grooming, importance of good, 14-15

H

Hand tools, 15-16
Headers, classified ad, 90-95
Health, maintenance of, 277
Home:
. the "right," 136-37
. touring the, 137-38, 141-42, 156-57
Home ownership, trends in, 212-14
Honesty in advertising, 101
Hotels, listing and sale of, 255-56
Hotspots, accentuation of, 141-42

I

Illness and real estate transfer, 3
Indecision, overcoming, 18
Independence, development of, 87-88
Identification:
. of contracting parties, 162
. of deposit monies, 159, 161
Influence, the center of, 204-5
Information:
. in ads, sufficiency of, 95
. questions that elicit, 108-11
. sources of, 28
Information forms, 241
Inquiries, telephoned, 103-4, 105-9
Inspection:
. for termites, 166
. tours of, 55-60, 125-28, 137-38, 141-42, 156-57
Institute of Farm and Land Brokers, the, 270
Institute of Property Management, the, 270
Institute of Real Estate Appraisers, the, 270
Institute of Real Estate Brokers, the, 270
Insurance, real estate, 268
Insurance companies as listings source, 38
International Traders Club, the, 270
Interest, arousing the client's, 146
Interviews:
. qualifying, 118-21
. telephone, 103-4, 105-9, 119
Investment, properties for, 233-35
Investments:
. appreciation of, 241, 243
. liquidity of, 241, 242
. stability of, 241, 242-43
. tests for sound, 241
. yield on, 241, 243

INDEX

K

Keys, 16
Knowledge:
. of oneself, 278
. use of, 271-72

L

Land:
. appreciation of, 66
. listing and sale of, 256-62
Layout of ads, 100-1
Lead lines, classified ad, 90
Leases, non-residential property, 256
Legal notices as listings leads, 37
Leverage, the principle of, 243-44
Life insurance companies, lending practices of, 217
Liquidity, investment, 241, 242
Listening, the importance of, 139
Listing book, the, 15
Listing forms, 16
Listing kit, the, 16
Listings:
. canvassing for, 22-23
. comparable to advertised, 104
. expired, relisting of, 34
. information on, sources of, 28
. marketability of, 68-69
. post-servicing of, 75
. pre-show inspection of, 125-28
. prospecting for, 22-23
. sources of, 30-31, 33-40
. types of, 78-80
Loan commitments, 74
Loan correspondents, 267
Loans:
. assumption of, 166
. buyers' qualifications for, 166
. conventional, 215-18
. government insured, 218-29
Lock-boxes, 16

M

Magic moment, fallacy of the, 151
Map book, the, 15
Marketability:
. enhancement of, 73
. factors of, 68-69
Marriage and real estate transfer, 4
Marriage notices as listings lead, 35
Measurement of property, 58
Memoranda, use of, 11
Military personnel as listings source, 39

Mortgage amortization tables, 16
Mortgage bankers, 267
Mortgage brokers, 267
Mortgage companies, 16
. as listings source, 37
Mortgage indebtedness, owner's, 62
Mortgage payments, 223
Mortgages, assumption of, 166
Mortgage yield guide, the, 16
Motels, listing and sale of, 255-56
Motivations, buyers', 91-95, 122-25, 203
Moving companies as listings source, 34
Multiple listing, 80

N

Names, 1, 32-33, 105, 150, 207-8
Neglected property, 38
Negotiator, the salesman as, 133, 178-85
Neighborhoods:
. amenities of, 135
. inspection of, 55-56
Neighbors as source of listings, 33
Net listing, the, 80
New business, development of, 60-61, 129-30
News, developing a nose for, 40-41
Non-exclusive listing, the, 78-80
Notebook, the salesman's, 11-12

O

Objections to closing, 150, 155-56
Obsolescence:
. factors of, 56-57
. forms of, 266
Offers:
. acceptance of, 187-88
. buyer's cushioned, 157-58
. counter-offers to, 188-90
. negotiation of, 178-85
. presentation of, 174-75
Open listing, the, 78-80
Owners, absentee, 34
Ownership of property, 1

P

Personnel counselors as listings source, 38
Persuasion, defensive, 149-50
Physical deterioration, 56
Physical obsolescence, 266
Planning:
. of daily advertising, 101-2
. of work, 8-11
Policy, floor time, 86-87

Possession, agreements on, 167
Preferences, conflicting, 125
Presentation, the listing, 69-70
Price:
. determination of selling, 62-63, 72
. and marketability, 68
. statement of, in adds, 95
Price range approach, the, 71-72
Pricing methods, 42, 65
Problems, facing up to, 208-9
Profession, real estate as a, 2-3
Professional associations, 269-70
Professional men as listings sources, 37
Professionalism, importance of, 49-50
Promotion and real estate transfer, 4
Properties:
. investment, 240-41
. listing of comparable, 104
. selection of, for showing, 121-23
Property:
. appraisal of, 51-53, 65
. defense of, 138
. description of, 62
. documents pertaining to, 57
. exchanges of, 249-50, 262
. inspection of, 57-60
. measurement of, 58
. ownership of, 1
. the pricing of, 42, 65
. the showing of, 119-20
Property Description Form, the, 64
Property management, 262
Property values, determination of, 23-24
Prospect Card, the, 104-5
Prospect Form, the, 106
Psychology, closing session, 168-69
Public relations, importance of good, 49-50
Purchase agreement, writing the, 154
Purchase price (see Price)

Q

Qualification for financing, 233-35
. FHA loan, 224-26
. GI loan, 227-28
Questions:
. asking the right, 41
. closing, 155
. tie-downs phrased as, 149
. the uses of, 108-11
. for "yes" responses, 148-49

R

Real estate specializations, 267-69
Real estate transfers, causes of, 3-5

Receipts, deposit, 162-67, 198
Records:
. of comparable properties, 104
. of deposit monies, 159-161
. processing control, 199
. property appraisal, 51-53
Referral business, building a, 200-2
Referral file, the, 205-7
Referrals, sources of, 33-40
Refinancing arrangements, 166
Remembrances, 208
Rental agreements, 167
Repetition, the value of, 101
Residential cost handbook, 16
Romance as a factor in home selection, 122
Rushing the showing, 137-38

S

Sale:
. assuming the, 147-48
. closing the, 151-52
. service after the, 196
Saleability (see Marketability)
Salesman, the:
. attitude of, 12-14
. as negotiator, 133
. tools of, 13-16
Salesmen:
. listing, cooperation with, 175-76
. presence of, at closing, 197-200
Salesmanship:
. as communication, 13
. creative, 2
Sales personality, development of, 270-71, 272-73
Savings banks (see Banks)
Savings and loan associations, lending practices of, 216
Seller, the:
. as center of influence, 22
. closing the, 174
. educating the, 176-77
. as employer, 20
. enlisting the cooperation of, 73-74
. listing salesmen as agents of, 175
. as payer of commissions, 21
Selling forms, 16
Selling price (see Price)
Selling procedures:
. FHA, 222-23
. Veteran's Administration, 228-29
Selling process, the:
. preparation for, 72-75
. steps in, 146

INDEX

Service, post-sale, 196
Services, selling one's, 42-45
Showing of property, 119-20
. inspection prior to, 125-28
. rules of effective, 139-40
. rushing the, 137-38
. selection of properties for, 121-23
Showing sequence, the, 128-29
Showmanship, the value of, 140
Signs, 16
. "For Sale by Owner," 34
Silence, the value of, 139, 152-53
Sincerity, the quality of, 272
Smile, the worth of a, 273-74
Smile-a-phone concept, the, 111-12
Social contacts as listings source, 35
Solicitation (see Canvass)
Specializations, real estate, 267-69
Stability, investment, 241, 242-43
State loan programs, 229-31
Status and real estate transfer, 4
Success:
. factors of firm's, 85-86
. factors of personal, 1-3
. the image of, 274-75
Syndication, 268-69

T

Tape measure, the, 15
Tax advantages, 247
Telephone:
. effectiveness on the, 111-12, 119
. handling inquiries via, 103-4, 105-9
. solicitation of listings by, 28-33
Telephone directory, reverse, 23
Termite inspections, 166
Terms, statement of, in ads, 95
Tests for investment soundness, 241
Themes, classified ad, 90-95
Tie-downs, 149

Time, management of, 8-11
Title policy schedule of fees, 16
Tools:
. hand, 15-16
. the real estate salesman's 13-16
Total Market Analysis Report, the, 53
Touring the home, 137-38, 141-42, 156-57
Trade-in plans, 35
Trades, property, 249-50, 262
Tradesmen as listings source, 38-39
Trailer parks, listing and sale of, 255-56
Truthfulness in advertising, 101

U

Urgency:
. determination of, 60
. and marketability, 68

V

Vacant properties as potential listings, 39
Validity of contract changes, 190-91
Value:
. the nature of, 5
. owners' concepts of, 60
Veterans loans:
. State of California, 229-31
. Veteran's Administration, 227-29
Voice, cultivation of the, 275-77

W

Wardrobe, the salesman's, 14-15
Work:
. planning of, 8-11
. weekly program of, 27-28
Written agreements, 154-55

Y

"Yes" responses, querying for, 148-49
Yield:
. on equity, 244-46
. investment, 241, 243